Theatre History Studies

2016 VOLUME 35

Edited by

SARA FREEMAN

PUBLISHED BY THE MID-AMERICA THEATRE CONFERENCE
AND THE UNIVERSITY OF ALABAMA PRESS

Manufactured in the United States of America

Template Design: Todd Lape / Lape Designs
Production by Publications Unit, Department of English, Illinois State University
Production Director: Steve Halle
Production Interns: Madeline Cornwell and Kara Hamilton

Essays appearing in this journal are abstracted and indexed in
Historical Abstracts and *America: History and Life*

∞

The paper on which this book is printed meets the minimum requirements
of American National Standard for Information Sciences-Permanence of
Paper for Printed Library Materials, ANSI Z39.48–1984.

Theatre History Studies is an official journal of the Mid-America Theatre Conference, Inc. (MATC). The conference is dedicated to the growth and improvement of all forms of theatre throughout a twelve-state region that includes the states of Illinois, Iowa, Nebraska, Kansas, Missouri, Minnesota, North Dakota, South Dakota, and Wisconsin. Its purposes are to unite people and organizations within this region and elsewhere who have an interest in theatre and to promote the growth and development of all forms of theatre.

Theatre History Studies is devoted to research in all areas of theatre studies. Manuscripts should be prepared in conformity with the guidelines established in the most recent edition of the *Chicago Manual of Style*, and emailed to Sara Freeman at sfreeman@pugetsound.edu. Consulting editors read the manuscripts, a process that takes approximately four months. The journal does not normally accept studies of dramatic literature unless there is a focus on actual production and performance. Authors whose manuscripts are accepted must provide the editor with an electronic file, using Microsoft Word. Illustrations are welcomed and should conform to the instructions listed in the style guide on the website: http://matc.us/theatre-history-studies-4/theatre-history-studies-the-matc-journal.

This publication is issued annually by the Mid-America Theatre Conference and the University of Alabama Press.

Subscription rates for 2016 are $25 for individuals, $35 for institutions, and an additional $10 for foreign delivery. Subscription orders and changes of address should be directed to Allie Harper, The University of Alabama Press, Box 870380, Tuscaloosa, AL 35487; (205) 348-1564 phone; (205) 348-9201 fax.

Any single current-year issue or back issue is $34.95 each if ordered through the Chicago Distribution Center. (Please note: there was no issue published in 2013.)

Theatre History Studies is indexed in *Humanities Index, Humanities Abstracts, Book Review Index, MLA International Bibliography, International Bibliography of Theatre & Dance, Arts & Humanities Citation Index, IBZ International Bibliography of Periodical Literature*, and *IBR International Bibliography of Book Reviews*, the database of *International Index to the Performing Arts*. Full texts of essays appear in the databases of both *Humanities Abstracts Full Text* and *SIRS*. The journal has published its own index, *The Twenty Year Index, 1981–2000*. It is available for $10 for individuals and $15 for libraries from Sara Freeman, Associate Professor, Theatre Arts CMB 1084, University of Puget Sound, 1500 N. Warner St., Tacoma, WA 98416; (253) 879-2438.

CONTENTS

CONTENTS

CONTENTS

ILLUSTRATIONS

Introduction

—SARA FREEMAN

With this issue, I begin editing *Theatre History Studies*, and I am honored to follow in the steps of Ron Engle, Robert Schanke, Rhona Justice-Malloy, and Liz Mullenix. Because *Theatre History Studies* is an annual publication, my goal is to make each year's offering a substantial collection of historical, historiographical, and dramaturgical-historical pieces about the practice of theatre, the impact and meaning of theatre and theatrical representation in culture, and the role of performance in historical events.

To that end, each issue under my editorship will feature a selection of probing essays drawn from the general submissions we receive from scholars around the world, and there will also be a curated special section that allows for editorial shaping and commissioning around topics of current attention or emerging interest in the field of theatre studies. The contents will also feature the Schanke Award–winning paper from the previous year's Mid-America Theatre Conference (MATC), published as it was presented.

The Schanke Award, endowed by this journal's second editor, Robert A. Schanke, recognizes the outstanding essay by an untenured faculty presenter at the MATC conference. The 2015 award-winning paper, by Chandra Owenby Hopkins, investigates and documents the mode of "theatrical installation" employed by the Atlanta-based Alliance Theatre for their 2014 staging of former poet laureate Natasha Trethewey's collection of poems *Native Guard*. Hopkins positions the production as an intervention in theatrical form around race and the history of the Civil War that suggests ways of "reshaping interactions in the contemporary southern United States."

Hopkins's essay is also joined by an article-length version of Irma Mayorga's powerful keynote address from the 2015 conference, "En Ser Inspirado | *On Being Inspired*." When delivered in Kansas City, Mayorga's speech lit the room on fire. The authority and intimacy of Mayorga's argument about how not to ignore or neglect Latino/a theatre in the United States and her history of the inception of the Latina/o Theatre Commons demand attention from theatre scholars.

Moving back to the start, this issue begins with two essays that look closely at moments in German theatre, recovering, as Hopkins and Mayorga do, genealogies of cultural ideas about artistic forms and recording the work of theatrical "first responders" to huge social and political changes. Rebecca Rovit's microhistory about the immediate reinstatement of theatre production in Berlin "from the rubble" of the war with a 1945–1946 season recovers figures like Fritz Wisten and Gunther Weisenborn for the same type of serious consideration afforded Brecht and his company's work a decade later. Scott Venters does close reconstructions of two mass spectacle performances—the Nazi-tinged *Olympic Youth* performed at the opening of the 1936 Olympic Games and an 1817 commemoration day event supporting German nationalism staged by the gymnastic students of Friedrich Jahn—to uncover the functioning of a commemorative body in German cultural performance.

Both Rovit's essay and the one by Brian E. G. Cook go deep into a particular archive of materials. Cook's discussion of Cherub Theatre company's paradoxical position in British theatre from the 1970s to the 1990s harnesses both first-person narratives and seemingly impersonal institutional documents held in official and personal collections to highlight what range of concepts might matter to scholars looking to chart the artistic success, influence, or historical importance of theatrical production. Steve Tillis's article dilates out even farther around the notion of canonization and importance, arguing for scholars and teachers to take a "long view" of theatre history. Tillis especially shows how durational histories that include world theatrical forms, not just Western aesthetic traditions, reveal different patterns and turning points in theatre history. From the microhistory to the long view, these four essays all affirm that the work of theatre history research is to go deeper and to see more specifically how historical developments and theatrical forms related to one another.

The central curated section, "Rethinking the Maternal," presents a strong focus on dramatic literature. Collaborating with Sheila Rabillard and Karen Bamford, two Canadian scholars of drama, on this special section has been a great pleasure. I presented at the conference they hosted on the topic at Mt. Alison University, New Brunswick, in 2008 and am pleased to see this selection of essays coalesce for publication. Their introduction and the assembled essays create a compelling case that motherhood is an aspect of human experience that presents formal and symbolic difficulties for theatrical representation and, importantly, that modes of engaging with motherhood in theatrical meaning-making have been until recently under-researched in histories of dramatic literature and histories of stage production.

Elaine Aston's germinal article "A Critical Step to the Side Performing the Loss of Mother" came out in *Theatre Research International* in 2007. Jozefina Komporaly's *Staging Motherhood: British Women Playwrights 1956 to the Present* came out the same year. In 2013, Palgrave published Bailey McDaniel's *(Re)constructing Maternal Performance in Twentieth Century American Drama.* Rabillard and Bamford's special section joins these scholarly currents, providing the types of histories that emerge from analyses of the action and imagery of playscripts, revealing how works that perform motherhood contain potent documentations of culture and gender.

We study theatre history for both the big ideas and the revealing details. This range of articles has both, urging us to document, rethink, and breathe in (*inspire*) the potentials and material impacts of theatrical form and production.

Part I

STUDIES IN THEATRE HISTORY

Berlin's "First Responder" Artists, 1945–1946

Theatre and Politics from the Rubble

—REBECCA ROVIT

"We are alive. Our house is still standing; and I am engaged in the general theatre business again," Fritz Wisten reported from Berlin in 1946 to a fellow artist.[1] Born Moritz Weinstein in Vienna (1890), the former director of an all-Jewish theatre in Nazi Germany (1939–1941) survived the war in Berlin. His non-Jewish wife and his position at the helm of an eight-year cultural organization and its theatre, the Jewish Kulturbund, had afforded him some protection within the Nazi regime. But Nazi law mandated that he wear the Star of David as he labored in a Berlin factory. He was not permitted to join non-Jews in his neighborhood bomb shelters during frequent air raids that occurred during the 1940s. Like other Jews left in Berlin, he waited for the Soviet military to liberate the city from the Nazis. Still reeling from the devastating events of World War II, in spring 1945 Wisten nonetheless enlisted considerable effort in reviving Berlin's cultural landscape. He was one of the "first responder" theatre artists to forge a new direction in an environment that lacked a "cultural compass." By the time Germany capitulated to the Red Army and the Allied Powers arrived in Berlin later that summer, the physical devastation and the administrative upheaval that accompanied the war had destroyed the city's infrastructure, eradicating all "familiar points of reference—of community, of social and cultural networks" for disoriented Germans caught in the transition.[2] The vibrant reemergence of culture in the direct wake of war resulted from the way leading theatre directors and performers in Berlin coordinated their artistic endeavors even before Soviet and Anglo-American power put into policy the parameters for a new cultural life.[3]

Theatre historians have not adequately documented this "zero hour" (Stunde Null) for theatre practice, the moment so aptly described by historian Richard Bessel as when Germans, having experienced "destruction, defeat, disease, death and destitution on an unimaginable scale . . . went to hell and, in 1945, began to come back."[4] My focus on the immediate aftermath of World War II in Berlin (1945–1946) uncovers a surprising resurgence of cultural life in Berlin as the Red Army took over, sharing governance with the Allied Western command, from April 1945 through that autumn. Cultural officers in all of the occupied zones recognized the political power of culture, which led them to subsidize theatre. Officers in the Soviet-led Magistrat and the Allied forces also knew that the theatre could be a useful conduit for bringing recent history to the public. This article adopts a microhistorical lens to highlight the cultural and sociopolitical aftermath of war in Germany's capital city.[5] My reliance on archival research of previously unpublished documents and personal interviews reveals how a loosely connected group of seasoned theatre artists, including Wisten, directors Wolfgang Langhoff and Karl-Heinz Martin, and playwrights Friedrich Wolf, Hedda Zinner, and Günther Weisenborn, for example, began to restore cultural life as early as spring 1945. These artists—Jews, non-Jews, and German citizens of predominately leftist political leanings—had been at the forefront of the avant-garde prior to the war.[6] Their commitment to producing socially relevant and topical dramatic work conveyed an insistent appeal for audiences to take moral responsibility for a postwar Germany in transition. Their active engagement with the theatre season of 1945–1946 discloses how an emerging cultural policy in the newly occupied East sector versus the West would shape the dramatic repertoire for years to come.

This exploration of an under-researched but significant turning point in twentieth-century history allows us to consider the reappearance of a cultural conscience in Berlin in the direct aftermath of war before the Federal Republic of Germany and the German Democratic Republic were officially founded, in 1949. Why has the artistic work achieved in the twilight years of regime transition received so little attention in theatre scholarship? By focusing on a group of theatremakers and their early collaboration we may readdress historiographical questions about the prevalent notion, particularly in the United States, that Bertolt Brecht, Helene Weigel, and their Berliner Ensemble predominately steered the direction of postwar German theatre, especially in the East.[7] I suggest that we reevaluate the cultural significance of the immediate postwar period by crediting the contributions of those first-responder artists who began to restore theatre in Berlin three years before Brecht emerged from exile (1948) to manage the Theater am Schiffbauerdamm (1954) that Wisten had led for seven years.[8] To this end, this article highlights the interrelated web of artistic cooperation that existed among directors, playwrights, and performers, particularly Wisten, Weisenborn, Wolf, and Langhoff, whose collaborative work significantly influenced the programming of the repertoire at the Hebbel Theater and Deutsches Theater. If we agree with Peter Davis that a microfocus on individual artists may reveal the larger structures of cultural and sociopolitical power, thereby correcting "grand historical narratives," as noted by Filippo de Vivo,[9] then a microhistorical gaze within the "gaps" of theatre history in the immediate aftermath of World War II may expose an extraordinary interplay of forces that defined cultural policy for the ensuing decades.

Germany's division into four occupied zones affected the development of culture in the summer of 1945. The three major military victors considered Berlin a special case: each of them, the Soviet military, American-Anglo forces, and the French, would govern separate city sectors and manage cultural output. Cultural activities resumed more quickly in Berlin than in other occupied zones in Germany, where 86 percent of all theatres had been destroyed or badly damaged. Between June and December 1945 in Berlin alone, 121 theatre premieres took place outdoors, in half-ruined theatres, or in taverns, district halls, and school auditoriums.[10] Long before it was clear what kind of society would emerge from the rubble of war in the "fifth zone" of Berlin, the newly installed Soviet Military Administration (SMAD) under General Nikolai Bersarin made it a priority to enlist intellectuals, theatre and opera directors, and performers to fill the cultural vacuum. How did SMAD and the Allied Western Command broker cultural policies to shape early postwar theatre in what by autumn 1948 would be an increasingly divisive city?[11] This question is essential to my exploration into the continuity of theatremaking, including repertoire, by artists like Wisten who, while advancing the artistic avant-garde in the Weimar Republic, had been pushed into exile or incarcerated in the Third Reich, yet returned to aid in rebuilding Berlin's cultural life after 1945.[12]

The theatre season of 1945–1946 represents a transitional period in Germany's theatre history. During this year, Wisten reengaged himself in theatre, while Langhoff and playwrights Wolf, Zinner, and Weisenborn returned from exile and from Nazi prison camps to resume their theatre careers in Berlin, the former epicenter of culture. I will consider two play productions staged two months apart at one theatre in Berlin's West sector, the Hebbel Theater, marking the start of 1946 in Germany's capital: Friedrich Wolf's *Professor Mamlock: A Tragedy of a Western Democracy* (1933), directed by Wisten, and Günther Weisenborn's world premiere of *The Illegals* (1942–1945), directed by Franz Reichert.[13] Both plays draw directly on the experience of ordinary Germans during the Third Reich, highlighting anti-Semitism, opportunism, and complicity with—versus resistance to—the Nazi state tyranny. Even while Soviet and Anglo-American sector administrators were at odds in defining a new German theatre culture, the playwrights promoted their activist belief that theatre could be used as a "weapon"[14] to jolt audiences into an awareness of their recent history. Did their plays provide directors like Wisten with a paradigm for politically engaged theatre that would characterize the repertoire in the East and West zones? Or were these staged productions exceptions in a repertoire given to featuring classics rather than new work and to emphasizing freedom of spirit rather than the reality that citizens colluded with the Nazis? Wolf and Weisenborn chose different ideological alliances—and district zones in which to work—but their shared vision of humanity for their country's future necessitated a communal reckoning about Germany's difficult past.

Such an analysis inevitably points to the intricate planning initiatives of the competing occupying powers responsible for reestablishing a national and local infrastructure in the immediate aftermath of World War II. Wolf and Weisenborn's plays came to the stage amid the disjunction between the Soviet push for a "hasty normalization of cultural life"[15] in Berlin based on New Socialism and the Anglo-Saxon forces' more cautious efforts to "de-Nazify" the German populace and guide a broken nation toward a Western-style democracy. As Josef Foschepoth reminds us, although the Americans wanted to oversee "structural changes" within the conquered nation, the aim of American Occupation policy was primarily to make sure that Germany would not endanger international security.[16] This objective had ramifications for cultural policy. David Monod has made clear, for example, that cultural officers in the American occupation zone had to reestablish the arts in an environment tainted by the fact that many performing artists, especially in the music sector, had collaborated with the Nazi regime.[17] Officers thus focused their reeducation efforts on a denazification program. This caused a conflict, however, between core American goals for formulating cultural policy under a military occupation: how to both control and democratize the arts and punish those artists who had worked with the Nazis yet still allow for some freedom of the arts.[18]

Berlin 1945: Recircuiting the Theatre Infrastructure

It is vital to understand the complexity of Berlin's situation in 1945. By many accounts, the first three years of foreign occupation appear to have been marked by an openness that, according to Wolfgang Schivelbusch, embodied "a relative cultural independence, and power," even on the part of the Soviets.[19] Manfred Uhlitz points to the speedy implementation of cultural life by the Magistrat. This included the publication and posting of a spate of newspapers as early as June, even while 1.5 million refugees roamed Berlin, public transportation was nonexistent in the city's core, and one-third of the urban street grid would still need repair as late as October.[20] About the surprising reemergence of cultural life during the spring of 1945 Günther Rühle refers to an extraordinary "will" among artists to create theatre, which showed that respect for the power of art remained intact despite the "burdensome situation" in Germany.[21] Hermann Glaser writes about the aftermath of World War II as a time of cultural euphoria and celebration by citizens yearning for "cultural riches."[22] Indeed, eyewitness accounts by theatremakers attest to the postwar demand for cultural events: Late in 1945, Friedrich Wolf reports from Berlin on the high attendance at theatres despite such hindrances to theatregoing as steep prices, early curtain times, and difficult evening traffic jams so soon after the war's end. "It is ever clearer," he writes to his friend Langhoff, "what a decisive function a *goal-conscious* theatre serves especially these days."[23]

Retrospective reports by eyewitnesses about the "theatre fever" that pervaded the devastated city refer to what Bärbel Schrader calls "an almost nostalgic awe at the unimaginable enthusiastic spirit" that allowed theatre to take place at all.[24] Fritz Wisten's daughters corroborated this when they spoke about the extraordinary sense of opportunity that existed in Berlin after the oppressive years of the Nazi regime. Their father took advantage of this freedom and used it to make a difference in postwar theatre.[25] In considering the response of citizens—particularly theatre artists—to a new postwar freedom under foreign military rule, it is useful to recall Schivelbusch's description of the historiography of victors and those vanquished, which he has described in terms of a "defeat empathy." Such a postwar dynamic involves the occupying military force and those conquered at the "home front." Detailing the psychological phases that civilians undergo, Schivelbusch notes the initial "elation" at having survived. However, this "Dreamland period" is jolted by an "Awakening," wherein people seek to remove the "victor who freed us" and sense a betrayal when the occupying forces do not leave.[26] According to Foschepoth, the Germans resisted the occupation forces, though the "first year under Soviet policy was better than expected," especially as the Americans behaved more like occupiers than liberators.[27] The paradigm of how civilians respond to military occupation in the wake of war offers a provocative way to think about the reaction of cultural leaders in post–World War II Berlin to the control of their country by international forces. During the first months and year, the liberating "Dreamland" of opportunity appeared to outweigh the very real impediments to life under a recent dictatorship, subsequent war zone, and government takeover by multinational forces.

At the same time, evidence exists to suggest that well before an eventual German defeat seemed inevitable, Soviet leaders planned how to "Sovietize" local populations in their zone of occupation; and in 1943 and early 1945, Stalin, Roosevelt, and Churchill met to discuss how they would lead as victors over the Nazis.[28] More specific to cultural policy, a group of German Communists in Moscow exile (including Friedrich Wolf) gathered in late September 1944 to discuss the guidelines for a cultural policy modeled on the Soviet Union for the new Germany they envisaged after a Red Army victory.

The Ulbricht Group centered around members dedicated to the German Communist Party (KPD) who would become political leaders of the German Democratic Republic: Wilhelm Pieck, Walter Ulbricht, and Otto Grotewohl. Besides the playwrights Wolf and Hedda Zinner, the group included theatre directors, actors, and literary critics with Communist sympathies: Maxim Vallentin, Gustav von Wangenheim, Fritz Erpenbeck, and Johannes R. Becher (the future Minister of Culture for the GDR), all of whom a year later would head theatres and promote through their plays and publications a politicized concept of theatre. Their idea of a "unified and continuous production of literature and criticism" would initiate a "new German national theatre culture" whereby plays and staged productions could be used as an "antifascist action" to "re-educate the German soul of the people" (Volksseele).[29] The guidelines emphasized a commitment by the Communists to "antifascist programmatic goals" through propaganda and artistic means, repertoire, cadre (elite activists), and organization. With the Nazis' capitulation in May 1945 and the concurrent return to Berlin of the Ulbricht Group, the literary and performing arts featured prominently in the "master plan" for Berlin's political future. By looking at the relationship that artists like Wisten, Wolf, and Weisenborn, for example, developed with authorities in the East and West sectors, a link may be made between the early cultural agenda in Berlin and the repertoire in the first theatre seasons. This, in turn, points to the potentially significant role of theatre to extend beyond mere entertainment, to create dialogue, and thereby to enlighten people (Volksbildung).[30]

The Cultural Chamber (Kammer der Kunstchaffenden)

General Commander Bersarin, a former ambassador to Berlin in the 1920s, entered the capital city with the Red Army during the Battle for Berlin in late April 1945. Days before Hitler committed suicide, and amid battles in the streets of Berlin, Bersarin swiftly set rules for public life under the new occupation. It is noteworthy that in establishing evening curfews for citizens, he specifically permitted the attendance of theatre, circus, and cinema in events in Berlin until nine o'clock in the evening.[31] One of his first appointments in late April was to delegate Clemens Herzberg as the Magistrat's managing representative for Cultural Affairs, an office that became the Chamber of Creative Artists (Kammer der Kunstschaffenden) in the ensuing Soviet Military Administration (SMAD), located—and not by chance—at the former site of the Nazi Reich Chamber of Culture in what would be the British-occupied district. The Jewish-born Herzberg assembled Berlin's artistic directors of opera and theatre and reconvened acting ensembles so that cultural life could resume quickly. Former artistic directors on site were best situated to restart their cultural undertakings. Heinz Tietjen (State Opera), Gustaf Gründgens (National Theatre), Ernst Legal (Schiller Theater), and Paul Wegener were among those directors who led theatres under Nazism. Wegener was the only one of the group who openly had espoused an antifascist stance during Hitler's regime. Within two weeks, he replaced Herzberg at the helm of the cultural chamber. For the sake of expediency, SMAD officials tried to reestablish a cultural infrastructure right away.[32]

Walter Ulbricht's returning group of party functionaries was keen to create a Communist German state based on Stalinist principles. The avowed Communists worked closely with Bersarin to implement guidelines for the development of theatre, setting the stage for what would become standard artistic policy in the Soviet-occupied East zone and the future GDR. David Pike acknowledges that the Communist Party's cultural policy was not firmly set in mid-1945, nor were its prearranged plans all realized by 1949. However, he claims an early and pervasive role of Soviet foreign policy and the KPD in cultural affairs. He suggests that the party adopted rhetoric that emphasized the "political 'nonpartisanship' of organized cultural pursuits" in Germany while "managing the affairs surreptitiously" until the Communist Party was ready to discuss its priorities openly.[33] Although the Western Allied forces together with the Soviets had negotiated the imminent occupation of Germany before the war ended, significantly, Russian military and intellectual leaders governed Berlin alone for what Schivelbusch terms "two decisive months" before American troops even entered the city. This gave the Russians a considerable advantage over the other occupying powers when it came to policy.[34]

Under Berlin's Magistrat, administration members from Ulbricht's group decreed in mid-May 1945, for example, that ration cards would be distributed according to four classes of citizens whose food allotment was linked to their occupation status. The rules stipulated that "qualified scholars, engineers, and artists were eligible" for the top category (class I), with writers and actors in the top two classes, ranking their worth to the new Germany in terms of food privileges.[35] The administrators thus created an incentive for artists to register as such and contribute to the intellectual and creative pursuits encouraged by the Soviets. This affected the number of artists (and "would-be" artists) who jockeyed for status and established themselves as cultural trailblazers. Playwrights who returned with Ulbricht, like Friedrich Wolf and Hedda Zinner, profited from this arrangement. As a director, Wisten also belonged to the highest class, receiving the most generous rations available, which according to Manfred Uhlitz amounted to what a heavy laborer would receive: 20 grams of meat and one half of a loaf of bread.[36] By registering as a theatre director at the Cultural Chamber in the wake of war, Wisten also reconnected with leaders in Berlin theatre, benefiting personally and professionally.

Rehabilitation: The Case for Günther Weisenborn

The Russians relied strongly on rebuilding Germany with German antifascists and unsung "heroes" who had been persecuted by the Nazis or chased into exile. These men and women lent social and symbolic merit to the new Germany in the eastern sector.[37] As the Red Army moved through Brandenburg toward Berlin during the last days of April, they released political prisoners, appointing them to administrative positions to weed out the Nazis from local office. Günther Weisenborn had been serving a three-year prison term for "high treason" against the Nazi state because of his role in the antifascist resistance network dubbed the "Red Orchestra" by the Gestapo. After the playwright was freed from a labor prison, he became mayor of Langengrassau-Luckau. While in prison the prolific writer wrote poems, memoirs, and plays. Weisenborn's new dramatic writing was stylistically reminiscent of the antiwar dramatic work he created with Brecht during the Weimar Republic (1928–1932). The 1928 premiere of his *U-Boot-S4* at the Volksbühne had established Weisenborn's reputation in the avant-garde just as Brecht's *The Threepenny Opera* had for him that same year. After Brecht attended the premiere of the younger playwright, the two collaborated artistically with Hannes Eisler. Weisenborn cowrote the 1931 play of *The Mother* with Brecht (starring Helene Weigel in 1932).[38] And the two joined a collective authorship of the screenplay for the leftist film *Kuhle Wampe or Who Owns the World?* (1932). Less than a year later, the Nazis censored the film, directed by Slatan Dudow (with music by Eisler). Was it due to a twelve-year lapse in theatre historiography during the Third Reich that proof of Weisenborn's collaboration with Brecht has become little more than a footnote to the record? Or might it be more likely a consequence of Weisenborn having gone into "inner exile" instead of opting to leave Germany?

Blacklisted by the Nazis like Brecht had been, Weisenborn nonetheless adopted several pseudonyms and continued to write in Germany. Nor did his theatre work cease under Hitler's regime. Besides writing plays that premiered in the Third Reich, he became chief dramaturg at the Schiller Theater under Heinrich George, who had starred in *U-Boot-S4*. None of Weisenborn's colleagues knew about his engagement in resistance actions against the Nazi state. Beginning in 1937, while he worked in theatre, radio, and film, he socialized with various circles of people who distributed illegal leaflets, sought radio communication with the Soviets, and infiltrated organizations of Hitler's state. In autumn 1942, the Gestapo arrested Weisenborn for his association with the Harro Schulze-Boysen/Arvid Harnack resistance network. Sentenced to death for being a traitor, Weisenborn had received a reduced sentence by 1943. He was relocated to several prisons before the Red Army freed him in 1945.[39] Weisenborn turned to theatre to attend to the discord of a traumatized Volk. Of the plays he had begun to write in prison, his tribute to the German resistance, *The Illegals*, would premiere in 1946 at the Hebbel Theater, where he shaped the repertoire with his former colleague from the combined Schiller and Renaissance Theater during the Nazi Reich, theatre director Karl-Heinz Martin. But in May 1945, when their former boss, Heinrich George, negotiated with SMAD officials the reopening of his former theatre, Weisenborn was still in Luckau serving as mayor.

Planning a New Theatre Season: 1945–1946

The Soviet Military Administration sanctioned the city's first official production of a popular farce, *The Rape of the Sabines* (by the brothers Franz and Paul von Schönthan), for late May at the bomb-damaged Renaissance Theatre in Berlin west (what would be the American zone). At the premiere on May 27, Ernst Legal presided over his former ensemble members as a producer of the play, directed by Egon Brosig. The play had been scheduled for several days earlier, but spectators were sent home twice due to electric outages in the theatre. Thereafter, when a loss of electricity interrupted a performance—a frequent occurrence—the actors played by candlelight. According to one reviewer, the audience's resounding applause at the opening performance showed that the "exquisite" experience of the liberating play meant more to spectators than their lack of physical comfort in the theatre's cold and sparsely furnished, improvised space.[40] This was not an isolated example of the poor conditions at theatres during the summer of 1945. Throughout six weeks of rehearsals for a revival of Brecht's *The Threepenny Opera* at the Hebbel Theater in Kreuzberg, in addition to surmounting problems with faulty electric cables and stolen costumes, actors often rehearsed in the dark or with umbrellas because the rain leaked through holes in the theatre's roof onto the stage.[41]

Meanwhile, in another district of Berlin, the Soviet Command had granted Fritz Wisten protection and permission to move about the city freely by bicycle. His identification papers designated him "Director of the Office for the Enlightenment of the People" in Berlin-Nikolassee and in charge of "artistic events."[42] By June 1945 Wisten reported to the director of the Cultural Chamber, Wegnener, whose office belonged to the "Department for Popular Education," led by Otto Winzer. In exile in Moscow, Winzer had detailed pedagogical objectives for audience education in a new Germany. He could implement those principles as he reestablished Berlin's cultural elite with directors like Wisten and dramaturgs like Weisenborn.[43] Winzer also helped to found a Cultural League for the Democratic Renewal of Germany to encourage left-leaning artists to move to the Soviet occupation zone, where the Deutsches Theater was located. The group deliberately located the league in Berlin-Dahlem, which fell into the American-occupied zone. But it was the Russians who gave the new cultural alliance a license late in June 1945, just days before the Allied troops arrived in Berlin to occupy their city sector zones.[44]

When the American military entered Berlin early in July and took over Wisten's residential zone, the Soviet-controlled offices at Schlüterstraße had already officially registered him as a "director and actor in the Stage Commission of the Chamber of Working Artists." The Western Allied Command endorsed Wisten's theatre-related work, granting him unhindered mobility throughout the city so that he could carry on his artistic endeavors.[45] He had received permission from Wegener and Wangenheim to stage one of the first serious postwar productions at the Deutsches Theater, a revival of Lessing's classic drama of tolerance, *Nathan the Wise*, which the Nazis had banned. The production premiere on September 7, 1945, was something of a theatrical coup: Wisten not only cast Wegener as Nathan, but Wangenheim's influential father, Eduard von Winterstein (stage name), also played a lead role. The politically powered production run coincided with the performance run of another once-banned play, *The Threepenny Opera*, less than a mile to the West at the Hebbel Theater, whose poor conditions had plagued the rehearsals. Karl-Heinz Martin directed the production.[46] Martin had gained his reputation through his expressionist productions of plays by Ernst Toller and Georg Kaiser at the Volksbühne, where he served as artistic director between 1929 and 1932. Together with Weisenborn, Martin had also worked at the Schiller-Renaissance Theater from 1938 to the war's end. Much like Wisten, Martin's artistic credentials ensured him a major role in rebuilding Berlin's theatre scene.

By 1946 the Allied Command in Berlin had compiled an A-list, known as the "White List" (weiße Liste), including more than fifteen hundred names of Germans who might become part of the society elite.[47] In addition to Martin, Wisten was listed among the "most significant artists." The commanding officials deemed his cultural work at Max Reinhardt's former theatre important to the well-being of the city's residents. They even granted him an exemption from the electricity-saving measures prescribed by Allied authorities, because his preparatory stage work and rehearsal time required a higher use of electricity than allotted to standard households.[48] In spring 1946, the American Command praised Wisten's cultural contribution, once more making an exception for the director in determining that the Army could not "requisition" the apartments he occupied at the Deutsches Theater with his set designer, Ernst Schütte.[49] Soviet officials and Allied forces had ample time to see Wisten's production of *Nathan the Wise*. It played in repertory and celebrated its one hundredth performance on November 7, 1946, which was open to audiences from all city sectors.[50]

Repertoire in Berlin's Occupied Zones

Wisten wanted to lead his own theatre. To achieve his goal, he worked tirelessly as a freelance director at the Deutsches Theater and at the Hebbel Theater, where Martin presided, located in the city's Anglo-American sector. One of the most difficult issues that concerned theatre directors was what plays belonged in the repertoire. This was particularly problematic for German-language work. After twelve years without cultural influences from the outside, the German repertoire was dependent on pre-1933 plays and blacklisted works, as well as foreign plays. Those plays that were confiscated and forbidden in the Third Reich therefore were not always easy to find, or to stage, because of issues related to permissions and royalties. Directors had little flexibility about what could be produced in the 1945–1946 season. Nonetheless, the Deutsches Theater produced ten plays during this period: three classics (including *Nathan the Wise*), two modern plays (among them, Wisten's production of Sternheim's comedy *The Snob*, starring Gustaf Gründgens), and four contemporary pieces, including Thornton Wilder's *Our Town*. A former assistant to Gründgens surprisingly had procured the American play in German translation. *Our Town* premiered on August 3, 1945.

The production of Wilder's play puzzled German critics, who found little to praise. There were only two performances before SMAD officials told Wangenheim to remove the play from the repertory. Readers in all of the occupied sectors read Paul Rilla's opinions on theatre, which he published in the Soviet-sector *Berliner Zeitung*, the official publication for the city. In the first days of August, after the Potsdam Conference, SMAD officials placed all publishing and printing companies under military administration, subjecting newspapers to censorship. Rilla pronounced Wilder's dramatic "experiment" a failure, because its focus on a new scenic form did not justify the content, with which Germans could not identify.[51] For him, the repertoire in the new Germany must engage theatregoers with topical subjects that reflected the present German situation. As editor of the *Berliner Zeitung*'s feuilleton section, Rilla could sway public opinion. The first newspaper with an American license would not be printed until September 1945. In fact, it was not until autumn 1945 that the Allied military forces determined that all cultural activities, including publications, theatre, music, and radio, would be overseen by a Cultural Affairs Committee of the Allied Command.[52]

It took until the summer of 1946 for the Americans to compile for German stages in their city sector an authorized list of stage-worthy playwrights, including Wilder. The list took into account new work by American playwrights Eugene O'Neill (*Mourning Becomes Electra*) and Lillian Hellman (*Watch on the Rhine*) besides Wilder (*The Skin of Our Teeth*). As noted, both the Renaissance and the Hebbel Theaters were located in Anglo-American zones of influence. *Our Town* had a repeat performance at an outlying theatre district in the British zone early in 1946. The French sector had few theatres, but cultural officers there maintained a connection to publishers with Berlin affiliates, ensuring an eventual channel for French plays.[53] In the East sector the new Henschelverlag enabled directors to procure the rights to scripts easily. The clear influence from the Soviets also facilitated the staging of Russian classics and contemporary Soviet drama in districts under their jurisdiction.

In the East, the Soviet strategy encouraged the production of work that stressed the Nazi past so as to point toward antifascism, its heroes, and the conquest of dictatorship. In the West, the cultural strategy was also connected to the political: to highlight the past to "de-Nazify" the populace and move beyond the past to start anew. The problem with the theatre repertoire in the first year was a lack of "proportion between the stage and the life of the times," as critic Friedrich Luft stated. Luft was a proponent of Günther Weisenborn's new drama. Bärbel Schrader invokes Luft to claim that only two contemporary productions successfully made visible the proper proportion between life onstage and in "real time" that Luft encouraged: the first one being Weisenborn's play, *The Illegals*, at the Hebbel Theater (March 1946). But Schrader believed that these productions were relegated to mere "experiments" and thus produced in the theatre's small studio space for fear of how the public would receive the play's content.[54] Significantly, however, Schrader ignores an earlier play production in early January 1946 that effectively offered audiences in equal proportion "the stage and the life of the times," namely Friedrich Wolf's *Professor Mamlock: A Tragedy of a Western Democracy* (1933), which premiered on the Hebbel Theater (Mainstage), under Fritz Wisten's direction.

Friedrich Wolf and *Professor Mamlock*: Diagnosing Anti-Semitism within the Populace

Karl-Heinz Martin, the artistic director of the Hebbel, urgently summoned Wisten to his office in the autumn of 1945 to discuss Wolf's play about a Jewish German surgeon and anti-Semitism in Hitler's regime.[55] Martin, together with Weisenborn as the theatre dramaturg, wanted to produce some of Wolf's new work, planning *Mamlock* for the second half of the new season, 1945–1946. "Give us *Mamlock*," Martin wrote to Wolf, adding that the actor Walter Frank was excited and eager to start right away on the German premiere.[56] Wisten knew Wolf personally from the playwright's agitprop theatre work in Stuttgart during the early 1930s, when they both had lived and worked there. A Jewish-born physician and writer, Wolf immigrated to the Soviet Union directly after the burning of the Reichstag late in February 1933. He returned to Berlin with Ulbricht group members, keen to promote ideas initiated in Moscow, including the creation of an organization with shared cultural, moral, and intellectual objectives to "overcome the past."[57]

Wolf's clear-cut allegiance to the Communist Party (KPD) and his politically infused writings endangered his well-being in Germany when the Nazis came to power. His 1928 essay, *Art as a Weapon* (*Kunst als Waffe*), advocated using the theatre stage as a "battleground" for ideas. No stranger to controversy, the 1929 Berlin production of his play *Cyankali* sparked a debate about the federal law that banned abortions. Wolf volunteered as a physician for the International Brigades in the Spanish Civil War, but he was arrested en route and sent to the Le Vernet internment camp in Vichy (France). He returned to Moscow after his release in 1941.

The Hebbel Theater premiere of Wolf's *Professor Mamlock* five years later on January 9, 1946, should be viewed as a cultural touchstone production for the times. The play had never been produced in Germany. The world premiere took place in Warsaw in Yiddish. The first German-language production took place at the Zürcher Schauspielhaus in 1934. But by the twenty-second repeat performance, Swiss fascists had cordoned off the theatre and street battles raged between a polarized Right and Left in a neutral Switzerland. In 1937 the Jewish Unit of the Federal Theatre Project Theatre in the United States staged the play in English translation. The play was so popular outside of Germany that it had Hebrew, Russian, Swedish, and even Japanese-language runs.[58]

Wisten's 1946 production of *Professor Mamlock* introduced Germans to the play and marked a rerouting of repertoire choices for those theatregoers chastened by recent history. The four-act play indicts patriotic and professional Germans like the character of Mamlock and those who work with him at the hospital. Although he is a Jew, he holds conservative political views and does not recognize the dangerous anti-Semitic attitudes of those around him. The imminent theatre premiere of Wolf's play gained significance in providing a forum to make public what Martin referred to as "the foundation and the genesis of those incidents that led to this nous accusons! [we acknowledge!]"—in other words, the starting point for an anti-Semitism that led to ostracism and extermination and, ultimately, to an acknowledgment of a country's crimes.[59] Ironically, after the start of the international Nuremberg Trials in November 1945, the political officer of the US Control Commission expressed his concern about the Hebbel Theater's choice of *Mamlock*, Martin informed the playwright: plays of "this type" were "not desired," because, as Martin put it, they were not optimistic.[60]

Wolf, however, had no interest in writing or staging merely uplifting "feel-good" plays. He expressed far more optimism about the timeliness for remaking Berlin into a first-rate cultural center. "Come here as soon as possible; you will easily have opportunities," he wrote to his friend Wolfgang Langhoff about the "great potential" of theatre work in Berlin.[61] Langhoff, who had left his Swiss exile to settle in Düsseldorf, however, had decided that while he "must return to Berlin," it seemed to him more important—at least in the short term—to stay in the Rhineland, where there was a "great need" for people trained in cultural work. Berlin had "enough" people in place for the time being.[62] Wolf's excitement about the quality of postwar theatre in Berlin and the Allied forces' strong encouragement and support for theatre venues would lure Langhoff to Berlin in autumn 1946, less than a year after assuming the directorship of the Municipal Stages in Düsseldorf. For something else especially appealed to Langhoff; according to Wolf, it was "truly astonishing" the extent to which Berlin theatregoers actively sought "good theatre" and intellectually resonant events to attend: "They really seem to be starved" for culture, Wolf reported as he enumerated a wealth of daily newspapers (ten) and journals (eight), including one satirical magazine that appeared twice a week. Meanwhile, significantly, his *Professor Mamlock* had been successfully dramatized as a radio play, broadcast six times to great acclaim over the previous months. How would German theatre audiences understand his play politically? he mused two weeks before the 1946 premiere. One thing he knew for certain: His play would be "the first 'directly' political play" since the end of the war.[63]

Figure 1. Friedrich Wolf's *Professor Mamlock*, January 9, 1946. Director Fritz Wisten. Walter Franck as Mamlock, Act III. Courtesy of SLUB Dresden, Deutsche Fotothek. Photo by Abraham Pisarek.

Professor Mamlock onstage showed audiences a mirror of themselves almost in real-time. As noted, the production run took place while the Nuremberg war crime trials were underway. The play's chronology parallels the historically quick ascension of the Nazis to power, beginning in May 1932, before the

Hindenburg election. Act 2 takes place the day after the burning of the Reichstag in late February 1933. Act 3 opens less than two months later on the day of the April boycott against the Jews by the Nazis; and the final act ends on the next day, at the end of which Professor Mamlock commits suicide, when barred by his surgical staff and the SA from his hospital operating room for being a Jew. The designer Heinz Pfeiffenberger used a stage revolve to portray two main playing areas for the production: Acts 1 and 4 were set in the hospital's preparatory room for surgery, an atmosphere of clinical sterility that exuded a starkness and "hygenic coolness," according to a reviewer for the *Tägliche Zeitung*. Acts 2 and 3 took place in Mamlock's home living room.[64]

Wolf uses Mamlock as a spokesperson for the fight against narrow-mindedness and intolerance in his polemical play. Political discussion pervades Mamlock's operating room, where his assisting physicians make their anti-Semitism apparent in act 1 before Mamlock's entrance. They prepare their patient, an editor of a major newspaper, for surgery: "Who are the owners of the big department stores like Tietz, Wertheim, Alsberg, Karstadt?" Dr. Hellpach asks the young intern Dr. Inge Ruoff, to which she answers with recognition, "The Jews . . . the Jews."[65] The play's characters can easily be divided into politically Left and Right ideological camps, further indicated by the appearance in act 1 of a wounded worker, injured in a street fight between Nazis and Communists. By the end of the first act, Mamlock has asked his staff to keep politics out of his operating room, which he wishes to reserve for doctors and patients only.

By act 2, however, Mamlock has admitted "political surgery" to his daily chores. His former patient Dr. Seidel comes to warn him of slander in the newspaper that Jews are working with the Communists. Mamlock may want to disappear for a few days, Seidel suggests, because the Sturmabteilung (SA) is arresting Jews for instigating the Reichstag fire. On the home front, despite her political leanings to the Right, Dr. Inge too tries to warn the family. She is in love with Mamlock's son (Rolf) who has joined the city's leftist political cause. The playwright uses the triggering event of the Reichstag fire to drive the plot, revealing the escalating political situation for Jews in Germany.

As act 3 opens after the 1933 boycott of Jewish businesses, the demarcation lines between Right and Left politics are clearly drawn for the characters. Mamlock's young daughter has been harassed at school for being a Jew. Rolf cannot be found. Sturmabteilung men have escorted Mamlock home from his clinic. Wearing a cardboard sign around his neck marked "Jew," he is humiliated and uncomprehending that he has been asked about his lineage. We hear him mutter "defenseless, defenseless," then he goes to get his revolver. Dr. Hellpach, Mamlock's former assisting surgeon, has become an official ideologue in an SA uniform. He dismisses Mamlock from his duties at the hospital and forbids his return to the clinic. In response to Hellpach's anti-Semitic rant, Mamlock is resolute about his intentions not only to return to his clinic but also to stand his ground: "We will stay in Germany. We can no longer leave this land. We are part of this country."[66]

Mamlock remains defiant in the final act showdown at the clinic with Hellpach and his craven operating staff. The surgeon refuses to sign his dismissal papers. Instead, he rips them up and throws the pieces in Hellpach's face. Then he shoots himself in the chest. Mamlock's dying words make clear the playwright's intention: "Fight . . . but with whom, but for whom . . . to be caught with cut off trousers, with the sign around one's neck; to be paraded through the streets by these heroes . . . and yet to fight . . .. How can one forget that . . . too bad! One only thinks in the end of oneself."[67] As he bleeds to death, Dr. Inge despairs. She has had a change in conscience since the first act, partly due to her love for Rolf, who represents an alternative political path in the play. She asks Mamlock whether he has chosen the only way to resolve the situation. His response is telling: "For me the only way . . .. Maybe (*he looks at her*) you . . . you must go another way, a new way (*insistent, softly, but with all his strength*). Listen to me. Take that path . . .. Greet my son . . . Rolf, when you meet him on the other path, on the other path (*falls back*)." Will Inge choose the "other path," a way that appears connected to Communist resistance and revolt? It is another young character, the nurse's aide, Simon—a Jew—who closes the play with a repeated warning: "We will never forget what we have seen these past days and weeks!"[68]

Wisten's politically tinged production in 1946 offered audiences a didactic warning to remember not only what they have seen onstage but also what they likely saw and experienced in the years that led to Hitler's takeover. Critics praised Fritz Wisten's direction of the play and its attention to the political times.[69] The director's renewed acquaintance with Wolf deepened an emerging collaborative artistic relationship between the men that would continue through the 1950s.[70] It also paved the way for the next significant artistic collaboration at the Hebbel: the return of Günther Weisenborn's dramatic work to the Berlin stage. The stage production of his newest work further enhanced the Hebbel's theatre repertoire.

Weisenborn's "Place-less Dramaturgy" and *The Illegals*

Weisenborn coproduced the world premiere of his play about anti-Nazi resistance, *The Illegals*, on March 21, 1946. He wanted to offer audiences cultural diversion and spiritual uplift, much as directors Wisten and Martin did. At the same time, like Friedrich Wolf, he also tried to "jolt" theatregoers publicly so that what they saw onstage would help them to see and think.[71] His play premiered in Studio 46, an experimental space for new forms of performance in an intimate setting. Weisenborn's new play was not an "experiment," however. Wolf wrote plays with the intention of provoking audiences to reflect upon what was happening around them politically; in the case of *Mamlock*, on the attitudes of ordinary and apolitical Germans. Weisenborn also drew on the immediate aftermath of cataclysm, personal and national, to craft a dramaturgy that tapped into the trauma of the recent past. Like Wolf, he hoped that audiences would recognize their recent history and begin to accept it. Both Wolf and Weisenborn and their respective directors at the Hebbel in 1946 shared a common purpose: The two productions attest to the men's adherence to an antifascist Germany. They wanted to renew the national repertoire, encouraging people of all ages to assume collective moral responsibility for their country's past crimes and for the future. Weisenborn noted that the Hebbel Studio 46 was specifically organized to "change and activate" spectators through their exposure to new plays as well as to "combative" old ones. Young actors, directors, and designers would use their art to speak to youth in the theatre audience.[72]

Weisenborn's play straddles autobiographical confession with a commemoration of those who opposed the Nazi regime from within. He acknowledged that he wrote *The Illegals* "in shock" during nights of a "desperate winter": "We survivors in the service of the dead have the very concrete duty to make memorials in the present for the 'departed.'" He wrote in the post-trauma of war, dedicating his play, as he put it, "as a memorial of the Schafottfront." The "Front" was characterized by the scaffold for execution where his fellow "soldiers" in the resistance were beheaded. He wrote as an eyewitness clandestinely in the early 1940s and then during 1945. For Weisenborn, keeping the historiographical record straight was vital. As noted in his dedication to his play, he also wrote for posterity: "We have the duty to make clear their deeds to our German people and especially to the youth . . .. The world must know that countless people in our 'Fatherland' existed, who pure as ice, believing and freedom-loving, fought for humanity and died as a result. This play might be the catalyst for the deeds of illegal organizations to be reported and discussed publicly. It is time. The way that our beloved Germany, marked by pity, will behave at home vis à vis the deeds of the 'Illegals' will be a determining factor in how we are judged by the world."[73] Weisenborn ensured that the resisters who died for a cause received recognition. Yet it also was imperative for his message to reach future generations. In his struggle to fight against the Nazis, the playwright used theatre to reconcile himself with his active work in resistance circles, as well as his survival against the odds. At the same time, he reached out to shaken audience members, many of whom were in deep denial about the extent to which ordinary citizens contributed to the twelve-year reign of terror and oppression within Germany and outside its borders.[74]

The reception of Weisenborn's play was mixed even before its premiere. A critic for a leading Soviet-sector newspaper previewed the play two weeks before it opened. Fritz Erpenbeck claimed that the content outweighed the dramatic form to the point of being less dramatic and more polemical. He thought that rhetoric replaced dialogue, and that the play seemed contrived, "dominated by cabaret-like inlays." He preferred the "purpose play" (Tendenzstück), wherein the ideological content would be organically linked to form.[75] Weisenborn referred to a mode of postwar writing as embodying a "place-less dramaturgy" (*ortlose Dramaturgie*) in time and space.[76]

Weisenborn's concept of a "place-less" dramaturgy is reminiscent perhaps of Thornton Wilder's experimental dramaturgy and includes aspects of Brecht's concept of an epic theatre. Like Wilder, Weisenborn believed in engendering in the audience an intensive empathy and accompanying catharsis. Unlike Brecht, however, he favored "strong and passionate dramatic scenes" that escalated. Weisenborn adopted an episodic format, yet he divided those episodes within acts. Despite his insertion of a narrator/character and songs in his play, he worked against the aesthetic distancing effect that Brecht used. The songs that he included, for example, are organically integrated into the text and are not in juxtaposition to it.[77] His idea of the "place-less" stage softened the didactic edge of his play, encompassing the philosophical and moral realm. He was never interested in avoiding the illusion of theatre or solely "undergirding his plays with ideology." Instead, the playwright tried to portray a story in scenic episodes whose import might provoke ideological changes within a reflective spectator.[78]

Weisenborn was concerned that reports about a kind of "inner emigration" during the war obfuscated the real actions of the resisters (or illegals), relegating their actions into what was a parenthetical. He saw their "inner refuge" as something obviously necessary but not as the point of his play. Rather, he wanted to portray human relationships within the circles of resistance, not to offer numbers and hard facts about the resistance movement.[79] He had written a report on the resistance, documenting the fact that Germans rebelled against their dictatorship: "It is time for the world to find out what happened here in this country," he wrote. "We owe it to the world . . . and particularly to the dead . . .. We survivors have a duty to bear witness . . .. The time for silence, secrets, and whispers is over. We can speak! We must speak! And so the play *The Illegals* is a beginning."[80]

His play in forty-one episodes opens with a narrator, the character of the "Good Neighbor" who propels the action not unlike how Wilder's Stage Manager opens *Our Town.* Leaning against a fence and smoking a pipe, the character speaks about the shortsightedness of Germans: "The German does not see that the sun is made of the tin of smoking propaganda and dripping with blood. The German must learn to see. Like a child, he must learn the alphabet of soft violence. To this end, several men and women have decided to teach the German a lesson. It is autumn. The Maple [tree] is bare and the leaflets fall!"[81] By setting the scene in the autumn of 1942—the actual time of his arrest—Weisenborn presents a version of his story, weaving in a love story at the core of his memoriam to his lost circle of fellow resisters. Lill (played by Lulu Säuberlich) works in the Resistance and as a waitress in the café bar run by Manna, whose son Walther belongs to another resistance group. Walther as protagonist is likely Weisenborn's alter ego: like Weisenborn, the character Walther engages in illicit work that goes beyond pasting leaflets against the regime. He sends illegal radio broadcasts. After Lill recruits Walther and seduces him politically, the two join forces romantically (for one night), before he is discovered and kills himself at his arrest.

Figure 2. Günther Weisenborn's *The Illegals: Resistance and Romance*, March 1946. Director Franz Reichert. Ernst Wilhelm Bochert (Walther) and Lulu Säuberlich (Lill). Courtesy of SLUB Dresden, Deutsche Fotothek. Photo by Abraham Pisarek.

In a powerful passage in scene 12, Lill speaks to Walther about the resistance group for which she recruits him, setting it within the greater network of the fight against tyranny: "All that members ask is 'Is the man good?'" she tells him, then forcefully makes clear the need to create a united front for freedom, despite the ostensibly low number of those engaged in the fight. She enumerates how out of four million residents in Berlin, three million do not reflect about fighting for freedom. This leaves one million, of whom nine hundred thousand are fearful, or followers. That leaves one hundred thousand, of whom ninety thousand have too much to do or claim to be apolitical or to lack the opportunity to get involved in politics. She further whittles down the remaining ten thousand people to one thousand, because, as she claims, nine thousand are otherwise engaged: "One thousand determined men and women in all of greater Berlin, of whom 993 are unknown to me, leaving seven—that is our group . . .. But somewhere in Berlin there must be others." To this, Walther responds: "Maybe they are not so far from you all, the others—only you don't know about one another."[82] He belongs to another resistance group. Lill's passage is a strong condemnation of the German populace during the Third Reich.

Weisenborn has written about how the ordinary German (bystanders and opportunists alike) were in the same German "boat," so to speak (and Walther espouses this idea in the play). The small group of resisters, which included ordinary workers, members of the upper social classes, and the military, was for the most part scorned and detested, because its members fought against their own people and the German nation, sacrificing their lives for the defeat of the Fatherland. By serving as the surrogate bearer of memory for those who died in his stead, Weisenborn as survivor-witness and writer could speak to the complicated psychological terrain of German complicity in allowing the Hitler regime and to the minority of resisters who defied the state.

In this way, Weisenborn captures in his play the immediate history of the resistance. He calls attention to the fact that resistance cells did work against the murderous regime from inside Germany. By referring to actual people, to statistics regarding the number of people in the resistance, and to how the resistance worked, the playwright effectively uses Walther's dramatic illegal broadcast in the penultimate scene 40 to "whisper the 'sacred names' of those real-life resisters who were executed by order of the Nazis: Schulze-Boysen, Husemann, Schumacher (Kurt and Elisabeth), Walter Küchenmeister."[83] Weisenborn's play ends in a similar way to Wolf's *Professor Mamlock*: Walther is arrested (scene 41) and shots are fired outside. Did he commit suicide to protect the others in the resistance group? Or was he killed by the men in civilian dress who took him away? It appears that he killed himself, as did Wolf's Mamlock.

The play's final stage image is a sobbing Lill, who lost her love but remains safe to continue her resistance activity. The play ends in death coupled with the hope of redemption for the next generation. The resistance circle was not breached completely. Others were able to carry forth the fight against tyranny. And Weisenborn knew that better than anyone did. He had not let his former compatriots die in vain. The sacrifice of the play's main resister protects the resistance group so that it could continue at the play's end. Walther's final broadcast within the play is directed to young Germans—the next generation—to explain the difficulty of being a German resister during the Third Reich (read: traitor) and to ask them how they might remake their future.

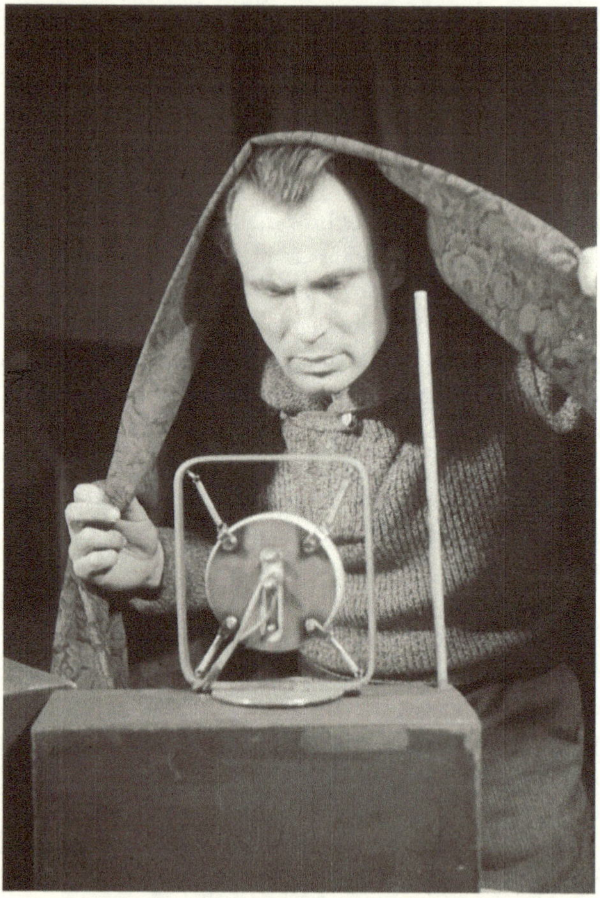

Figure 3. Günther Weisenborn's *The Illegals: Resistance and Romance*, March 1946. Director Franz Reichert. Ernst Wilhelm Borchert as Walther. Courtesy of SLUB Dresden, Deutsche Fotothek. Photo by Abraham Pisarek.

It is doubtful that German audiences in March 1946 could readily identify with the "heroes of the resistance" at the "scaffold-front." With his play, Weisenborn confronts the mass denial that ultimately led to the rubble that Germany had become only a year earlier. The playwright tried to create a theatre experience that could shock theatregoers into a reflection that would deepen as they watched actors inhabit their roles. In performance, the play's mise-en-scene suggested that the scripted "form" enhanced the content's drama and thus the experience for theatregoers. Weisenborn reported on the premiere's "huge success" and its rapid adoption into theatre repertoires in Germany's West zone. His words to a director in Darmstadt who produced the play show the playwright's commitment to the dramaturgical transposition from text to the theatre stage. He meticulously described the use of technical elements of lighting and scenic design for the Berlin premiere: "The scenery was sparse with a large projection in the background which changed: roofs of the city, etc. During the first broadcast, the projection dissipated. The light shone on a group with radio headphones on. Walther plays the broadcast with a blanket over his head. A weak greenish light emanates from the radio sending device, otherwise it was dark. During the second broadcast, the light was extinguished so that the naming of the five names took place in absolute darkness."[84]

Weisenborn aimed to actively engage spectators in the total theatre experience. Vital to a production of the play would be the use of the stage and its formalistic elements (projection, sound, lighting, and performing bodies) to highlight the content and create in spectators an emotional connection. *The Illegals* enlightened audiences about their past. A spate of productions took place in the East and West zones on radio broadcasts and in theatres from Berlin to Schwerin, from Darmstadt to Munich, between March and May 1946. This attests to the play's appeal for Germans in the wake of war.[85]

Casualties of the Cold War?

Between 1945 and 1948, Weisenborn's work as dramaturg at the Hebbel Theater reflected his ongoing resolve to create a repertoire that did not shy away from difficult subject matter even as East-West party line positions hardened. In crafting his dramaturgy, he compelled audiences to confront their immediate collective past. His idea of a "place-less" stage (Ortslose Bühne)[86] suggests an "unfixed" time and location, reminiscent of the actual "place-less-ness" of Berlin between 1945 and 1946, when the city's new cultural shape began to emerge from the rubble. Weisenborn's own displacement may be gauged by the numerous times he relocated, first to Hamburg in the early 1950s to work as the Chief Dramaturg at the Kammerspiele, only to return to West Berlin in the 1960s. Yet, his ongoing desire to document the German resistance to Hitler, reminding Germans about the need for moral freedom, garnered more sympathy in the 1960s than in the 1940s.

Fritz Wisten, on the other hand, adopted a more pragmatic approach to establishing himself as a director of what would be known as "komödiantisches

Theater," entertaining and enlightening social commentary onstage. He maintained a highly visible presence as an efficient director-manager. When he proposed to Langhoff that he direct Sternheim's satire about social class, *The Snob*, at the Deutsches Theater Kammerspiele in 1946, the appeal of the production lay in the actor cast to play the leading role: Once more Wisten envisaged a star-studded cast of old and new faces onstage. His casting of his old friend Gründgens as Christian Maske enabled the famous actor's return to the German stage, in May 1946, after an eight-month Soviet internment.[87] Wisten had a knack for bringing people together around theatre and positioning it as a vehicle for restoration. In the summer of 1946 the Soviet Military Administration officially presented him with a legitimate license to lead the Theater am Schiffbauerdamm. Major Alexander Dymschitz recognized Wisten's value in "re-educating the German people." As a director, the cultural officer said that Wisten saw "theatre as a weapon" by which one could expose the "social struggle and educate society."[88] In his acceptance speech, Wisten spoke of the ubiquitous nature of politics and the political nature of all plays: "When politics means the attempt to overcome reality through action, that does not mean that humanity divides into those who act and those who do not act; rather, into a group that acts and one that allows themselves to be acted upon. The seemingly unpolitical person; that is, one who allows things to happen, actually supports the one who does something: not to stop something from happening is the same thing as permitting it: political neutrality . . . does not exist. Nor do unpolitical plays."[89] Fittingly perhaps, Wisten would choose Friedrich Wolf's plays as staples for his repertoire at the new Schiffbauerdamm Theater and, subsequently, as part of the Volksbühne.

Only one year after the German capitulation, citizens were returning to the theatre in large numbers. Berlin had three major venues in different city sectors and a dedicated group of artists who established a new direction for German cultural life. Many of these men and women had been blacklisted and even incarcerated by the Nazis for their political beliefs and actions, or for their religion (being Jewish by birth). They were ideologically on the Left, and several of them (Wolf, Wisten, Zinner, and Langhoff) joined the Communist Party and worked in the East sector, especially after the division between East and West resulted in two Germanies. During the first postwar theatre season of 1945–1946, however, Wisten, Weisenborn, Wolf, and Wolfgang Langhoff, as new director of the Deutsches Theater (autumn 1946), put aside ideological differences to work together in their common desire to create a more profound confrontation with recent history in order to move beyond it.

In hindsight, one must ask why some of these theatre artists have been consigned to footnotes in historiographical accounts of theatre immediately following the war. Fritz Wisten served a pivotal role in the resurgence of culture in the immediate aftermath of war. He led the new Schiffbauerdamm Theater for eight years before Brecht and Weigel returned to jockey for its management. Nonetheless, his contribution to postwar theatre has been mostly fleeting in literary and theatre histories of the period. Why is a political hero of the resistance and a prolific writer like Weisenborn not better known as a playwright in the West? Despite his commitment to living and working in the West, his significance to theatre history has been marginalized, particularly in the United States. His literary work found more resonance in what would be the GDR than in the West. Yet he lived and worked in the West, never joined the Communist Party, and remained largely nonpolitical.[90] Are these theatremakers ultimately "casualties of the Cold War"? The playwrights who belonged to the Ulbricht Group, Friedrich Wolf and Hedda Zinner, chose ideological sides early on, cementing their dramaturgical and literary significance in what became East Germany. Their contribution to theatre history as first responder artists in the aftermath of war remains underdocumented in the West. Weisenborn's status, on the other hand, is puzzling.

Part of the answer may come from Brecht himself, in a letter he wrote to Weisenborn in 1949. Regarding their coauthorship of *The Mother* in 1931–1932 and some discussion of royalties, Brecht writes: "As far as the 'Mother' is concerned, your name was left out during the Hitler years on my initiative, because you otherwise might have been endangered. Now that will not be the case again."[91] The omission of Weisenborn's name from his dramatic work meant that in historiographical terms, Brecht received sole credit for *The Mother* during the years he spent in exile, especially in the United States. As Brecht gained primacy in East Berlin after 1949, Weisenborn worked in West Germany. His "internal" German exile, his double life in the resistance, and his incarceration by the Nazis complicate the reconstruction of his postwar theatre profile. He was firmly rooted neither in the East nor in the West; in effect he was "place-less."

Likewise, how may one "place" Fritz Wisten in the greater scheme of rebuilding Germany's cultural terrain? Like Weisenborn, his postwar reputation rested, in part, on how he maintained his professional life within the Third Reich at the helm of the Jewish Kulturbund theatre. After the war, he placed hope in the burgeoning antifascist state that replaced the dictatorship. Like Weisenborn, he worked to create theatre for future German audiences. Yet he admitted to being disillusioned with the growing rigidity apparent in the East sector after 1947 (the year he joined the SED party). Of their father, Wisten's daughters outlined how he "toed the line," so to speak, adapting to being at odds with the political system in the GDR. It became increasingly clear to him that the new regime represented a too-familiar image of what he remembered from the Third Reich. He made a careful compromise as he led the Volksbühne through the 1950s: to work in the East and retain his residence in the West, breathing freely in the evenings at home in Berlin- Schlachtensee.[92]

Late in 1945, Friedrich Luft commented on Berlin as a haunted city whose residents needed clarity and solace that could come from art. His words echo with a sense of displacement as he refers to the "loneliness of the building of our destiny" amid the rubble: empty, broken, yet cleared of "false landlords." Luft characterizes the first sound of the poet-dramatist Weisenborn, who emerged from the shadow of rubble, as a "plaint," followed by an accusation confronting the denial that created the "field of rubble" in the first place.[93] This is the strength of spirit that Weisenborn, Wisten, Wolf, and others brought to theatre during the transitional year of 1945–1946: They first responded to a cultural crisis, remaking theatre with a new urgency for the times.

Notes

1. Fritz Wisten to Camilla Spira, March 1946, FWA 74/86/434, Stiftung der Akademie der Künste (AdK), Berlin. A well-known cabaret actress in the Weimar Republic, Spira performed with Wisten in Berlin through 1938. She performed under Wisten's direction in 1946. All translations from German are mine, unless otherwise stated. All subsequent archival holdings related to Berlin's Akademie der Künste will be referred to as AdK, Berlin.
2. Richard Bessel, *Germany 1945: From War to Peace* (London: Simon and Schuster, 2009), 6.
3. Until the publication of Günther Rühle's 2014 German-language survey of German theatre between 1945 and 1966, no serious full-length scholarly work addressed Berlin theatre and politics during the transitional years of occupied Germany (1946–1949) before the founding of the German Democratic Republic. See Rühle's *Theater in Deutschland, 1945–1966: Seine Ereignisse—seine Menschen* (Frankfurt am Main: S. Fischer Verlag, 2014). Using broad strokes, the renowned critic (born 1924) incorporates a wealth of detail into his fifteen-hundred-page survey. He includes a section on theatre under early military occupation in Berlin and other German cities (through 1948).
4. Bessel, *Germany 1945*, 4.
5. See Peter A. Davis, introduction to his guest-edited issue on microhistory, "Asking Large Questions in Small Spaces," *Theatre Survey* 55, no. 1 (January 2014): 3–5.
6. Several artists, like Gustaf Gründgens, and directors Ernst Legal, Heinz Tietjen, and Paul Wegener managed theatres or worked within the Nazi regime and did not espouse leftist political sensibilities. Gründgens, for example, would be incarcerated for eight months in Soviet internment for his collaboration with the Nazis as Intendant of the National Theatre in Berlin.

7. Stephen Parker, *Bertolt Brecht: A Literary Life* (London: Bloomsbury Methuen, 2014), 3. The scripting of Brecht's "iconic" stature as an artistic and his far-reaching influence in the English-speaking world may be tied to his lengthy exile abroad, including in the United States, facilitating the dissemination of foreign- and English-language translations of his plays, and productions of his plays, written in exile, notably in Zurich during the war.
8. Parker refers to Brecht's contentious struggle to wrest the artistic leadership of the Theater am Schiffbauerdamm from Wisten in 1949 (523).
9. Davis, 3. Compare to Filippo de Vivo, "Prospect or Refuge? Microhistory, History on the Large Scale: A Response," *Cultural and Social History* 7, no. 3 (July 2010): 387–97, wherein the historian suggests that microhistory serves as a corrective to "address large historical problems" (387).
10. Hermann Glaser, *Kulturgeschichte der Bundesrepublik Deutschland: Zwischen Kapitulation und Währungsreform 1945-1948*, vol. 1 (Munich: Carl Hanser, 1985), 244.
11. My inquiry builds on an analysis of the developing cultural politics of the Soviet zone and its influence on the emerging GDR; for a thorough study, see David Pike, *The Politics of Culture in Soviet-Occupied Germany, 1945–1949* (Palo Alto: Stanford University Press, 1992).
12. See John London, ed., *Theatre under the Nazis* (Manchester University Press, 2000), wherein multiple authors show how the German cultural output continued even under censorship within Nazi Germany. Anselm Heinrich has written about the remarkable continuity of German- language theatre in Łodź (Litzmannstadt) during World War II; see Heinrich, "Germanification, Cultural Mission, Holocaust, Theatre in Łodź during World War II," *Theatre History Studies* 33, no. 1 (2014): 83–107. I have documented the continuity of theatre within Nazi Germany, in ghettos like Łodź, and in concentration camps by Jews and political prisoners; see my *The Jewish Kulturbund Theatre Company in Nazi Germany* (Iowa City: Iowa University Press, 2012) and "Cultural Ghettoization and Theatre during the Holocaust: Performance as a Link to Community," *The Journal of Holocaust and Genocide Studies* 19, no. 3 (2005): 459–86.
13. The theatre was known as the Theater in der Stressemanstraße.
14. This is the term that Friedrich Wolf used to describe the power of theatre as a transformative means to reach audiences.
15. Bärbel Schrader, "Die erste Spielzeit und die Kammer der Kunstschaffenden," in *Unterm Notdach, Nachkriegskliteratur in Berlin, 1945–1949*, ed. Ursula Heukenkamp (Berlin: Erich Schmidt Verlag, 1996), 233.
16. Josef Foschepoth, "German Reaction to Defeat and Occupation in West Germany under Construction," in *Politics, Society, and Culture in the Adenauer Era*, ed. Robert G. Moeller (Ann Arbor: University of Michigan Press, 1997), 75.
17. David Monod, *Settling Scores: German Music, Denazification, & the Americans, 1945–1953* (Chapel Hill: University of North Carolina Press, 2005), 10.
18. Monod, Settling Scores, 12–13.
19. Wolfgang Schivelbusch, *In a Cold Crater: Cultural and Intellectual Life in Berlin, 1945-1948*. Trans. Kelly Burry (Berkeley: University of California Press, 1998), 37.
20. Manfred Uhlitz, "Das Kultur Leben zur Stunde Null," *Berliner Geschichte, Kriegsende in Berlin, 1945* (April 2015): 38–47.
21. See Rühle, *Theater in Deutschland, 1945–1966*, 33–4.
22. See Glaser, 19–20.

23. Friedrich Wolf letter to Wolfgang Langhoff, Friedrich-Wolf-Archiv #303, Correspondence. 27 December 1945, AdK, Berlin; my emphasis.
24. Schrader, "Die erste Spielzeit und die Kammer der Kunstschaffenden," 251.
25. Author Interviews with Eva Wisten and Susanne Wisten-Weyl, September 7, 2011; June 12, 2014, Berlin. In 1946 Eva and Susanne were sixteen and twenty-one years old, respectively.
26. Wolfgang Schivelbusch, *The Culture of Defeat: On National Trauma, Mourning, and Recovery*, trans. Jefferson Chase (New York: Henry Holt and Co., 2003), 18.
27. Foschepoth, "German Reaction to Defeat and Occupation in West Germany under Construction," 79–80.
28. See Anne Appelbaum, *Iron Curtain: The Crushing of Eastern Europe, 1944–1956* (New York: Doubleday, 2012), xxvii, 19–20, on Tehran and Yalta Conferences of Big Three Allies; Schivelbusch, *In a Cold Crater*, 46. See also Pike, *The Politics of Culture in Soviet-Occupied Germany, 1945–1949*, chap. 1, "Sovietization or Democracy?"; and James E. Tent, *Mission on the Rhine: Reeducation and Denazification in American-Occupied Germany* (Chicago: University of Chicago Press, 1982), 13–17.
29. Maxim Vallentin, *Einleitende Bemerkungen zur Ausarbeitung von Richtlinien (Theater)*, September 25, 1944, appendix in *Petra Stober, Spielräume und Grenzen: Studien zum DDR-Theater* (Berlin: Christian Links Verlag, 1998), 260–61, emphasis in original. In *The Politics of Culture in Soviet-Occupied Germany*, David Pike draws a sharp contrast between Communist Party (KPD) aims and its outward rhetoric in calling for an "antifascist-democratic regime," whose allegiance to democracy, he claims, was "just a passing relaxation of the party's natural inclinations" (10).
30. The concept of cultural enlightenment for the people and edifying a nation (Volksbildung) is a longstanding concept in Germany.
31. Schrader, "Die erste Spielzeit und die Kammer der Kunstschaffenden," 235; Bessel, *Germany 1945*, 115. Also see Uhlitz, "Das Kultur Leben zur Stunde Null," 40–41.
32. Manfred Uhlitz writes that when Bersarin invited theatre directors like Gründgens in May to Friedrichsfelde to prepare for the opening of theatres, they agreed generally to exclude former National Socialists, 42–43. Only in a few cases did SMAD officials replace directors. For example, they arrested well-known actor-directors Heinrich George and Gründgens in June 1945 for having shown too much allegiance to the Nazi Reich.
33. Pike, *The Politics of Culture in Soviet-Occupied Germany, 1945–1949*, 72–73. Uhlitz also makes clear that the Communist-dominated Magistrat, with its influence on culture, was supervised by the Department for the Education of the People (Volksbildungsabteilung), 41.
34. Schivelbusch, *In a Cold Crater*, 10. Also see David Caute, *The Dancer Defects: The Struggle for Cultural Supremacy during the Cold War* (Oxford: Oxford University Press, 2005).
35. Pike, *The Politics of Culture in Soviet-Occupied Germany, 1945–1949*, 43. Susanne Weyl-Wisten corroborated this fact; interview with author, June 12, 2014, Berlin.
36. Uhlitz, "Das Kultur Leben zur Stunde Null," 46.
37. See Stephen Brockmann, "Heroes of the Zero Hour," in *Heroes and Heroism in German Culture*, ed. Stephen Brockmann and James Steakley (Amsterdam: Rodopi, 2010), 117. See also Janet Swaffer, "Heroes and Reunification: The Resistance of Cultural Memory from Two Germanies," in *Heroes and Heroism in German Culture*, 134.
38. Günther Weisenborn Archive, AdK, Berlin, #0028; Weisenborn wrote (n.d.) about

U-Boot S-4 (which Erwin Piscator initially signed for his theatre in 1927) and intimates that Brecht initiated their collaboration the day after the premiere; he cites Brecht verbatim, praising Weisenborn's boldness of vision. Weisenborn file #105: typewritten script, *Die Mutter* (1931–32). On Weisenborn's clear collaborative role on the play, see Parker, *Bertolt Brecht: A Literary Life*, 295.

39. See Anne Nelson, *The Red Orchestra* (New York: Random House, 2009). Compare to Günther Weisenborn Archives, Adk (Berlin); interview with author, Hans Coppi Jr., Gedenkstätte Deutscher Widerstand (German Resistance Memorial Center), Berlin, March 14, 2013. Coppi's parents were executed by the Nazis in 1942 and 1943 for their role in the "Red Orchestra" resistance network.
40. Friedrich Luft, cited in Schrader, "Die erste Spielzeit und die Kammer der Kunstschaffenden," 231–32.
41. Uhlitz, "Das Kultur Leben zur Stunde Null," 44. In early autumn, spectators paid admission with coal for the theatre's furnace.
42. May 20, 1945 (Russian and German), FWA 74/86/174,2, Wisten archives, AdK, Berlin.
43. Schivelbusch, *In a Cold Crater*, 49.
44. The American Allied Command would shut down the "cultural league" by 1947, when it was clear that their evolving cultural policies directly opposed those of Soviet powers.
45. June 29, 1945, FWA 74/86/174, 1. Bühnenausschluss der Kammer der Kunstschaffenden. AdK, Berlin.
46. Wolfgang Langhoff returned from Zurich in 1946 to lead the Deutsches Theater. It should be noted that Wangenheim called the shots, not Wisten, when it came to producing *Nathan* and casting his father. This is clear from correspondence (Fritz-Wisten-Archives) from Wangenheim to Wisten, FWA 74/86/963,964. AdK, Berlin.
47. This fact has been corroborated in the literature. On list, see Glaser, *Kulturgeschichte der Bundesrepublik Deutschland*, 26. David Monod writes that the list-making took place during the winter of 1945–1946, 5–6.
48. The certificate issued to Wisten on February 22, 1946, attests to his artist status as director at the Deutsches Theater, which fact is also noted on a list compiled by the Allied Command. The certificate also certifies his electricity usage waiver. FWA 74/86/74, 5, AdK, Berlin.
49. Wisten Archives, AdK, Berlin, FWA 74/86/1748, 2 (in English), April 16, 1946, letter from Commanding General Major in US Army, R. W. Barka, assures the director of the Deutsches Theater that the apartments are safe.
50. "Hundertmal Nathan," *Berliner Zeitung*, November 7, 1946. In Wisten Clipping, FWA 74/86/26, AdK, Berlin.
51. Schivelbusch, *In a Cold Crater*, 63; Wilfried Scheitlein's translation of Wilder's play was used for its Zürich premiere in 1939; Schrader, "Die erste Spielzeit und die Kammer der Kunstschaffenden," 242–46, who cites Rilla's reviews in the *Berliner Zeitung* of *Our Town*, August 7, 1945, August 23, 1945 (243, 251).
52. Uhlitz, "Das Kultur Leben zur Stunde Null," 40–41. See also Rühle, *Theater in Deutschland, 1945–1966*, 47, 1214n38.
53. See plan for Hebbel Theater repertoire by Karl-Heinz Martin (1946), Weisenborn Archives, AdK, Berlin. Correspondence with West-Theaters, 9339, H. In 1948, Jean-Paul Sartre's *The Flies* was produced, albeit in the American sector.
54. Schrader, "Die erste Spielzeit und die Kammer der Kunstschaffenden," 247. The second

"experiment" was a production of Fred Denger's *Wie Heissen* a month later at the Deutsches Theater.

55. Fritz Wisten Archive, Adk, Berlin: See correspondence from Karl-Heinz Martin to Wisten, 1945–1946, FWA 74/86/663–665.
56. Friedrich-Wolf-Archive M303, AdK, Berlin. Correspondence, Karl-Heinz Martin to Wolf, October 22, 1945.
57. Schivelbusch, *In a Cold Crater*, 74–75.
58. See Brooks Atkinson, "Culture under the Nazis," *New York Times*, April 25, 1937. Electronic access on July 15, 2015.
59. Friedrich-Wolf-Archive M303, AdK, Berlin, Correspondence, Karl-Heinz Martin to Wolf, October 22, 1945.
60. Friedrich-Wolf-Archive M303 AdK, Berlin, Letter to Wolf from Martin, November 21, 1945; letter from theatre secretary to Wolf, December 30, 1945, included headlines from the *Berliner Zeitung* about the ongoing Nuremberg Trials.
61. Also see correspondence from Friedrich Wolf to Wolfgang Langhoff, December 27, 1945. (Rehearsals were underway for the *Mamlock* production.)
62. Wolfgang Langhoff Archive #128, AdK, Berlin. Letter to Renate Langhoff, November 22, 1945.
63. Friedrich-Wolf-Archive M303, AdK, Berlin, correspondence. Letter from Wolf letter to Wolfgang Langhoff, December 27, 1945. Part of the letter is also cited in Schivelbusch, *In a Cold Crater*, 25, 197n57.
64. Ilse Jung, *"Um die Menschenrechte: Professor Mamlock in Hebbel-Theater ein grosser Erfolg," Tägliche Rundschau*, January 11, 1946. FWA 74/86/ 25, Wisten Clipping Sammlung. See set design drawing, FWA 74/86/20, 72, AdK, Berlin.
65. Fritz-Wisten-Archive, AdK, Berlin. Friedrich Wolf, *Professor Mamlock (Tragödie des westlichen Demokratie)*, Director's annotated production script. FWA 74/86/50, act 1, 4.
66. Director's script, *Professor Mamlock*, act 3, 41, 43.
67. Director's script, *Professor Mamlock*, act 4, 64–65.
68. Director's script, *Professor Mamlock*, AdK. Compare to *Professor Mamlock* in Friedrich Wolf: *Dramen* (Frankfurt am Main (Röderberg-Verlag, 1979), 306–7.
69. See Fritz-Wisten-Archive, FWA 74/86/ 25, Wisten Clipping Sammlung for 1945–1946, AdK, Berlin. Included are reviews: Fritz Erpenbeck, "*Professor Mamlock* im Hebbel-Theater: Ein Zeitstück, wie es sein soll." *Deutsche Volkszeitung*, January 11, 1946; Ernst Lewalter, "Ein Rückblick auf 1933: Friedrich Wolfs Prof. Mamlock im Hebbel-Theater," *Der Kurier*, January 11, 1946; "Ein politisches Stuck in Berlin" *Der Tagespiegel*, January 13, 1946 (WK).
70. After Wisten became artistic director of the Theater am Schiffbauerdamm in August 1946 (through 1956) and the Volksbühne (through 1961), Wolf's works were regularly performed.
71. Weisenborn cited from October 1945 in Ilse Brauer, *Günther Weisenborn*, introduction by Ingeborg Drewitz (Hamburg: H. Christians, 1971), 163.
72. Günther Weisenborn Archive #99, AdK, Berlin. In the program for *The Illegals*, Weisenborn jotted down handwritten notes about these goals, using "kämpferisch" to designate old plays.
73. Günther Weisenborn, *Die Illegalen* (Berlin: Aufbau, 1946), front matter.

74. For a provocative perspective about the difficulty that postwar Germans had coming to terms with the enormity of German crimes during the Third Reich, see Alexander and Margarete Mitscherlich, *The Inability to Mourn: Principles of Collective Behavior*, trans. Beverly R. Placzek (New York: Grove Press, 1975). The authors address how Germans constructed a protective fantasy about the Nazi past. They state that if Germans denied that the events of the Third Reich took place, then they would not have to acknowledge them (4).
75. Fritz Erpenbeck, *Deutsche Volkszeitung*, March 4, 1946, cited and trans. by Pike, *The Politics of Culture in Soviet-Occupied Germany, 1945–1949*, 197–98.
76. Weisenborn Archives #107, AdK, Berlin, "Wie wir Gorkis *Mutter* dramatisierten," Lecture delivered on Volga boat in honor of the 100th Gorki Jubliaum, June 1968. The author writes about dramatizing the original script for *The Mother*, and his subsequent collaboration with Brecht and Eisler in conceiving an anti-Aristotelian dramaturgy that became "epic theatre." The goal was to change how a spectator may think about the world, Weisenborn wrote in reference to his "ortslose Dramaturgie" (2).
77. Weisenborn, *Die Illegalen* (Berlin: Aufbau, 1946). In the first act, Walter's mother sings the "Song of the Scream" (Lied vom Geschrei); Walter sings the "Song of the Illegals" in act 2; and Manna incants a soft song toward the play's end.
78. Weisenborn Archive (3), correspondence with Theater-West G-H, AdK, Berlin. See Henry-E. Simmon, "Kein Brecht Epigone" published in *Hamburg Blätter* (1964–65). Also in Weisenborn Archive #107, "Wie wir Gorkis *Mutter* dramatisierten," 3.
79. Weisenborn Archive, Notes and plans, 1945–1969, Hamburg/ Berlin, n.d. #2, 2.
80. Weisenborn Archive #387, Bericht über die Widerstandsbewegung (n.d., n.p.), an allusion to the previous April suggests the date is likely early 1946 (2).
81. Weisenborn Archive # 99, 100, original typewritten script, *Die Illegalen*, AdK, Berlin; compare to Weisenborn, *Die Illegalen* (Berlin: Aufbau, 1946), 15.
82. Weisenborn, *Die Illegalen* (Berlin: Aufbau, 1946), 32.
83. Weisenborn, *Die Illegalen* (Berlin: Aufbau, 1946), 90.
84. Weisenborn Archive (2) 1339 Briefwechsel, West-Theater, C-F. Weisenborn to Karl-Heinz Stroux, director at Darmstadt Staatstheater: 29.3.1946. AdK, Berlin.
85. Weisenborn Archive (2) 1339 Briefwechsel, West-Theater, C-F. See correspondence between theatres and Weisenborn regarding projected dates for performances in spring 1946.
86. See note 79. Weisenborn Archive #107, AdK, Berlin.
87. While Wisten was active, he deferred to those who led the theatres, like Langhoff, who produced *The Snob*. See Fritz-Wisten-Archive correspondence between Deutsches Theater (Langhoff) and Wisten, FWA 74/86/962–966. AdK, Berlin.
88. The license was dated July 11, 1945, but made official on August 1, 1946.
89. See FWA 74/86/545, AdK, Berlin.
90. Wolf Köppe, "Günther Weisenborn's Ballad of His Life," *Flight of Fantasy: New Perspectives on Inner Emigration in German Literature 1933–1945*, ed. Neil H. Donahue and Doris Kirchner (New York: Berghahn, 2003), 245.
91. Weisenborn Archive, AdK, Berlin. Correspondence # 694: Brecht to Weisenborn, November 29, 1949: Brecht did not remember how they had arranged for the payment of the royalties.

92. Author interview with Eva Wisten and Susanne Wisten-Weyl, September 7, 2011, Berlin.
93. Weisenborn Archive, #19, AdK, Berlin: Friedrich Luft, November 1945, "Über das Tröstliche: Als Einführung zu G.W. Berliner Requiem" (Geschichte für 14 Schauspieler u. Chor, 1946), 2, 5.

"Would You Die for the Fatherland?"

Disciplining the German Commemorative Body

—SCOTT VENTERS

Leni Riefenstahl's 1938 film *Olympia* opens with a lyrical montage of the ruins of the Acropolis slowly breaking into view through a blanket of haze. The heroic sounds of Windt's and Gronostay's neo-Wagnerian score function as a docent, leading the viewer to marmoreal visions of the supple *Medici Venus* and the taut *Myron Diskobolus*. The latter deliquesces before the eyes to be replaced by the sinewy body of German decathlete Erwin Huber. The antique past is tenderly fleshed out by the German body, and classical Greece is sutured onto the present as an act of commemoration in this documentary of the 1936 Olympic Games in Berlin. Yet there was another conversation with antiquity occurring during the opening ceremonies of the Olympic Games, a conversation edited from Riefenstahl's final cut; this conversation was a more subtle, more circuitous, more tendentiously manipulated dialogue between the Nazis and the ancients that produced an embodied transcript of Foucauldian-defined discipline enacted by the youth of Germany. Along with his fabricated torch-lighting ceremony and its spurious classical origins, the chief architect of the ceremonies, Secretary General of the Organizing Committee Carl Diem, entertained the crowd from forty-nine nations assembled in the newly constructed Olympiastadion with a four-part mass spectacle entitled *Olympic Youth*. Hans Niedecken-Gebhard, a pupil of Rudolf von Laban, directed an international agglomeration of children between the ages of eleven and eighteen through a series of lavish displays. The first scene consisted of games and dances culminating in a human formation of the rings on the Olympic flag. Next followed a mass dance titled "Maidenly Grace" in which 2,300 youthful girls danced in circular, liquid motion and then parted to reveal the venerated modern dancer Gret Palucca, gracefully sliding through the steps of a waltz. In the third scene the children of all participating countries marched into the stadium with their respective national flags. But in the final movement this international harmony was shattered by a call to the youth of Germany to sacrifice their lives when the fatherland was in danger. Drilled into a rigidly formal position on the field by the upper ranks of the Hitler-Jugend (Hitler Youth), the affirmative answer was reinforced by the unrelenting mass of assembled young bodies beckoned by the Führer. A mock sword battle between professional dancers followed, culminating in Schiller's "Ode to Joy" sung by fifteen hundred voices in the last movement of Beethoven's Ninth Symphony, which attempted to reestablish a rapprochement. However, the unsettling call upon the youth to die for Deutschland and the intimations toward war had been made. In just a few years, many would die for or because of the fatherland.[1]

It is at this performative moment, caught in valorizing official reports published without the benefit of hindsight—when the trained, docile body appears most at odds with the Athenian-Hellenic notion of liberty, when play rubs against war, and when the antinomies of youthful innocence and political ideology become a tangled mass—that disciplinary power is most evident. It is also at this moment—when the corporeality of youth seems completely confined by militaristic discipline, when freedom is coerced from their limbs, and when the romantic oath elicited from the young wears only the mask of voluntarism—that a disturbing call to antiquity is being made. It is in this moment that the hoarse whispers of antiquity mingle with the cries of modernity. Those young, pliant, healthy bodies that would go on to join the SS and gas those deemed adulterated, deformed, and impure—Jews, Poles, Gypsies, the hereditarily ill, and homosexuals—had actually been conditioned into premilitary formation by a complex genealogy that had its roots in a sublimated homoeroticism. In a sense, that very same desire, through a complex historical process, had turned in upon the non-normative "abject" parts of itself. I am referring not to the facile association between the Hellenic Olympics and its original culture's valorization of same-sex desire but to the distinctly German influence that laid the foundations for Riefenstahl's celluloid aestheticization of masculine beauty. This paper tracks the embodied coupling of homoerotic desire with nationalism (ostensibly quashed by the Nazis) through a sinuous return to the antique past, and contends that such desire enabled the mechanisms by which the Nazis' spectacular and cohesive forces were shaped. Under the guidance of state teacher of gymnastics Friedrich Ludwig Jahn (1778–1852), the practices and rhetoric of the German Gymnastics Movement (Turnen) and its nineteenth-century push for national confederation subsumed Johann Joachim Winckelmann's (1717–1768) eroticized yet sublimated exhortation of the Hellenic body as national emblem. The Nazis later co-opted but reengineered the protocols and aesthetics of Turnen as the basis of premilitaristic discipline for the Hitler-Jugend, an organization upon which a racially sanitized, coordinated, and hierarchized vision of national unity could be projected. Since the birth of German physical culture in the early nineteenth century, the body of male youth functioned as the commemorative site of the nation, a spectacular but uncontainable, obstinate nexus for the revivification of a romanticized Teutonic past and the prognostication of a utopian national futurity. The Third Reich, by enclosing the body's semiotic and erotic excess through exhibitions of restriction, management, and mortification, disclosed the unavoidable pain that accompanied stitching those temporal longings onto a present material reality of "pure" German nation.

Friedrich Ludwig Jahn's Turnen and the Commemorative Body

In his first major work, an essay titled "Reflections on the Painting and Sculpture of the Greeks," Winckelmann states, "There is but one way for the moderns to become great, and perhaps unequalled; I mean, by imitating the antients [*sic*] . . . especially the Greek arts." Additionally, Greek sculpture should not only function as the basis for aesthetics but also serve as the blueprint for a superior physical basis of German Kultur: "The most beautiful body of ours would perhaps be as much inferior to the most beautiful Greek one, as Iphicles was to his brother Hercules." In this vision Germany maintains a fraternal bond with the ancients but also stands in a degraded position due to its artistic and physical deficiency. According to Winckelmann, this is due partly to the ancient Hellenes' racial ties to a superior climate and partly to a socially reinforced regimen of exercise and competition among the Greeks: "The Spartan youth . . . familiar with wrestling and swimming from his infancy . . . [and] the grand games . . . [were] always a strong incentive for every Greek youth to exercise himself."[2] Suzanne Marchand characterizes Winckelmann's return to representations of Greece as an effort to rid German society of corruptive elements. In Winckelmann's philosophical revitalization of Greek sculpture, Marchand identifies an ascetic principle of aesthetic appreciation at work: a principle seeking to slough off early modernity's penchant for impure ornamentation and the cultural degradation inscribed on the effete body, and a principle linked directly to racial typing, though far from late-nineteenth-century notions of Aryanism.[3]

Above any idealistic illusions of "nature" it was the art object that Winckelmann privileged, for it was "the beauties of the Greek statues being discovered with less difficulty than those [beauties] of Nature [that were] of course more affecting."[4] The very notion of an object to fixate erotic and speculative energies upon held an affective potential beyond the banality of the so-called natural and present world. For Winckelmann the art object par excellence, the nude male statue, carried the capacity to stand in for the love object, resulting in an erotic point of contact gesturing toward (but never achieving) closure otherwise withheld from him in his many relationships with men, and denied him culturally in its overt, public manifestation.[5] The object mediated and prolonged the same desire that urged his pen toward verbal climes of abstraction and sublimation. Through his frequent writing for publication, Winckelmann repeatedly transformed Eros into Platonic promulgations and utopian corporeal landscapes as a matter of cultural necessity to avoid criminalization and to give his opinions philosophical gravitas. But this personal sublimation of erotic potentiality and longing for beauty also formed the basis of a national vision. As Winckelmann states in his magnum opus, *The History of Ancient Art*, "beauty was thus desired and prized by the Greeks . . . [and] every beautiful person sought to become known to the whole nation by this endowment . . .. Beauty was an excellence which led to fame."[6] The body was not just an individual's; it bespoke the community and reflected a shared national glory.

Winckelmann's Greek corporeal model for German nationalism had a profound impact upon the first wave of Romantics, which included Herder, Lessing, Schiller, Goethe, and Humboldt, and their works of the last decades of the eighteenth century. F. A. Wolf continued this racial-aesthetic schematic in his *Darstellung der Altertumswissenschaft* (1807), separating Greeks and Romans from Egyptians, Jews, Persians, and other "Orientals" as a "higher Geistescultur [sic]" (intellectual or spiritual culture).[7] In the case of the ancient Hellenes, the health of the Greek body was repeatedly united with the health and valorization of the Greek spirit (intellect), making the two inextricable. Looking at Plato's dialogues as a celebration of the union of intellect and the youthful male body, while seeing the productive collision of aesthetics and the beautifully masculine physical attributes of a virile race in sculpture, both Winckelmann and Wolf averred that the physical culture of the Greeks was a necessary background to the sublime cultural and aesthetic articulations.[8]

The Greek marriage of physical form and cultural perfection as a model for the German nation reached a new pinnacle when Wilhelm von Humboldt incorporated the writings of Schiller into his methodology of social and pedagogical reform. In *Latium und Hellas oder Betrachtungen über das classische Alterthum* (1806) Humboldt affirmed, "The value the Greeks placed on a freely formed [*gebildet*] body distinguishes them before all nations. In it lies the delicate and deep sense that the intellectual must not be separated from the physical, but rather must express itself in it . . . and this care in honouring physical strength and agility was . . . maintained . . . by the fame of the winners in the public games."[9] In this passage there is no division between mental life, physical exercise, and national prowess; all were legibly inscribed upon the individual body as national representative in the athletic, panhellenic *agones* of ancient Greece. The Olympic Games of Greece was an event and symbol of unity achieved by bringing together superbly conditioned and racially similar Greek bodies. For Humboldt and a coterie of other nationalists, such a paradigm of confederation supported perfectly the aims of German unification. Unity could be achieved through play, through the body in motion and in competition with other racially identical bodies.[10] These pendant hopes of Humboldt's were concretized in the pedagogic programs of physical exercise and play (known as Turnen) under the direction of one man, Friedrich Ludwig Jahn (1778–1852).[11] Jahn incarnated theory and worked through earlier doctrines to make physical culture the basis of a collective that would define a new German nationalism.

Marion Kant states that since Turnen's inception, "Jahn defined movement as a patriotic exercise that promised national as well as individual 'liberation'" from French hegemony.[12] Since the end of 1794, France had controlled all of Germany west of the Rhine, a condition that persisted until the war of liberation in 1814 and the international settlement reached at the Congress of Vienna the following year.[13] Although Prussia, where Jahn lived and worked, was technically free from French tyranny, at the Peace of Tilsit in 1807 the kingdom lost "all territories west of the Elbe" and several territories in the east, and had to offer up indemnities and men to aid Napoleon's drive across Europe.[14] Suffering from the wounds inflicted upon his German pride, between 1811 and 1819 Jahn founded and maintained the Turnplatz at the Hasenheide in Berlin, where he combined pro-confederation speeches with displays of physical prowess, turning his educational system into a pulpit from which he could preach and perform a liberal strain of nationalism. During these same years Jahn organized a Freikorps in the struggle against Napoleon, carried out several secret assignments for the Prussian statesman von Hardenberg, and was involved in numerous insurrections to thwart French dominance until after the war of liberation in 1814 (in which he fought with many of his gymnastics students known as Turner). Additionally, Jahn published a pro-unification doctrine, *Deutsches Volksthum*, and aided in founding the Burschenschaften, a liberal, nationalist student fraternity, in Jena in 1815. Jahn's insurrectionist activities and the development of Turnen coincided in time and political objectives. Battle readiness and youthful games were integrated into a crusade for the reclamation of the country and the casting off of French oppression.

The marriage of nationalist goals and physical education was accomplished in great measure because of Turnen's elasticity. Turnen shares much with modern-day gymnastics. Emphasis was placed on balance, endurance, and strength in exercises like swinging on bars, vaulting from a "vaulting horse" (shaped like a mammalian horse replete with tail, head, and saddle) and executing differently styled mounts and landings, and balancing between various horizontal (including parallel) bars and vertical posts. But Turnen also encompassed multiple preparatory and basic exercises, akin to track and fieldwork: walking, running, calisthenics, hopping, kicking, crouching, skating, skipping, climbing, throwing, wrestling, and even shooting. Turnen was not a form of competitive athletics, conceptualized as sport in its English variation. There was no quantitative measure for victory over competitors. Instead, there was an embodied repertoire of movements, rituals, and protocols that allowed for personal creativity, self-improvement, and spontaneity to flourish alongside group drills and ceremonies that fostered cohesion. Take, for instance, the different modes of running that students would engage in individually or as units (referred to as squads): running straight, running in the circle, racing, running in straight lines and angles, running in a spiral line, running backward, and running uphill.[15] Jahn encouraged students to explore the possibilities of adapting to unusual conditions and pushing their bodies beyond perceived limitations. Through numerous group exercises and games offset with rest periods, students also learned the possibilities of collective action, but always with an eye on military preparedness and the potential of mobilizing the prepared body in the service of the German national cause.

Sifting through the pages that outline Jahn's gymnastics, one detects a pyramidal formation with the most directly militaristic exercises resting at the pinnacle. In a sense, all other feats of physical agility and strength (jumping, swinging, climbing, and running) were preparations for the most difficult and offensive maneuvers of throwing and shooting. Jahn details no fewer than eleven of these exercises in his manual. These include shooting with firearms, cross-bows, the bow, and darts; throwing heavy bodies, iron-bars, and ducks and drakes; and slinging. Jahn declares that "throwing is one of the most important exercises" and that shooting should be considered an extension of throwing; hence, it "would be very desirable to have a particular shooting place connected to every gymnasium."[16] In Jahn's opinion the male body is unabashedly a weapon; throwing is the natural segue into shooting a gun. And agility with knives is a test of fitness, as one exercise reveals: "Drawing out a knife, stuck in the ground, near to the little toe, the hand of the opposite side passing around behind the feet which are standing fast and straight out; right and left."[17] What Jahn diagrams is no mere child's play; it is situated just beyond the scope of the child but along his particular form of play's trajectory. One has only to read over the extremely detailed instructions Jahn provides on charging a rifle to realize that the act of shooting is just another activity like jumping, disciplined and ingrained into the body.[18] Shooting and knife-work are placed on the continuum of physical activity so that they become a natural supplement to bodily health, which has been elaborated, managed, codified, and reinforced by horizontal (peer) pressure and supervisory oversight, developing into what Foucault calls the "automism of habit" and, ultimately, actions that define the spatio-temporal identity of a collective.[19] It is not that the knife and gun are necessary to develop a boy's strength, dexterity, or agility; a stick could be substituted for the knife, and the use of a gun precludes the necessity of throwing (a much better activity for muscular development). These items are important because they are weapons, and not metaphors for obstacles one might encounter or abstract pieces of equipment that resemble objects in nature. Engaging with them is certification of accomplishment and group identity. They are essential to the health of the specifically German body. To say that the Turnvater was weaponizing his students would be an exaggeration, but Jahn was certainly equipping his young gymnasts with the necessary skills and predispositions to become future soldiers.

Romanticism became integral to creating this German national identity. Arising from the Sturm und Drang movement of the late eighteenth century, which denounced the vapid French and their effete form of rationalism, acolytes of Romanticism looked to the past and the tradition of the Volk for inspiration. In his fourteen "Addresses to the German Nation," delivered between 1807 and 1808, Fichte apotheosized a German cultural identity that was coherent only within a racialized spatiotemporal imaginary: "Our most urgent present problem is to preserve the existence and continuity of all that is German. All other differences vanish before the higher point of view. Love for the Fatherland must reign supreme in every German state."[20] As a solution to the "French problem," Fichte proposed a union cemented by a uniquely "German" adhesive, but a subsidiary problem was that the precise characteristics of just such an adhesive were being hotly debated. The referent "German" was still in the process of becoming. The roots had to be dug up, and the French residue had to be scraped off.

To free the German body from the heavy dross left by French conquest, Friedrich Ludwig Jahn prescribed a litany of precise and detailed exercises "to regain manliness" and "to restore the lost balance in human education."[21] As early as 1810 Jahn assembled groups of youths at Hasenheide in Berlin "to swing, jump, run, march [and] play patriotic games."[22] Youthful male German bodies moved in aesthetic harmony with other similar bodies through coordinated and communal exhibitions of physical prowess. Although Jahn shunned the execution of strict military drills, his exercises tended to take paramilitary shapes that reinforced group solidarity. Monika Zechetmayr summarizes the stages of gymnastic periods as "based upon a common core of Teutonic enculturation" that moved individuals though isolated squads into a final formation of the entire group.[23] Squads were always headed by a young leader who took students through various exercises like running with "the breast out, [and] shoulders back" in tautly unified lines, circles, and spirals, "following each one the man before him."[24] All students understood the chain of command and came to recognize the unique vocabulary, system of regulations, and signals of the Turnplatz. Equally as important as the exercises were the rest periods. At the close of the afternoon session "all Turner were called together by the ringing of a bell . . . to gather at the Tie."[25] The Tie was the time and location set aside to promote community building through social mingling, meals, announcements, singing, and the public expulsions of students for various infractions. Although Jahn stressed the importance of spontaneous and free participation, the Turnplatz transformed into a site of coordinated movements, enforced athleticism, and the semiotics of unity. Uniforms of not-yet bleached linen jackets and pantaloons became mandatory, squads became more rigidly organized, and spectators were barricaded off from the gymnasts, dividing the initiated from the perpetual outsiders.[26] The Turnplatz increasingly transmuted into a locale reserved for disciplined bodies that had drunk deep the draughts of patriotism to stand as exemplary physical statements of the national spirit.

Concomitant with his program of physical education, Jahn publicized his ideological and political positions through frequent lectures and writings, which over time shaped the gymnastic-union into something of a cult. In arguing for German cultural confederation, Jahn not only openly detested all things French but also avowed anti-Semitism and rejected all things that fell outside the traditional ideological boundaries of Germania. Jahn, like other Romantics, looked longingly to the quasi-mythic bygone era of the Volk: "German means national. Our feeling of nationalism, or Germanness, has been disappearing more and more because of our sins. We must return to the past and re-create Nation, Germanness, Fatherland."[27] For Jahn and his like-minded contemporaries, the true German race was not only something to be differentiated synchronically but also something to "resurrect" diachronically from the German past. German Kultur had been lost through the deprivations of time, the infectious European mentality of cosmopolitanism, and most sinfully, through German complacency. The sins of "merely one-sided intellectualization" and "excessive refinement" had sapped Germany of its masculinity and national spirit,[28] just as much as the sins of "laziness, lustfulness, and uncontrolled sexual passion" corrupted the mind, atrophied the body, and taxed one's health.[29]

This perceived temporal displacement from the national past is perhaps why Jahn felt most at home in charting a consanguine relationship between Hellas and Germania. "Which nation has the noblest character, closest to that of mankind itself? Only those who have incorporated the sacred notion of humanity [can aspire to this] . . .. In ancient times the Greeks did in their popular culture, and the cosmopolitan Germans still do—both [are the] sacred peoples of humanity."[30] In this statement Jahn does not hesitate to draw a direct line between the Greeks of time past and the Germans of his own day, as if the history and culture standing between the two societies could be omitted. Despite the temporal chasm separating them, the Germans and the Greeks share space in this humanistic taxonomy. What collapses this gulf is the material and empirical continuity of the similar Greek and German body, which was, in Jahn's opinion, the most visible, verifiable, and veracious site for this revelation of aesthetic, cultural, and "human" affinity between the Greek and the German nations.

Such an affinity between nations was not a self-evident and durable substance; it had to be created and re-created through a dramaturgy equivalent to its cosmic symbolism. Ensuring that the materiality of the body remained crosshatched with the phenomenology of nationalism, a way of being in the world with the promise of German unification at the horizon of expectations, was the responsibility of the spectacular, or of making the body a spectacle. This is where the homoerotics of Winckelmann's idiosyncratic Graecophilia informed Jahn's particular brand of corporeal nationalism. Both men diagnosed a deficiency in their contemporary epochs and began constructing Hellenic and homogenously masculine utopias as reparative strategies. These "no-places" occupied simultaneously the phantasmal past and a promised futurity, but certainly not the present; only their reified fragments could take the gaze of the spectator in the here and now. For Winckelmann, it was the image of the beautiful, "the great and manly Contour observed in [Greek] statues," that granted access to this bygone utopia, whereas Jahn charted the coordinates of a utopian zone of national unity mediated by the spectacularity of the German masculine figure, or rather, figures always in a collective.[31] Only the homosocial zone of the Turnplatz could mitigate an aching desire for the not-yet nation of a united Germany. Like Winckelmann's transcendent Greek imaginary, the Turnplatz was an exclusive arena where the serious contemplation and creation of beauty was done. Jahn admonishes in his writings that the gymnasium "is no theatre . . .. No one has a right to expect a spectacle"; but, at the same time, he accepts, even embraces, its value only because one can, even must, gaze upon it. "The fairest youths danced undressed on the theatre" and filled the "Gymnasies [sic]" in Winckelmann's ideal.[32] In Jahn's, "all who [were] too small or weak, or ha[d] not yet passed through the preparatory exercises [were] excluded from gymnastick [sic] plays."[33] Both imaginaries contain an impossible perfection based on exclusions of the insufficient or degenerate and the fixation of erotic, productive energy upon the impossible masculine ideal.

With the publication of his treatise Die Deutsche Turnkunst (The Art of German Gymnastics) in 1816, Jahn's amalgamation of nationalism and gymnastics crystallized into a how-to manual for training one to become a true member of the Volk. The text proudly and baldly exhibited its political ideology, with adolescent play serving as preparation for future military action. The second section of Jahn's treatise elaborates upon the format and purpose of games, but most of the games lean toward group coordination in paramilitary exercises with political objectives. The first game, simplified as "Capture the Enemy," is played by between twenty and one hundred boys and involves the seizure and public display of a member of the opposing army. "One is chosen who, distinguished by some mark, takes his place on the opposite side. He asking: are you afraid of your enemy? advances, and the others, answering with no! start from their goal, endeavoring to reach the opposite side without being caught. He who is caught receives three claps in succession by the single one."[34] The game is replete with its own aggressively militant rhetoric that establishes an outsider from a cohesive group. The repeated answer of "no" to the question "are you afraid of your enemy?" is a rehearsal for political identification and action, and the "claps" willingly received by the prisoner coerce from the participants a toleration of a certain degree of physical abuse, inuring them somewhat to pain.

As part of his grand narrative of German nationalism, Jahn aimed to combine gymnastic days with state "commemoration days marking the salvation, resurrection and rescue of the German people."[35] The new national festival calendar was to become synonymous with the celebration of the German body, drawing attention to the material presence of a strong Germany, rather than a purely intellectual assertion of cultural superiority. The Wartburg Festival marked a crucial date on this calendar. On October 18, 1817, the three hundredth anniversary of Luther's Ninety-Five Theses and the fourth year since the Battle of the Nations at Leipzig, approximately five hundred students and faculty from several German universities gathered together at Wartburg Castle in Eisenach to demonstrate for a German nation-state cemented together by a new constitution and an old common language. The festival was a manifestation of liberal, youthful, fiery yearnings for a racially united culture of the German Volk.[36] At this massive participatory event, several "oppositional books" were burned, including Napoleon's Civil Code and German playwright August von Kotzebue's *History of the German Nations*. However, Steven Michael Press in his article "False Fire: The Wartburg Book-Burning of 1817" has provided evidence that the burning was not the result of a "spontaneous overflow of powerful feelings" reflective of the Romantic zeitgeist in its yearnings for national identity.[37] It was, in fact, planned in advance and carried out by Jahn's gymnastic students. The whole event was a political performance made possible and enhanced by the spectacular coordination of young Turnen adherents.

At the festival in the days prior to the book-burning, Jahn's young assistant, Hans Ferdinand Maßmann, was placed in charge of several leaders who publicly conducted squads of young men through exercises and drills. The whole event was highly organized. "Maßmann had prepared a set of instructions for the guidance of these leaders, and there were written lists of exercises in tabular form to show the steps of progression in each group."[38] Games filled the days, while the nights were passed in haylofts where Jahn read aloud "prophetic passages from the Old Testament."[39] The gymnastic-union's participation in the festival was not just a series of random or haphazard displays but was shaped by a rigorously detailed teleological narrative that relied upon the white German body as the prophetic fulfillment of national destiny. And these drills and games were also a prelude for the final game of book-burning atop the Wartenberg Hill. On the hilltop Hans Ferdinand Maßmann "carried a basket with roughly thirty-five packets of paper bundled together to resemble books."[40] Upon the conclusion of a terse speech, Maßmann read a number of titles from a list nicknamed "the list of lies," each time asking if a title should "be condemned."[41] Several of Maßmann's companions were planted in the crowd and would solemnly shout in the affirmative at each interrogative statement. But the books were, in fact, "nothing more than pieces of paper torn from dictionaries and romance novels."[42] The content of the event was vacuous, but the formal elements were convincing, unless one took note of Maßmann's frequent mispronunciations of book titles and his companions' intense desire to obstruct all of those present from viewing the texts.

Both the games frequently enjoyed in the Turnplatz (gymnasium) and the games of the festival had been rehearsals for a political performance whose stagecraft was intentionally obscured. The young and physically sculpted Maßmann, as Jahn's second-in-command, led a small group of gymnastics students through the typical call and response game of "Capture the Enemy." Only this time instead of asking "are you afraid of your enemy," Maßmann queried, "should this book be condemned," and the negative used in the gymnasium was now turned into a "yes!" A book was then set ablaze. The paradigm and militant nationalistic intention was the same; only the content had been slightly altered. The performance was just that, a performance, rehearsed and drilled as many times as the German body in the gymnasium. A body does not spontaneously attain fitness; it must be stretched and tested, forced to exert against a contrary force. In a similar manner, the myth of a true Germanic cultural identity (that such an identity could be rediscovered in the past or uncovered in the present body) had to be made and re-made all the time. The choreography of the book burning encircled the myth of nationalism in a halo of performativity (in the Austinian sense); it ushered in a new relation to reality and disciplined those present to accept that relation. Through the enactment of biblical motifs of conflagration and destruction, the corps of male youth elevated the body conditioned to communality above the word. Only the voice and body together in their presence and united in their purpose, and shared among a collective, had the power to incinerate what opposed that national collective; mere text was powerless. Notions that legitimate rule should be reserved solely for the aristocracy or Junkers (landed nobility) dissolved before the power of the masculine assemblage. Evaporated, too, was the valorization of university education as the only proper path toward self-governance and social advancement. Physical fitness and involvement in its institutional praxis was not the only test of national allegiance, but it was presented as a decisive one. It came from below, from the Volk, and provided a model of physicality and ritual that could be reperformed daily—a regimen of nationalism that cut across class lines to all those with body and passion enough. In time, such a mentality of rational body practice, health, and hygiene would be a normative brick in the edifice of bürgerlich (bourgeois) culture, and one often synonymous with nationalism.[43] In time, the formal evidence of national allegiance and racial purity, mandated through fitness programs, eugenics, and physical policing, would be imposed from above, the Nazis being the far-off oppressive extreme (and an organization that also burned books).[44] The form of the spectacle on the Wartenberg Hill mattered more than the indiscernible content. The form was the desire of future fulfillment, the male body its promissory note, its mediation, the concretized object of insatiable fixation. There were no actual books being burned, and several of the authors proclaimed as enemies before the assembled crowd agreed with the liberalist principles of German union.[45] But those facts were clouded by what was on display: the youthful German body, ostensibly rising from the soil like a warrior spawning fully formed from the dragon's teeth sown by Cadmus, fervent and adamant in his call for solidarity, for vengeance against the French, and for a German national consciousness. This was the stuff of the literature of Pindar, but in a vastly superior sensual presence; it was the subject of a new heroic ode—a racial-cultural ode that could be read upon the body.

Hitler's Youth and the Greek Body: Eros as Discipline and the Construction of an Aryan Racial Ode

Amid the ruins of World War I and the Weimar Republic, Anton Drexler and Adolf Hitler founded the National Socialist German Worker's Party in 1920 by making appeals to a lower middle class drawn to the Nazis' combination of "anti-Semitism with hostility to large commercial enterprises, attacks on cooperatives and hostility to immigration."[46] Centralization and militarization were identified as the only valid rescuers of *völkisch* spiritual life. Hitler's Nazis, by the end of the 1930s, had carried these notions to an extreme form of totalitarian violence, but similar ideological currents of untainted racial origins and the educational infrastructure to shape future German citizens through physical conditioning and doctrinal immersion had been in place since the latter nineteenth century. Under the penumbra of the revolutionary fervor of 1849, Wagner, in his essay *Art and Revolution*, rallied for a return to "the Grecian spirit" to inculcate a "fair, strong manhood of freedom."[47] But after the defeat of liberal reformers at the Revolution's close, the Grecian spirit of physical and aesthetic education was slowly transfigured into a coupling of militarization and biological theories of racial nationalism taught in the school system. This led not to an increase in freedom but to its restriction by the establishment of state-driven mechanisms of discipline for youth demarcated along ethnic lines. The organic metaphor of racial origins (Welcker's idea of "a nobler origin, greater historical beginnings, [and] grander calling" linking a people to its soil) was increasingly linked to advances in virological and bacteriological sciences.[48] Biological theories of race began to dominate as language was being filled out with metaphors of parasitism, disease, and abnormality to classify as degenerate those such as Jews,

Roma, Sinti, the hereditarily ill, and homosexuals, most consistently the targets of prior, nonmedically based forms of xenophobic nationalism.[49]

Hand in hand with this new emphasis on national racial identity was the military's takeover of education and childhood socialization. Heinz Stübig has charted the negotiations between the German military and Volksschule teachers, which resulted in the extension of military service privileges and new opportunities for career advancement to a class of grammar school teachers once rejected by the military establishment.[50] In a reciprocal exchange, teachers were coming to and from the military ranks while prepping young students for a soldier's career. Grammar school education took a decidedly belligerent turn. A handbook for school instructors, *Basic Features of Evangelical Volksschule Education*, resurfaced in eight editions between 1873 and 1890, a testament to the overwhelming intrusion of military protocol into childhood socialization: "*At the start of the lesson*, one should announce: 'Books open! Get ready to write! To do your sums! To draw!' . . . to ensure the lesson is started with precision. *During the lesson*, commands such as the following are necessary when, for example, the class is expected to respond in unison: 'Stand up! Sit down! Altogether! First! Etc. Seats! Boys! Girls!' When slates or notebooks are to be exchanged for mutual inspection: 'Exchange slates to the right! Exchange slates to the left! Return slates!'"[51]

As is evident, educational materials were weaponized while the body was disciplined for armed service. It was not solely that disciplinary and pugilistic values were taught in the classroom but that the youthful body was constrained by recurring drills and urgent exhortations that entrenched obedience at the level of unconscious habit. The above example of instruction is the very epitome of Foucault's characterization of how discipline functions as "a policy of coercions that act upon the body . . .. Discipline increases the forces of the body (in economic terms of utility) and diminishes these same forces (in political terms of obedience)."[52] Power in the classroom was augmented for a body, but it was a body conditioned for expedient uses of the state and military. In 1872 Wilhelm Liebknecht condensed all pedagogical objectives into a single directive: "The principal purpose of school, however, is definitely to provide usable raw material for the barracks . . . the molding of men *cum* machines . . .. It would be simply impossible to do this with human beings educated in a human manner."[53] Jahn's Hellenic roots of physical education had sprouted into a mechanistic view of humanity. Beauty was no longer the individual body signifying its cultural origins through movement, or even a squad of self-directed young men aiding each other through gymnastic exercises, but the unthinking corporality following bureaucratic dictates—a "usable raw material" at the disposal of the state. The grammar school and playfield were incubators for battlefield fodder.

Gertrud Pfister has stated that nationalisms have specific forms that adhere to and arise in their own distinct epochs.[54] Structures speak to broadly shared desires, and desires speak through structures. Formal arrangements of bodies are de facto coconstructers of ideology, not just expressions. Like other aspects of the *Volksschule* curriculum and pedagogy, the resurgence of Turnen participated in adapting bodies to a more overt, militaristic idea of nation and authoritarian governance, and, more specifically, one that could communicate an image of empire through the mass articulation of visual excess. In her article "Cultural Confrontations: German Turnen, Swedish Gymnastics and English Sport—European Diversity in Physical Activities from a Historical Perspective," Pfister enunciates the changes that occurred within the Turnen movement's organization and style in the second half of the nineteenth century. Once banned because of Jahn's allegiance to nationalism and his willingness to crossfertilize his politics and his pedagogy, Turnen was resuscitated as a part of secondary education in two greatly altered forms in which "systematization of exercises and external discipline gained increasing importance."[55] The first was a mode of exercise known as puppet Turnen, "the systematic movement of single limbs"; the second was called mass Turnen, which involved "large numbers of people doing free exercises [calisthenics] on the ground or drill-like exercises." In the first of these forms, the body was broken down into parts to command and motivate. Emphasis on the self as an organic whole and the coordination of autonomous parts was reduced to unilateral directions from center to extremity. In the second, Jahn's smaller and more numerous squads under the command of separate leaders (who instructed squad members but still actively worked with them through exercises) were amalgamated into a giant "mass" receiving orders from a nonparticipating, authoritative voice. Gone was any semblance of self-governance of the Turnvereine (gymnastics clubs). The regulation of membership, the circulation of thoughts and expression at the *Tie*, and the segregated but relatively free involvement of spectators: all were abandoned and replaced by the spectatorial gaze of the school board and its staff. Jahn's lyrical "cosmic humanity" of culture, which he located between the similar bodies of Germans and Greeks and which served as his foundation for a rising German nation, was reanimated as an authoritarian mode of oversight and discipline, preparing young bodies for an imperial form of national identity.

This type of embodied national narrative of mechanical precision and conformist principles latched upon modernity favorably as integral to the nation's economic and global advancement, but such a tale of progress vied with another, equally pandemic narrative of nation that rejected instrumentalization of the collective in favor of a return to folk culture as the wellspring of a unique sense of German nationhood. *Ausdruckstanz* (expressionist dance) was an example of the latter tendency, and the Nazis' cultural ministry under Goebbels would capitalize greatly on and alter its aesthetics to accord with the regime's own fascistic performance rhetoric (which will be examined later). Dianne S. Howe charts two main lines of *Ausdruckstanz*, both intersecting with the form's major figure and popularizer, Mary Wigman. The Emile Jaques-Dalcroze School outside Dresden, where Wigman, Valeria Kratina, and Edith von Schrenk trained, is the first major line. Here, "students performed in large pageant-type productions," and these "group-movement compositions" would tour extensively as part of an ideological mission.[56] Valeria Kratina, who became the director of a branch outside Vienna, summed up the social function of the new form: "Dance must become an art form for the general public—that is its future. That means, an art for everyone . . .. The great work of dance must become, beyond personal expression, the expression of the all-too-common element of humanity in order to find its way into the heart of everyone."[57] Dance was not to be merely a formal display of virtuosity set at a distance from the observer's own life-world, such as ballet, which had been drawn from Baroque court culture, but a shared "expression" of that life-world, an intelligible language that elevates the "all-too-common" because of its universality, its in-commonness.

The second major line of *Ausdruckstanz* emanated from Rudolf von Laban's "movement choirs." Again, turning to Howe for clarification, "The Movement Choir was a form of artistic body culture which Laban hoped would become a new type of folk dance."[58] It relied upon the use of persistent rhythms of interlocking but individuated motions that worked together as an organic whole. The *choir* did not aim for precision or the appearance of discipline among its many participants. Unity was not achieved from above but from within, by individuals guided by their own impulses and movement dialogues. The reviewer John Martin deridingly described one choir event as "two hours without pause [in which] fifty or sixty dancers—men, women and children—stamped and jerked about upon the stage . . . to the accompaniment of piano, drum or gong."[59] The choreographers of the Movement Choir put into rhythmic communication an assortment of men, women, and children (generally untrained). A display of deft skill or tightly wound aesthetics was obviously not Laban's primary theatrical goal. Laban desired to create a folk community onstage, in all its ages of man and divisions of sex. It was a valorization of the body of the *Volk*, freed in its individuated-togetherness. But according to Susan Manning, "National Socialist patronage and policy rigidified the modernist project of *Ausdruckstanz* while supplanting the avant-gardist project with a compulsory physical education program."[60] The image of the *Volk* in *Ausdruckstanz*, which was originally set in motion to militate against the dehumanizing and dislocating effects of industrial capitalism and the *technologizing* (and militarization) of social life, would, by the 1930s, spiral into lustful and violent intimacy with is dreaded opposition.

At first the Nazis formed a point of mediation between these two polarized extremes of a forward looking techno-modernity and a backward glancing romanticized *Volk* sprung from the soil, to all appearances leaning toward the latter, which greatly appealed to national conservatives. As the Nazis gained political momentum, the romantic rhetoric, whether appearing to some as political posturing or as sincere expression, rested uneasily next to the party's co-optation of the invasive bureaucratic machinery, militaristic programming, and disciplinary measures of Bismarck's infrastructure, even adding to them new positivistic sciences and technologies. Looking at the 1920s while the Nazis were still on their ascent, Tobin Siebers goes so far as to assert that in the Nazis' conservative social ethic, they "wanted to represent themselves as latter-day Greeks" (the same rhetorical positioning that Wigman appropriated).[61] Homoerotic male nudes were frequently legislated into public spaces, but in Siebers's final analysis the use of masculine nudity amounted to a "banal form" of homoeroticism—that is, a desexualized symbolism based in replication and political instrumentalization.[62] Peter Guenther's firsthand observations of the Grosse Deutsche Kunstausstellung (Great German Art Exhibition) in Munich during July 1937 seize the meaning: "I thought that they were intentionally attempting to imitate famous Greek sculptures . . .. These were simply large, primarily male, nudes. People around me marveled at the craftsmanship . . . [and] realism of these figures (although certainly none of us looked like any of these giants). The visitors whom I overhead seemed not to recognize by the titles given to the statues—*Kameradschaft* (Comradeship), *Sieg* (Victory)—that they were meant to be symbols."[63] The imagery was first and foremost a reminder of the individual's obligation to sacrifice to what was larger-than-human, the Reich and the German race. They communicated the German race's physical imperative toward perfection—that which is beyond the bodily summation of the human ("none of us looked like any of these giants").

Although repressed in the accompanying symbolism, the homoerotic element in the statues was essential and quite visible. The figures in *Kameradschaft* are fully nude, muscled beyond nonsteroidal attainment, and feature prominently placed genitalia. With a single leg-locked, the men clasp right hands in front of the posteriorly positioned comrade's pelvis, his left hand resting upon the anterior figure's backside. The erotic is not missing at all; it is not even just under the surface. The erotic radiates between the figures. The male sexual organ is what brings the men together, fixing their hands in a bronzed embrace. These comrades appear united in the shared avowal of their sacrificial nudity before the nation. But the sculpture also *contains* the desire between the men within in its over-metaphoric symbology.

A certain homogenization was always the underlying principle for Hitler's deployment of the Hellenic past—to reinforce the breeding of a pure stock and the extirpation of racial and physical degeneration. In his 1933 Party Day speech in Nuremberg, Hitler declared, "The Ideal of Beauty, of antiquity, will be eternal as long as the same pure character and race exist."[64] In his push for unadulterated racial stock, Hitler openly rejected forms of modern art deemed degenerate for their embrace of "misshapen cripples," their attraction to corrupted forms, and their association with the Jews.[65] More than 650 paintings, sculptures, prints, books, and other visual art pieces were culled from museums and ridiculed in a four-month exhibition beginning in July 1937, *Entartete Kunst* (Degenerate Art).[66] Artifacts were attacked for their representations of racial impurities and physical deficiencies or for their makers' misplaced sociopolitical allegiances. The gymnastics movement and physical youth culture (revived and refined by the Nazis) were part of a same program of social modeling as the Nazis' castigation of art and artists. Both used the science of eugenics to justify the correction or banishment of "horrendous, disabled, and sickly" bodies (or their representations). National Socialist–approved aesthetics and physical training worked to purify and reproduce the body of the future Aryan war machine. This was Hitler's primary motivation for increasing the national focus on German youth groups beginning in the 1920s, but the "science" behind the program was opaque and circuitous—the domain of specialists. Therefore, the Reich resurrected one of modern Germany's romantic forebears, a man who captured the spirit of the *Volk* and the virile spectacle of the male body: Friedrich Ludwig Jahn and his gymnastics movement with all its Hellenic trappings.[67]

Drawing upon the "Jahn Renaissance" of the preceding Weimar period, the Hitler Youth under von Shirach's direction laid its foundation upon Jahn's motto "from the gymnasium to a new national life," circulating the phrase widely in its own unique application of his methods.[68] But organizational differences between Jahn's loosely confederated gymnastics-union and the Nazis' centralized command of its youth soon translated, and intentionally so, into differences in praxis. The top-down hierarchy of the Hitler-Jugend descended from the Führer to bands of the young, classified by age, sex, ability, and district. The taxonomy was almost overwhelming. Like Russian nesting dolls, the smallest groups of ten were enveloped by the larger districts of up to two hundred thousand, which were firmly situated within the grasp of central command. Boys were divided into two age groups, ten to fourteen and fourteen to eighteen, while girls formed a larger cohort between the ages of ten and twenty-one. The girls were trained to become mothers and housewives (this model was already in place in the Bund Deutscher Mädel, or League of German Girls, begun in the later years of the Weimar Republic but intensified under Nazi administration and eugenics legislation), while the boys were essentially treated as future soldiers. Even the youngest at ten years of age were forced to answer in the affirmative to the repeated appellation of "soldier."[69] "Evenings of 'comradeship,' folk customs, [and] out-of-doors activities" consumed much of their time, but these "Boy Scout-like" pursuits were secondary to more bellicose activities.[70] Michael H. Kater informs us that regular academic instruction for members of the Hitler-Jugend amounted to only one and a half hours each day, whereas five hours were given over to sports and severe physical training.[71] Jahn's physical "games" had most certainly kept the nineteenth-century French threat in their purview, but direct military preparation in the forms of battle maneuvers and drills was not a factor in his gymnastics program. The Nazis, by contrast, capitalized on a methodology of offensive planning achieved by constant drilling, forced marches, grenade lobbing, and rifle practice. As Gerhard Rempel states, "The apparently spontaneous play of young boys was organized to develop follow-the-leader relationships."[72] The more innocuous athletics like calisthenics, swimming, ball games, and soccer were interspersed with the violent activities of boxing and fencing. Yet perhaps the most egregious abuse was the violence enacted in Turnen-based (though highly restrictive) drills justified as ethical practices.

These undertakings evolved into paramilitary exercises whose functions were not only battle preparedness, such as learning to throw stick grenades, but also wearing down the individual's soul. One boy reported, "We had to run for hours, crawl through filth, and hop up and down," while another rhetorically asked, "Did we feel degraded, drilled, demeaned, or caught?"[73] These operations to increase physical endurance and capacity for work were coupled with group sadism, torture, and peer shaming. Boys divided into "platoons for war games, and they hunted down the 'enemy.' . . . Stronger boys often pummeled weaker boys, throwing them to the ground."[74] In one incident, a midlevel teenage officer tied the wrists and ankles of his charges and beat them with a steel-studded belt once their heterosexuality had been thrown into doubt.[75] In another, a unit leader ordered 160 boys to march into a freezing river.[76] And as part of the same process, each activity was accompanied by a recitation maintaining that all pains and sacrifices were patriotic and honorable in nature. Chants like "Our Flag is Showing Us the Way" reassured the boys that what was being enacted on their bodies and against their psyches was for the good of the nation.[77]

The 1936 Olympics in Berlin was the prime opportunity for an international staging of Hitler's vision of Germania. That year the Reich promulgated the order that alongside a "curriculum for hereditary and racial science," a mandatory "ideological training camp" in Bad-Sooden-Allendorf for all teachers in the colloquium was to culminate in "gymnastics presentations by all the classes."[78] One month later the Chancellor introduced "army training" into the regular classroom.[79] Carl Diem's spectacle that involved thousands of young bodies during the opening ceremonies of the games was, in many ways, to be the official model for future education, though it was already a model that had been developed in public education's extracurricular activities—the Hitler-Jugend. Like most Nazi rhetoric and its applications, Diem's *Olympic Youth* (first presented during the opening ceremonies on August 1, 1936) vacillated between the extremes of overt militarism that announced Germany's capacity for efficient production and a spirited Greek ideal of romanticism that gestured toward a *teutonisch* ethnicity. As Michael Mackenzie acknowledges, Diem was "playing on the philhellenism that was such an integral and ingrained element of educated German society," but Diem, who never joined the Nazi Party, was, nevertheless, also gratifying the ideological penchant of his overbearing patrons.[80] The mass-play's director, Hans Niedecken-Gebhard, likewise, was no National Socialist. He had been a student of Rudolf von Laban and worked closely with the republican government of the 1920s in the organization and execution of festival sporting events.[81] His allegiance was to the sports community and its value for Germany, but under the oversight of Goebbels and his ministry, aesthetic advocacy for the Nazi regime proved ineluctable in the spectacle's dramaturgy.

Susan Manning has said of *Olympic Youth* that it "epitomized the fusion—and confusion—of nationalism and internationalism," with its blending of traditional Olympic symbols (the torch, the rings, the bell, flags of many nations) and the "the body politic of the Third Reich."[82] To lend weight to the games' avowed purpose of international conciliation, Diem and Gebhard focused on what all nations had in common—the young—though some ideological disjunctions and semiotic baggage proved irreconcilable with the aims of internationalism. Their adept staging targeted spectator empathy and aimed at a participatory aesthetic by crafting "a festive community [of youth] that frame[d] and carrie[d] the play."[83] Diem had already used the Kampfspiele (the German or "bourgeois" Olympics) of 1926 as a laboratory for his aesthetics of "unity and order" bound and made impactful by the aggregation of youth.[84] Together with

Reich Chancellor Marx, Diem treated the youth as a blank slate on which to compose the bland prose of German uniformity: "We look delighted and hopeful to our youth who is not divided anymore by social, economic or class differences but united in the thought: we are united and recover in sports, differences do not matter and we want to serve the German nation."[85] Jahn's young students at the Wartburg festival of 1817 said as much a century prior. The physically trained body of the young had the ability to destroy antinational sentiment (in the form of books) and unite Germans across divisions of class, region, and custom. In 1936 the long-standing rhetoric of a potential and desired German "unity" was established by law through the exclusion of non-Aryan raced bodies, and whatever republicanism infused the nationalist ethos of the preceding years was transmuted into a disturbing inversion of Oedipal drama oscillating between mechanism and spiritual romanticism.

In the *Official Report of the Eleventh Olympic Games*, Carl Diem writes that the mass play was "not to be a theatre-festivity" but instead "a loosely-constructed series of several pictures show[ing] youth of various ages in playful and sportive movements . . .. The intention was to show again and again: 'It is in this way that youth shapes its youthful world; it is thus, obeying its own innate and sacred instincts, that it gives form to its still undeveloped forces.'"[86] Diem here stresses the agency and intentionality of children to shape a world, but that trope, just like the terms "innate" and "sacred instincts," as we will observe, will assault the eye as discordant when placed next to the symbolic counterweight of the Third Reich.

In the first picture, "Children at Play," the Olympic Bell rang out and a voice boomed, "I summon the youth of the world."[87] Trumpets blared from the top of the Marathon Gate, through which rushed 2,500 girls between the ages of eleven and twelve, clothed in plain white smocks, while from the Marathon Tunnel streamed 900 boys to settle on the arena field. The boys were outfitted in "training suits and hoods in the colours of the Olympic Rings."[88] The children formed into five groups and executed dances in the round that eventually congealed into the colored rings of the Olympic flag. The *Report* states, "The intention was to make a choric dance which would be a notable rhythmical experience for all participants. No technical demands were to be made which could not be executed by non-professional dancers."[89] This was also the moment at which the least differentiation appeared between the sexes: through the similar styles of their movements, their shared formal objectives (shaping the rings), and their working in heterogeneous groups. This sexual and international combinatory cooperation degraded as the plot advanced, or, to slightly alter the statement, homosocial groupings and conflict were *necessary* for the plot to advance. Leaving childhood meant leaving mixed company and differentiating how one moved through the world. Manning identifies that any unity present in the text is illusory and that the play "actually divides men from women, young from old, mass from leader, German from Jew . . . in other words, it functions as a metaphor for the *Volksgemeinschaft*" (people's community).[90] Even in this first picture of the production, divisions appeared. The girls were dressed in white, hinting to the spectator their future bridal raiment, and chained together delicately with ribbon and hoops. The boys were allowed more freedom in the symbolic clothing of future athletes. In the final tableau, the girls were pushed to the periphery and formed the border around the boys, who comprised the central arrangement of the rings, as if the serious business of the games meant splitting apart the naturally unisex experiences of youth. Through this action the performance unconsciously portrayed an anxiety about the coexistence of immaturity, internationalism, and sexual heterogeneity. Growing up means growing apart, leaving proximity to the multisexed community, and (as we will see) leaving behind the enjoyment of liberty.

"Maidenly Grace," the second picture, continued the classification and separation of bodies, rhythms, and voices. Two thousand three hundred pairs of lithe female limbs (aged 14–18 years) trickled in from the eastern steps and adorned the field with a series of round dances while the Olympic rings broke apart and exited from sight. Wearing simple, "unbleeched [*sic*] natural coloured costumes with a rust-red border," one could easily catch sight of Gret Palucca, a foremost figure of *Ausdruckstanz*, in a fiery red dress, as she emerged "from their midst . . . and danced a waltz."[91] Her mellifluous solo contrasted with the militant march of adolescent males that was soon to follow. But before the young soldiers arrogated the arena, the girls' dances took the shape of games with balls, hoops, and clubs.

The second movement staged a coming to sexual awareness with the complete absence of sex. If anything, there was a regression to childlike behavior for the women. The maidens appeared donning smocks trimmed with what could easily be interpreted as the first signs of menstrual blood, but the sensual rhythms of the dances were replaced with frivolity and the desultory arrangement of discrete games. Choreographed by Dorothee Günther and Maja Lex, the circular dances were executed to the accompaniment of "flutes . . . a shawm, a chorus of bass viols, wood and metal stares, glass bells and chimes, large and small kettle-drums and drums, cymbals, triangles, tambourines and small percussion instruments of all kinds," which emphasized sensuousness and accented the body's cadences.[92] Palluca's emergence in apparel of ardent red appeared at first to be the climax of the disparate explorations of femininity—the arrival of womanhood. She danced her modernized adaptation of the waltz, a dance Andrew Hewitt calls a representation of "the very essence of dance itself, the most intoxicating and energizing force of human movement."[93] Not to mention that it is a social dance with all the eroticism that a social dance (as opposed to courtly dance) entails. When the waltz was introduced into social life, "men and women paired off exclusively and in immediate physical proximity in public space."[94] Palucca, sporting the color of blood and fire, danced her waltz alone. The *Official Report* informs the reader that she danced not only alone but also with egress denied within an enclosed circle of young girls. In effect the waltz's eroticism was contained and the waltzer's sexuality nullified. Manning characterizes Palucca in this solo as a matronly figure, but she could just as easily have been a "negative example" of insatiable feminine passion, running amok and exhausting itself. Whatever her metaphoric role, her physical presence prompted the women to turn away from their bodily explorations and channel their sexual energies toward the inconsequential and inane objects (balls, hoops, clubs) of girlhood games.

For the boys becoming men, the tale moved on a different trajectory. In the third picture, "Youths at Play and in a Serious Mood," the spectator again witnessed a segregation of the biological sexes. Girls withdrew to the end of the arena while "thousands of boys from the east and west steps storm[ed] into the field of play, resounding with the romance of all young life."[95] The girls passively watched while the boys of different nations formed their own camps around fires and "sang the national songs of their homeland."[96] The boys' style of play was sexually differentiated as well, which in this case meant "militarized," but whose bellicosity was offset by the shorts they sported in a variety of brilliant colors. The "boyish gambols" on the field "in spite of their gay liveliness maintained [their] symmetrical formation [in] all the many groups."[97] Absent was the spontaneous interaction of child with ball, hoop, and club; present was the formation as drilled and rehearsed. Then the sportive interactions were swept away in the flood of "a thousand silk flags of all nations" rolling down the stadium stairs upon the shoulders of older, adolescent boys. The standard bearers of each country, the Hitler Youth among them, "marched" their flags around the course and saluted each other as they crossed paths. The multitude of flags finally came to rest around the Olympic flame as a boy recited the "Hymn of Fire."[98]

In this picture becoming a man amounts to finding a nation—of other men. The girls were exiled from the masculine communities, in essence, validating the spectacle of the body politic as only spectators can. Becoming a nation amounts to organizing a homogenously sexed camp of individuals. It also means replacing "boyish gambols" with the "march" of flags and sacrificing play to discipline.

Is this the moment of transition into utopia, when smoothed-out nationalisms recline comfortably on the texturized plane of international difference? Or did that moment just pass with the innocence of childhood: not a sexual awakening but an awakening to national allegiance, to banners, to marches, to a loss of individual will, to a flame at the altar burning for immolation, in sum, to "adulthood" under the Nazis?

There is a similarity in narrative pattern between Diem's third picture, "Youths at Play and in a Serious Mood," and the fate of Jahn's Turnen in the Reich's educational system. The Turnvater's system of peer-led exercises and games "always played with zeal and interest" transmogrified into mass drills regulated by governmental agencies and laws.[99] The third picture of *Olympic Youth*, by its creators' own admission, was made possible only by "the generous and willing cooperation of the Central School Administration of Berlin," which oversaw "the technical and organizing work [that] took up a year and a half."[100] This is not to mold the school administration and Jahn's early practices into an absolute dichotomy or to say that Jahn was guiltless of manipulating the young to serve his nationalist motives (which were rather blatant). But his was a system that encouraged self-organization and allowed space for critique, and if there was a utopia to be gained through bodily discipline, Jahn had to have suspected, staring out from the window of his prison cell (under the conservative imperial government from 1819 to 1825), that it might never be realized during his lifetime; only its traces and impressions as an open-ended spectacle of youth could be sensed.

The creation of utopia requires the artist-observer to complete it. Jahn simply created a space for the elements of his vision to be absorbed: the gymnasium filled with the struggle to produce German masculinity. Winckelmann, too, saw the ideal as impossible to make concrete in his present day: what was "natural among" the Greeks "might seem ideal to us," but touched through the imagination the ideal could serve as a source of artistic nourishment.[101] "I imagine myself appearing in the Olympic Stadium . . .. Indeed, my imagination has several times plunged me into such a reverie, in which I have likened myself to those athletes, since my essay is to be regarded as no less doubtful in this issue than theirs. I cannot but think of myself thus, when venturing on the enterprise of elucidating the principles and causes of so many works of art . . . I see before me, not one, but numerous enlightened judges."[102] Winckelmann's theoretical writings are an Olympic contest because they mediate his desire, along with the art object, to grasp the elusive ideal. In his reverie he becomes the athlete. He inhabits an imagined masculine near-perfection, and because he allows himself to be penetrated deeply and completely by its representative artifact that penetration (or the utmost need for it) prevents mastery of the vision evident in the implications of the subject's standing before "enlightened judgment." Neither Winckelmann nor Jahn aimed to control, collapse, or close his utopic vision; to do so would have been to destroy it. In their creation they allowed to their raw materials, whether nude statuary or the adolescent German male, an agency, an ability to perforate the observer. This strikes a chord with Ernst Bloch's visualization of utopia in an anti-Marxist or anti-Hegelian dialectical frame, that is, as a pure potentiality embedded in the subject's and object's interactions, embedded in the ongoing, never consummated relation of the materials themselves: "So far does utopia extend, so vigorously does this raw material spread to all human activities, so essentially must every anthropology and science of the world contain it. There is no realism worthy of the name if it abstracts from this strongest element in reality, as an unfinished reality."[103] Bloch deracinates dialectical materialism from a universal teleology (for example, the resulting proletarian society that can be found in Marx) in favor of individualized and multiple temporalities that add up to a phenomenology of the "not-yet," a phenomenology that posits being as always in a process of creating utopian possibilities. Utopia is conditioned by the material world's interaction with the hermeneutic positioning of the subject and constitutes a perpetual coexistent alternative to the present, much like dreaming or, to borrow from Winckelmann, "reverie."

Olympic Youth, by contrast, struggled against the realism of nationalism and Hitler's closure of utopian possibility. When the girls left the field and the flags replaced frivolity, adolescent male sexual virility was sublimated into adult homosocial communes and preparations for the possibility of combat. Undercurrents of bilateral homoerotic flows, functioning (ostensibly) as an adhesive for homosocial group arrangements akin to the Greek gymnasium or boys' clubs, cowered before a unilaterally shaped spectacle of disciplined youth. The dreamlike quality of youth at play was forced out of the arena by nationalism's symbolic accoutrements of flags, uniforms, and marching formations that appeared all-too-compulsory and contrived from without. Gathered around the edges of the field, the Hitler-Jugend constrained the international community within a circle of swastikas and by their mere presence silenced any proposals of lasting amity. The labored and thick Nazi symbolism the youth supported at the Olympics had already been worked out and was at its height in the Thingspiel movement: a multidisciplinary, multimedia form of theatre that "tried linking alleged Germanic traditions to National Socialist festive practices."[104] A völkisch brush painted the colors red, white, and black onto a mélange of choirs, solo arias, orations, pantomime, parades, gymnastics, pageants, ballet, modern dance, and ceremony. At the Olympics those same Thingspiel symbols of a National Socialist vision of the Volk nudged aside international accord and encircled once independent entities. Even the mention of the Hitler-Jugend's name exposed the loss of boyhood independence, a filial submission to the call from an overbearing father, his ownership and particularism supplanting extra-familial obligations.

The fourth picture, "Heroic Struggle and Death Lament," began with just such a fatal call. A single speaker (Joachim Eisenschmidt, assistant to the director of the Festival Play Bureau) dressed in pure white hailed the young soldiers: "All games / divine purpose; / fatherland / greatest win. / Fatherland's greatest command / in adversity: / Sacrificial death!"[105] Then sixty male dancers bearing swords commenced a mock feudalistic dance-battle. From the edges of the stadium at midfield advanced the opposing "phalanxes of dancing warriors."[106] The first battalion was bedizened in rust-red costumes trimmed with gold, while the second wore yellow bordered by silver, all designed by Lotte Brill. Their leaders, played by Harald Kreutzberg and Werner Stammer, presented themselves and began to "duel." Both were wounded to the death, and their slow choreographed demise attenuated the luminescence from the searchlights surrounding them. Having breathed their last, the "fallen heroes [were] borne away from the arena in solemn procession."[107] Famed instructor of modern dance, Mary Wigman, and her eighty female dancers bedecked in different shades of grey then performed a dance of mourning for those slain in battle. In the prototypical choreography of Lament for the Dead (for the 1934 Tanzfestspiele), Wigman juxtaposed Greek classicism with modern expressionist movement.[108] The dance involved mourners initially moving in loose clumps, each expressing sorrow in her own particular way, but as the lament increased in intensity the gestures and vocal paroxysms transitioned into a "strong homophonia" with all moving together in a giant circle "as a symbol of sorrow they all have in common." The dancers eventually kneeled slowly and lugubriously to the ground, overcome by their shared grief.[109] Choric unity was able to absorb the individual's struggle to express suffering, and the fate of collapse under sorrow's load was experienced equally by all. "As the anguish of the sorrowing women die[d] away in hopeless monotony the closing hymn beg[an] to be heard."[110] All the participants coalesced into a mass on the stadium's field while above them a vault of light blazed in the sky from a ring of searchlights around the arena, or as the *Report* grandiloquently puts it, "Flames of fire encircled the edge of the Stadium, which was filled with thousands of flag-wavers, and the chorus [sang] the 'Seid umschlungen, Millionen! Diesen Kuss der ganzen Welt! Freude, schöner

Götterfunken!' (May millions be embraced! This kiss to the whole world! Joy, divine spark!)"[111]

For the staging of *Olympic Youth*, foreigners were obviously included (since without them, presenting the international community would be impossible), but Jewish dancers had been prohibited. The American dance community boycotted, but most nations (Hungary, Bulgaria, Yugoslavia, Austria, Switzerland, Holland, Greece, and Italy) agreed to Hitler's terms.[112] Thus, the performance community on the field during the mass-play had been policed and supposedly cleansed of racial "pollution." When in the fourth picture of *Olympic Youth* the call went out to the young crowd assembled to "sacrifice" for the fatherland, it landed upon a racially regulated society. Rossol states that to interpret this summons to death for the nation as a component of Nazi programmatic thinking "is to miss the point."[113] She views the demand instead as a "universally usable theme" with a long track record. Although I agree with Rossol that the theme is widespread and had a convoluted history prior to Nazi appropriation, under the specific conditions of performance, interpreting the call to the children as an extension of Nazi discipline is an unavoidable semiotic resonance, if not the point. It cannot be forgotten that the request, though directed to the international community, was made in German; that the community of internationals had been racially policed; that the Hitler-Jugend stood among that community and had been fed the same doctrine while their bodies had been made docile objects. Through a dance of death, the boys' bodies answered the Führer's question posed by his proxy: "Will you die for the Fatherland?"—"Yes!" In this call and response one can hear the echoes of Jahn's games: "Are you afraid of your enemy?"—"No!" And the echoes of student political schemes atop the Wartenburg hill resound even more loudly: "Should this book be condemned?" "Yes!" Except this time the voice of authority is not a young gymnast asking the boys to burn books; the sovereign is commanding that they burn bodies—the bodies of soldiers, Jews, Gypsies, homosexuals, degenerates, old or unproductive people, all those unwilling to transform Eros into efficiency for the Führer. And perhaps as a coded symbol of this burning, the Olympic Games of 1936 closed with a novel spectacle of "a dome of light" hovering above the international community. The dome of light might have been interpreted as the Holy Spirit beckoning to his creation, but the unforgettable call of the Father had already been made—that is, the call to war.

But we must be cautious not to darken this luminous moment with what we think of as history's inevitable slide into the genre of tragedy. Not yet had those assembled nations descended into the inferno of World War II, and, recalling Bloch, it is the "not-yet," the tear in the fabric, the rupture in the seal, where utopia is to be found. The event as a whole disclosed the contemporary split psyche of what Jahn's Turnen had become. On the one side, there was the ideal of Greek forms beautifully "Germanized": the women sent the boys off to war and then lamented their sacrifice, motifs working through a gendered Wagnerian social ethic. On the other side was the male Aryan body rigidified by modernity and the promotion of a capacity for technical warfare. The erotic plenitude of Winckelmann's Greek nudes and Jahn's use of it as a model for national-racial conditioning were present on both sides of this bodily aesthetic divide, though continually shifting in their legibility. When the two-hour performance is comprehended in its entirety, the taint of the Nazis is visibly infused throughout, but still there is a prodding from the "not yet" contained within but also disrupting Hitler's national mimetic at Berlin in 1936, when totalitarian discipline failed to claim total victory over the demos. Harald Kreutzberg, one of the foremost dancers of Ausdruckstanz, performed the role of the sacrificial commander on the field of battle, but he also performed his queer being-in-the-world on the field of the Olympiastadion. According to Buch and Worthen, "Kreutzberg, a homosexual, had long used androgynous personae in his work," and he had long been acclaimed for his virtuosic brilliance in those personae.[114] His charisma upon the stage attracted recurring support from the National Socialists, which suggests that the Nazis intentionally overlooked, and in a way relied upon, his sexual inclinations and homoerotic attachments. His queer presence was undoubtedly essential to the narrative of *Olympic Youth*. When Kreutzberg erupted from the phalanx of soldiers, a "Greek ballet warrior" in "pink and saffron," as Janet Flanner of the New Yorker described him, he compelled the young men of his army and the spectators in the stands to view, follow, desire, and emotionally invest in his queer corporeality.[115] The censured, suppressed, and banished body of the homosexual was in that moment the cynosure of nations, and its sacrifice was the ultimate scene of pathos. Kreutzberg revivified Winckelmann's Greek nude as the erotic mediator of the unforeclosed, the "not-yet" utopia, the material being that could absorb the spectator's desire for an abstract ideal and maintain that desire as a sense of hope.

Notes

1. For a more detailed description, see Nadine Rossol, *Performing the Nation in Interwar Germany: Sport, Spectacle and Political Symbolism, 1926–36* (New York: Palgrave Macmillan, 2010), 125.
2. Johann Joachim Winckelmann, *Reflections on the Painting and Sculpture of the Greeks*, trans. Henry Fusseli (London: Henry Fusseli, 176), 2–5.

3. Suzanne L. Marchand, *Down from Olympus: Archaeology and Philhellenism in Germany, 1750–1970* (Princeton, NJ: Princeton University Press, 1996), 9.
4. Winckelmann, *Reflections on the Painting and Sculpture of the Greeks*, 17.
5. More than any other biographer, Alex Potts has made it a mission to connect Winckelmann's embodied sexual self to his aesthetic theories and histories. Winckelmann's highly charged and emotionally invested "friendships" with younger men can be tracked back to his great reluctance to cease an affair with a former pupil of his while teaching in Seehausen. This was stopped by violent threats from the young man's family. The repeated lack of consummation in his passionate ventures functioned as kindling for Wincklemann's bountiful desire, particularly demonstrated in his letters to the young Latvian nobleman, Friedrich Rheinhold von Berg. Quoted in Alex Potts, *Flesh and the Ideal: Winckelmann and the Origins of Art History* (New Haven: Yale University Press, 1994), 204.
6. Johann Joachim Winckelmann, *History of Ancient Art*, vol. 2, trans. Alexander Gode (New York: Frederick Ungar, 1968), 177.
7. Marchand, *Down from Olympus*, 21.
8. For an expansion upon this idea, see Felix Saure, "Beautiful Bodies, Exercising Warriors, and Original Peoples: Sports, Greek Antiquity and National Identity from Winckelmann to 'Turnvater Jahn,'" *German History* 27, no. 3 (2009): 360.
9. Quoted in Saure, "Beautiful Bodies," 365.
10. Undergirding this philhellenic pedagogic take on German nationalism was Schiller's Romantic theory of aesthetics. In his 1794 treatise on aesthetic education Schiller posits two human drives in the production of art: the sensuous and the formal. What is required is an amalgamation of the two drives brought about by Beauty. This amalgamation is called the "play-drive" and it "annul[s] time within time, reconcil[es] becoming with absolute being and change with identity." Schiller locates the apogee of the play-drive as exhibited by Beauty "not in Rome, but in Greece," where it was revealed that "with beauty man shall only play, and it is with beauty only that he shall play. The bloodless combats of strength, speed, and agility" in the agonistic rivalries at the Olympic Games are exemplary of achieving that "world at play." See Friedrich Schiller, *On the Aesthetic Education of Man in a Series of Letters*, trans. Elizabeth M. Wilkinson and L. A. Willoughby (Oxford: Clarendon, 1967), 81, 91, 97, 105–7.
11. Two treatises on physical education modeled on the Greek gymnasium appeared prior to Jahn's foundation of the Turnplatz (open-air gymnasium) in 1811. Gerhard Ulrich Anton Vieth's two-volume *Versuch einer Encyklopädie der Leibesübungen* (1794) and Johann Christoph Friedrich GutsMuths's *Gymnastik für die Jugend* (1793) were major influences on Jahn's own design, but it was Turnvater Jahn who, according to Charles Beck, the original English translator of Jahn's treatise on gymnastics, *Die Deutsche Turnkunst*, first "established a gymnasium on a scale, appropriated for the community at large." See the preface to Friedrich Ludwig Jahn, *Treatise on Gymnasticks*, trans. Charles Beck (Northhampton, MA: Simeon Butler, 1828), iii.
12. Marion Kant, "The Moving Body and the Will to Culture," *European Review* 19, no. 4 (2009): 581.
13. For a digestible summary of events, see Mary Fulbrook, *A Concise History of Germany* (Cambridge: Cambridge University Press, 1992), 95–104.

14. Fulbrook, *A Concise History of Germany*, 99.
15. For a complete list of exercises, see Jahn, *Treatise on Gymnasticks*, vii–xviii.
16. Ibid., 104–5.
17. Ibid., 133.
18. Ibid., 106–7.
19. Michel Foucault, *Discipline and Punish: The Birth of the Prison*, trans. Alan Sheridan (New York: Vintage, 1995), 135.
20. Louis L. Snyder, *Roots of German Nationalism* (Bloomington: Indiana University Press, 1978), 61.
21. Saure, "Beautiful Bodies," 370.
22. Kant, "The Moving Body," 581.
23. Monika Zechetmayr, "A Clarification of the Contribution of Friedrich Ludwig Jahn (1778–1852) to the Development of Modern Gymnastics" (master's thesis, University of Washington, 1977), 76.
24. Jahn, *Treatise on Gymnasticks*, 9–10.
25. Zechetmayr, "A Clarification," 80.
26. Jahn, *Treatise on Gymnasticks*, 156–57.
27. Quoted in Snyder, *Roots of German Nationalism*, 61.
28. Quoted in Saure, "Beautiful Bodies," 369.
29. For a short summary of Jahn's notion of sinfulness in his *Deutsches Volkstrum*, see George L. Mosse, *Nationalism and Sexuality, Middle-Class Morality and Sexual Norms in Modern Europe* (Madison: University of Wisconsin Press, 1985), 78.
30. Quoted in Saure, "Beautiful Bodies," 371.
31. Winckelmann, *Reflections*, 6.
32. Winckelmann, *Reflections*, 11.
33. Jahn, *Treatise on Gymnasticks*, 161.
34. Ibid., 142.
35. Saure, "Beautiful Bodies," 370.
36. After the defeat of the French in 1815, a number liberal organizations pushed for unification of the German states or an alteration to the privileges of the nobility. The more extreme sects of leftist liberals included student leagues (*Burschenschaften*) who lobbied for immediate confederation and an end to the estate system. Many of these student fraternities were present at Wartburg and participated in the populist Hambach Festival of May 1832. Although the generation of students under Jahn's tutelage, in many ways, grew more radical in their activism than the Turnvater condone, Jahn, nevertheless, continued to be an influential figure in their midst.
37. William Wordsworth, *William Wordsworth: The Major Works* (Oxford: Oxford University Press, 1984), 611.
38. Fred Eugene Leonard, "Friedrich Ludwig Jahn and the Development of Popular Gymnastics (Vereinsturnen) in Germany," *American Physical Education Review* 10, no. 1 (1905): 3.
39. Ibid.
40. Steven Michael Press, "False Fire: The Wartburg Book-Burning of 1817," *Central European History* 42 (2009): 624.

41. Ibid.
42. Ibid., 625.
43. That physical culture was a defining characteristic of *bürgerlich* sensibility able to move through economic class structure is one of Hau's central theses in examination of Life Reform movements between 1890 and 1930.
44. Michael H. Kater informs us that regular academic instruction for members of the Hitler-Jugend (Hitler Youth) amounted to only one and a half hours each day, whereas five hours were given over to sports and physical training. See Michael H. Kater, *Hitler Youth* (Cambridge, MA: Harvard University Press, 2004), 50.
45. See chapter 2, note 36 for a summary of liberal movements for unification.
46. Alexander J. De Grand, *Fascist Italy and Nazi Germany: The 'Fascist' Style of Rule* (London and New York: Routledge, 1995), 12.
47. Richard Wagner, *The Art Work of the Future and Other Works*, trans. W. Ashton Ellis (Lincoln and London: University of Nebraska Press, 1993), 32.
48. See Brian Vick, "The Origins of the German Volk: Cultural Purity and National Identity in Nineteenth-Century Germany," *German Studies Review* 26, no. 2 (2003): 246.
49. See George L. Mosse, *Nationalism and Sexuality, Middle-Class Morality and Sexual Norms in Modern Europe* (Madison: University of Wisconsin Press, 1985), 23–47. The physician and anthropologist Carl Heinrich Stratz's *The Racial Beauty of Woman* (1901) is indicative of this turn, as Michael Hau has exposed. In his study Stratz combs the writings of medical practitioners and compares body measurements and phenotypical features of women belonging to various races of his own classification (Mongols, *Mittelländer*—whites, *Nigritier*—blacks) and, not surprisingly, determines that the white race (particularly the German woman) is, in Hau's words, "the most capable and ha[s] the most perfect and beautiful individuals." See Michael Hau, *The Cult of Health and Beauty in Germany: A Social History, 1890–1930* (Chicago: University of Chicago Press, 2003), 87.
50. Heinz Stübig, "The Prussian German Army: School of the Nation in the Nineteenth Century," *European Education* 34, no. 3 (2002): 11.
51. Quoted in Stübig, "The Prussian German Army," 13.
52. Foucault, *Discipline and Punish*, 138.
53. Quoted in Stübig, "The Prussian German Army," 14.
54. Pfister, "Cultural Confrontations," 63.
55. Ibid., 76.
56. Dianne S. Howe, *Individuality and Expression: The Aesthetics of the New German Dance, 1908–1936* (New York: Peter Lang, 1996), 25.
57. Quoted in Howe, *Individuality and Expression*, 26.
58. Howe, *Individuality and Expression*, 29.
59. Quoted in Howe, *Individuality and Expression*, 29.
60. Susan A. Manning, *Ecstasy and the Demon: Feminism and Nationalism in the Dances of Mary Wigman* (Berkeley: University of California Press, 1993), 9.
61. Tobin Siebers, "Hitler and the Tyranny of the Aesthetic," *Philosophy and Literature* 24, no. 1 (2000): 101. Mary Wigman spent three years at the commune working closely with Laban. She was the node where the two lines of *Ausdruckstanz* met, and her passionate modern dance solos and all-female ensembles of the teens and mid-twenties gathered up

those strands. To Wigman, that Germanness was only conscionable and cognizable because it was thoroughly Greek: "The Greeks had a theatre that was inseparable from religion and the state, that embodied their being as *Volk*, nation, family, and individual. A theatre that belonged to all, that served God and humanity, that became a festival [*Fest*] in the highest sense." Quoted in Manning, *Ecstasy and the Demon*, 193–94.

62. Siebers, "Hitler and the Tyranny of the Aesthetic," 104.
63. Peter Guenther, "Three Days in Munich, July 1937," in *"Degenerate Art": The Fate of the Avant-garde in Nazi Germany*, ed. Stephanie Barron (Los Angeles: LACMA, 1991), 33.
64. Quoted in Siebers, "Hitler and the Tyranny of the Aesthetic," 104.
65. George L. Mosse, "Beauty without Sensuality: The Exhibition *Entarte Kunst*," in *"Degenerate Art": The Fate of the Avant-garde in Nazi Germany*, ed. Stephanie Barron (Los Angeles: LACMA, 1991), 26.
66. Stephanie Barron, *"Degenerate Art,"* 9.
67. Quoted in Gerhard Rempel, *Hitler's Children: The Hitler Youth and the SS* (Chapel Hill: University of North Carolina Press, 1989), 173.
68. Quoted in Rempel, *Hitler's Children*, 175. During the volatile period of the Weimar Republic the gymnastics youth culture of Jahn had once again stepped onto the stage of German sociopolitics. In 1923, Reichskunstwart (Imperial Protector of Art) Edwin Redslob proclaimed a return to Jahn's original and chaste ideas of national spectacle, except that the former commemoration days once celebrated with gymnastics extravaganzas that had aimed at nineteenth-century German unification were now to be massive participatory events that valorized the unstable republic. See Rossol, *Performing the Nation*, 49–57.
69. Kater, *Hitler Youth*, 29.
70. *German Youth Activities Army Assistance Program Guide* (S.l.: s.n., 1948), 27.
71. Kater, *Hitler Youth*, 50.
72. Rempel, *Hitler's Children*, 176.
73. Quoted in Kater, *Hitler Youth*, 31.
74. Susan Campbell Bartoletti, *Hitler Youth: Growing Up in Hitler's Shadow* (New York: Scholastic, 2005), 28.
75. Kater, *Hitler Youth*, 53.
76. Bartoletti, *Hitler Youth*, 28.
77. Kater, *Hitler Youth*, 33.
78. Anson Rabinbach and Sander L. Gilman, *The Third Reich Sourcebook* (Los Angeles: University of California Press, 2013), 245.
79. Ibid.
80. Michael Mackenzie, "From Athens to Berlin: the 1936 Olympics and Leni Riefenstahl's *Olympia*," *Critical Inquiry* 29, no. 2 (2003): 333.
81. Rossol, *Performing the Nation*, 125.
82. Manning, *Ecstasy and the Demon*, 195.
83. Quoted in Rossol, *Performing the Nation*, 126.
84. Rossol, *Performing the Nation*, 46.
85. Quoted in Rossol, *Performing the Nation*, 45.
86. Organisationskomitee für die XI. Olympiade Berlin, 1936, E.V., *The Eleventh Olympic Games, Berlin, 1936: Official Report* (Berlin: Wilhelm Limpert, 1937), 577.
87. Ibid.

88. Ibid., 580.
89. Ibid., 583.
90. Manning, *Ecstasy and the Demon*, 195.
91. Organisationskomitee, *Official Report*, 577.
92. Ibid., 581.
93. Andrew Hewitt, *Social Choreography: Ideology as Performance in Dance and Everyday Movement* (Durham, NC: Duke University Press, 2005), 27.
94. Ibid., 33.
95. Organisationskomitee, *Official Report*, 577.
96. Ibid.
97. Ibid., 580.
98. Ibid., 577–78.
99. Jahn, *Treatise on Gymnasticks*, 142.
100. Organisationskomitee, *Official Report*, 584.
101. Winckelmann, *History of Ancient Art*, vol. 2, trans. G. Henry Lodge, 286.
102. Ibid., 300.
103. Quoted in Vincent Geoghegan, *Ernst Bloch* (London and New York: Routledge, 1996), 144.
104. Rossol, *Performing the Nation*, 109.
105. This is a translation taken from Susan Manning, but I have altered her original translation of "Not" from "need" to "adversity," line six. See Manning, *Ecstasy and the Demon*, 199. The original German is taken from the *Official Report*. "Allen Spiels / heil'ger Sinn; / Vaterlandes / Hochgewinn. / Vaterlandes höchst Gebot / in der Not: / Opfertod!" See Organisationskomitee, *Official Report*, 578.
106. Organisationskomitee, *Official Report*, 578.
107. Ibid.
108. Buch and Worthen, "Ideology in Movement," 236.
109. Quoted in Manning, *Ecstasy and the Demon*, 181.
110. Ibid.
111. Organisationskomitee, *Official Report*, 580.
112. Manning, *Ecstasy and the Demon*, 195.
113. Rossol, *Performing the Nation*, 127.
114. David Joseph Buch and Hana Worthen, "Ideology in Movement and a Movement in Ideology: *The Deutsche Tanzfestspiele* 1934 (9–16 December, Berlin)," *Theatre Journal* 59, no. 2 (2007): 227.
115. Janet Flanner, "Berlin Letter," *New Yorker* (August 15, 1936), 35.

Shocking the System

The Arts Council, the British Council, and the Paradox of Cherub Theatre Company

—BRIAN E. G. COOK

On its surface, this article is the story of the Cherub Company, London, which between 1978 and 2003, under the leadership of Andrew Visnevski, premiered nearly forty professional productions of British and European classic plays in London. Many of those productions subsequently toured nationally, and several were sent overseas by the British Council to tour internationally to countries including Germany, Spain, Zimbabwe, Sudan, Iraq, and Pakistan. The company won a Fringe First at the Edinburgh Festival for its production of *Kafka's THE TRIAL* (the production's official title) and had several national theatre critics as champions, especially B. A. Young of the *Financial Times*. Visnevski, the company's founding artistic director, is now ensconced at the Royal Academy of Dramatic Arts as the head of the academy's MA programs.

However, this is not the story of a company that is widely recognized for its successes, and, in fact, it is currently one of the few published stories of this company in any scholarly or critical record. In this article, I will provide a brief historical accounting of the company and its work, though my larger purpose is to expose the process by which it (and potentially other companies like it) has been excluded from the historiographic record. Cherub's case prompts a reconsideration of the connection between "success," financial stability, and historiographic importance, for its history is still accessible through archival research and interviews, and those records provide a window into the way artists either become canonized by the cultural field or are forgotten. By telling the story of a company that almost no one has ever heard of and whose work has largely been forgotten, I will begin to unpack the motivations that drive canonization.

Despite Cherub's exclusion from the historical record, an examination of the company's work reveals much about the human biases inherent in processes of artistic validation, especially validation connected with receiving a monetary subsidy. Cherub produced much of its work over its twenty-five-year history without any consistent government subsidy or corporate sponsorship (which is arguably a success in its own right). From August 1979 to May 1982, Cherub gave nearly four hundred performances of eleven different productions at theatres all over Great Britain and Europe. Audiences were receptive, newspaper critics generally positive, and touring-house producers satisfied.[1] But agencies responsible for funding artistic work were mixed on whether Cherub's work was successful, and a key part of Cherub's story is how two government agencies looked at the same company and saw something completely different. Its lack of success with the Arts Council of Great Britain (ACGB), the primary agency providing subsidies to artists within the United Kingdom, meant that Cherub could never grow into a stable company with a consistent group of actors and a permanent home, which was its goal. Faced with rejection after rejection for its subsidy applications to the ACGB, the company had little of the funding needed to develop new productions, and the resulting instability caused its productivity to slow in the mid-1980s. Visnevski constantly had to recruit new young actors and technicians willing to work for what Cherub could afford to pay instead of being able to work with actors already accustomed to his style, and the company began to focus on remounting old productions for overseas touring.

Unlike the ACGB, the British Council (BC) was happy to send Cherub to tour abroad, and though it wasn't able to pay for the company to develop new productions to be in seen in Britain, its largesse served as a lifeline for the company. The BC was part of the Foreign and Commonwealth department and had been created in the mid-1930s "to promote abroad a wider appreciation of British culture and civilization," and it regularly funded international tours of existing productions by companies like Cherub.[2] These two agencies saw Cherub completely differently, and that's partially because Cherub was, and is, a notoriously a difficult entity to pin down and define. Because Visnevski sought a company that would be artistically diverse and that enabled him to explore the scripts he chose to produce, the company actively resisted codification. If Cherub's story tells us anything, it is the importance placed upon definition in historiography and upon artistic branding in the British theatre economy in the last decades of the twentieth century. That quality is likely the most important factor in this story, for the company's reluctance to brand itself meant that others were free to do the defining, leaving Cherub particularly subject to external opinion.

Cherub was started by Visnevski and actor Simon Chandler in 1978 with a mission "to prove against all current odds that great plays can be made accessible and exciting to a wide audience at comparatively low production costs."[3] Their choice to produce "great plays" (read: classics) caused the company to be viewed in a specific way by audiences, critics, and government representatives in the British context. Cherub was not, by and large, a company focused on producing new work but rather one that wanted to reinvestigate or revive often-ignored English and Continental classics. The company's artistic choices were predicated on the founders' view that mainstream British theatre in the late 1970s was overly naturalistic and hidebound. In particular, Polish-born Visnevski sought to reinvigorate it by using a more physical, Eastern European approach to his productions of classic texts. It was this artistic choice that doomed the company. As I'll show, representatives of the ACGB largely viewed Cherub's attempts as unnecessary and unsuccessful, and rejected nearly every request the company made for a subsidy.

Visnevski had come to Britain after being exiled from Poland in 1971, and he initially struggled to fit into the culture in which he was now immersed. During a 2010 interview, Visnevski remembered: "I became very very conscious of the fact that in the United Kingdom there was an obsession with pigeonholing. And in my personality-forming years, I developed a resistance to the idea that anybody should be able to pigeonhole anything—certainly not me. I suppose this came to a head while I was studying at [the] Central [School of Speech and Drama], where I had certain difficulties as I was classed as 'stylistically incompatible' for a while. I knew that I was marrying in me at the time—this difficult time—I was trying to marry what I had brought out of Poland and my admiration for certain styles of theatre and ways of performing with what was being instilled to me at Central, which was trying to be the 'boy next door.'"[4] Visnevski brought with him the methodologies of the theatre he had grown up with: a focus on actors' physical and emotional investment, a willingness to fully engage the body, the use of mask and mime, and the view of the play text as but one of many equally important parts a director might utilize to tell a story. Those methodologies formed and marked Cherub's style and approach. Visnevski directed nearly all of Cherub's productions over its twenty-five-year history; it is nearly impossible to see Cherub independent of Visnevski. Some of his most notable early work with Cherub includes a production of John Fletcher and William Shakespeare's *Two Noble Kinsmen* (1979), in which Visnevski used an all-male cast and the London punk style of the era to create a potentially dangerous and certainly edgy world. The actors wore tight leather pants and little else; female characters were denoted by painted breasts and male characters by leather codpieces. The central story of two knights' battle over the same "woman" thus took on more complicated meanings in an era when homosexuality on British stages was hardly commonplace (though no longer illegal).[5]

The company's 1980 adaptation of Franz Kafka's novel *The Trial* played to sold-out crowds at the Edinburgh Festival Fringe, some of whom brought their own ladders to see over the multitudes. *Kafka's THE TRIAL* put Kafka's protagonist Joseph K in the center of a world empty of trappings but full of malice, suspicion, and fear. The novel was adapted by Visnevski. Five actors played twenty-odd characters on an incredibly simple set, with masks and white makeup distorting their features, inspired by the paintings of expressionist George Grosz. The production of *Macbeth* (1981) utilized Japanese theatre's stylized movement, with actors wearing long wigs, grotesque make-up, and heavy fur costumes reminiscent of Medieval European garb. The production featured ten actors playing all of the various roles and lasted just under two hours without an intermission. The set comprised a white shag carpet (part of which had been cut up to make the costumes), three sets of footlights, and "weird sounds and anguished cries of an alien, hellish world[, which] echo from the shadows and silhouettes that flit across a white screen [upstage]," noted Keith Nurse in his review for *The Daily Telegraph*.[6]

Cherub's productions were usually both lauded by newspaper critics with a fondness for continental European theatre AND castigated by representatives of the ACGB, who felt that Cherub's physicality had no place in text-centric British theatre. As the reports and correspondence in the ACGB's archive show, the ACGB's staff and advisers had trouble deciding what Cherub was and what it could become. It was purportedly a fringe company doing classics in an "alternative way," but alternative in this case did not necessarily mean political. Unlike other, now-famous companies producing with European models like Cheek by Jowl (founded 1981) or the later Complicité (founded 1983), who were both founded by British people who had studied European methods, Cherub was founded by someone who was tailoring his native Eastern European-ness to fit the British cultural field. As a result Cherub's aesthetic gave the ACGB's staff pause because it was so different that they couldn't often figure out how it could be improved, and generally they just labeled the company's work "bad." One noted report, written by ACGB drama officer Jon Plowman, criticized the physicality in Visnevski's work as being derivative of the 1960s European-inspired "experiments" of Peter Brook.[7] "No clear reason for treating the play in this way beyond a visual one," Plowman writes about *Two Noble Kinsmen*, "and I think one might put it in a new category along Brookian lines marked jerk-off theatre. Should not be encouraged in front of a paying public—they might not go blind!"[8] Cherub was a British alternative theatre company that avoided the blatantly left-wing political play favored by much of the rest of the "alternative" segment, and it utilized "foreign" techniques that often did not maintain the integrity of the classical texts it chose to produce.[9] It was an alternative company that didn't do typically alternative work, a British company that didn't work in a British way, an ensemble of young theatre people who produced work more "foreign" than many of the ACGB's officers seemed ready for.

The ACGB's leadership and staff had worked hard from the agency's postwar days to cultivate its place within the British theatre mainstream. From its earliest days, it had struggled to find the right balance between two parts of its chartered mission, one being "to improve the standard of execution of the fine arts" and the other "to increase the accessibility of the fine arts to the public."[10] In other words, it was supposed to both make art "good" and make it available to everyone, a mission it found to be completely challenging to fulfill. The ACGB had to both "raise" and "spread," and eventually, the ACGB adopted a specific policy that chose to prioritize the former over the latter. It was elaborated by Secretary General William Emrys Williams (served 1951–1963) in an annual report: "Might it not be better to accept the realistic fact that the living theatre of good quality cannot be widely accessible and to concentrate our resources upon establishing a few more *shrines*. . . . In reconsidering the exhortation of its Charter to 'Raise and Spread' the Council may decide for the time being, to emphasise the first more than the second word, and to *devote itself to the support of two or three exemplary theatres which might re-affirm the supremacy of standards in our national theatre*. . . . High standards can be built only on a limited scale."[11] With its new policy, the ACGB was, in the 1950s, merely heeding a call that had already been fairly prominent in arts circles since the nineteenth century, essentially a trickle-down of culture. John Christie, founder of the Glyndebourne Opera, an organization fully supported by private donors, wrote a letter to a member of the Arts Council, in which he said, "Our view is that the method, which can achieve this purpose, is to light incandescent fires in a few places, the sparks from which will fall far and wide and are likely to set alight whatever material will burn."[12] The danger for Christie in opting to spread the arts without first raising firm centers of excellence was that "mediocrity" would reign. "Mediocrity will set nothing on fire. . . . Mediocrity is like damp sheets. The way to distribute Art is by creating great Artistic achievement. Light a few fires in the Country and raise these to incandescence."[13]

Within the theatre segment, the ACGB of the 1980s could look back and attribute many successes to the focus on raising specific institutions. Public subsidy had been given to sustain the Royal Shakespeare Company and for the establishment of the Royal National Theatre, and these would become two of the primary centers for excellence. A subsidy had also been used to support the work of the English Stage Company at the Royal Court, the site of the "revolution" of 1956 in British theatre with the production of John Osborne's *Look Back in Anger*. Through the 1950s and 1960s, "Raise and Spread" helped to reestablish British theatre on the world stage. As Dan Rebellato has documented, London's stages would usher out the posh and supposedly soulless work of Noel Coward and Terrance Rattigan to welcome the work of "Angry Young Men" like Osborne, John Arden, and Edward Bond.[14]

Cherub came on the scene in the midst of the great upwelling of theatrical practice that had followed the withdrawal of official censorship in 1968. Many British alternative theatre companies emerged in the 1970s and sought to open up theatre's potential to revitalize society by depicting and reflecting what the mainstream theatre had previously ignored. Indeed, many of the most noted companies also sought to provoke radical political revolution through theatrical production. Interestingly, most of these artists still acquiesced to working with mainstream institutions like the ACGB, choosing to not directly challenge the notion that such agencies had the authority to make distinctions about who should have funding and who should not. That is not to say that the ACGB's funding decisions were welcomed without controversy; indeed, widespread outrage often came with specific subsidy announcements, becoming especially pronounced as the Thatcher government's budget cutting reduced the overall amount of subsidy the ACGB had to give away, thus forcing it to make tough decisions about which companies it would cease to support. Nevertheless, the ACGB held a tremendous amount of cultural (and economic) capital, and it was not an entity that could be avoided in the 1970s and 1980s. Its granting of subsidy was a de facto acknowledgment of a company's acceptance by the mainstream, even if the company remained alternative in mission. Thus, a company granted a subsidy could see itself (and be seen by others) as "successful" and to have won a tremendous victory by being granted legitimacy.

The ACGB developed specific funding streams to direct to the new "alternative" segment, though many both inside the ACGB and elsewhere wondered about the wisdom of supporting companies whose quality was sometimes secondary to political motivation. The ACGB often paid lip service to the idea that it was working to "develop" such companies, at least those that it generally found to have value. Both mainstream and alternative companies pressed for funding, and the ACGB did its best to acquire as much information on all of the various companies who wanted something from it. The ACGB was hierarchically organized, with the full council meeting regularly to make "decisions" based on the work and reporting of the full-time staff. Each "art" had a department, and theatre was funded by the Drama Department. Generally, the ACGB Drama Department would send reviewers to report on the performances of any company who wished to seek a subsidy. Those reviewers were sometimes direct employees of the ACGB: officers, who did the daily work and were the immediate face of the ACGB that most companies saw regularly; or the drama director and his assistants, those in charge of the departments and who oversaw the work of the officers. Other reports were written by members of the drama advisory panel, who were unpaid "professionals" from whom the ACGB saw fit to request advice. Sometimes even full members of the council itself were asked to write reports, and occasionally reports were requested from people outside the council, especially from those who worked for Regional Arts Associations (RAAs) or who were notable figures in the field.

The ACGB's decision-making was an intensely human process, fraught with both the benefits and deficits of human interpretation. The various reports on Cherub's productions place the ACGB's staff and advisers squarely in the position of producing and defending particular theatrical production practices within the cultural field of Great Britain to the exclusion of others. Cherub's alterity was synonymous with its foreignness. The company was never overtly political; instead, Visnevski in particular saw himself as opposed to the dominant theatrical practices within mainstream British theatre, seeking instead to use his native East European aesthetic in his productions. "Maybe I lacked the vocabulary at the time to express what I would want my company to be seen as," Visnevski told me. "I've always hated this Arts Council question, 'But what are you? What is your identity?'" For Visnevski, definition was, and is, confining: "The identity has the right to change, and it should otherwise you're dead creatively. And I've tried to change my way of looking, my interpretation, my way of communicating with an audience from show to show. . . . The word alternative means that you are an option. The theatre's not an option; there are many kinds of theatre. I am one of many, I represent one of many kinds of theatre . . . which has a right to shift and change. And at one point I may be seen as more mainstream and another point as less mainstream, but again, what is mainstream theatre?"[15] Although Cherub sought funding from the ACGB, it was never granted it because of the ACGB's misrecognition and rejection of their foreignness. Even so, Cherub could likely never have conformed to the ACGB's expectations, largely because the ACGB did not articulate them and partially because Cherub did not initially recognize the consequences of defying those unspoken expectations and refusing to define itself. The company's aesthetic prompted a specifically different style of theatre and performance that the ACGB, ever in its pursuit to reward excellence, decided to define as "bad."

From the company's earliest days, the ACGB's officers were flustered by Cherub. Because they could not place the company's work in a style or genre of performance they were accustomed to seeing, the Arts Council's reviewers would often attribute the intentional rawness of the company's productions (usually arising out of the visceral and emotional nature of the actors' performances) to "youth" or "inexperience." The Arts Council of Great Britain drama officer Jonathan Lamede noted that for Cherub's first production, *Life is a Dream* (1978): "This new young company had bitten off far far more than they could chew. . . . It was surprising to learn afterwards that the majority of the cast had had professional experience; the standard seemed to me to be that of a group of people barely out of drama school, raw, unvariegated and without much grasp of rhythm, pace or inflection."[16] Only about twenty years before, in 1949, the ACGB's Llewellyn Rees was horrified by the "debasing [of] human nature" that he witnessed in a training session at the Old Vic School, and Simon Shepherd has documented the rejection of the "physical" in acting across the 1960s with the emergence of the Royal Court's emphasis on "kitchen sink realism."[17] As many of the ACGB reports demonstrate, this realism was the norm by which they judged Cherub's performances.

Drama officer Plowman, responsible for the "jerk-off theatre" review of *Kinsmen*, reminisced in his report on *Life is a Dream*, "It reminded me in production of nothing so much as the Eastern European films which were shown for children on the BBC in the early 60's [*sic*], were always presented by Peggy Miller and seemed always to be dubbed by the same four radio actors."[18] Plowman associated Cherub's productions with East European performance techniques, though by saying the production was "nothing so much as" these films, he reveals that he views such techniques with little regard. Indeed, Plowman's particular conceptualization of Eastern Europe and its culture would be a yardstick that the ACGB would continually use for Cherub's productions. The films Plowman refers to were shown on the BBC in the 1960s and 1970s under the collective series title *Tales from Europe*.[19] Most of the films shown on *Tales from Europe* had been heavily subsidized by various European governments, and thus were inexpensive for the BBC to purchase broadcast rights to. Former BBC executive Edward Barnes said that after purchasing them, the BBC "would re-edit them into short series, and because we couldn't afford dubbing we'd add narration over the dialogue. This became virtue from necessity, because the viewers could hear the original language and it gave them a taste of other cultures and other worlds."[20] It is not accidental that Plowman should specifically recall in his report the overdubbing of the German actors' lines by the narration of a British actor. In *The Singing Ringing Tree*, for example, the European-ness of the film is foregrounded and is virtually unobscured, with only a hastily added Britishness (the narration) scrawled over the top of it. I think that a similar case could be made for many of Cherub's productions, especially the early ones like *Life is a Dream* and the next production, *The Two Noble Kinsmen*. As Visnevski has said, he felt that he was always trying to marry his Eastern European self with the British milieu he was now in, sometimes uneasily. A Cherub show was like a *Tales from Europe* episode; its European-ness was writ large, and its lack of Britishness was perhaps off-putting to those accustomed to traditional British performance.

The ACGB tried numerous times to put Cherub in a box by asking the company to define itself, something it refused to do; and because the staff did not sympathize with Visnevski's mission and could not associate the company within conventional designations, they began to see Cherub as a problem.[21] As Plowman's reports particularly make clear, when the ACGB's staff was left to draw its own conclusions, the reviewers often imagined the worst. Because the ACGB could not both fund the company and keep it marginalized (as it tended to do with other "token" companies), they opted to ignore the company's need for funding in the hope that Cherub would just go away.

On its side, Cherub's biggest fault was that it didn't play by the ACGB's rules, and its desire to be contrary showed up both in its work and in its interactions with the ACGB. The company's determination to be different was what drew critics and audiences to its productions, but it also alienated the ACGB. To be able to do what one wanted in the 1980s (and probably still today), companies had to be very adept at "playing the game" with the ACGB to get financial support. Those who could not or did not play the game successfully were often in trouble. Cherub's founder, Visnevski, tried to walk the line between his own artistic principles and the ones that he could perceive the ACGB was placing on his productions, but even he admits now that he was not a good politician with the ACGB. That, coupled with the fact that the company did not know specifically what the ACGB's objections were because the ACGB officer reports were not available to the artists, placed them at a severe disadvantage. All Visnevski knew was that his company wasn't being funded, and in desperation, he and his company made some decisions that led them into an even more complicated relationship with the ACGB.

Cherub's first misstep came when Visnevski attempted to obtain a program rather than a project subsidy on a couple of occasions. The ACGB preferred to test the waters when working with a new company by offering a project subsidy, or small grants only for specific projects, a fact that Visnevski did not understand. After a number of project grants, a company could be considered for a program, or annual, subsidy, a more sizable grant intended to support the work of a company over the course of a year, as Lamede explained to Visnevski in a letter dated May 31, 1979.[22] In its early days, Cherub didn't operate on a traditional, seasonal model, and in part, the misunderstanding between Cherub and the ACGB seems to have come out of the rather chaotic nature of Cherub's production schedule. Without a subsidy, the company had to constantly perform *something* if it was to stay alive (the more tickets sold, the more money to produce). Having become a cooperative in 1979 before *Two Noble Kinsmen*, the actors and crew were being paid only from box office receipts, after expenses were deducted. In its first five years of operation as a cooperative (1979–1984), Cherub put up seventeen new productions, half of the total number of shows that Cherub would produce over its twenty-five-year lifespan.

Cherub's hectic schedule of performances and rehearsals and organizing tours didn't line up with the Arts Council's timeline. "You will of course be entitled to submit project applications in 1980/81, once the Council makes funds available," ACGB drama officer Jonathan Lamede wrote to Visnevski in August 1979 after noting that the company's application for program subsidy had been denied. "I would suggest you contact me no later than January 1980 if you intend to put in an application for the period starting April 1980."[23] At the time, Visnevski was preparing to leave for Edinburgh for the premiere of *Kinsmen* at the Festival Fringe, a production produced and subsequently toured without a subsidy. He was also planning the company's next productions. In February 1980, Visnevski sent a letter to drama director John Faulkner, seeking "financial support for . . . work in 1980–81." The letter also detailed the company's plans for *Barabbas* and the two children's plays, *Donkey Work* and *Monster Man*, which were planned to tour to schools. Visnevski, because he had so many plans for future productions, hoped the council would extend program funding to continue his work so that Cherub didn't have to wait for the project grant deadlines. Lamede's response, sent through his assistant Sarah Golding, was to once again explain that the company had already applied for a program subsidy and had been rejected. Individual project applications, Lamede said, were only to be used for future, as-yet-unproduced work as "the Council cannot offer subsidy in retrospect."[24] Lamede's written responses increasingly express frustration with what he perceives as Visnevski's incompetence.

Although it made several other applications over the next year, Cherub did not receive a subsidy until 1981. This was £5000 for a tour of Thomas Middleton's *A Chaste Maid in Cheapside*. The tour followed the premiere and subsequent positive response at Edinburgh and in London to *Kafka's THE TRIAL*, and this probably assured the funding for *Chaste Maid*. Lamede admitted in a letter that he "managed to see *THE TRIAL* at the Young Vic recently and enjoyed it a great deal."[25] Significantly, Lamede's report on *THE TRIAL* also notes that it was "a Cherub show which I actually liked." He goes on to write, "Being an old Kafka buff, I was inclined to be even more critical than usual, so I'm being won over against some odds when I say that this show was the closest to the feel and spirit of Kafka's works that I've seen on stage."[26] Although the funding application was handled by the touring department, Lamede was aware of the application, and likely the combination of a different set of officers in touring and the positive response to *THE TRIAL* greased the wheels for the application to be accepted.

However, the grant for *Chaste Maid in Cheapside* was the only project subsidy Cherub received from the Arts Council in its twenty-five-year lifetime. In May 1981, just two weeks after Cherub had received the news that the previous application had been accepted, Drama Director John Faulkner notified the company that two project applications (for productions of *Macbeth* and an adaptation of Daniel Defoe's *The Journal of the Plague Year*) had not been funded. In his letter, he writes that "advisers and officers had the benefit of referring to no less than sixteen written reports and two verbal reports on seven different productions," a number, he assures Visnevski, that is more than average and that "the balance of these reports was not favorable."[27] The rejection put the company into a couple of binds. First, since plans were underway for a tour of *Macbeth* prompted in part by the ACGB-funded tour of *Chaste Maid* (including some promised bookings for the production in theatres across the country), Cherub's ability to meet the scheduled demands of the *Macbeth* tour was greatly in doubt. Second, and more importantly, the company was once again in the position of having to defend itself to the ACGB, a state Cherub believed itself to have surpassed once it received the £5000 for *Chaste Maid*. Visnevski and his team assumed that the funding meant that the ACGB had finally relented and that they'd have less trouble in the future securing a subsidy.

The company found itself in a rather Kafkaesque position: The ACGB had funded one application and then rejected another based on the same set of reports that Faulkner claimed were "not favorable." Visnevski responded to the rejection letter by writing: "Based on [the advisers' and officers'] reactions the Company was at that time [one month earlier when *Chaste Maid* had been funded] judged worthy of financial support, and we have done *no new work since then* which might have led them to change their opinions. Does this mean that decisions are again based on reports made in 1978 and 1979, and the consideration recently given to the reputation we have built up since last September over twenty weeks touring and several highly successful London appearances is no longer valid?"[28] Visnevski has a point. Of the sixteen reports, most of the stridently negative ones are from the company's early productions in 1978–79. Later reports on Cherub's work had been much better, which should have indicated precisely what the ACGB said in numerous letters it was looking for: the company's "development," or an improvement over time. That these improvements were being made essentially without subsidization should have boded well for the company. If one filtered out the oldest responses, Cherub at least should have warranted a second look based on its newest productions. Visnevski was pointing out a flaw in the ACGB's rhetoric: if we've done such poor work, why did you give us money? And, of course, the real question underlying everything was a clarification of the *specific* objections the ACGB used in determining that Cherub was not worthy of subsidization. Since Cherub was not allowed access to the confidential ACGB show reports, it had never received a straight answer to this question, one Visnevski asked repeatedly.

Lamede's response to Visnevski's letter was typically understated. He notes that "the Drama Director's letter was quite clear about the reasons for the rejection of your applications," and that there was "leeway within the system for us to proceed as we did in your case" by funding the tour of *Chaste Maid*. He concludes, "When the advisers and officers together considered all the information, it was felt that in the final analysis Cherub's work was not in the forefront when compared with that of other applicants."[29] This letter prompts a huge question of what "leeway" existed and why the ACGB saw fit to use it to fund a Cherub show when they felt the company's work was "not in the forefront." It also implies that there's far more at issue in the granting of a subsidy than just artistic quality. Cherub had, of course, made some rookie mistakes: for one, repeatedly asking for program subsidy when it had been warned against doing so, perhaps "demonstrating" to Lamede that the company was not administratively ready for subsidy. The company was beginning to develop a reputation for fighting back against the ACGB and for questioning its decisions, and this surely did not ingratiate them with Lamede and Faulkner. This refusal to "play the game" would come back to haunt Cherub as it repeatedly sought subsidies from the ACGB in future years.

The Stage caught wind of the controversy (perhaps tipped off by Cherub), and in an article a spokesman for the ACGB provided another Kafkaesque twist. The article's author summed the explanation up by writing: "Touring money and project grants come from separate funds and applicants had to meet different sets of criteria. She [the spokesman] said the touring department had decided there was a good case for taking 'A Chaste Maid' on the road and had recommended it a guarantee. When the two project applications . . . were received, the drama department had given them a low priority in the present financial climate. But the *decision was no reflection on the company's work*, the spokesman stressed, only comparative importance of its chosen projects. Cherub should feel free to seek support for its next production, she added."[30] In its explanation to *The Stage*, the ACGB's spokesman directly contradicted the explanation Cherub had been given by both Faulkner and Lamede.[31] The spokesman did not mention "leeway" within the system and specifically said that the decision was not based on the company's work, despite the fact that Faulkner had so clearly articulated that it was. The spokesman's acknowledgement that the touring department and the drama department had separate, yet unspecified, sets of criteria must have been maddening for Cherub. Visnevski didn't know on what basis the ACGB was rejecting his applications, though he now knew that one department's criteria were so different that it allowed the company to receive funding when the other's did not. Like Joseph K in *The Trial*, Visnevski knew that the company was disliked, but he didn't know who was writing about their productions or what these people's complaints were. The ACGB also had no specified policy for specifically addressing complaints or any appeals process for those companies who were denied subsidies.

The reports in the ACGB archives reflect the view that if Visnevski (and by extension Cherub) could be made to conform to the ACGB's expectations, whatever those were, then this would yield a "better," more fundable product. In many of the ACGB reports, the company is patronizingly described, with officers using words like "young" or comparing the cast to "students." The status afforded to those writing the reports (both the drama officers and the advisory council members) allowed them to see themselves as significantly above those who would otherwise have been their peers, who would never gain access to the reports. The association with Eastern Europe—which, for often blatantly political reasons, even scholars have considered "backwards"—made it even easier for the ACGB to view Cherub and its productions as less than capable. This view persisted over time, with officers and advisers often listing in their reports the things they felt Cherub lacked, sometimes agreeing and other times contradicting one another. One adviser wrote of Cherub's *Journal of the Plague Year*: "He [Visnevski] hasn't the experience or the knowledge to function as the artistic director of a company; it all ends up like a show by students. He has a strong visual sense, might develop into a most interesting director, but needs to work as a subordinate for a while."[32] For the company's *A Chaste Maid in Cheapside* in 1981, a drama adviser wrote that the production "reminded [him] of a University drama group" and that he'd "like to see him working with better actors."[33] Another adviser writes of the same production that the acting was "good," though he says, "I'd like to see more of the company's work. They still seem to be searching for the right play." Exactly what type of play this reviewer or the ACGB in general would have liked to see is unclear, though he does say that he feels "the company has a tendency to swamp content in technique."[34] Lamede himself, in his review of *Kafka's THE TRIAL*, commented on "the aptness of this company's style to the work of Kafka," and I wonder if the ACGB would have been happier if Cherub had not been producing "classics" but instead adaptations of modernist literature.[35] However, the ACGB never made its wishes clear, and Visnevski chose to produce the plays he was interested in, thus missing another opportunity for the ACGB to provide feedback that could have positively impacted Cherub's suitability for funding.

Several reviewers praise aspects of Cherub's productions, and a few even say that they're surprised the company isn't yet receiving subsidy. Sometimes a sense of doubt would creep into the reports: a sense that though a firm decision had been taken about the company, some officers and advisers were having second thoughts. One drama officer wrote: "I was of course anxious to put to the back of my mind the discussions I had heard in Projects Committee about Cherub, but I found it difficult to do so. I find I am no nearer an answer to the question: 'should this company be subsidized by us?' This is precisely the kind of theatre I do not like. . . . BUT lots of people think otherwise. They had houses of 600 at Leeds, I was told. Is it possible that the demand for this work is so great that the company's style and standard is *disregarded* by its audiences?"[36] This report is especially revealing, because for the first time, someone from the ACGB intimates that there might be something the council isn't seeing in Cherub's work. He rationalizes this by saying that the *audience* must be "disregarding" the problems otherwise apparent with the company's "style and standard." He does not consider that his (and the other ACGB officers') expectations for style and standard might not jibe with that of the audiences or theatre critics who admired Cherub's work.

In short, the company felt that the ACGB was backing it into a corner. Its shows were popular, and between recurring appearances at the Edinburgh Festival Fringe and national tours, the company was known and respected by both national theatre critics as well as small regional touring venues. The company's international profile was also increasing: it had been invited to take *Kafka's THE TRIAL* on tour to the Netherlands by the British Council, and it had already taken *Two Noble Kinsmen* to Stuttgart, Germany. Yet Cherub could not secure funding from the ACGB, and despite those successes, Cherub's issues with the ACGB would continue. In a January 1982 article in *The Stage* titled

"Cherub Seeks Grant Support," Cherub's funding issues with the ACGB would be writ large, as *The Stage* once again discussed the question of Cherub's receipt of money for *Chaste Maid in Cheapside* but subsequent rejection for a subsidy for a tour of *Macbeth*. "I am not fighting the Arts Council," Visnevski was quoted as saying, "but I want them to be more aware of outside opinion, particularly the opinion of critics and directors."[37] Cherub also began to seek support directly from its audience, asking them in programs and lobby displays to write to the ACGB and tell them to reconsider Cherub's funding. A move made out of desperation, it irritated the ACGB's staff and likely solidified already widespread opposition to granting the company any further subsidization.

Without a subsidy, the company had no choice but to produce as rapidly and as often as it could. Increasingly desperate for funds to create new productions that could tour, the company posted letters from the council in the lobby in the theatres it performed in, and handed around circulars that explained the company's financial status and listed the Arts Council's address with the plea, "If you have enjoyed the show, please help us by writing to say so. . . . Your enthusiasm will help to persuade them we are worthy of support."[38] The ACGB's officers and advisers saw the display when they attended performances, and the ACGB received many letters from audience members, and from RAA representatives, theatre critics, and theatre producers.

Eventually, the head of the British Council's Drama and Dance Department, Robert Sykes, decided to write his own letter to the ACGB in support of Cherub. Writing in March 1983 that he wanted to "take an opportunity of noting formally a British Council view of this Company's value," he specified that the BC can only support artists overseas, and that it thus must rely upon artists who have the ability to develop their work within the United Kingdom prior to tour. This required a subsidy from the ACGB. He then detailed Cherub's history with the BC, complimenting the company for both its efficiency and its quality. He also wrote, "Sometimes [Cherub] may shock the systems of a conventional theatre going public, but [it] has a proven track-record of communication with the minds of young audiences." He concluded the letter by saying: "In view of the British Council's association with Cherub Company's overseas visits, I think it is probable that my staff have a rather closer contact with the development of its work than other Advisers or Assessors. If, in the course of looking at future applications from Andrew Visnevski for Arts Council support you wished to get an opinion from any of us, we would be very happy to help."[39] In a remarkable moment, one government agency in support of British arts (the one sending artists abroad) was defending and promoting a company that had been derided by another (the one supporting artists at home). Further, the BC was offering its own assessment criteria as a basis for an ACGB reassessment. Sykes's letter seems to have had little impact, for the ACGB continued to defend its position and did not take Sykes up on his offer. Acting Drama Director Dennis Andrews replied by saying that the ACGB *had* taken into consideration outside views, and that these outside views are the only reason why Cherub is so heavily scrutinized, "since I have to add that the main burden of *our* reports has not and does not recommend support for the company."[40]

A holdover from Britain's imperial project, the BC sent British artists overseas to encourage "the study and use of the English language, and thereby, to extend a knowledge of British literature and of the British contributions to music and the fine arts, the sciences, philosophic thought and political practice."[41] This mission required that the BC work to make connections between Britain and other countries, and the fact that exchange, and not just dissemination, was involved meant that the BC was much more amenable to difference than was the ACGB. In contrast to the trenchant ACGB opinion of Cherub, the BC found value in almost everything that comprised Cherub's ethos: small, efficient, visual, inventive. The BC sent Cherub overseas eight different times between 1981 and 1989, and as a result Cherub made a decisive but necessary shift toward international touring in the mid-1980s as the BC welcomed them with open arms. By 1989, an article in the *Independent* dubbed Cherub "cultural ambassadors,"[42] a phrase picked up for an article on the company in *Direct*, the journal of the British Director's Guild.[43] The company would later use "Britain's cultural ambassadors" in much of its subsequent publicity. In a way, the BC and Cherub were perfect partners, and the relationship was somewhat symbiotic. In the midst of a budget crisis prompted by Thatcherite cuts, the BC was particularly attracted to small companies with efficiently packaged shows. In a memo to the BC representative in Iraq, the BC London representative pitched: "[Cherub's] production of *Twelfth Night* is one I would recommend . . .. The production has a bright, visual impact enlivened by an attractive musical score. It is inventive without being particularly bizarre or esoteric and its inventiveness is not . . . of a kind which would offend any Iraqi cultural taboos . . . Cherub may not be cheap but you won't find cheaper. Their costings are very economical."[44] The memo praised the company's work ethic and described them as being very "devoted to the Council" as well as flexible and understanding of working in difficult conditions. The BC found Cherub to be a useful commodity: Its productions allowed the BC, for comparatively less money, to send what it considered a quality production overseas for the delight of overseas corporate sponsors and foreign nationals. Further, though Cherub produced plays in English, its "visual" approach bridged the language gap, and thus its productions could more easily be sent to non-English speaking countries.

British Council tours like Cherub's to Iraq in 1988 reflect that the BC's motivation to send theatre companies abroad was as much political and economic as it was artistic: the end of hostilities in the Iran-Iraq War brought untold opportunities for British business. Cherub's crews would become, as several memos in the British Council's archive note, some of the first Westerners to go into Basra and Mosul following the end of the conflict. To fund the overseas tours, the BC coordinated with corporate sponsors in the receiving countries as part of the work of developing ties between Britain and countries abroad. Much of the company's time was spent attending parties that the sponsors used to show off the company to their associates and employees. Cherub did find the time, however, in both Iraq and Pakistan, to accept invitations to performances at the local theatres and to perform for local audiences. The corporate sponsors were induced to arrange matinees for school audiences, and in Iraq, the company did several workshops with school groups. Similar arrangements were made for Cherub's later tour to Africa in 1989.

The pretour newspaper coverage (with copy likely supplied by the BC) often made Cherub's visit seem an important cultural event for those who would be able to see it. *The Herald* in Harare, Zimbabwe, wrote that "the chances are that tickets for the second evening performance will be at a premium" and profiled the "impressive six-person cast of highly seasoned professionals" who were featured in *Twelfth Night*.[45] In Karachi, Pakistan, the *Morning News* described Cherub as having "an ongoing reputation as a leading medium-scale company specializing in lively productions of the classics."[46] Overseas, the buzz around its performances remade Cherub into something it was not acknowledged to be in the United Kingdom: an important company of substantial skill and reputation. While this narrative certainly suited Cherub, it also suited the BC and its corporate sponsors. Unlike Cherub's shows in small, cramped theatres in the United Kingdom, where the audience was made aware of the company's financial plight, the audiences abroad entered some rather grand theatres with the expectation of seeing an important international company. Where Cherub had seen itself as pioneering a particular type of theatre within Britain and been rejected by the ACGB, the company was now being sent into former war zones to showcase its style of theatre as some of the best of Britain. And the audiences in those countries were being told that they could like Cherub and appreciate it for what it produced. The difference in how the ACGB and the BC saw Cherub can perhaps best be summed up by how they expected Cherub to be understood by specific audiences. The ACGB thought Cherub unfit for mainstream British audiences and refused funding that would have allowed the company to grow and move off the Fringe. The BC, on the other hand, funded overseas tours because it saw the possibilities for Cherub to impact diverse audiences and reflect well on arts in the United Kingdom.

The BC tours didn't change the ACGB's mind, and the regularity with which the ACGB turned Cherub down caused the company's status as unworthy to become definitive. Without the imprimatur of the ACGB, most other (private) funders followed suit and refused Cherub's requests for money. That the company managed to continue on for twenty-five years is remarkable in and of itself. Indeed, the company's duration begs the question of its influence upon the cultural field. Cherub, though it saw itself as "innovative" and perhaps even aspired to be "avant garde," never gained enough symbolic capital to be able to modify or escape the classification placed upon it by the dominant forces of the cultural field. It *seems* to have had no clear influence in reshaping the definitions of theatre practice in Britain between 1978 and 2003, but the company did produce nearly forty shows seen in countries around the world. Can it really have had no impact on the cultural field? Did its productions truly fail to alter the landscape?

In *Staging the UK*, Jen Harvie writes an "alternative British theatre historiography" that locates a wide range of performances in Britain by foreign artists as potential sites of influence. Her examples include the Berliner Ensemble in London in 1956; the Comédie-Française at Edinburgh in 1948 and in London in 1951; Peter Daubeny's World Theatre Seasons on the West End from 1964 to 1973, featuring major companies from Western and Eastern Europe, Asia, the United States, and Japan; the Glasgow Citizens' Theatre; London's Gate; the London International Festival of Theatre (LIFT); and several other "important (if often repressed) instances where twentieth-century mainland European theatre in particular has been introduced to and has influenced British theatre."[47] Cherub does not have the symbolic capital of any of these companies, but does that mean it had no impact on the cultural field? Most of the theatrical performances Harvie cites were one-time occurrences (or short runs) in London or Edinburgh. The only interaction any British audience member might have had with those companies was to view their performances or (for those lucky enough) to participate in a workshop or talkback event that may have been scheduled. This is no different than how anyone might have experienced Cherub's work.

The primary difference is in how each event was sold (their branding): those viewing Brecht or attending the LIFT festival understood that these companies were important because they were told as much through the marketing of the productions. Cherub could not make that claim for itself at its own productions in the United Kingdom (though, significantly, the British Council had done exactly that on Cherub's tours abroad). The importance of the event in both instances comes out of a desire to convey a type of meaning to the audience in advance of the production. That it can be applied contextually is an indicator that it is a subjective designation and can thus be employed at will; importance is, after all, granted by the primary arbiters of the cultural field. Importance is also a means by which historians prioritize the history they wish to tell. One cannot tell the entire history of the world; one must pick and choose what will be included in the narrative when everything cannot possibly be included. That we will inevitably leave some history out of our narratives is not in doubt, but that doesn't mean that we must base our own priorities exclusively upon those who have gone before. By continually reinscribing the notion of importance, we cannot imagine what we have lost.

Despite the disjunction between the ACGB and the BC in supporting the company, Cherub's story enables us to see how institutions tend to reaffirm the standards set by another, more powerful institution within the cultural field. Institutions (families, schools, churches, the military) shape people. The field of cultural production contains numerous institutions engaged in assorted cultural projects, and these institutions train people to develop likings for a particular type of cultural good and to train people to create that type of good. Over time, certain practices within the field become normalized, and various institutions are expected to cater to those norms. In Cherub's case, one institution, the ACGB, made a determination about Cherub and its work. The ACGB's stamp of approval was a significant determining factor for how other institutions came to understand the company. For a time, Cherub's productions were able to convince enough people (especially media institutions and the British Council) that the company was worthy of attention in spite of the ACGB's decisions. This position was not ultimately sustainable, because with little money Cherub could not continue to produce enough shows to keep themselves in the minds of the media and the British Council. Over time, especially as the critics and British Council staff members who were sympathetic to Cherub moved on, even the institutions that supported them began to look elsewhere. By the time of Cherub's *Edward II* in 1998, most of the media ignored Cherub's shows, and some of the few critics that did review the production were hostile. The ACGB's determination ultimately was adopted by all of the other institutions within the field, save for some educational institutions that now view Visnevski as a worthy candidate to train their students in a different type of performance mode.

Cherub's success, then, is in the eye of the beholder. The company did not develop into a theatrical powerhouse like Cheek by Jowl or Complicité.

Visnevski has never been asked to direct at the RSC, the Royal Court, or the National (nor at any regional theatre, for that matter, though he has directed numerous productions abroad for other companies). Neither he nor any other member of the Cherub Company ever became rich or famous directly as a result of their work with Cherub. In conventional terms, Cherub was not successful. And yet, as I've shown, if one looks at Cherub genealogically, we cannot even begin to calculate the company's impact. The company managed to create thirty-six productions over twenty-five years without government subsidization. The company's shows were seen in England, Scotland, and abroad, and we cannot calculate who saw these productions and what impact their attendance might have had. Visnevski and many other members of the company have since entered the theatrical mainstream, going on to work with, teach, and potentially influence multitudes of others. We may never be able to estimate how the company's practices spread through the continued work of the various company members as they've moved from institution to institution within the cultural field. The so-called innovations that became "physical" theatre in the late 1980s and early 1990s and that have now become canonical are often described as being dance-inspired or the result of Britons going abroad to study with European practitioners. However, Cherub was already utilizing many of the methods that would become hallmarks of the later physical companies ten years before. If historical importance is rooted in notions of conventional success, Cherub cannot be considered important. However, a wider view of the circumstantial evidence lends weight to a reassessment of Cherub's historical value.

Notes

1. See reviews from B. A. Young, "Life is a Dream," review of *Life is a Dream* by Cherub Company, *Financial Times*, March 1, 1979; "The Two Noble Kinsmen," review of *The Two Noble Kinsmen* by Cherub Company, *Financial Times*, November 26, 1979; "Young Vic Studio: *Barabbas*," review of *Barabbas* by Cherub Company, *Financial Times*, May 9, 1980; and "Twelfth Night/Upstream," review of *Twelfth Night* by Cherub Company, *Financial Times*, October 18, 1982, among many others. Several critics, audience members, and producers wrote to the ACGB in response to a plea from Cherub; I found letters from Stephen Boyce, Christopher Hudson, Raphael Gonely, and others as well as responses from ACGB officers to those letters in the ACGB archive.
2. Frances Lonsdale Donaldson, *The British Council: The First Fifty Years* (London: J. Cape, 1984), 1.
3. "Cherub Company at the Upstream Theatre Club," undated information guide, ca. 1982. Cherub Archive (currently privately held by author).
4. Andrew Visnevski, interview with author, December 12, 2010.

5. The Lord Chamberlain began allowing homosexual themes in 1958 prior to the abolishment of theatre censorship in 1968. Homosexuality was generally decriminalized in 1967. Specifically gay companies like Gay Sweatshop, which was touring its productions *Mr X* (1975) and *As Time Goes By* (1978), were actively performing at the same time as Cherub, with a more direct mission to bring homosexual storylines to the stage. The appearance of homosexuality in the theatre was not without controversy. From October to December 1980, the production of Howard Brenton's *The Romans in Britain* appeared at the National Theatre, directed by Michael Bogdanov. The play featured the homosexual rape of a Celt by a Roman soldier, and while the rape was simulated and not literal, moralistic gadfly Mary Whitehouse filed charges of indecency against Bogdanov for directing the scene. While the prosecution was ultimately abandoned, the judge in the case ruled that simulated acts in the theatre could be considered for prosecution as indecent acts, setting a precedent that has not yet been overturned in British law (though no additional prosecutions have been brought).
6. Keith Nurse, "Macbeth in an Alien World," Review of *Macbeth* by Cherub Company, *The Daily Telegraph*, November 20, 1981.
7. Perhaps not insignificantly, Visnevski's key productions fall perfectly between Brook's 1960s work and the "emergence" of physical theatre companies like Complicité in the late 1980s.
8. "PJP" [Jon Plowman], Drama Officer's Report, March 26, 1980, ACGB Archive, V&A Theatre and Performance Archives, London, UK. Plowman is actually implying that audiences would prefer to go blind rather than see this show. See also Brian Cook, "'They Might not Go Blind': Cherub's Kinsmen and the Drama Officer's Report," *Performing Arts Resources: A Tyranny of Documents: The Performing Arts Historian as Film Noir Detective* 28 (2011): 314–21.
9. For more on the literary bias of British theatre, see Jen Harvie, *Staging the UK* (Manchester: Manchester University Press, 2005); and Alison Oddey, *Devising Theatre: A Practical and Theoretical Handbook* (London: Routledge, 1994).
10. Andrew Sinclair, Arts and Cultures: The History of the 50 Years of the Arts Council of Great Britain (London: Sinclair-Stevenson, 1995), 51.
11. Ibid., 88. Emphasis mine.
12. Ibid., 118.
13. Ibid.
14. Dan Rebellato, *1956 and All That* (New York: Routledge, 1999).
15. Visnevski, interview with author, December 12, 2010.
16. "Jonathan [Lamede]," Drama Officer's Report, June 25, 1979, ACGB Archive.
17. Simon Shepherd, *The Cambridge Introduction to Modern British Theatre* (Cambridge: Cambridge University Press, 2009), 81–82.
18. "PJP," Drama Officer's Report, March 22, 1979, ACGB Archive.
19. "Tales From Europe," http://thewhitehorses.angelfire.com/002-talesfromeurope1.html (accessed September 15, 2011).
20. Mark Hudson, "Return of the Teatime Terror," *Daily Telegraph*, March 30, 2002, 7.
21. Visnevski told me that after *Two Noble Kinsmen*, Jonathan Lamede asked him if Cherub was a "gay" company. Visnevski was offended at the question, because he said his personal life was none of the ACGB's business. If he'd said yes, what might that have meant for the company's funding prospects? The full answer will have to be explored elsewhere,

but the ACGB did fund many companies with a specifically political mission, as part of demonstrating its inclusiveness. But Visnevski did not wish Cherub to be "political" and to play only to a specific demographic community; Visnevski wanted the company's work to have a wide appeal. He rejected the label "gay" for his company because he felt it did not match his company's mission, which he never viewed as a political one.

22. Jonathan Lamede, letter to Andrew Visnevski, May 31, 1979, Cherub Archive.
23. Jonathan Lamede, letter to Andrew Visnevski, August 7, 1979, Cherub Archive.
24. Sarah Golding (for Jonathan Lamede), letter to Andrew Visnevski, February 27, 1980, Cherub Archive.
25. Jonathan Lamede, letter to Andrew Visnevski, January 30, 1981, Cherub Archive.
26. Jonathan Lamede, ACGB Drama Officer Report, April 2, 1981, ACGB Archive.
27. John Faulkner, letter to Andrew Visnevski, May 14, 1981, Cherub Archive.
28. Andrew Visnevski, letter to John Faulkner, May 26, 1981, Cherub Archive. Emphasis in original.
29. Jonathan Lamede, letter to Andrew Visnevski, May 28, 1981, Cherub Archive.
30. *The Stage*, June 18, 1981. Emphasis mine.
31. The identity of this person is a mystery, though the fact that the author writes "she said" leaves out the options that it's either Lamede or Faulkner.
32. John Bowen, Drama Department Show Report, November 9, 1981, ACGB Archive.
33. Nicholas Barter, Drama Department Show Report, July 7, 1981, ACGB Archive.
34. John Bond, Drama Department Show Report, September 18, 1981, ACGB Archive.
35. Jonathan Lamede, Drama Officer's Report, January 15, 1981, ACGB Archive.
36. "AMcK," ACGB Show Report, July 6, 1981, ACGB Archive.
37. "Cherub Seeks Grant Support," *The Stage*, January 21, 1982, Cherub Archive.
38. Undated program insert, ca. 1981, Cherub Archive.
39. Robert Sykes, letter to Dennis Andrews, March 9, 1983, Cherub Archive.
40. Dennis Andrews, letter to Robert Sykes, March 17, 1983, Cherub Archive.
41. Donaldson, *British Council*, 1.
42. Emma Crichton-Miller, "Getting on Famously," *Independent*, August 12, 1989, 30.
43. "On a Wing and a Prayer," *Direct: The Journal of the Director's Guild of Great Britain*, October 1989, 9.
44. Paul J. Smith, memo to Peter Elborn, October 8, 1987, British Council Archive, British Council, London, UK.
45. Ian Hoskins, "Theatre: Man with the Midas Touch," *Herald* (Harare, Zimbabwe), April 28, 1989, British Council Archive.
46. "Cherub Theatre Challenges Rigid Approach towards Classics," *Morning News* (Karachi, Pakistan), November 25, 1988, British Council Archive.
47. Harvey, *Staging the UK*, 119.

The Long View of World Theatre History

—STEVE TILLIS

In the fourth edition of their textbook *Living Theatre: A History of Theatre*, Edwin Wilson and Alvin Goldfarb state the historiographic principle that still underlies much scholarship of theatre history: "By definition, a history is a chronicle—a recapitulation of events from the past"[1]—a definition, by the way, that the authors wisely cut from subsequent editions. Still, those editions are no less stuffed with events than are the earlier ones.[2] The result is the sort of chronicle to which Wilson and Goldfarb had referred: history as little more than the proverbial "one damned thing after another." The problem affects not merely this particular textbook. Here is Thomas Postlewait on one of the most frequently used textbooks: "[Oscar] Brockett's chronicle of information lays out the theatre for the reader as a register of names, places, titles, techniques, terminologies, and events." The advantage to such a presentation of history is that it allows interpretive freedom; the disadvantage "is that many classes remain committed to the memorization of facts rather than cultural studies and social history."[3] Postlewait's claim about memorization is no doubt exaggerated, and there is undeniable value in Brockett's assemblage of facts. But as with all chronicling, it falls short of a basic goal of history writing, which is to make sense of the past, not merely to note its passing. Let me take a quick example. One might easily note that spoken theatre in Europe emerged in cities such as London and Madrid, while Japan's *kabuki* had its origins in Edo (Tokyo). But why did these urban forms emerge when and where they did, and how did their urban origins shape their performance? Examining them in the context of the global trend toward urbanization can help elucidate the curious parallels between these very different forms of theatre. But lacking textual guidance, students (and their professors) might easily overlook any relationship between the forms, leaving them to founder in the depths of theatre history's endless catalog of events.

Of all the available textbooks, *Theatre Histories: An Introduction*, by Phillip B. Zarrilli, Bruce McConachie, Gary Jay Williams, and Carol Fisher Sorgenfrei, makes the strongest effort to move beyond chronicling. In addition to being the most inclusive *world* theatre text, the authors structure their history "in relation to key developments in human communication."[4] This emphasis on communication is borrowed from Walter Ong and Tobin Nellhaus;[5] Nellhaus himself correctly speaks of "communication technology" to characterize key developments such as writing and print, as well as film, television, and so on, emphasizing the "communication frameworks" that follow in the wake of changes in that technology.[6] *Theatre Histories*, in other words, focuses on an important aspect of one of the historical trends I will be discussing later in this article: technological development. Other historical trends, however, are given far too little discussion in the textbook, while historical continuities (a result of what I will shortly speak of as structures) receive scant notice, leaving unanalyzed why many things remain more or less unchanged *despite* technological developments. *Theatre Histories*, in brief, is an important first step toward moving beyond chronicling, but one that leaves much conceptualizing to be done.

Arguably the most significant way of conceptualizing long stretches of history was pioneered by the historian Fernand Braudel, long the leading light of the Annales school of historiography. Braudel takes issue with the historiographic tradition that sees the past as a "mass of diverse facts," contending that "this mass does not make up all of reality."[7] He argues that history can fruitfully be understood in terms of multiple, though interrelated, scales of time. The historian Patrick Manning likewise argues for the importance of multiple time scales, adding that "at any given scale . . . the experience of that level is influenced by phenomena at both smaller and broader scales," while at "any given scale there exist patterns and phenomena that are unique to that level."[8] But if the broadest temporal scale is treated simply as a chronicle, its particular "patterns and phenomena" remain hidden from sight.

Braudel's idea of using multiple time-scales has only occasionally been applied to theatre history. Postlewait gives Braudel a shout-out, commenting that his methodology "offers one means for getting beyond the pervasive historical practice of giving each period its single identity";[9] he clearly has misgivings, however, which will be noted shortly. Stefan Hulfeld, meanwhile, uses

Braudelian terms to discuss "modernist theatre" in Europe, observing that "distance" is important to the historian and that "unless we take a larger time-frame into consideration, connections will remain hidden."[10] A handful of other scholars have also made explicit use of Braudel's ideas for very specific purposes, such as examining Dutch theatre audiences in the "long nineteenth century."[11] As best I can tell, however, Braudel's conception of history has not been systematically applied to world theatre history. This article seeks to show that when we take what can be called a "long view," we can identify "patterns and phenomena," to use Manning's words, that are identifiable only through the use of an appropriate scale of time; in this way we can clarify the relationships between "phenomena at both smaller and broader scales." When we move beyond chronicling the multitudinous events of theatre history, new questions can be raised about those events, and new interpretations can be suggested that might help us to make sense of them.

Time-Scales and Agency

Rather confusingly, it must be admitted, Braudel has offered two somewhat different iterations of his approach to history. In the first version, he sets forth a tripartite scheme whose most encompassing scale of time involves phenomena "whose passage is almost imperceptible." Specifically, this concerns "man in his relationship to the environment," and he refers to it as "geographic time." The middle time-scale is what Braudel calls "social time," which concerns "the history of groups and groupings" and includes such phenomena as "economic systems, states, societies, and civilizations." Finally comes traditional history: a history of "brief, rapid, nervous fluctuations," which is "the most exciting" time-scale of history, but one whose "resounding events are often only momentary outbursts, surface manifestations of these larger movements [observed in the more expansive time-scales], and explicable only in terms of them."[12]

In the second version, Braudel somewhat rearranges the material under discussion, though he retains a tripartite scheme. He introduces a new name for the most expansive time-scale—the *longue dureé*—which concerns "history measured in centuries" or longer.[13] As such, it includes geographic time as well as the longer-lived phenomena associated with what he had previously called "social time." Central to analysis on this time-scale are two concepts: "structures," a term that encompasses both geography and all manner of "fairly fixed . . . relationships between realities and social masses"; and "the secular tendency," which means, in effect, long-term trends.[14] The longue dureé will be of primary concern in this article. As we will see, its structures are a powerful influence for historical continuity, while its trends often create opportunities for change. Braudel's middle time-scale in the second version of his approach is now one of "conjunctures," and it deals above all with economic cycles and what he calls "inter-cycles"; its time-span is roughly ten to fifty years.[15] Finally comes the history of events, which is understood as in his earlier version.

To speak of the longue dureé, I should make clear, is not just another way of referring to one or another period of history, however long that period might be. Indeed, taking the long view can undermine facile periodization by bringing to light continuities that endure through multiple periods as well as forces for change that operate even in the midst of given periods. As we have seen with Postlewait, this can help break down the historiographic habit of instilling each period with a "single identity."[16] Manning, meanwhile, asserts that there is value in research on any scale, but that each scale makes its own particular demands on the historian.[17] The scale of the longue dureé can certainly be helpful in understanding periodicity, but the "patterns and phenomena" to be discovered with it are by no means limited to one period or another.[18]

Braudel's scheme of time-scales (in both its iterations) is certainly open to criticism, especially in its diminution of events. One can easily accuse him of dehumanizing history when he speaks of events as "the ephemera of history."[19] Although he later states that "the only error . . . would be to choose one of these [time-scales] to the exclusion of all others,"[20] he has, in fact, regularly been accused of doing just that. According to François Dosse, in his book-length analysis of the Annales school, "Braudel was steadfast against traditional history . . . , showing an antipathy to events that Jack Hexter calls passionate and sometimes unreasonable."[21] And I alluded earlier to Postlewait's misgivings about Braudel, the most notable of which is along the same lines: however much Braudel "has taught us about the *longue dureé*, he has not demonstrated that the study of specific events, places, individuals, and groups lacks significance."[22] Indeed, the Annales school itself has in some respects moved away from studying the longue dureé. Dosse speaks of the "continuities and discontinuities," in the school,[23] and one of the most famous of its post-Braudelian works is Emmanuel Le Roy Ladurie's *Montaillou: The Promised Land of Error*, an extremely detailed study of life in a single medieval French village.[24] World historians such as Manning, however, continue to find much value in it, and Jo Guldi and David Armitage make an impassioned plea for it in their *The History Manifesto*.[25] In theatre, Tobin Nellhaus's *Theatre, Commination, Critical Realism* is notable for its long-term historical perspective in examining the impact of changing communication technologies and networks.[26]

Because events are, above all, the immediate product of people's actions, Braudel's perspective inevitably raises the question of human agency. Given the existence of long-term structures and trends, how are we to understand human agency?

Braudel himself wrestles with this question. He asks, "By stating the narrowness of the limits of action, is one denying the role of the individual in history? I think not." He offers, "The paradox [is] that the true man of action is he who can measure most nearly the constraints upon him, who chooses to remain within them and even to take advantage of the weight of the inevitable, exerting his own pressure in the same direction." This is all well and good. He goes on, however, to say that "all efforts against the prevailing tide of history . . . are doomed to failure." He asserts, "When I think of the individual, I am always inclined to see him imprisoned within a destiny in which he himself has little hand, fixed in a landscape in which the infinite perspectives of the long term stretch into the distance both behind him and before."[27] This is scarcely a ringing endorsement of agency.

Michael Adas is one of many historians who, while deeply sympathetic to Braudel, has pushed back against him, insisting that human agency (along with contingency and ideology) is a significant factor in history. Thus: "In and of themselves, institutions, systems, and processes cannot account for historical change or causality. Rather, they comprise the contexts (essential to historical analysis) in which human agents, both as individuals and as members of social collectives, make history."[28] Along the same lines, Postlewait insists, "We need a model of action that includes both motivation and aim within the framing conditions of material culture and cultural conditions."[29] While human agents operate within the historical contexts of the longue dureé, they are, in fact, responsible for their actions.

All that said, Braudel is surely correct that there is more to history than mere chronicle. When we pull back from the "history of events," the long view can expose the structures and trends within which the creators of those events must work. And no less than the "material culture and cultural conditions" to which Postlewait refers, it offers a deep appreciation of that which lies beneath the turbulent surface of history. If, as I have suggested, a key goal of the historian is to help us make sense of history, the long view offers a useful, even necessary, perspective, helping to expose contexts that can otherwise be obscured by the luminosity of events.

Structures

According to Braudel, a historical structure is "a construct, an architecture, but over and above that it is a reality which time uses and abuses over long periods. Some structures, because of their long life, become stable elements for an infinite number of generations. . . . Others wear themselves out more quickly. But all of them provide both support and a hindrance." In addition to the example of geography, Braudel comments on the "mental tools available to French thought at the time of Rabelais." Structures, in other words, need not be physical. Also, Braudel speaks of structures as being "fairly fixed."[30] By this he means that while they endure through time, they are dynamic and susceptible to a certain amount of change. These structures are not essentialist entities.

Theatre forms themselves are the most immediately significant structures in theatre history. They are made up of populations of associated theatrical events that have a coherent and distinctive system of performance and reception: Despite their many points of connection, *kabuki*, *bunraku*, and *noh* are separate theatre forms, as are European spoken theatre, opera, and ballet.[31] Let me be clear that when I write of "European spoken theatre" (or, when the context might allow it, the less unwieldy "spoken theatre"), I am referring to a specific theatre form, not the particular performance trait that the form shares with numerous other forms, including medieval cycle plays; moralities such as *Everyman*; the Greek New Comedy of Menander, with its choruses shunted to interludes between the episodes; the shadow theatre of in Kerala, India, with its very few songs primarily limited to the plays' introductory segment; and *sandiwara*, a form found in Malaysia and Indonesia.[32] Theatre forms cannot be characterized by any one trait, since it is almost inevitable that other forms will share that trait. One needs, instead, to consider the whole range of traits identifiable in the form. Using the long view allows us to place particular events within the structural context of their forms, clarifying their relationship to similar events and explaining how they are distinct from the events of other forms.

Theatre forms are never static but maintain key continuities even as they undergo inevitable change over time and across space. Within each form, there is a tension between continuity and change, with one or the other being dominant depending on the form and the time. Spoken theatre has been an unusually changeable form, but it is still easy to a trace a clear line back to, say, Shakespeare and Molière. It must, however, be distinguished from the theatre of the European Middle Ages: For hundreds of years, writers saw Renaissance theatre as revolutionary, with little or no continuity from theatre forms that were previously extant. In the nineteenth century, for example, Augustus Schlegel's highly influential lectures on theatre history did not even deign to discuss theatre from the many centuries between Seneca and Tasso.[33] Theatre historians of the past half-century have emphatically rejected this position, paying close attention to medieval theatre and emphasizing continuities with the spoken theatre that followed. Theatre history courses have widely followed suit, and the year 1642 (or, to the same effect, 1660) is often taken as the breaking point between the first and second semesters of two-semester survey courses. This is, however, an overreaction. The fact remains that Corpus Christi and morality plays have no continuous performance history subsequent to the mid-sixteenth century, and their use of allegorical characters has been entirely superceded by characters conceived to have at least a degree of psychological development. Moreover, the manners of performance typical of Corpus Christi and morality plays (including performance venues and means of support) have long been disused, while at least some plays from the sixteenth and seventeenth centuries have seen continuous performance, in theatres that continue to be purpose-built and commercial, however much their physical contours (particularly in England) might have changed.

The support offered by the structures of theatre forms scarcely need be detailed. Among many other things, theatre artists (including playwrights, performers, designers, and so on) are provided with a tradition to work within, while established scripts serve as models and are often, in themselves, performed; also, performance techniques that have been honed for years, even centuries, serve as guides for new performances. Theatre forms, moreover, provide audiences with some foreknowledge about the type of performance they might be seeing, allowing them to make an informed choice to attend; most people, for example, find it helpful to distinguish between a musical and an opera. Also, audiences are informally trained, to a greater or lesser degree, in how to understand performances of particular forms. Given the highly distinctive performance traits that these forms often exhibit, this sort of training is often critical for adequate comprehension of a play.

It must be noted, however, that theatre forms can also provide a hindrance. The long shadows of respected scripts can intimidate playwrights, and new works must compete with older ones even to reach the stage. Established performance techniques can stifle creativity, while the theatres themselves can limit performance possibilities. Audiences, meanwhile, can easily get bored with fare that is "more of the same," leading them to seek out different kinds of theatre; alternately, their competence as viewers can become a straightjacket, limiting performers to that which their audience best understands and supports. In sum, the structure of theatre forms is an immensely powerful force for continuity, whether for better or for worse.

As noted earlier, Braudel considers human geography to be a component of the longue dureé. I have elsewhere discussed theatre's geography,[34] so I will limit my comments here to a single example of how the structure of geography has significantly affected world theatre history. Thus, the various regions of Eurasia have long been linked together, thanks to the relative ease of movement across the entire landmass. The upshot of these interregional linkages was the easy spread of crops, domesticated animals, and technologies, along with the economic stimulus of trade. Although the various societies of the landmass were primarily agrarian, they had growing populations and boasted towns and cities that served as focal points for power, religion, and commerce: These characteristics offered fertile soil for theatre. As early as the fourteenth century, complex and professionalized forms (among them Japan's noh and China's Yuan *zaju*) could be found in much of Eurasia. By the seventeenth century, interregional contacts had significantly increased, and economic gains led to the explosive growth of cities: commercial forms such as kabuki, *kunqu*, and European spoken theatre emerged across Eurasia. In the case of kabuki, this emergence came after the Tokugawa regime had sought to limit foreign influences, but by then, Japan had long been part of the Eurasian economy.[35] None of this is to suggest that these various theatre forms are "genetically" related—but all are dependent on a socioeconomic context that was at least partially the result of Eurasia's geographic unity. The long view here provides us with at least a partial explanation for why Eurasia's disparate forms can share many traits. It also helps explain why those traits are often absent from traditional theatre in much of sub-Saharan Africa, which was in large part removed from intercourse owing the barrier of the Sahara, and among Amerindians, who for countless generations had no contact with Eurasia.

Of appreciably less age than geography are theatrical structures that might span entire regions but are wholly man-made. These regional structures can often be found in multiple theatre forms, both contemporaneously and through time. Two important examples come quickly to mind.

The first is the use of "role categories" (also called "role types") in East Asia, most especially in China. According to William Dolby, their purpose "would seem to be to facilitate the organisation of the actor's training," but no less importantly, they "give the audience a feeling of familiarity and connoisseurship, in that they would to a considerable degree come to know what to look for and expect of the actor."[36] For the past millennium, "their use has been one of the main characteristics of Chinese drama."[37]

Even as they lent continuity through the centuries, role categories have not remained static. The early *yuanben* and the zaju of the Song Dynasty had categories appropriate to their limited comedic content. With the emergence, however, of the more sophisticated Yuan zaju and *nanxi* ("southern plays") in the fourteenth century, the constellation of categories established the outlines of an enduring structure. Relatively little is known about nanxi, but Yuan zaju had the main role categories of *zhengmo* ("main man"), *zhengdan* ("main women"), and *jing*, a clown or villain type. As early as Yuan zaju, jing roles were notable for their painted faces. There were also a few subcategories within each of the main ones, usually predicated on age or significance to the play's action.[38]

With the emergence of kunqu (in the sixteenth century), role categories saw significant elaboration, the main categories being *sheng* ("the more serious males roles"), *dan* (female roles), *jing* ("forceful" male characters, such as warriors or villains), and *chou* (comic characters). Both of these latter categories customarily have painted faces, and the impression one receives is that the *jing* category from Yuan zaju split into its component parts of clowns and villains. Within each of the major categories, a range of more specific role subcategories developed, such as the *laosheng* ("dignified middle-aged or elderly roles").[39]

Jingju (also known as *jingxi* and Beijing opera) emerged a few hundred years later. It retains the basic categories of *sheng*, *dan*, *jing*, and *chou* but offers an even more elaborate set of subcategories. Thus, the earlier *laosheng* was now subdivided into *wulaosheng* roles ("middle-aged or elderly dignified warriors" who typically wore white beards) and *changkao* roles ("high-ranking dignified warriors" who typically wore full armor, complete with flags attached to their shoulders to signify that they lead armies).[40]

European theatre does not have anything quite like this Chinese tradition of role categories, although opera (with its vocal categories) and the Italian *commedia* (with its young lovers, various *zanni*, braggart soldiers, and so on) are vaguely similar. Europe does, however, have its own region-wide and long-lived theatrical structures, one of which will serve as my second example.

In a provocative article mainly concerning periodicity in English theatre, Margreta de Grazia suggests that 1660 might well be a more important historical marker than 1576 because "when the theatres reopened [in 1660], a new kind of stage was on view. The proscenium stage had replaced the platform stage; a perspectival space set off from the audience had supplanted an open stage continuous with the audience."[41] According to de Grazia, "What was once a place in which action occurred becomes a *representation* or *picture* of a place where action occurs," with this sort of representation being "a perfect materialization of [the] modern condition of visibility and knowability."[42] As I discussed earlier, I would take 1576 to be the more significant turning point for English theatre; among many other reasons, the changes in staging brought about by purpose-built theatres were in themselves revolutionary. De Grazia's point, however, is well taken: 1660 also saw the emergence of "a new kind of stage," which is with us to this day.

This new model for theatres had its origins in sixteenth-century Italy, and over the next century it was transmitted through much of Europe, owing in large part to the labors of various members of the Galli-Bibiena family. In cities that were strongly influenced by Italian art, it was almost inevitable that Italian principles of theatre and stage design would be generally adopted.[43] These principles—including a proscenium, perspective scenery, and machinery for elaborate stage effects—found their first expression in opera houses but soon diffused into theatres of all types.

Here then is a European structure that has existed for more than three centuries and has quite literally shaped performance in opera, spoken theatre, ballet, and musicals, among yet other forms. The opportunities presented to theatre artists by Italianate staging have been enormous, so its endurance should not be surprising. It offered what amounts to a clean canvas, a performance area that constituted its own set-off world; this was especially the case after theatre reforms banned audience members from sitting on the stage. But this sort of staging has also restricted the possibilities for most European theatre forms, being inimical to the intimacy and interactivity of theatres such as the Elizabethan playhouses. Italianate staging has not, of course, held exclusive reign in Europe: platform staging has had a long, if not illustrious, half-life, while folk forms such as the English Mummer's play traditionally make do with streets, pubs, or private houses. Still, it clearly has been the dominant way to stage a show. By the early twentieth century, this dominance had come under a sustained attack that targeted many established theatrical conventions, but it is not easy to do away with such a long-lived structure, and to this day most theatres in Europe, the Americas, and Australasia are still built with prosceniums, perspective scenery, and elaborate stage machinery.

The long view, as these examples illustrate, helps us to understand the regional theatre contexts in which entire forms are situated. As such, it can provide insight into why those individual forms are structured as they are, and why their events have some of the traits they do. It can also help bring to light the genetic relationship between different forms by demonstrating influences they have in common.

Beyond these regional theatrical structures, we can also identify structures that do not arise specifically in theatre but have a huge impact on it: language, religion, and race or ethnicity are three of the most important. Although they might be self-evident in given theatrical events, they are critical aspects of the social context of an event. In practice these structures are often intertwined, but for explanatory purposes it will be useful to discuss each in turn.

Language is probably the most significant of these structures, at least in regard to theatre, if only for the elementary reason that words (either spoken or sung) are one of the most widely used means of conveying dramatic action. It is reasonable to suggest that, as a general rule, audiences desire to understand what the actors are saying, so that they might more fully appreciate a show. This is not to gainsay the possibility of enjoying a performance whose language one does not understand. European opera is perhaps the most obvious example of this kind of performance. Its success in lands where the vernacular differs from the language of the opera probably results in large part from the fact that it can be enjoyed on a purely musical basis, as well as from the social cachet it is accorded. A rather different kind of example would be noh, which employs an archaic vocabulary and densely allusive literary style. The difficulties it now presents even to native-Japanese speakers, however, are mitigated by the form's emphasis on movement and musicality, as well as to the study given to the plays.[44] The fact that theatrical writing has been marked by a flood of translations and adaptations serves to support the contention of language's importance: when plays are read or performed in the vernacular, the foreign, which otherwise might have only a very limited audience, becomes accessible. Translation, however, is inevitably problematic, because the particularities of any given language will, at least to a degree, shape the thinking that is being expressed by it, as is evidenced by the greater-or-lesser incommensurability of different languages.[45] Language, in brief, is at once a means of theatrical expression and a constraint on both the potential audiences for, and the content of, a performance.

The structure of religion, to continue on, has had a massive impact on theatre history, as is particularly clear when one looks beyond secular European theatre forms. My point here is not to rehash the debate about whether theatre has descended from religion but to note the way that religion has shaped innumerable theatre forms. Obviously not all theatre has a religious dimension, but religious belief can be found in every society (however attenuated it might be in some places) and is taken very seriously in most. The result is that one or more theatre forms in most societies are involved in some way with local understandings of the sacred. In numerous theatre forms, religion can account for a play's plots, characters, and themes, as well as the occasions and locations of performance.

The Shi'ite *ta'ziyeh*, for example, presents cycles of plays that focus on the stories of Hussein, with an emphasis on the battle of Karbala, at which he and his followers were slaughtered; the *ram lila* of Northern India relates stories about Rama, the seventh incarnation of Vishnu; the passion and Corpus Christi plays of medieval Europe presented stories from throughout the Bible, focusing in particular on the Passion of Jesus; and on and on. The importance of religion is such that differing religious stories can sometimes be at the basis of theatre forms that share particular structures. The performance of the European Jewish *purimshpieln* (Purim plays) closely follows the conventions of European spoken theatre but uses Old Testament narratives (especially from the biblical Book of Esther) and themes from Jewish experience such as perseverance in the face of oppression; also, the specific occasion of performance is the Jewish holiday of Purim.[46] Likewise, most of the stories told in *wayang kulit purwa*, perhaps the oldest form of shadow theatre in the insular region of Southeast Asia, are drawn from the classical Hindu epics, the *Mahabharata* and the *Ramayana*;[47] similar in its performance traits is *wayang kulit menak*, but this form focuses on legendary stories from the life of Amir Hamzah, an uncle of the Prophet Mohammad.[48] In these last two cases, shared formal structures exist in forms that rely on distinct religious structures.

Finally, we come to race or ethnicity. One's racial or ethnic identity is often very closely associated with that of language and/or religion, but it is still possible to separate it out in cases where different ethnic or racial groups are not separated by language or religion yet have theatre forms that are theirs alone. These conditions obtain between black and white Americans. I need scarcely note that activity in many theatre forms (especially the musical and spoken theatre) is shared by both groups; there are, however, some forms that are specific to black communities.

Most striking is a form, generally unnoticed by theatre historians, that is "of black folk, by black folk, and for black folk—a genuinely sequestered cultural preserve," known as the Chitlin Circuit (also known as the Chitlin' or Urban Circuit). According to Henry Louis Gates Jr., its plays tell of "matters that are of immediate concern" to their urban audiences, such as "gang violence, crack addiction, teenage pregnancy [and] deadbeat dads."[49] They are clearly not a celebration of, say, the black struggle for equality; in fact, "the subject of racism—or for that matter, white people—simply never arises."[50] Rather, they reflect realities that have become part of many African American lives. But despite subject matter that is sometimes ugly, there is an "audience communion" with the performance;[51] as such it becomes a celebration of the community. It is worth observing, though, that Chitlin Circuit theatre makes use of the aforementioned Italianate staging. Further, it is, as Gates says, "basically a melodrama, with abundant comic relief and a handful of gospel songs interspersed."[52] As such, it belongs to a family of theatre forms whose existence dates back more than two centuries, with an additional connection to a musical structure that evolved from an African American tradition of worship.[53]

Some of the structures I have discussed will be apparent in studies that are concerned with single theatrical events, but their endurance through time and across space renders them of far more significance than is often recognized. Various structures can unite seemingly distinct theatrical events or theatre forms; they can bind together entire regions, or even multiple regions. They provide a range of contexts within which theatre artists operate and have a direct and important bearing on their work. They are significant forces for conservatism that provide a specific range of opportunities to, or limitations upon the options of, those artists, inescapably shaping their work.

Trends

Counterposed to the structures of the longue dureé are the long-term trends that have no less effect on it. Even to speak of trends is to risk the sort of progressivism that is still prevalent in many discussions of theatre history. The progressivist argument—a transposition from Whig historiography into the realm of theatre—holds that theatre history demonstrates an inexorable progress from ritual, with its emphasis on dance and music, to the realistic theatre of the spoken word. As I have argued elsewhere, this suppositious trend relies on cherry-picking evidence from theatre history, as well as on an assumption that "Western" theatre is in some way both the mainstream and pinnacle of such history.[54] Obviously, this is not the sort of trend I seek to identify.

The trends I will be discussing are sometimes called "secular." In the sense used here, the term has nothing to do with an absence of religion; it refers, rather, to trends that endure over extended periods of time, beneath any shorter-term variations.[55] These trends can operate directly or indirectly on theatre. Either way, they are often implicated in theatrical change, as theatre develops in response to them. The long view helps clarify this important context, thereby also helping to explain why theatrical change in different theatre forms, even different regions, will sometimes happen in tandem.

The historian Jerry H. Bentley gives the clearest exposition of secular trends, noting three in particular—"three realities of global human experience"—that have been of huge importance. As Bentley suggests, they "reinforce one another with powerful effects throughout human history." These trends are "rising human population, expanding technological capacity, and increasing interaction between peoples of different societies."[56] To these we can add the trend of accelerating urbanization, which derives from, but also helps to stimulate, the other three.

Evidence of rising population is all around us. The historian David Christian provides a historical perspective that shows the trend in its broadest configuration. To take only a few numbers: ten thousand years ago, the total human population was approximately six million people; a thousand years ago, it was roughly two hundred fifty million; two hundred years ago, it was nine hundred fifty million; at present, it is around six billion.[57] As Bentley recognizes, "Population has risen at different rates in different lands, and . . . has been subject to numerous constraints," such as famine, war, and plague.[58] Still, "for any given thousand year period since the invention of agriculture, population has been higher at the end than at the beginning."[59] On a century-by-century basis, a chart provided by the historian Andre Gundar Frank shows that only the fourteenth century (out of the past thousand years) exhibited a decrease in the global population, owing to a dreadful series of famines and plagues, most notably the Eurasia-wide Black Plague.[60]

The rise in global population is of interest here primarily for its relationship to the other three trends. Human population has surged along with technological development, most notably since the invention of agriculture, making further development all the more essential. Increases in population, in conjunction with technological developments, have also helped to shrink the world, as it were, making interactions between societies increasingly possible. Finally, a rising population has made urban growth not only feasible but also necessary, as loci for production, trade, and power (both civic and religious). In brief, then, rising population is a critical aspect of the three other trends, to which I will now turn.

The expansion of technological capacity is in evidence all around us. Subsequent to the use of fire, the first great technological advance dates back to the invention of agriculture some seven thousand years ago. Technological advances have taken place all through the ensuring years; since the late eighteenth century, they have been as breathtaking as seemingly inevitable. Henry Petroski, a professor of civil engineering, has said, "Form follows failure"; that is, when available technology does not quite fit an immediate need, people will seek to improve its functionality. "This principle," he argues, "governs all invention, innovation, and ingenuity." Moreover, "since nothing is perfect, and, indeed, since even our ideas of perfection are not static, everything [technological] is subject to change over time."[61] Expanding technological capacity has, of course, been no less uneven than population growth. And we should not forget that older technologies can have surprisingly long half-lives. Still, a general expansion is undeniable, despite the "appalling cruelty, suffering, and environmental damage" that has accompanied the "increased human power, comfort, and safety."[62]

In theatre, the application of new technologies has been a regular practice. As we have seen, *Theatre Histories* plots the history of theatre according to the development of communication technologies and the communication frameworks that they spawned—but that is by no means the only kind of technological development to affect theatre. The technology of lighting, for example, has had a striking impact. The first major development, after the long use of torches, was the invention of oil lamps, followed by mass-produced candles. The most radical development in the technology of lighting, however, was probably the introduction of gaslight. The technologies that preceded gaslight cast a mediocre light at best, were awkward to maintain, and, above all, were often the cause of devastating fires. Moreover, from the Renaissance until the beginning of the nineteenth century, the stage space in Europe was, in effect, "like a painting or a bas-relief," with the actors "normally lined up across the stage" in the available light, "utilizing very little of the open space behind them, which was dedicated to moveable scenery."[63] A better kind of light was highly desirable, especially in indoor theatres. Gas-lighting was introduced in 1815, in London's Covent Garden—but apparently it was used only to light some of the public areas of the theatre. Lighting of the performance itself was not to come for another two years, when, on August 6, 1817, the playbill at the Lyceum Theatre in London announced, "The GAS LIGHTS will this evening be introduced over the whole stage."[64] The *London Times* called the innovation "a considerable improvement," in part because it allowed for variable lighting according the needs of each scene.[65] Curiously, it took some twelve years before most of the major theatres in London had gas lighting.[66] This was due both to the sheer cost of installing gas and the rather common complaint that gas-lighting "allowed people to see too much": the "poverty" of scenic, costume, and prop materials was "instantly discovered by an excess of light."[67] Performers were compelled both to use higher quality materials and to modulate the intensity of light.

By brightening the stage, gaslight made possible an increase in theatre sizes (an increase further abetted by changes in construction technology) and a general move toward more realistic materials—two of the signal developments of nineteenth-century European spoken theatre.

Associated with the introduction of gas was the ability to darken the house during performances. In 1821, the Lyceum began experimenting with lowering the houselights during performances, though the practice was used "sparingly," at least in England, for much of the century.[68] Reasons for this delay are interesting. Primary among them was the complaint, from long-time attendees, that "a darkened auditorium . . . demanded and focused their attention on the stage," thus restricting the social aspect of theatregoing.[69] As the practice became widespread, however, it helped to reinforce a key idea of Italianate staging: the inviolate stage-picture—but now with the added benefit of clearly visible depth—that was disassociated from the (now-darkened) world of the audience.

The 1878 introduction of gaslight into kabuki also brought about "a considerable change in the aesthetics" of the form, since the stage had previously been illuminated only by candles, torches, and the daylight that came through paper windows. Given the brightness of gas lighting, however, the make-up was too garish; the movement was too broad and stylized, appearing "simply ridiculous"; and the *kōken* (stage assistants), dressed in black, became clearly visible for the first time.[70] Much of this sounds remarkably similar to European complaints lodged against gaslight: In both places the technological development was desirable but discomforting. Although the kabuki audience remained lit to reduce the shock effect of bright gaslight, more subtle makeup and movement were required of the performers, and the "invisibility" of the *kōken* became more a convention than a reality.[71]

In addition to the trends of rising population and expanding technological capacity is Bentley's third trend: the increase of societal interactions, which has taken place both within and across regions. Bentley suggests that "from remote times to the present, interactions have had significant political, social, economic, and cultural ramifications for all the people involved."[72] Among the historical processes involved in these interactions have been "large-scale migrations, campaigns of imperial expansion, long-distance trade, the spread of biological species, and encounters and exchanges of religious and cultural traditions."[73] As with the previously discussed trends, we must recognize that inter-societal contact has occurred at a highly uneven pace through history. Despite those fluctuations, however, the trend has had a massive impact on history. Indeed, the historian William H. McNeill goes so far as to argue that "through the larger part of recorded history, the main drive wheel of historical change was contacts among strangers, causing men on both sides of such encounters to reconsider and in some cases to alter their familiar ways of behaving."[74]

Interactions have played a crucial role in theatre history. Sometimes theatre is simply an indirect beneficiary of intersocietal contact. For example, the spread of Buddhism from India to China (and thence to Japan) had a profound impact on the development of theatre in those lands. In China, Buddhism provided the subject matter for numerous plays, including *Journey to the West*, whose narrative concerns the pilgrimage of the Xuanzang to India, seeking sacred Buddhist texts; the play contains "copious quotations from the Buddhist scriptures and the theme of Buddhist morality."[75] And although noh bears the spiritual influence of the indigenous Shinto of Japan, Komparu Zenchiku, a leading playwright and theorist of the fifteenth century, writes: "At the foundation of every performance, as well as all art, all life, and all existence, is the fundamental Buddha nature."[76]

Sometimes, though, theatre is directly affected by societal interactions. Their increased rate in the past two centuries (made possible especially by new technologies of transportation) has wrought profound developments as theatre forms from different regions have been brought into contact with one another. The emergence of the Yoruba popular theatre in present-day Nigeria is a fine example of the interaction between foreign and domestic traditions. The most obvious, yet fundamental, indigenous element in the emergence of Yoruba popular theatre is the Yoruba language in which the plays are performed. By contrast, the plays of such estimable ethnic-Yoruba playwrights as Wole Soyinka are written and performed in English. The popular theatre's vernacular has been crucial to the success of the form throughout Yorubaland, which has the "largest urban concentration" in Nigeria.[77] By contrast, again, Soyinka's plays have tended to be of interest primarily to the educated elite of Nigeria and to the world beyond Nigeria's borders.

Two additional indigenous elements were also crucial to the emergence of Yoruba popular theatre. First is the ethnic heritage of Yoruba folklore. According to Oyekan Owomoyela, this folklore provides "a vast treasury of theatre material": plots, proverbs, "ornamental dialogue," and so on.[78] Also, it is "nationalistic," and the twentieth-century "reaction to foreign oppression meant . . . [a] return to the native culture."[79] Second is an earlier form: *Apidán* theatre, which emerged more than two hundred years ago and has lasted to the present day.[80] All of the folkloric aspects mentioned earlier are to be found in Apidán, and to these we must add that form's ever-present drums, its regular recourse to dance and chant/song, and the professional status of its performers.[81]

And yet nonindigenous theatre forms also played a huge role in the emergence of the Yoruba popular theatre. British colonialism had introduced

Christian missions into Nigeria; before long, some churches broke away from the missions to hold their services in the vernacular.[82] Within these churches, a popular form of performance was the "cantata": "dramatized versions of well-known Bible stories, rendered entirely or almost entirely in song."[83] In typical European fashion, these cantatas were mounted on stages that separated the performers from their audience. In the mid-1940s, Hubert Ogunde began staging original cantatas. At first, they were rather typical church productions, although from the beginning he included vernacular music along with the more hymn-like music of earlier cantatas. In the next few years, however, he took a series of steps that exploded the cantata form: he introduced secular plots and themes of direct local relevance (including folkloric and anticolonial material); he professionalized his troupe; and he made extensive use of drums and chanting, as well as of improvised dialogue between the set-piece songs. Perhaps most importantly, he took advantage of the astonishing increase in population and wealth in Lagos and other Yoruba cities and began touring his troupe through the urban and semiurban enclaves of Yorubaland, performing in such venues as movie houses, nightclubs, town halls, and community centers.[84] The Yoruba popular theatre, in sum, was made possible by the societal interactions between Britain and the Yoruba people; those interactions were the essential context within which Ogunde created the form.

The final global trend to discuss is accelerating urbanization. Regarding cities in Eurasia and North Africa, Christian notes that "in the third millennium BCE, there were perhaps eight cities with at least 30,000 inhabitants"; by 100 CE, there were some seventy-five cities of at least this size, with the largest of them holding 450,000 people. A downturn in urban development, owing to plagues and the turmoil of foreign invasions, took place in the first millennium CE, but by 1000 CE there were again seventy such cities.[85] And although we tend to think of urban development as a Eurasian phenomenon, it is worth noting that, at its height, the Aztec capital, Tenochtitlán, is estimated to have had between 150,000 to 250,000 people;[86] cities also existed in precolonial Africa, most notably the Yoruba cities of Oyo and Ibidan. There are currently over five hundred "urban agglomerations" in the world with populations of a million or more each; indeed, half of the total global population is now urban-dwelling.[87]

Peter Hall, an urban historian, has argued that some cities become what he calls "cultural crucibles";[88] his examples are ancient Athens, Renaissance Florence, Elizabethan and Jacobean London, nineteenth-century Vienna, late-nineteenth-century Paris, and post–World War I Berlin; no doubt at least as many non-European cities could be added to this list. According to Hall, these cities all shared the traits of increasing populations along with "rapid economic and social transformation."[89] They were cities "in transition," heading "into new and unexplored modes of organization," with "transformation in social relationships, in values, and in views about the world."[90] Not all transitions, however, are created equal. While conservative, stable societies will not prove particularly creative, neither will "societies in which all order, all points of reference, have disappeared."[91]

A critical trait of these cities is their concentration of population. This has an impact on both the people who create theatre and those who attend it. For the creators, it allows for collaborations, rivalries, and influences. Gary Taylor asks whether the playwrights of Elizabethan England were "rivals or partners." The answer, of course, is both. But the more important point is that "each playwright's individual success contribute[d] to the collective health of the theatrical economy on which they all depend[ed]."[92] And thanks to that economy, a steady pool of actors and playwrights could be drawn to the city and developed into experienced professionals.

In regard to the audience, the concentration of urban populations makes theatre physically accessible to potential audiences. Forms such as Greek comedy and tragedy, kabuki, jingju, and European spoken theatre have often made their appeal to the large but socially diverse audiences that lived in close proximity to their performance venues. As H. T. F. Kitto puts it: "If the Greek was not within a day's walk of his political center, then his life was something less than the life of a real man."[93] Technological developments have made large, centralized theatres accessible to increasingly dispersed audiences: trams, buses, and subways serve city-dwellers far beyond comfortable walking distance; more recently, automobiles have brought entire urban agglomerations within their sphere, while airplanes have brought international audiences.

Another important trait of these cities is their function as creators and controllers of wealth—and for better or worse, at least a modicum of wealth is crucial for the arts in general and theatre in particular. Whatever the origins of such wealth might be, one of its most notable effects is that it frees a number of people (at least some of the time) from more immediately productive labor, allowing them to work in the service industry of theatre. This is not to say that all theatre requires money. As in other service industries (such as medical care), the service can be performed for nonmonetary remuneration, or even for free. Still, performers must survive, and that survival depends on earning enough (one way or another) to survive. According to Hall, "It [is] true that, as D. H. Lawrence once said, culture [is] founded on the deep dung of cash."[94]

A city in the sort of transition discussed by Hall not only sees an increase in its overall wealth but also sees that wealth distributed in new ways, sometimes among its established segments, but sometimes to segments that were previously nascent or even nonexistent. I mentioned earlier that the Yoruba popular theatre was associated with the development of Lagos and neighboring Yoruba cities. At the start of the twentieth century, Lagos had a population of some 50,000 people.[95] By 1948 it had reached 333,000, and it had grown to over a million by 1960. Intersocietal contact was the prime cause of Lagos's growth. Colonialism "accelerated the formation of new classes: cash-cropping framers, an educated elite, and, between them, an amorphous urban 'intermediate class,' made up of wage laborers, artisans, traders, providers of services of all kinds, low-paid civil servants, [and] employees of big trading companies."[96] It was by and for this last new segment of Nigerian society that the Yoruba popular theatre was created; without this segment and its newfound wealth, the form would have lacked the material support necessary for its prolific growth.

Our four secular trends, in sum, have had a profound impact on theatre history. Primarily they have fostered change—as opposed to the continuity that structures reinforce—by altering the social contexts within which theatre artists work, thereby creating new opportunities for them. But an understanding of the long-term secular trends can also help us understand the radical decline, over the past hundred years, of many established theatre forms. Modern media has siphoned away theatre artists and audiences; societal interactions have had a globally homogenizing effect, diminishing interest in localized theatre forms; and the immiseration sometimes associated with contemporary urbanism—especially in poorer countries—can render insupportable the costs (however minimal) of theatre. The long view provides a key to understanding these theatrical changes, even though they might well be for the worse.

Conclusion

Each theatrical event is a unique entity, and the study of even a single event can be highly rewarding. As Braudel himself admits, such events are "the most exciting" part of history, "the richest in human interest."[97] Not even Braudel would discourage historians from studying them, however much he himself might prefer to focus on the longue dureé. Indeed, event-based studies are the necessary base on which any history taking the long view must be constructed. The problem arises when historians move beyond such localized study but do little more than string together a chronicle of events.

Postlewait's claim, mentioned at the start of this article, that textbooks such as Brockett's lead "many" classrooms to emphasize "memorization" is rhetorical overkill. The larger point, though, is that texts such as Brockett's leave students with little more than facts, while professors are offered scant guidance in developing teachable interpretations of history. Although *Theatre Histories* is a marked improvement in this regard, it is only a first step to fulfilling the promise of the long view.

How might theatre professors attend to the longue dureé in classroom discourse? Part of the answer would be to introduce the idea at the start of the semester; a general discussion of structures and trends, along with examples of their effects, will cue students to their significance. This would be followed up by regularly encouraging students to look beneath the surface of events for the structures and trends that bear upon them. Just as the authors of *Theatre Histories: An Introduction* discuss the impact of developments in communication technology, so might one look more broadly at technological developments as well as the other long-term trends that can prompt theatre artists to work in new and different ways. No less importantly, one might also highlight the various structures that can endure for centuries or longer and both support and constrain the ways in which those artists go about their work.

The upshot would be to move beyond the singularity of events. Let me return to the example I gave near the start of this article, regarding the role of urbanization in the emergence of European spoken theatre and kabuki. London, Madrid, and Edo were all "cities in transition," to use Peter Hall's term. The population of London grew from 120,000 (in 1550) to 200,000 (in 1600) to nearly 500,000 (in 1650). It was the epicenter of an economic revolution that saw "unprecedented social mobility and the breakdown of traditional class distinctions."[98] Madrid, meanwhile, had been a minor city until Phillip II moved his court there in 1561, making it the de facto capital of the country. The population at the time was roughly 30,000; by 1598, it had risen to 60,000, while by 1656 the city had 100,000 inhabitants.[99] The case with Edo was similar. It was a "wretched struggling village" until 1603, when the Tokugawa shogunate established it as their capital; by 1723 the population was over 500,000, not counting the samurai class, which was not yet included in the register.[100] In all three cases we see exploding populations that were filled not only with nobles (and, in Edo's case, samurai) but also with large classes of professionals (such as lawyers), merchants, petty officials, craftsmen, shopkeepers, and apprentices, most of whom had money to spend: By and large, these were potential audiences that had scarcely existed in those cities.

None of this is to suggest that this sort of growth in itself creates a new theatre form; the point is that it creates opportunities for new forms, which theatre artists can then exploit if sufficiently talented. Each of the cities I have mentioned quickly saw purpose-built theatres constructed within walking distance of the bulk of its population, offering tickets in a range of prices that allowed attendance by those of relatively little means as well as those who could afford to pay more but insisted on a higher quality of seating. These theatres were, above all, commercial enterprises that needed to appeal to the broadest possible audiences. As a result of that need, the plays of spoken theatre (in London and Madrid) and kabuki mixed historical pieces starring kings or warriors with domestic pieces centered on life in the contemporary city: think *Richard III* and *Bartholomew Fair*; *The Siege of Numantia* and *The Trickster of Seville*; the *jidaimono* (history plays) and *sewamono* (plays about contemporary commoners) in kabuki.

As I hope is evident, the near-contemporaneous emergence of spoken theatre and kabuki was no mere coincidence. In both cases, rapid urbanization was a critical prerequisite, but that urbanization itself was spurred in England and Spain by the societal interactions that followed in the wake of the so-called voyages of discovery; Japan, meanwhile, was deeply involved in international trade, as noted earlier. One might also note the importance of new technologies, in particular regarding the shipbuilding technologies that provided the physical means for advancement of intersocietal contact. And as we have already seen, the emergence of Yoruba Popular Theatre took place in a surprisingly similar socioeconomic context of rapid urban growth that was spurred by intersocietal contact and that created new classes with money to spend. It must be added, though, that each of these forms (and, in the case of spoken theatre, the English and Spanish variants) was shaped in part by continuities with earlier forms of theatre and, more broadly, with other societal structures. Trends and structures alike were of profound importance in the emergence and development of these forms.

Whatever else might be said of it, history is not random, and historical development cannot be understood through chronology alone. Historical events are the result of human actions, but those actions do not take place in a vacuum. They are shaped by structures, which generally support continuity, and trends, which open up new opportunities for change. By highlighting those structures and trends, the long view can help us better understand why events take the shape that they do and how they are related to one another. In this way it adds a vital dimension to the study of world theatre history.

Notes

1. Edwin Wilson and Alvin Goldfarb, *Living Theatre: A History of Theatre*, 4th ed. (New York: McGraw-Hill, 2001), vii.
2. The concept of a historical "event" can be, as Thomas Postlewait notes, "quite ambiguous, complicated, obscure, and even [self-]contradictory"; Thomas Postlewait, *The Cambridge Introduction to Theatre Historiography* (Cambridge: Cambridge University, 2009), 89. Use of the word, however, seems unavoidable, so the reader must simply be aware of its complexities. For a fuller discussion, see Postlewait, *Cambridge Introduction*, 89–116.
3. Ibid., 169. The text to which Postlewait refers is Oscar J. Brockett, *History of the Theatre*, 4th ed. (Boston: Allyn and Bacon, 1982). There have been numerous further editions, with the more recent ones having been coauthored by Franklin J. Hildy. Despite the changes made over the years, Postlewait's criticism is still germane.
4. Phillip B. Zarrilli, Bruce McConachie, Gary Jay Williams, and Carol Fisher Sorgenfrei, *Theatre Histories: An Introduction*, 2nd ed. (New York: Routledge, 2010), 19.
5. Ibid., xix.
6. Tobin Nellhaus, *Theatre, Communication, Critical Realism* (New York: Palgrave Macmillan, 2010), 8, 54–55; note that Nellhaus distances himself from Ong, whom he accuses of "technological determinism," 6.
7. Fernand Braudel, *On History*, trans. Sarah Matthews (Chicago: University of Chicago Press, 1980), 28.
8. Patrick Manning, *Navigating World History: Historians Create a Global Past* (New York: Palgrave Macmillan, 2003), 267.
9. Postlewait, *Cambridge Introduction*, 168.
10. Stefan Hulfeld, "Modernist Theatre," in *The Cambridge Companion to Theatre History*, ed. David Wiles and Christine Dymkowski (Cambridge: Cambridge University Press, 2013), 15–32, on 17.
11. Henk Gras and Harry van Vliet, "Paradise Lost nor Regained: Social Composition of Theatre Audiences in the Long Nineteenth Century," *Journal of Social History* 38, no. 2 (Winter, 2004): 471–512. Braudelian time-scales—in reference to literature as whole—are also discussed in Franco Moretti, *Distant Reading* (London: Verso, 2013), 85–87.
12. Fernand Braudel, *The Mediterranean and the Mediterranean World in the Age of Philip II*, trans. Siân Reynolds (New York: Harper & Row, 1972), 1:20–21.
13. Braudel, *On History*, 27.
14. Ibid., 30–31.
15. Ibid., 27.
16. Postlewait, *Cambridge Introduction*, 168.
17. Manning, *Navigating*, 266–67.
18. Ibid., 267.
19. Braudel, *Mediterranean*, vol. 2, 901.
20. Braudel, *On History*, 34.
21. François Dosse, *New History in France: The Triumph of the Annales*, trans. Peter V. Conroy Jr. (Urbana: University of Chicago Press, 1994), 93.
22. Postlewait, *Cambridge Introduction*, 109.

23. Dosse, *New History*, 215.
24. Emmanuel Le Roy Ladurie, *Montaillou: The Promised Land of Error*, trans. Barbara Bray (New York: Vintage Books, 1968).
25. Jo Guldi and David Armitage, *The History Manifesto* (Cambridge: Cambridge University Press, 2014). A somewhat different example would be Barry Cunliffe, who was influenced by Braudel's ideas in writing *Europe Between the Oceans: 9000 BC–AD 1000* (New Haven: Yale University Press, 2008); see especially 17–18.
26. Nellhaus, *Theatre, Communication, Criticism Realism*, 57–141.
27. Braudel, *Mediterranean*, 2:1243–44.
28. Michael Adas, "Bringing Ideas and Agency Back In: Representation and the Comparative Approach to World History," in *World History: Ideologies, Structures, and Identities*, ed. Philip Pomper, Richard H. Elphick, and Richard T. Vann (Oxford: Blackwell, 1998), 81–104, on 87.
29. Postlewait, *Cambridge Introduction*, 100.
30. Braudel, *On History*, 31–32.
31. One might speak of "genres" or "styles" rather than "forms," but both of those terms are regularly used for literary discussion, so it seems advisable to follow the practice of many scholars of Asian theatre and speak of "forms." I take the term "theatrical event" from, above all, Willmar Sauter; see his *The Theatrical Event: Dynamics of Performance and Perception* (Iowa City: University of Iowa Press, 2000).
32. George E. Duckworth, *The Nature of Roman Comedy: A Study in Popular Entertainment*, 2nd ed. (Norman: University of Oklahoma Press, 1994), 29; Stuart Blackburn, *Inside the Drama-House: Rāma Stories and Shadow Puppets in South India* (Berkeley: University of California Press, 1996), 40; and Ghulam-Sarwar Yousof, *Dictionary of Traditional South-East Asian Theatre* (Kuala Lumpur: Oxford University Press, 1994), 237–38.
33. Augustus William Schlegel, *A Course of Lectures on Dramatic Art and Literature*, trans. John Black, rev. A. J. W. Morrison (London: Henry H. Bohn, 1846); the break is between Lectures XV and XVI, 212.
34. Steve Tillis, "Conceptualizing Space: The Geographic Dimension of World Theatre," *Theatre Survey* 52, no. 2 (November 2011): 301–27.
35. Andre Gundar Frank, *ReOrient: Global Economy in the Asian Age* (Berkeley: University of California Press, 1998), 104–7.
36. William Dolby, *A History of Chinese Drama* (London: Paul Elek, 1976), 8.
37. William Dolby, "Early Chinese Plays and Theater," in *Chinese Theater: From Its Origins to the Present Day*, ed. Colin Mackarras (Honolulu: University of Hawaii Press), 7–31, on 21.
38. Dolby, *History*, 60.
39. Ibid., 105.
40. Ibid., 180–81.
41. Margreta de Grazia, "World Pictures, Modern Periods, and the Early Stage," in *A New History of Early English Drama*, ed. John D. Cox and David Scott Kastan (New York: Columbia University Press, 1997) 7–21, on 18.
42. de Grazia, "World Pictures," 19.
43. George C. Izenour, *Theater Design*, 2nd ed. (New Haven: Yale University Press, 1996), 47.
44. Zemmaro Toki, *Nō Japanese Plays* (Tokyo: Japan Travel Bureau, 1954), 113.
45. For a general discussion of this issue, see Howard Stankey, "Incommensurability,

Translation and Understanding," *The Philosophical Quarterly* 41, no. 165 (October, 1991): 414–26.

46. Eli Rozik, *The Roots of Theatre: Rethinking Ritual and Other Theories of Origin* (Iowa City: University of Iowa Press, 2002), 139.
47. Ghulam-Sarwar Yousof, *Dictionary of Traditional South-East Asian Theatre* (Kuala Lumpur: Oxford University Press, 1994), 291.
48. Ibid., 290.
49. Henry Louis Gates Jr., "The Chitlin Circuit," in *African American Performance and Theater History: A Critical Reader*, ed. Harry J. Elam and David Krasser (Oxford: Oxford University Press, 2001), 132–48, on 140.
50. Ibid., 141.
51. Ibid., 141.
52. Ibid., 140.
53. For reviews of current Chitlin Ciruit plays, see chitlincircuitreviews.com. For discussion of Chitlin Circuit theatres as venues for music, see Preston Lauterbach, *The Chitlin' Circuit: And the Road to Rock 'n' Roll* (New York: W. W. Norton, 2012).
54. Steve Tillis, "Theatre History's 'View of the World,'" *TDR (The Theatre Journal)* 48, no. 3 (Fall 2004): 6–10, on 7–8.
55. This usage of "secular" might seem strange to some readers, but it is commonly employed in social sciences such as economics. It derives from the Latin *saecularis* "relating to an age or period"; see http://www.oxforddictionaries.com/us/definition/american_english/secular (accessed April 4, 2016).
56. Jerry H. Bentley, "World History and Grand Narrative," in *Writing World History: 1800–2000*, ed. Benedikt Stuchtey and Eckhardt Fuchs (Oxford: Oxford University Press, 2003), 47–65, on 51.
57. David Christian, *Maps of Time: An Introduction to Big History* (Berkeley: University of California Press, 2011), 143.
58. Bentley, "World History and Grand Narrative," 53.
59. Ibid., 53.
60. Frank, *ReOrient*, 168. The global population as of 1300 is given as 384 million, while by 1400 it had dropped slightly, to 373 million; by 1500, however, it had vigorously rebounded to 446 million.
61. Henry Petroski, *The Evolution of Useful Things* (New York: Vintage Books, 1992), 22.
62. Bentley, "World History and Grand Narrative," 54.
63. Marvin Carlson, "Space and Theatre History," in *Representing the Past: Essays in Performance Historiography*, ed. Thomas Postlewait and Charlotte M. Canning (Iowa City: University of Iowa Press, 2010), 195–206, on 200.
64. Terence Rees, *Theatre Lighting in the Age of Gas* (London: Society for Theatre Research, 1978), 9; small caps in the original.
65. Ibid., 9.
66. Ibid., 12.
67. Ibid., 189.
68. Ibid., 187.
69. Ibid., 188.
70. Thomas Leims, "Kabuki Goes to Hollywood: Reforms and 'Revues' in the 1980's," in *The Dramatic Touch of Difference: Theatre, Own and Foreign*, ed. Erika Fischer-Lichte,

Josephine Riley, and Michael Gissenwehrer. (Tübingen: Gunter Narr Verlag, 1990), 107–17, on 113.

71. Ibid., 113–14.
72. Jerry H. Bentley, "Cross Cultural Interaction and Periodization in World History," *American Historical Review* 101, no. 3 (June 1996): 749–71, on 750.
73. Bentley, "World History and Grand Narrative," 58; see also Patrick Manning, "The Problem of Interactions in World History," *American Historical Review* 101, no. 3 (June 1996): 771–81.
74. William H. McNeill, *The Shape of European History* (New York: Oxford University Press, 1974), 42.
75. Dolby *History*, 142.
76. Benito Ortolani, *The Japanese Theatre: From Shamanistic Ritual to Contemporary Pluralism*, rev. ed. (Princeton: Princeton University Press, 1990), 128.
77. Biodun Jeyifo, *The Yoruba Popular Travelling Theatre of Nigeria* (Lagos: Nigeria Magazine, 1984), 51.
78. Owomoyela, Oyekan, "Folklore and Yoruba Theater," in *Forms of Folklore in Africa: Narrative, Poetic, Gnomic, Dramatic*, ed. Berth Lindfors (Austin: University of Texas Press, 1977), 258–70, on 264.
79. Owomoyela, "Folklore," 263.
80. For a succinct summary of Apidán (also known as Alarinjo) theatre, see Joel Adedeji, "Alarinjo: The Traditional Yoruba Travelling Theatre," in *Drama and Theatre in Nigeria: A Critical Source Book*, ed. Yemi Ogunbiyi (Lagos: Nigeria Magazine, 1981), 221–48.
81. Adedeji "Alarinjo," passim.
82. Karin Barber, John Collins, and Alan Ricard, *West African Popular Theatre* (Bloomington: Indiana University Press, 1997), 38.
83. Ibid., 39.
84. Ibid., 39–40; Jeyifo, "Yoruba Popular," 70–73.
85. Christian, *Maps of Time*, 326.
86. Dirk R. Van Tuerenhout, *The Aztecs: New Perspectives* (Santa Barbara: ABC-CLIO: 2005), 147.
87. United Nations, Department of Economic and Social Affairs, Population Division (2014), *World Urbanization Prospects: The 2014 Revision, Highlights* (ST/ESA/SER.A/352), 13; http://esa.un.org/unpd/wup/Highlights/WUP2014-Highlights.pdf (accessed April 6, 2016).
88. Peter Hall, *Cities in Civilization* (New York: Pantheon, 1998), 1.
89. Ibid., 284.
90. Ibid., 284, 285.
91. Ibid., 286.
92. Gary Taylor, *Cultural Selection: Why Some Achievements Survive the Test of Time—And Others Don't* (New York: Basic Books, 1996), 53, 54.
93. Cited in Hall, *Cities*, 36.
94. Hall, *Cities*, 284–85.
95. The "turn-of-the-century" figure is from *The Encyclopedia Britannica*, 1911 edition, under the heading of "Lagos."
96. Barber et al., *West African*, 2.
97. Braudel, *Mediterranean*, vol. 1, 21.

98. Hall, *Cities*, 117.
99. http://academic.eb.com.stmarys-ca.idm.oclc.org/EBchecked/topic/356111/Madrid (accessed April 4, 2015).
100. G. B. Sansom, *Japan: A Short Cultural History* (Stanford: Stanford University Press, 1978), 469.

Part II

SPECIAL SECTION
RETHINKING THE MATERNAL

Introduction to Part II

—KAREN BAMFORD AND SHEILA RABILLARD

In Dael Orlandersmith's *Forever* (onstage at the New York Theater Workshop, May 2015), the author performs an eighty-minute monologue in which her protagonist battles to speak the truth about herself, truth that is at the same time inevitably truth about her mother.[1] The difficulty of truths about the mother, the drama it generates, and how those dramatic truths enter stage history are the concerns of the essays presented in this special section.

In what sense does the maternal need to be re-examined, why now, and why pursue this inquiry via studies of British and North American theatre and drama since the 1970s? One answer lies in the inadequate social support, and contradictory cultural concepts, surrounding contemporary Anglo-American motherhood. Although "motherhood and apple pie" refers to something regarded as an unquestionable good, maternity is presently both problematic and potentially dangerous for individuals and states.[2] Most women in Western societies appear to have greater reproductive control than ever thanks to reliable contraception, new technologies for circumventing infertility, and sophisticated means of monitoring pregnancy; nevertheless, maternity remains a significant risk to health. According to Amnesty International's report "Deadly Delivery: The Maternal Health Care Crisis in the USA" published in 2010, two to three women die every day during pregnancy and childbirth in the United States; an update one year later indicated that the United States' maternal mortality rate had worsened from forty-first to fiftieth (as compared to other Amnesty-ranked countries). Figures published in the *Lancet* in May 2010 also show increasing maternal mortality in Canada, Denmark, Austria, and Norway.[3] While Western societies struggle to find effective policies to promote mothering that will support development of the community and the individual, actual conditions for mothers in some of the wealthiest countries are deteriorating.

A UK government study reported in the *Guardian* in 2008 revealed employment discrimination against pregnant women and those of childbearing age;[4] according to Save the Children's 2007 "Mother's Index," employment conditions are worse for mothers in Canada and the United States than in the United Kingdom. Analysis published in the *New York Times* (August 9, 2014) summarizing recent economic research concluded that generous maternity leave policies in European countries inhibited women's job opportunities and promotions while lack of leave in the United States discouraged labor force participation outright. "Mothers on both sides of the Atlantic, then, pay a price for the structure of family leave policies."[5] As the conditions of motherhood change, the demography of motherhood is changing also, affected by social and economic pressures not fully understood. European governments attempting to reverse the downward trend of birth rates (falling, for native-born women, since the 1970s) have met with scant success.[6] At the same time, racialized discourse has framed the reproductive rates among marginalized populations as a social danger: the British *Daily Mail* raised the issue of what was seen as excessive Muslim fertility.[7] While some demographic change may be comparatively uncontroversial, such as the increase in average maternal age in the United States, it nevertheless entails an alteration in individual maternal experiences and in family histories. Other changes, such as the number of births to unmarried women—almost four out of ten in the United States in 2015; rising faster in the United Kingdom during the 1980s and 1990s than at any time in history—require adaptations in political, social, and economic structures even as they indicate shifts in sexual mores, family patterns, and maternal responsibilities.[8]

If adequate support for maternity is often wanting in stable and privileged nations, more disturbing still is international inaction concerning the use of rape as a part of warfare, the subject of a widely publicized conference: The Global Summit to End Sexual Violence in Conflict, London, UK (June 2014). Although the example is extreme, and military conflict lies outside our purview, the phenomenon to which the Summit draws attention—rape as an instrument of war—illustrates a central concern of the essays presented here: maternity as a contested terrain, wherein political, economic, and cultural forces are at work often in ways obscured by emotion ranging from deep affection to the horror evoked by violation. "Rethinking" in the title above proposes that the essayists, and the playwrights they consider, participate in a reimagination of mothering.

Phrased slightly differently, "re: thinking the maternal" announces an equal interest in disclosing forces and issues expressed indirectly via conceptions of, and responses to, maternity.

The Power of Contemporary History

In the last fifty years the structure of families and the performance of mothering grew more visibly various and fluid. At the beginning of this period birth control became widely available. The Abortion Act of 1967 made abortion legal on a number of grounds throughout England, Wales, and Scotland. The US Supreme Court decision in *Roe v. Wade* (1973) legalized abortion based on the right to privacy. Abortion was decriminalized in Canada in 1988, making it a medical matter. Notably, Ireland was an exception to this pattern, and the essays in this issue treating Irish drama explore distinctive approaches to maternity marked by Irish history and culture. The Republic of Ireland did not permit abortion until 2013, and then only under limited circumstances; at that date Northern Ireland still had not legislated abortion rights.[9] As with abortion, so too was access to contraception delayed in the Republic of Ireland (permitted via prescription in 1980, and nonmedical contraceptives legalized for those over eighteen in 1985). Elsewhere, however, contraception became increasingly accessible during this period in North America and the United Kingdom due to changes in law and the introduction of oral contraceptives. Contraception was decriminalized in Canada in 1969; it was made legal in the United States for married couples in 1965, and for all US citizens regardless of marital status in 1972. In the United Kingdom, the birth control pill was made available through the National Health Service in 1961, chiefly to married older women who already had children; by 1974, family planning clinics were permitted to prescribe the pill to single women.[10] Thus, beginning in the 1970s, maternity increasingly became seen as a choice. The right to choose is still contested, however: legislation in the United Kingdom has reduced the period in which abortion is legal from twenty-eight to twenty-four weeks; various states in the United States have introduced restrictions on the circumstances under which abortions may be provided; and the US Supreme Court ruled (on June 30, 2014) that a publicly traded company can refuse on religious grounds to provide insurance coverage for contraception, coverage otherwise required by federal healthcare legislation.

While changes in medicine and law make maternity a choice (albeit a contested one), the choosing may be neither free nor fully understood, and thus it is rich territory to explore in drama and scholarship. In Lynne Van Luven's anthology *Nobody's Mother*, writers weigh the satisfactions of having refused maternity; many attest to the difficulty of persuading others that theirs was a valid, rewarding decision.[11] In *Le conflit: La mère et la femme*, French philosopher Elisabeth Badinter argues powerfully that women are still choosing between motherhood and career in Western societies (between being "mother" and "woman") because of the ways in which motherhood is currently constructed. She makes the case that, while reproductive technologies widely available since the 1970s promised to provide all women in industrialized societies the same freedom to choose when, or whether, to become mothers, in fact economic pressures have produced very different choices—depending upon class, level of education, and job opportunities—and along with those choices different concepts and valuations of motherhood.

Far from being a unifying element in women's perception of their gender identity, contemporary motherhood in Badinter's analysis seems sometimes less and sometimes more important than career: for some women their definitive work in society, and for some a purely personal means of enriching their experience. These disparate conceptions of motherhood—crucially unexamined and potentially divisive politically—are vulnerable to the influence of cultural and commercial currents, including conflicting maternal ideals of the sexualized consumer "yummy mummy"; the multitasking executive; and the good ecological mother who devotes her time to breast-feeding.[12] As Jacqueline Rose points out, idealization of motherhood (now arising in new and contradictory guises) is rightly "one of the earliest and foremost targets of feminist critique."[13]

If maternity during the later decades of the twentieth century was redefined as a choice, by the beginning of the twenty-first century medical interventions produced new possibilities for multiple mothers (genetic, gestational, social) and plural maternal genders and sexualities, including concepts of motherhood challenged and expanded by transgender identities. In 1996 news media announced the cloning of Dolly the sheep and debated the implications for human reproduction, implications explored in Caryl Churchill's play *A Number* (2002). *New York Times* reports in June and early July 2014 described in vitro fertilization involving three genetic parents, and medical tourism to the United States to obtain the services of surrogate mothers.[14] Paid surrogacy is permitted in very few countries (and is illegal in the United Kingdom and Canada). However, the *New York Times* noted "an increasing flow" of the affluent (married and single, gay and straight) from Europe, Asia, and Australia seeking paid surrogacy in the United States. The article further noted that such developments have raised "fundamental questions about what constitutes a family" and in particular about the nature of maternity. "In many nations, a situation that splits motherhood between the biological mother and a surrogate carrier is widely believed to be against the child's best interests. And even more so when three women are involved: the genetic mother, whose egg is used; the mother who carries the baby; and the one who commissioned and will raise the child."[15]

Changes in laws and innovations in medical technology during the last several decades of the twentieth century and the early years of the twenty-first have also altered maternity by opening to view, respectively, adoption and gestation. Some of the complex consequences of the latter surveillance for pregnant women are dramatized in *My Glass Body* (see Komporaly's essay) and have played a part in the attempts of abortion opponents to endow the newly visible fetus with personhood and legal rights. See, for instance, Peggy Phelan's influential discussion of US activists who dramatize the voice of the fetus.[16] It scarcely needs to be added that changes in law and custom during this period demonstrated increasing acceptance of same-sex marriage (and same-sex couples as parents), divorce, single parenting, and working mothers. The pace and scope of transformations sketched in this brief introduction, transformations that have taken place in less than a life span, trace a history that makes the elusiveness and plurality of mothering critically evident.

Feminist Theatres and Theories

Early twenty-first-century work by emerging British and North American female playwrights suggests that this is a time for reflection on "the complicated and often contradictory legacy of various waves of feminism,"[17] in particular as this complex heritage relates to maternity. In *The How and the Why* (2011), which brings together an accomplished senior scholar and the daughter she gave up for adoption, US playwright Sarah Treem directs attention to women's still unresolved conflict between the demands of motherhood and career, between Badinter's "*la mère et la femme*." *The Village Bike* (2011), by British playwright Penelope Skinner, dramatizes charged psychic and social reactions to the maternal body, reactions fueled by confusion surrounding women's hard-won sexual freedom. The play concerns a young married woman who loses her sense of self, especially her sexual self, because of her own and her husband's responses to her pregnant body. Rising female playwrights, it seems, are finding this an appropriate time to explore maternity and with it the complexity of feminist heritages despite or perhaps because of the fact that, as Jill Dolan asserts, "women's stories, along with stories about men and women of color, are still tokenized in American theater."[18]

In a related sense, maternity is a timely subject for feminist criticism to take up again, as Elaine Aston argues in her landmark essay "A Step to the Side: Performing the Loss of the Mother" (2007). Aston's subtle analysis of key autobiographical performances demonstrates that such theatre prompts the spectator to question assumptions about likeness or liking between mother and daughter, about maternity and the (re-)production of identity both individual and collective. In her essay Aston, drawing on the work of Eve Kosofsky Sedgwick, proposes that we have reached a critically productive moment to loosen the antiessentialist stance achieved by feminism in the 1980s and 1990s and come back to the mother as a feminist subject.[19] While feminist antiessentialism was philosophically well-founded and more than merely strategic, its rhetoric emphasized experiences, bodies, and behaviors that challenged essentialist notions of woman by defying traditional gender and sexual categories. The move to understand gender as socially constructed and performative, as Judith Butler proposed—to "trouble" and "undo" gender conceptually—drew attention away from ways in which traditional women's roles such as motherhood were being reconfigured in practice. Jacqueline Rose's 2014 review welcomes the appearance of new scholarship on maternity; in the course of her essay she also reminds us of the significance of foundational feminist work on motherhood by Woolf, Rich, Arendt, Winnicott, and Loraux and conveys the rich possibilities of returning to the topic now.[20] Feminist criticism itself can be seen in terms of a history of changing, often conflicting, approaches to mothering.[21] A brief retrospect shows vital questions debated but unresolved and frames the challenge to recast such questions productively, and raise fresh questions still.

Virginia Woolf, in *A Room of One's Own* (1928), offered early evidence that maternity was a necessary and troubling subject for modern feminisms. She implies that daughters who deplore restrictions suffered by the maternal generation may also resent their mothers for bequeathing the consequences of oppression. "What had our mothers been doing then that they had no wealth to leave us?" Still more suggestive is her invention of Shakespeare's gifted sister, whose career is thwarted by every gender-based oppression of her era but who is finally doomed because of maternity: "She found herself with child . . . and so . . . killed herself one winter's night and lies buried at some cross-roads." Echoing (presumably male) economists Woolf advises women undergraduates to bear children "in twos and threes, not in tens and twelves." The reader is left to consider whether the works of Shakespeare might be written by a woman who has "borne and bred and washed and taught" three children "perhaps to the age of six or seven years," and whether no children at all might be a more prudent choice for a modern Judith Shakespeare.[22] Thus Woolf touches on many of the issues that will concern feminist thinking: the cost and the value of mothering in many senses—economic, psychological, political; the complexity of mother-daughter relations, and the distress or resentment that may arise when women recognize that mothers reproduce in their daughters their own oppression; the conflict between motherhood and career; restrictive sexual mores and patriarchal control of reproduction; the possibility that maternity might be an optional course of action rather than an expression of essential identity. In the years following Woolf's address to the "Fernham" undergraduates, feminists worked to remove barriers to women's economic and legal equality with men. As Woolf recognized, child-bearing had much to do with women's inferior status, and the 1970s saw an important milestone in this struggle when advances in medicine and changes in law (as mentioned earlier) granted women greater control of their reproductive capacities. In the wake of these newly won "immense privileges," as Woolf might have called them, the focus of feminist efforts shifted.

"Beginning in the late 1970s feminists looked beyond the economic, political and legal structures of society to the deeper levels of meaning production to explain and rectify the inferior status of women." A central element of this movement, Susan Hekman points out, "was the effort to analyse women's role in reproduction." For radical feminists it was not the biological fact that women have children that caused their subordination but rather the cultural construction of mothering and sexuality.[23] Contending solutions to this inequity ranged from refusal of motherhood (Shulamith Firestone) to calls for its reclamation and redefinition (Mary O'Brien, Adrienne Rich). Radical feminism's emphasis upon women's difference from men influenced a number of feminists who turned to psychology with interesting consequences for discussions of maternity. Theorists such as Dorothy Dinnerstein and Nancy Chodorow concluded that mothers raised boys and girls according to very different (socially constructed and policed) patterns; their ideas stimulated fresh debate concerning concepts and representations of motherhood. If the mother is the means whereby unequally valued gender differences are reproduced, is she not part of the technology of oppression? Do such theories reinscribe the mythic figure of the psychologically all-powerful mother? Are there disruptive ways to mother, especially given the increasing variety of family formations?

Theories grounded in the psychology of the individual and the mother-child dyad obscure the roles played by community both as nurturer of the young and as the (collective) body and identity to be reproduced. This crucial oversight has begun to be redressed by the path-breaking work of Patricia Hill Collins, who asserts the importance of mothering in reproducing threatened or marginalized communities and conceives mothering as a collective enterprise.

Hill Collins challenges Western feminist discourses that privilege individual autonomy and instead recognizes that individual survival, empowerment, and identity require group survival, empowerment, and identity. Critics building upon her work (see, for example, Haugo's essay in this issue), and playwrights such as Suzan-Lori Parks and Marie Clements, notably explore the politics of the communal dimension of maternity.

This highly selective account now reaches the point where Judith Butler's work definitively shaped the antiessentialist direction of Anglo-American feminist discourse. Her publication of *Gender Trouble* in 1990 established the dominance of postmodern feminism and the nonessential, performative, character of gender, of "woman." The influential work of French feminists such as Irigaray, Kristeva, and Cixous necessarily complicates the story. On the one hand, insofar as feminists from continental Europe participate in postmodernism's critique of dualistic discourse and the modern autonomous subject, their approach seems to accord with (and often anticipate) the antiessentialism of Anglo-American feminism in the 1980s and 1990s, which led away from the subject of the mother. Yet Cixous advocated writing with mother's milk; and it is not too much of a simplification to identify many influential European feminisms with feminism of difference. The question of how to negotiate the legacies of competing feminisms is raised by the history of earlier approaches to maternity as it is by Aston's call to return to the subject of motherhood in the wake of postmodernism.

Among the reactions against, and alternatives to, postmodern feminism are some that allow a return to the subject of maternity by loosening, but not abandoning, the antiessentialist stance. One such path is offered by feminist new materialists such as Elizabeth Grosz who shift the emphasis from linguistic constructs to the materiality of the body and to the interplay of technologies and practices, natural and built environments, that constitute women's realities. New materialist feminists ground arguments not in essential difference but in ontology reconceived as a matter of fluidity and interaction.[24] A second approach defined by recent feminist discussion is intersectionality, which attempts to take into account the myriad factors such as race, ethnicity, sexual orientation, class, and ableism that along with gender constitute a woman's identity. Both of these approaches suggest that maternity can return as a productive subject for feminism. New materialism gives the body a preeminent place in discussion, but in a theoretical move that precludes using the body to define a fixed essential identity. In some respects intersectionality, like new materialism, builds upon the insights of antiessentialism but loosens its stance by turning from the politics of undoing gender to the volatile project of exploring shifting interactions among multiple social and cultural factors.

Along with renewed interest in the work of psychologists such as Winnicott plus attention to the politics of motherwork in marginalized and racialized communities inspired by theorists like Hill Collins, these materialist and intersectional approaches show how present feminist discussion, informed but not limited by antiessentialism, can resume the subject of maternity. To this array of not incompatible practices and theoretical frameworks, one more might be added. Adriana Cavarero argues that the debate between difference feminism and antiessentialist feminism is a debate over "what" woman is, a stalemated contest between metaphysical positions. She proposes that feminists ask not "what" but "who" and that we attend in particular to "who" a woman is in relation to others in her life. Cavarero offers a distinctive example of how to achieve a "loosened" stance, after executing a nimble step to the side.[25]

Maternity is still poorly supported in privileged societies; debates about mothering initiated by second-wave feminists have not been resolved; and according to Badinter, motherhood is conceived in contradictory ways determined by socioeconomic forces, contradictions that divide women and thus threaten feminist politics. In short, "mother" is still a troubled and troubling term. The good news is that the recent history of feminist theory has made the subject more difficult—necessarily more entangled with bodies, technologies, communities, economies, genders, sexualities, racial and ethnic identities, and the interactions of all these. Recent feminisms have articulated evolving, loosened, ontologies suggesting that discussion of maternity can be deliberately contingent and contextual. The essays presented here respond to this opening with flexible methods informed by current feminist debates and adapted to the particularities of the plays examined and their circumstances.

Maternity in Drama

Scholarship such as Marianne Hirsch's influential *The Mother/Daughter Plot: Narrative, Psychoanalysis, Feminism*[26] and research fostered by organizations like the Motherhood in Post-1968 European Literature Network (Institute of Modern Languages Research, University of London) suggest that scholars have begun to investigate contemporary literary representations of maternity, particularly in European literatures, and to acknowledge the need to listen attentively for the voices of mothers, which continue to be scarce.[27] However, comparatively little of this work has been devoted to drama; theatre scholarship still needs to heed Aston's call to "come back to the mother" as a feminist subject. One might answer the question "why maternity in drama?" by pointing to characteristics of the genre: the medium of representation, the performer's body, allows for complex interrogations of concepts of maternity, which are so often entangled with philosophical and political debates about what constitutes our embodied human existence. For example, scholars such as Nicole Loraux and Janet Adelman, who, respectively, study maternity in ancient Greek and Renaissance drama, have disclosed deep-seated societal tensions and fundamental cultural matrices.[28] Further, the dialogic structure of the dramatic text as well as the interplay of actor with actor, and players with audience, suggest that drama provides a stage where playwrights and critics can take up Cavarero's invitation to see who mothers are, and in relation to whom—to ask not "what is Mother?" but "who is this mother?"

At the end of the nineteenth century, and through the first half of the twentieth century, playwrights deployed (or combated) what might be thought of as a conventional rhetoric of the maternal, a rhetoric in which mothers tended to be identified with altruism, conventional pieties, conformity, control, biological necessity, materialism, and the limitations of material existence itself.[29] Henrik Ibsen's Nora affronted audiences chiefly because she refuses to sacrifice her own self-development and instead walks away from her family; a prominent German actress of the day as well as theatres in Hamburg and Vienna famously required a revised ending that allows Nora to stay for the sake of the children.[30] Elizabeth Robins, in her suffrage drama *Votes for Women* (1907), gave an interesting twist to arguments that women could be trusted with the franchise because of their maternal commitment to stability and continuity, and deserved it because of their service as mothers in reproducing the existing social order. The play's heroine gives birth in secret to an illegitimate babe who lives just a few hours. This lost maternity seemingly drives her campaign for women's rights: the plot tacitly implies that greater access to participation in the public sphere might arm women against the exploitation she suffered. More mystically, her sacrificed maternity appears to be a source of inner strength, as if the loss of motherhood is so great it has steeled her against other, necessarily lesser, trials.

Synge's *Riders to the Sea* (1904) and Sean O'Casey's *Juno and the Paycock* (1924) must be mentioned in even the briefest survey of maternal piety, suffering, and power in early twentieth-century theatre; the essays by Douglas and Maresh speak to the political and cultural legacy of such maternal figures in contemporary Irish drama. If these landmarks of dramatized maternity explore the subtler complications of supposed maternal altruism,[31] Sidney Howard's *Silver Cord* (1926), a sensational hit written at a time of enthusiasm for Freudianism, emphasizes an extreme, negative version of maternal service to social stability and presents mother as a nightmarish embodiment of control and sexual repression. The protagonist brings his new bride home to mother, only to have mother literally interpose herself between husband and wife (she assigns the bride a distant room and her son a bedroom that communicates with her own), exploit her economic leverage, and figuratively strangle her son with a silver (umbilical) cord.

With two of the dominant playwrights of the midcentury, Tennessee Williams and Eugene O'Neill, mothers are creatures of great, even frightening, power, still linked to maternal ideals of self-sacrifice, piety, and social conformity: Amanda in Williams's *The Glass Menagerie* (1944) and Mary Tyrone in O'Neill's *Long Day's Journey into Night* (written 1941; produced 1956). Both playwrights also evoke sexuality and reproduction as disturbingly primitive forces when figured in maternal characters such as Stella (Williams, *A Streetcar Named Desire* 1947) and Josie Hogan (O'Neill, *A Moon for the Misbegotten* 1947). Despite the complexity of such characters, it might be argued that they are nonetheless depicted from a limited, masculine perspective insofar as maternity is perceived as other—the antithesis of the narrator Tom, as he sees himself in *Glass Menagerie*, for example; mysterious and chthonic to the protagonist James Tyrone in *A Moon for the Misbegotten*. Maternity as "other" finds its epitome in Harold Pinter's *The Homecoming* (1964), wherein Ruth takes the place of the dead mother in an all-male family and the play concludes with her enigmatically enthroned at the nexus of the men's desires for power, sex, and food.

These landmark plays roughly chart the theatrical terrain up until the 1970s, but what of subsequent plays that might be informed by the vigorous feminist debates about maternity? A series of interviews with women playwrights active in the late twentieth century conducted in the 1980s by Kathleen Betsko and Rachel Koenig presents considerable evidence that, during the early years of second-wave feminism, mother-daughter relationships in particular were too difficult for these playwrights to address immediately in their work. The problematic role of mothering within patriarchy was too recently articulated, the ensuing debate as yet too intense. Betsko, herself a dramatist, declares that mother-daughter dynamics are "the last, dark continent to be explored in dramatic material. . . . The love, savagery, and ambivalence between mothers and daughters is largely unexamined in theater."[32] Several of those interviewed (Ntozake Shange, Marsha Norman, Susan Yakowitz, Emily Mann, Tina Howe, Adrienne Kennedy, Gretchen Cryer, Anne Commire) are asked to comment on the topic, and the resulting informal survey shows that, with the notable exception of Norman (whose remarkable *'night, Mother* inspired Jill Dolan's equally insightful analysis of its gendered spectatorship),[33] many shared the feelings expressed by Shange:

> INTERVIEWER: Why do some women have a hands-off attitude toward presenting their own mothers in their work?
> SHANGE: What Adrienne Rich says in *Of Woman Born* is true: It is difficult to embrace the very female who taught you to be an oppressed person. I think it's going to take a long time for us to learn how to do that. Luckily, I've been able to start—but I, too, had a very "hands-off" attitude toward my mother for years. Its just since I've been able to start writing mother characters in the novel that I came to see the beauties in her and could transmit them to my audience.[34]

If the contemporary female playwrights interviewed by Betsko and Koenig found the mother-daughter bond too difficult at a time when the debates about motherhood ignited by second-wave feminists such as Rich were new, this bond (as envisaged by women) has now moved onto the stage in plays analyzed in our volume by Maresh, Douglas, Justice-Malloy, and Haugo. From the later decades of the twentieth century through to the teens of the twenty-first, playwrights both male and female have turned to the subject of motherhood with new freedom, and the result has been a variety of distinctive dramas that grapple afresh with maternity as concept and experience. Admittedly, it has not always been easy for plays on this subject to find a stage or an audience. Tina Howe's experience in this regard is instructive. "I plunged into *Birth and After Birth* in 1970," she writes, "eager to explore the wonder and terror of motherhood." "Three years later I emerged with an opéra bouffe in which couples spar over their fertility, a false birth is reenacted onstage and a large hairy man plays a four-year-old. Needless to say, every self-respecting theatre in the country turned it down. The Absurdists can shake up our preconceptions about power and identity, but for a woman to take on the sanctity of motherhood . . . even my agent at the time dismissed me."[35] Nonetheless, an encouraging number of plays have found their way onto the stage and into print.

The New York productions of plays by Orlandersmith (2015), Treem (2014), and Skinner (2014) are heartening indications of a receptive audience.[36] In addition to the plays discussed in this issue, a quick survey of contemporary dramas centrally concerned with maternity discovers plays addressing the class-inflected conflict between motherhood and career (Caryl Churchill's *Top Girls*, 1982, Wendy Wasserstein's *The Heidi Chronicles*, 1988); the entanglement of maternity, muse, and creativity (Wendy Lill's *Memories of You*, 1989; Michel Tremblay's *For the Pleasure of Seeing Her Again*, 1998); infertility, transnational adoption, and unwed motherhood (Timberlake Wertenbaker's *Break of Day*, 1995); the politics of reproduction in marginalized communities (Marie Clements, *Tombs of the Vanishing Indian*, 2012; Suzan-Lori Parks, *The Red Letter Plays*,

1998, 2000); a mother's death and its aftermath (Daniel MacIvor, *Marion Bridge*, 2006); mothering as the work of three generations and more (much of Marcie Rendon's theatre); mortal combat between mother and daughter (Martin McDonagh, *The Beauty Queen of Leenane*, 1996); childbirth and US medical practices (Karen Brody, *Birth*, 2008); mothering as struggle against the death wish (Marsha Norman, *'night Mother*, 1983); the ethics of caregiving and the politics of international conflict (Caryl Churchill, *Seven Jewish Children*, 2009; Lynn Nottage, *Ruined*, 2008); queer critique of maternal mythology (Maureen Angelos, Dominique Dibbell, Peg Healey, and Lisa Kron, *Oedipus at Palm Springs*, 2010); race, economics, and mother-substitutes (Tony Kushner [book and lyrics] and Jeanine Tesori [music], *Caroline, or Change*, 2003); and the benign rule of an immigrant matriarch (Quiara Algería Hudes [book] and Lin-Manuel Miranda [lyrics], *In the Heights*, 2008). These examples, limited as they are, suggest a context for the analyses included here; each of the plays discussed in this issue is part of a wider, ongoing, dramatic exploration of contemporary mothering. Recalling the complaint of Tina Howe, and Jill Dolan's diagnosis of a theatre in which women's stories still make token appearances, it has to be said that such dramatic explorations of maternity do not constitute a movement, an upsurge of hot tickets. Rather, they are pieces of a persistent, urgent, often-interrupted conversation, a conversation this special section of essays aims to make more audible and interconnected. In the essays that follow, we look to dramatic work from the later decades of the twentieth century and the beginning of the twenty-first for new understandings of motherhood as a collective, malleable enterprise subject to shifting cultural, economic, and political pressures, and often idealized in contradictory ways; for analyses of mother-child relations that take into account community and intersecting identities; for concepts of maternity affected by new medical technologies; for emerging maternities produced by reconfigured families and newly empowered genders and sexualities. We present new opportunities for apprehending who mothers are. We ask how maternities are being reconceived.

Maternities, Rethinking

Arden Thomas's essay in this volume confronts an old association between Mother and Nature deployed in the cause of environmental justice. Examining two plays from the early 1990s—José Rivera's *Marisol* (1993) and Cherríe

Moraga's *Heroes and Saints* (1992)—Thomas demonstrates that both Mother and Earth have been reimagined. In "Making a Spectacle: Motherhood in Contemporary British Theatre and Performance," Jozefina Komporaly addresses the issue of maternal agency. She argues that motherhood plays a significant role in the performance of power, discussing, for example, theatrical explorations of medical imaging of the pregnant body. Innovatively combining the theories of Judith Butler and Bracha Ettinger, Komporaly analyzes *Glass Body: Reflecting on Becoming Transparent* (2006) and *My Glass Body* (2007), by Anna Furse; *Once We Were Mothers* (2004), by Lisa Evans; and *Colder than Here* (2005), by Laura Wade. The essays by Karin Maresh and Jenny Douglas are devoted to the work of Marina Carr, one of the most prominent playwrights currently working in Ireland. Troubled maternity in Carr's acclaimed midlands trilogy is the focus of Maresh's "Un/Natural Motherhood in Marina Carr's *The Mai, Portia Coughlan*, and *By the Bog of Cats* . . ." Maresh situates this difficult material (maternal neglect, child abandonment, filicide and maternal suicide) in the context of traditional Irish idealization of maternity and construction of women as "naturally" maternal; she demonstrates how Carr opens space for aspects of maternity silenced and excluded by such constructs. In "Flying Babies and Pregnant Men: Staging Motherhood in Marina Carr's *Low in the Dark*," Douglas highlights Carr's first major play (1989), a brilliantly funny piece indebted to Beckett. Carr's absurdist strategy, Douglas argues, disrupts traditional assumptions that maternity is essential to womanhood and sexuality unnatural to motherhood. The psychological burdens of maternal presence, and the trauma marked by maternal absence, are the focus of essays by Rhona Justice-Malloy and Margaret Savilonis. Their essays interrogate the mother-child bond in ways that revise familiar psychological readings of identity-formation and demonstrate that the psychological difficulty of this bond must be understood in relation to maternity's position outside current power structures. Resisting the popular notion that daughters need to separate from their mothers to achieve an authentic identity, Rhona Justice-Malloy asks us to consider the notion of "daughtering" as a needed complement to the overburdened concept of "mothering." In her essay "Mothers, Daughters, Identity, and Impossibilities" Justice-Malloy draws on the work of Suzanna Danuta Walters to emphasize the active role of daughters seeking attention, affection, and answers in two contemporary American plays: *Memory House* (2005), by Kathleen Tolan, and *Well* (2007), by Lisa Kron. No mothers appear in the plays discussed by Margaret Savilonis in "'She Was Always Sad': Remembering Mother in Caryl Churchill's *Not Enough Oxygen* and *A Number*." Savilonis argues that the physical absence of mothers who feature instead in the stories of husbands and sons enacts their dehumanization via myth and memory and exposes their exclusion from power. By leaving maternal bodies offstage, Savilonis concludes, Churchill points to a gap in societal structures that needs to be filled. Jennifer Worth's essay examines the fascinating perversity of mothers as represented in the American musical. Engaging with D. A. Miller's queer theorization of "the Star Mother," Worth focuses on *Gypsy* (1959) and *Grey Gardens* (2006): musicals in which monstrous mothers compete with daughters for stardom. The conventions of musical theatre, she argues, marginalize and pathologize mothers (and by extension, all women) for merely attempting to carve out an identity for themselves. The final essay in this special section underscores the collaborative character of mothering and the importance of this work to the sustenance of communities, especially those of historically oppressed populations. Ann Haugo's essay "Decolonizing Motherhood: Images of Mothering in First Nations Theatre" argues that mothering is profoundly political for the colonized indigenous peoples of North America. Using the term "motherwork" coined by Hill Collins to theorize the reproductive labor of racialized minorities, Haugo touches on the work of Spiderwoman Theatre and Vera Manuel and explores in depth Marie Clements's *Unnatural and Accidental Women* (first produced 2000, published 2005). Haugo demonstrates the necessity of asking how theatre and performance by Native women engages with colonial narratives about mothering and illuminates the political significance of Clements's representation of mothers as archetypal figures of strength within community.

Considered together, the essays in this special section demonstrate the rewarding and wide-ranging conversations that result as contemporary theatre scholars take up the difficult subject of motherhood. The essays were born at a workshop generously sponsored by Mount Allison University and were fostered by discussion with Marcie Rendon, L. Bailey McDaniel, Christopher Mitchell, Sara Warner, and especially Sara Freeman. We trust the omissions and oversights inevitable in a small group of essays will spur readers to pursue in other plays by other playwrights the many further possibilities for reconceiving maternity.

Notes

1. Hilton Als, "I Remember Mama: Dael Orlandersmith's memory play," *New Yorker*, May 25, 2015, 74–75.

2. "motherhood, n. and adj.," *OED Online*, Oxford University Press, accessed September 5, 2015, http://www.oed.com.ezproxy.library.uvic.ca/view/Entry/122655?redirectedFrom=motherhood.
3. Amnesty International, "Deadly Delivery: The Maternal Health Care Crisis in the USA," March 12, 2010, and "Deadly Delivery: The Maternal Health Care Crisis in the U.S.A. One Year Update, Spring 2011," Amnesty International Secretariat, accessed September 2015, http://www.amnestyusa.org/research/reports/deadly-delivery-the-international-maternal-health-care-crisis-in-the-usa; Hogan, Foreman, Naghavi, Ahn, Wang, Makela, Lopez, Lozano, Murray, "Maternal Mortality for 181 Countries, 1980–2008: A Systematic Analysis of Progress Towards Millennium Development Goal 5," the *Lancet* 375 (May 8–14, 2010): 1609–23. http://www.journals.elsevier.com/the-lancet (accessed September 2015).
4. Kira Cochrane, "You're Fired," the *Guardian*, April 23, 2008, http://www.theguardian.com/money/2008/apr/23/worklifebalance.discriminationatwork (accessed September 5, 2015).
5. Claire Cain Miller, "Can Family Leave Policies Be Too Generous? It Seems So," The Upshot, *New York Times*, August 9, 2014. http://www.nytimes.com/2014/08/10/upshot/can-family-leave-policies-be-too-generous-it-seems-so.html?_rso (accessed June 2, 2015).
6. Elisabeth Badinter, *Le conflit: la femme et la mère* (Paris: Éditions Flammarion, 2010), 31–35.
7. Steve Doughty, "Number of British Muslims will double to 5.5m in 20 years," Mail Online, *Daily Mail*, updated January 28, 2011. http://www.dailymail.co.uk/news/article-1351251/Number-British-Muslims-double-5-5m-20-years.html (accessed July 10, 2014).
8. Gretchen Livingston and D'Vera Cohn, "The New Demography of American Motherhood," Pew Research Center, May 6, 2010. http://www.pewsocialtrends.org/2010/05/06/the-new-demography-of-american-motherhood (accessed September 5, 2015); Livingston and Cohn, "Share of Births to Unmarried Women Dips, Reversing a Long Trend," Pew Research Center, June 17, 2015. http://www.pewresearch.org/fact-tank/2015/06/17/share-of-births-to-unmarried-women-dips-reversing-a-long-trend/ (accessed September 5, 2015); Jacqueline Rose, "Mothers," *London Review of Books*, June 19, 2014, 17–22; Gretchen Livingston, "Less Than Half of US Kids Today Live in a 'Traditional' Family," *Pew Research Center*, December 22, 2014. http://www.pewresearch.org/fact-tank/2014/12/22/less-than-half-of-u-s-kids-today-live-in-a-traditional-family/ (accessed September 5, 2015).
9. Frances Perraudin, "When Will Abortion Become Legal in Northern Ireland?" *New Statesman*, September 28, 2013. http://www.newstatesman.com/uk-politics/2013/09/when-will-abortion-become-legal-women-northern-ireland (accessed June 25, 2014).
10. Rebecca Cafe, "How the Contraceptive Pill Changed Britain," BBC News, December 4, 2011. http://www.bbc.com/news/uk-15984258 (accessed June 25, 2014).
11. Lynne Van Luven, ed., *Nobody's Mother: Life Without Kids* (Victoria, BC: TouchWood Editions, 2006).
12. Susan Maushart, *The Masks of Motherhood* (New York: New Press, 1999); Sharon Hays, *The Cultural Contradictions of Motherhood* (New Haven: Yale University Press, 1996).
13. Rose, "Mothers," 17.

14. Kim Tingley, "One Child, Three Parents," *New York Times Magazine*, June 29, 2014, 26–31, 38, 49; Tamar Lewin, "Coming to U.S. for Baby, and Womb to Carry It," *New York Times*, July 6, 2014, 1, 12–13.
15. Lewin, "Coming to U.S. for Baby," 1, 12.
16. Peggy Phelan, *Unmarked: The Politics of Performance* (New York & London: Routledge, 1993), 130–45.
17. Alexis Soloski, "Sex, Violence and Power, With a Feminist Slant," *New York Times*, June 12, 2014. http://www.nytimes.com/2014/06/15/theater/sex-violence-and-power-with-a-feminist-slant.html (accessed June 15, 2014).
18. Quoted by Soloski, "Sex, Violence and Power, With a Feminist Slant."
19. Elaine Aston, "A Critical Step to the Side: Performing the Loss of the Mother," *Theatre Research International* 32, no. 2 (2007): 130–42.
20. Rose, "Mothers."
21. The chronology and focus of Anglo-American feminist scholarship differs from that of European feminist scholarship; Nicole Loraux's influential discussion of ancient Greek motherhood, *Mothers in Mourning* (1990; trans. 1998) belongs to a later generation of scholarship than Rich's *Of Woman Born* (1976). It should be noted, then, that in order to sketch the chronological background to Aston's call for a return to motherhood as a subject of feminist study, one must temporarily set aside the story of European adherents to feminism of difference, as well as many classical scholars both in the United Kingdom and in North America, feminists who never turned away from the subject.
22. Virginia Woolf, *A Room of One's Own* (Orlando: Harcourt, 2005), 21, 48, 111.
23. Susan Hekman, "Feminism," in *The Routledge Companion to Critical and Cultural Theory*, 2nd ed., ed. Simon Malpas and Paul Wake (London and New York: Routledge, 2013), 97, 98.
24. Diana Coole and Samantha Frost, "Introducing the New Materialisms," in *New Materialisms: Ontology, Agency, and Politics*, ed. Diana Coole and Samantha Frost (Durham: Duke University Press, 2010), 8.
25. See Adriana Cavarero, "*Who* Engenders Politics?" in *Italian Feminist Theory and Practice: Equality and Sexual Difference*, ed. Graziella Parati and Rebecca West (Cranbury, NJ, and London: Associated University Presses, 2002), 88–103; and Cavarero, *Relating Narratives: Storytelling and Selfhood*, trans. Paul Kottman (London and New York: Routledge, 2000).
26. Marianne Hirsch, *The Mother/Daughter Plot: Narrative, Psychoanalysis, Feminism* (Bloomington and Indianapolis: Indiana University Press, 1989).
27. Marina Bettaglio argues that although mother's voices are still relatively rare in literature, a growing number of women are communicating their experiences of motherhood via social media and the popular press, in formats ranging from blogs to diaries, comics, and so-called mommy memoirs. These popular gestational and maternal writings, Bettaglio's analysis shows, are commodified as they participate in the neoliberal market economy and enmeshed in the contradictions of postfeminism, often reinforcing the myths of maternity they purport to dismantle. See Marina Bettaglio, "(Post)Feminist Chronicles and Their Discontents," *Letras Femeninas* 41, no. 1 (2015): 228–45.
28. Nicole Loraux, *Mothers in Mourning*, trans. Corinne Pache (Ithaca: Cornell University

Press, 1998); Janet Adelman, *Suffocating Mothers: Fantasies of Maternal Origin in Shakespeare's Plays,* Hamlet *to* The Tempest (New York: Routledge, 1992).

29. Ann Douglas argues that American literary modernism defined itself in reaction against a "feminized" nineteenth-century culture; see *The Feminization of American Culture* (New York: Knopf, 1977) and *Terrible Honesty: Mongrel Manhattan in the 1920s* (New York: Farrar, Straus, and Giroux, 1995). Douglas's analysis of this perceived cultural "feminine" aligns it with what I have called the conventional rhetoric of maternity—an idealization of the maternal that readily lends itself to demonization as the epitome of oppressive moral, social, and aesthetic timidity.
30. Henrik Ibsen, "The Alternative 'German' Ending [to *A Doll's House*]," in *Four Major Plays,* trans. James McFarlane and Jens Arup (Oxford: Oxford University Press, 1981), 87–88.
31. There are also works from the early years of modern drama that develop characters who flout conventional maternal idealization even as they demonstrate its power: consider the shocking self-absorption of Arkadina in Chekhov's *The Seagull* (1896), who refuses to respond to her son's needs. And one must not forget Sophie Treadwell's extraordinary *Machinal* (1928) in which maternity, like every other aspect of the protagonist's life, is an excruciating imposition of gendered social norms and behaviors so extrinsic to her being as to be experienced as machinery.
32. Kathleen Betsko and Rachel Koenig, eds., *Interviews with Contemporary Women Playwrights* (New York: Beech Tree Books, 1987), 50.
33. Jill Dolan, *The Feminist Spectator as Critic* (Ann Arbor: University of Michigan Press, 1988).
34. Betsko and Koenig, *Interviews,* 375.
35. Tina Howe, introduction to *Approaching Zanzibar and Other Plays* (New York: Theatre Communications Group, 1995), ix–x.
36. See Soloski, "Sex, Violence, and Power."

Poisoning the Mother/Land

An Ecofeminist Dramaturgy in José Rivera's *Marisol* and Cherríe Moraga's *Heroes and Saints*

—ARDEN ELIZABETH THOMAS

In *Marisol* (1993) and *Heroes and Saints* (1992), the images that José Rivera and Cherríe Moraga contend with are of the poisoned earth and poisoned bodies, of deformed infants and bodiless heads, of a man giving birth and babies buried under concrete, of children crucified and the incarnation of la Virgen de Guadalupe, of Mother Earth as womb and tomb, of children and mothers and the earth screaming, burning, dying, yet refusing erasure and silence. When the title character in *Marisol* demands to know, "Why is there a war on children in this city? Why are apples extinct? Why are they planning to drop human insecticide on overpopulated areas of the Bronx? Why do cows give salty milk? Where did the moon go? How come nobody's seen it in nearly nine months?" Rivera leads us through a series of questions that conflate images of ecological apocalypse with recurring images of maternity and childbirth. And when Moraga's main character, Cerezita—a young woman born with only a head due to the toxic wastes infecting the land—takes on the ancestral images of the Virgin Mary and la Virgen de Guadalupe, she reclaims ancestral mothers and Mother Earth toward a conglomerate and powerful vision of a sustainable politics.

This essay reads the plays *Marisol* and *Heroes and Saints* through the lens of ecofeminist philosophy to see how the theatre might intervene on behalf of issues of environmental justice and ecological sustainability. Paying particular attention to the material conditions of women, children, and the land and interrelated issues of environmental destruction, race, and poverty, I examine how Rivera and Moraga incorporate metaphoric images of motherhood with concrete evidence of environmental toxins and policies experienced in the body. Ultimately, the playwrights articulate the material, physical consequences of political and ecological actions, calling for changed perceptions that empower individuals to work to transform communal, social, and even global ideologies of power that contribute to the destruction of the environment and the lives of women and children.[1]

With today's increasing anxiety about climate change and ecological disasters, it is particularly instructive to look at these two plays from the early 1990s that bring together interrelated issues of motherhood, environmental destruction, race, and poverty. As testaments to their contemporaneity, both plays are today often taught in college theatre classes and regularly revived on college campuses and in theatre companies across the country. Nearly two decades after their premieres, *Marisol* and *Heroes and Saints* continue to hold powerful resonances for current conversations about the material relationship between bodies and the detritus of environmental waste; about the damaging effects of globalization on the land and the community, and in the lives of mothers and children; and about the symbolic and linguistic analogies between woman and nature that foster systems of domination. By using an ecofeminist dramaturgy—a relatively recent theoretical model that examines dramatic playtexts or stagings through the lens of ecological feminist criticism—this essay offers new readings of these important plays. I argue that *Marisol* and *Heroes and Saints* reveal in concrete detail how policies that continue to be promoted by government and corporations against urban families and rural farming communities impoverish the planet and its peoples, with women and children as their primary victims. Additionally, this essay examines how these plays interrogate what Sheila Rabillard and Karen Bamford discuss in their introduction to this special edition of *Theatre History Studies* as motherhood's unstable cultural meaning in modern Western society. In particular, if *Marisol* and *Heroes and Saints* expose worlds of ecological destruction through metaphoric images of the maternal, this essay questions whether the plays go beyond Mother Earth as metaphor or essentializing myth, drawing on these archetypical precedents to foster an ecofeminist revision of such essentialism, or whether they are instead trapped by these culturally prevalent images.

It may be useful to define ecofeminism at this point. The term *ecofeminisme* was coined by French feminist Françoise d'Eaubonne in 1974 as a tool to assess interconnections between women's oppression and ecological crisis, or what Karen Warren calls the "twin and interconnected dominations of women and nature."[2] Ecofeminism has activist roots in antinuclear, antiwar, environmental, animal liberation, lesbian-feminist, women's health care, and labor movements and has emerged in the fields of philosophy, sociology, literature, and religious studies. Ecofeminism is a political intervention that connects ecological, feminist, and sociopolitical concerns; analyzes the effects of capitalist accumulation on women and the environment; and examines the critical links between sexism, classism, militarism, racism, and environmental destruction.

Clearly, ecofeminism consists of many different strains of thought and philosophy. In *Staying Alive: Women, Ecology and Development*, Vandana Shiva argues that environmental problems disproportionately affect women in most parts of the world where women are the primary caregivers who provide fuel, food, and water for their families and face increased burdens resulting from environmental deterioration.[3] For Shiva, male-dominated destruction within the global capitalist market system has destroyed ways of life in which women care for their families in often more sustainable ways. Further, she argues, Western science and technology have destroyed biological diversity and caused catastrophic ecological damage, impacting women and children with disastrous results. Similarly, ecofeminists like Ynestra King, Carolyn Merchant, and Rosemary Radford Ruether posit women's relation to the environment as socially constructed, putting less stress on the "naturalness" of women's identification with the environment and more on the structural and material relations of women to nature. In her introduction to *Women Healing the Earth*, Ruether writes, "We must recognize the ways in which the devastation of the earth is an integral part of an appropriation of the goods of the earth whereby a wealthy minority can enjoy strawberries in winter, while those who pick and pack the strawberries lack the money for bread and are dying from pesticide poisonings."[4]

Another area of ecofeminist thought that is particularly apt for this discussion is the argument that the ecological destructiveness of globalization and the oppression of women in modernity are results of dualist thinking and a logic of domination that rationalizes classism, sexism, racism, and environmental destruction. Two leading ecofeminist philosophers, Val Plumwood and Karen Warren, emphasize the problematic consequences of modernity's dualistic, hierarchical thinking that splits mind/body, culture/nature, reason/emotion, male/female. In these hierarchical relationships, women and nature are thrown into contingent relationships wherein "the dominant side is taken as primary [and] the subordinated side is defined in relation to it," the effect being to make domination appear to be inevitable or "natural." An ecofeminist philosophy breaks away from this logic of domination by creating counter conceptions of this mind/body dualism, attempting to achieve "non-hierarchal difference," and "recognizing continuity and reclaiming the ground of overlap between nature, the body and the human."[5]

Reading the plays *Marisol* and *Heroes and Saints* through this paradigm, however, draws attention to the fact that this strand of ecofeminism may not go far enough in destabilizing the relatively static nature of this mind/body dualism. As Catriona Sandilands argues in *The Good-Natured Feminist: Ecofeminism and the Quest for Democracy*, "What is necessary is a more thoroughly transgressive politics, one that shows the wielding of woman and nature as part of systems of domination, that shows dualism to be an oppressive fiction rather than a fact of nature itself."[6] By reading *Marisol* and *Heroes and Saints* through an ecofeminist dramaturgy, we can see that Rivera's and Moraga's imagistic texts and surreal staging spark a provocative challenge to the very idea of male/female, mind/body, and culture/nature as stable or coherent dualities. For example, when a man gives birth onstage in *Marisol* and a woman who is a head with no body stages an alternative motherhood in *Heroes and Saints*, the plays reveal notions of "mother" and "Mother Nature" as contingent and socially constructed, producing a transgressive politics that challenges the Eurocentric narrative of dualism. In this politics, these plays imagine the possibilities of a sustainable world that relies on the denial of such dualities as a means to suture cultural splits that have, in effect, ruptured human relationships to the earth.

Marisol opens onto a dystopian version of New York City in which ecological, social, and economic forces have imploded, creating an urban wasteland reeling from toxic poisoning, indebtedness, and violent crimes. One of the more uncomfortable elements of the play is that, though written twenty years ago, it feels disturbingly relevant to today's economic and environmental crises. Rumor has it that the "huge ugly windowless building with the smokestacks and armed guards" is a "federally funded torture center where they violate people who have gone over their credit card limit," and when the smoke from massive fires reaches New York City one character says she can smell "the defaulted loans . . . the unemployment."[7] Natural resources have disappeared or run amok: rainwater burns the skin, apples and coffee are extinct, forests are burning down, and the moon has disappeared (possibly, as one radio announcer says, to the orbit of Saturn). Throughout the city, Nazi skinheads set fire to homeless people while angels carrying Uzi submachine guns have declared war on God. Indebtedness, homelessness, unemployment, climate change, the degradation of natural resources: The world of the play "performs" the world of today. The ecological apocalypse of the play, then, is much more than a metaphorical representation of economic crisis. Rather, ecological disaster is a material consequence of tragic mistakes made in the name of economic progress.

The surreal, bizarre images of the play serve to highlight the egregiousness of materialism in a capitalist economy whose greatest product is waste, impoverishment, and a distorted, destroyed landscape.

In his review for the original production of *Marisol* in New York City, Frank Rich describes the set as a "heavy, graffiti-covered scenic environment" with a "curtain on which is emblazoned the message 'Wake up!'"[8] The play seamlessly combines gritty realistic elements with striking surrealism so that we are not surprised when Marisol, a young, professional Puerto Rican woman working in Manhattan and living in the Bronx, receives a visitation from her guardian Angel, "a young black woman in ripped jeans, sneakers, and black T-shirt. Crude silver wings hang limply from the back of the Angel's diamond-studded black leather jacket. She looks like an urban warrior, a burnt-out soldier of some lost cause."[9] The angel recollects another angel who appeared onstage, in Tony Kushner's *Angels in America* (1992)—arriving, as the character Harper notes, through the hole in the ozone layer. The angel in *Marisol*, however, presides over a planet that has deteriorated to the point of environmental apocalypse. In the first act Marisol's angel saves her from a fatal encounter with a homeless person, but in the second act, as Marisol tries to find her way through desecrated, nightmarish city streets, the angel has abandoned her to take up arms in a revolution against God, and Marisol must join forces with other similarly alienated street wanderers against neo-Nazi skinheads and the poisoned planet.

Most reviewers have argued that the play stages the plight of homeless people during the 1980s, or that it represents the violence and social upheaval in Los Angeles, which erupted in the riots of 1992. Frank Rich, of the *New York Times*, writes, "What is his war-torn New York if not the future he has already seen in his hometown of L.A.?" In a 2007 article J. Chris Westgate argues that *Marisol*'s "concern with the plight of the homeless suggests a rejection of municipal efforts during the 1980s . . . to criminalize those living on New York City's streets." Rivera himself discussed the play in relation to the urban homeless problems of the 1980s when he said in an interview, "There are walking nightmares out there that have to be dealt with—people who need help."[10] Appropriately, as Westgate notes, a character in his play threatens, "Homelessness is against the law in this city! I'm going to have you two arrested!"[11] Surely these are important concerns raised and examined by the play. But what this essay is most interested in are the ways in which the play shows an environmental crisis interwoven with maternal images out of their "natural" order as a direct result of market forces and social policies. The play reveals how devastation resulting from policies promoted by capitalist institutions and globalization includes ecological ruin, urban deterioration, increased social violence, and damaging conditions for women and children. In particular, I am interested in the ways in which the play poetically represents these socioecological issues by highlighting an environmental crisis interwoven with maternal images out of their "natural" order. In *Marisol*'s world, disruptive, "unnatural" images such as the disappearance of the moon (a feminine symbol) or a man's pregnancy and stillbirth represent an unnatural dislocation and the wasted, deadening landscape of a futuristic civilization debilitated by an environmental apocalypse.

In her article "*Fen* and the Production of a Feminist Ecotheater," Sheila Rabillard defines an ecofeminist theatre practice as that which works "to expose the cracks in the apparently seamless, and distinctly gendered, ideological structures governing our relationship to the environment." Using Shiva's work as a paradigm to discuss Caryl Churchill's engagement with ecological and socialist-feminist concerns, Rabillard argues that in *Fen*, the "sequence of 21 scenes offers a series of images that associate exploited land with oppressed women workers." Like Rabillard, Elaine Aston also examines Churchill's work in light of ecological feminist concerns. Aston writes that Churchill "introduces gender concerns into matters of ownership and ecology" and that Churchill's "'ideas of nature' bring materialism, ecology and feminism together."[12] In many of her plays, Churchill's work echoes the concerns of ecological feminists, who interrogate scientific, cultural, and historical shifts that celebrate commercial and industrial expansion, sanction the exploitation of nature, and perpetuate the subordination of women.

Unlike Churchill, however, José Rivera does not seem to be deliberately engaging in an ecofeminist theatre practice. What the play does do, as Una Chaudhuri critiques, is to create "an underlying and dystopic ecological condition," a condition that acts as a metaphor for the literal trashing of America and for persistent social concerns.[13] At some level I might wish for a more sustained engagement with the ecological destruction that pervades the world of the play, so that it is not open to a reading of the ecological destruction as mere background, metaphor, or "condition." For example, when Marisol interrogates the angel about the ecological destruction she sees all around her, the angel avoids challenging Marisol to consider the consequences of a human-made environmental apocalypse. Instead, she responds, "Because God is old and dying and taking the rest of us with him." So the angels decide to "stop the universal ruin" by declaring war on "our senile God" in the hopes that "when we do win . . . when we crown the new God, and begin the new millennium . . . the earth will be restored. The moon will return. The degradation of the animal kingdom will end."[14] Perhaps, however, it is in the very absurdity of this response that we are to find whatever message the play may wittily suggest about the devastation of the planet; in other words, human responsibility for the ecological crises is evoked by its noted absence.

But I am even more curious about what an ecofeminist *reading* of the play can reveal, even though the play itself does not overtly engage with activist ecological, and certainly not ecofeminist, concerns. For example, when the Angel visits Marisol one night in her cockroach-ridden apartment, she observes Marisol sleeping and begins to influence Marisol's body and dreams. Moving closer to Marisol, the angel causes her to feel heat, breathe faster, taste salt in her mouth, smell the ocean, and have an orgasm. Talking and laughing in her sleep and feeling "a wild energy" running through her body, Marisol touches her stomach "as she gets a wild, exhilarating idea." Marisol says, "*Am I pregnant with the Lord's baby*?! Is the new Messiah swimming in my electrified womb? Is the supersperm of God growing a mythic flower deep in the secret greenhouse inside me? Will my morning sickness taste like communion wine? This is amazing—*billions* of women on earth, and I get knocked up by God!" When she learns she is not pregnant, Marisol's questioning switches from motherhood and her own pregnancy to a concern for "Mother Earth," children, and the nine-month absence of the moon: "What's going *on* here, anyway? Why is there a war on children in this city? Why are apples extinct? Why are they planning to drop human insecticide on overpopulated areas of the Bronx? Why has the color blue disappeared from the sky? Why does common rainwater turn our skin bright red? Why do cows give salty milk? Why did the Plague kill half my friends? AND WHAT HAPPENED TO THE MOON? Where did the moon go? How come nobody's seen it in nearly *nine months* . . . ?"[15] As Marisol flips from her own maternity and pregnancy to anxiety about the earth and children, her questioning and sense of panic accelerate to the disturbing image of the moon, missing for nine months, a ghosted lunar pregnancy, as it were. Marisol's sexuality and maternity—the orgasm caused by the angel, and her thrill at the thought of being impregnated by God—are caught up in Marisol's concerns for the fertility of the earth and an invocation of the moon, traditionally a symbol for a woman's fertility, a symbol made all the more obvious with a reference to its disappearance for nine months. In Marisol's world, the disappearance of the moon reveals a profound sense of cyclical disruption, unnatural dislocation, and the wasted, "barren" landscape of modern civilization debilitated by an environmental apocalypse. It is as if the earth is so out of balance that the earth and its moon have slipped from their orbits.

But it is right here, in these seemingly "natural" ways in which the play combines images of motherhood, that an ecofeminist dramaturgy reveals the ways the play participates within a cultural complex that conflates women and nature as mothers. Phrases and associations such as Mother Earth, Mother Nature, fertile fields, barren landscapes, virgin islands, raping the land, and the popular slogan "Love Your Mother" show the long associations between mothers and nature in Western thought. These symbolic linkages between images of "mother" and "Mother Nature" tend to "feminize" nature and "naturalize" women, reflecting and perpetuating the inferiorization of both. As Stacy Alaimo writes in *Undomesticated Ground: Recasting Nature as Feminist Space*, "The dual meanings of nature converge at the site of woman, fitting her in a vortex of circular arguments: woman is closer to nature and is thus inferior; woman is inferior because nature has made her so."[16] These images of motherhood are central to the motif of environmental destruction in *Marisol* and reveal the deeply rooted, even unconscious, ways in which language describes and reflects the complex and ambivalent connections between women and nature in our society. In these ways the play participates in the pervasive association of mothers with nature, failing to intervene in a discursive terrain in ways that would shift and transform these sedimented notions of the maternal.

In another scene, however, *Marisol* challenges and destabilizes categories of motherhood, male, and female by staging a performance of motherhood in which a man gives birth onstage. Marisol's friend June had been living with and caring for June's brother Lenny, but June finally kicks him out of her apartment saying, "I can't mother you. Carry you around in my Epic Uterus anymore." While Marisol misinterprets the visitation from the angel thinking she is pregnant and June rejects the maternal role, it is Lenny himself who carries a child, entering the "radically altered" landscape of act 2, "pushing a battered baby carriage full of junk," complaining of hemorrhoids and nausea, and nine months pregnant. Marisol touches his belly, feels movement and pulls away, frightened and confused. She says, "I just don't know . . . what to think about this." In these moments of confusion, the staging of motherhood becomes a productive site for the transformation of meanings as Lenny's pregnancy challenges the nature of motherhood as a ground of fixed essences. Lenny, a man "nine months pregnant: huge belly, swollen breasts"[17] resembles Donna Haraway's image of the cyborg, a "boundary creature" that expresses discursive ambiguities between male and female, human and animal, nature and technology. This disruption of the rigid oppositions between male/female opens up a space for what Sandilands has envisioned as a democratic ecofeminism based on a transgressive politics rather than a concretizing of the boundaries that dualistic thinking perpetuates. As Sandilands notes, Haraway's cyborg "underscores a politics based more on transgression than on reification" of the limits of binary thinking.[18] Rivera's staging of a male mother giving birth onstage plays with uncertainty and ambiguity, provides a perspective shift, and creates a space for a decentered and imaginative politics that enables us to reflect on these categories of dualistic thinking.

Lenny-as-mother talks of digging through garbage bins to find some food, feeling the baby kick, and hearing its heartbeat. When he can't find anything but cigarette butts, cat food, and raw shoelaces to eat, he discovers that the Pentagon is hiding the last apple tree. He wheels and deals, "lots of weaseling around the black market, greasing palms, you know, giving blow jobs" until he finds the prize: an apple, small and withered, but enough to feel he is taking care of his baby. In this hierarchical market commodity where fresh food and other natural resources have disappeared, he does what so many women all over the world have done: he turns to sexual bartering to take care of his family. It turns out, however, that the apple is made entirely of salt. The city is wasted and desecrated, polluted by capitalist practices that trash the city and endanger the planet.

Lenny still has hope for the future, a hope embodied in the life of his baby and in the power he feels surging through his own body. He exclaims, "Every man should have this experience [of pregnancy]. There'd be fewer wars. *This* is power. *This* is energy . . .. [The] violent bloodstream sending food and oxygen . . . back and forth . . . *between two hearts*. One body. Two surging hearts! *That's* a revolution!"[19] If Lenny is similar to Haraway's imagined cyborg (though a creature not simultaneously animal and machine, but male and female), Lenny's revolution, like the cyborg's, is about what Haraway calls "transgressed boundaries, potent fusions, and dangerous possibilities," whose "slightly perverse shift of perspective" imagines new forms of power and pleasure. As Lenny has discovered by becoming a mother—becoming *other*—his seeing and experiencing from both perspectives at once reveals, as Haraway writes, "both dominations and possibilities unimaginable from the other vantage point."[20] By performing (m)otherhood, Lenny's lived reality becomes a symbolic political struggle whereby divisions of male/female and, by extension, such categories as self/other, culture/nature, refuse stable construction and instead thrive on contradiction, difference, and fluidity.

In *Marisol*, however, even this powerful maternal revolution is not strong enough to save Lenny's baby. In this world, it is not only the environment that is destroyed and dying off but children, too. The "ecosystem" of Lenny's body proves to be unhealthy and damaged, and his child dies before she is born. The labor and delivery enacted onstage is productive only of a stillborn child.

After the birth, Lenny embraces the dead baby and leads Marisol downstage to a rosary-covered fire hydrant. We see tiny crucifixes scratched into the sidewalk, but the stones of this walkway represent more than just slabs of concrete: these are individual tombs. Lenny says, "It looks like a sidewalk. But it's not. It's a tomb. For babies. *Angelitos*." Lenny removes a slab of the sidewalk and digs up the dirt beneath it to uncover a tiny wooden box. He gently lays the baby in the coffin, buries the baby under the concrete, names the baby Marisol, kisses the concrete, and falls asleep. In this wasted time, childhood deaths are a familiar sight, and Marisol reads the names scratched into the sidewalk: "Fermin Rivera . . . Jose Amengual . . . Delfina Peraz . . . Jonathan Sand . . . Wilfredo Terrón."[21] It is significant that these buried children are of many ethnicities, most of them with recognizably Latino/a names—"Fermin Rivera . . . Jose Amengual . . . Delfina Peraz . . . Jonathan Sand . . . Wilfredo Terrón"[22]—here, poverty and the destruction of natural resources disproportionately affects racial minorities and children.

Marisol lies down on top of the child cemetery and falls asleep. In the silence that follows we see only the (m)other who has just buried his child and Marisol, the midwife who first held her namesake, the dead baby. The violence, confusion, and energy that have been rushing forward in the play as if to represent the planet hurtling toward an inevitable apocalypse comes to an abrupt stop here in this moment of stillness. The action pauses, allowing the audience to take in the moments of labor, birth, and death to reflect on the dead babies and their mothers, victims of a city's oppressive social policies and the planet's tragic demise.

The finality of this scene evokes, by contrast, another play, Sam Shepard's *Buried Child* (1979). In this play when the dead baby's father, Tilden, digs up the corpse of his baby, the fields burst forth in a productive harvest of corn and sunshine. In Shepard's play, the unburied child and the fertile fields are figures of hope and renewal, suggesting that what had been lost by modern industrialization, forgotten identity, and dysfunctional personal history can somehow be "dug up," resurrected, and revived. This reclaiming of identity and the healing of the land are caught up together in a journey of recovery that promises a fecundity and an abundant future for the family and for the earth. In sharp contrast, *Marisol*'s dead babies remain buried under the impenetrable concrete city streets, and "Mother Earth" becomes both unhealthy womb and tomb. As metaphor and material-ecological presence, the poisoned land (apples that have turned into salt) and the buried children are weighty with an awareness of real ecological-material consequence. It *matters* that they are covictims of society's destruction of the environment.

This "buried child" motif recurs in Cherríe Moraga's *Heroes and Saints*, which begins with a radical subversion of this trope: The corpses of the children who have died from toxic pesticides on the grape crops are not buried but *crucified* in the vineyards. In the stunning opening tableau, a group of children walks into the grape vineyard, carrying a small cross—with a baby's dead body hanging from it. Once the children exit, the only movement is that of "the child's hair and thin clothing flap[ping] in the wind."[23] The wind subsides, and the stage is filled with silence and stillness. Whereas a similar moment of silence in *Marisol* occurs near the end of the play on a desecrated, barren city street, Moraga's scene takes place in the opening moments of the play in vineyards filled with ripening grapes. The contrast between the grape harvest and the dead baby silhouetted against the sky is shocking and marks the insidious nature of pesticide poisoning. The pesticide sprayings, used by corporate agricultural companies to create an abundant harvest, are literally killing the humans who live and work on the land. When a news reporter asks a villager, Amparo (the town's *activista* against pesticide poisoning), "Why would someone be so cruel, to hang a child up like that? To steal him from his deathbed?" Amparo replies, "He was dead already. Already dead from the poison. They always dead first. If you put the children in the ground, the world forgets about them. Who's gointu see them, buried in the dirt?"[24] The community resists the ritual of the burial ceremony, performing instead a new rite of bodily memory as an act of resistance and a call to arms. These unburied children on crosses both acknowledge the community's solidarity and mark the devastating effects of environmental poisoning.

Buried in *Marisol* and exposed in *Heroes and Saints*, born or crucified onstage in front of an audience, the bodies of dead babies are compelling enough to signify the world and be of the world at the same time, to paraphrase Bert States from *Great Reckonings in Little Rooms*. We know that the babies are actually dolls, yet the sight of tiny bodies being laid in tiny coffins or being hung on crosses makes us accept, if only for a moment, the "realness" of these bodies, the "thingness," as States says, of the coffins and the baby's hair rustling in the wind. Rivera and Moraga play on this tension, this vital aliveness between the image and the thing it signifies, to call attention to and arouse empathy for the very real plight of children and the planet. It is in these moments—moments of real materiality freighted with possibility and phenomenological "liveness"—that the plays do more than show an ecological wasteland as a metaphor for or condition of contemporary American society. If a production allows for the "upsurge of the real," as States calls it[25]—is the hair on the doll real human hair? Are the dolls wearing real baby clothes? Could those coffins actually be used for burying children?—the plays create a sense of urgency about the very real, personal consequences of ecological destruction. Just as Lenny's pregnancy acts as a catalyst for his new understanding of environmental destruction, the materiality of dead babies as well as the staging of mothers (male or female) holding their babies position the audience as witnesses to the devastating effects of environmental destruction, witnesses who might act on behalf of environmental injustices. It is precisely in moments such as these that the theatre's agile ability to move effortlessly between metaphor and physical presence reveals its power to be a particularly apt medium to tell stories in ways that can activate shifts in perception and action.

Although a piece of fiction, *Heroes and Saints* is based on real events. In the late 1980s in a small San Joaquin Valley farming town in California's central valley, a so-called cancer cluster was recognized, wherein pesticide spraying in vineyards caused high incidences of cancer and birth defects. Agricultural corporations employ Mexican immigrants at survival wages to work in these fields poisoned by pesticides, and the housing developments have built their homes over dumps where toxic waste pollutes the water. Moraga's main character, Cerezita, is an extraordinary character, both buried and unburied, in her own way. She is based on the story of a child Moraga saw in a film, *The Wrath of Grapes* (1986), which the United Farm Workers made to document the effects of pesticide poisoning and toxic waste dumping in the town of McFarland. Moraga describes the boy as "a child with no arms or legs, born of a farm worker mother. The mother had been picking in pesticide-sprayed fields while her baby was still in the womb." In the play, Cerezita is a teenager, but she is also only a head without a body: "a head of human dimension, but one who possesses such dignity of bearing and classical Indian beauty she can, at times, assume nearly religious proportions."[26] She is positioned on a rolling platform, or raite, that she operates with a mouthpiece under her chin. It is as if her body is buried beneath the toxic ground that surrounds the community.[27]

Over the course of the play we learn that the community is experiencing its own devastating environmental apocalypse: children and babies are dying from cancer and bodily mutations resulting from the pesticides sprayed on the crops, and the town itself was even built on toxic waste dumping grounds. The houses were sold inexpensively to the immigrant farm laborers, but the toxins have seeped into the drinking water and babies are being poisoned in their mothers' wombs and through the pesticide-laced breast milk. The community members begin to protest the companies that spray the fields with pesticides and the government agencies that build the houses, even taking their protest from the Central Valley of California to the state capitol in Sacramento.

The story of this town—McFarland in "real life" and McLaughlin in the play—is the story of environmental racism, in which people of color are disproportionately affected by environmental hazards in places where they live, work, and play. In the introduction to his book *The Quest for Environmental Justice*, Robert Bullard cites a 1999 study that documents how "communities populated by low-income groups and people of color are exposed to higher levels of pollution than the rest of the nation, and . . . these same populations experience certain disease in greater numbers than more affluent white communities."[28] In the play, much as in life, mothers take the leadership role in protesting the pollution.[29] Just as Dolores Huerta, vice-president at the time of the United Farm Workers, was brutally beaten by a police officer in 1988 at a peaceful demonstration in San Francisco protesting the policies of George W. Bush, the character in the play, Amparo Manríquez, the founder of "Mothers for McLaughlin," is beaten by a police officer during their demonstration in Sacramento. Chicana/o cultural studies scholar Yvonne Yarbro-Bejarano writes, "Perhaps because pesticides target the female reproductive system so devastatingly, women have assumed vocal leadership in the fight against these practices." And, ecofeminist scholar Karen Warren writes that "whether it is trees, forests and forestry, unsanitary water, food production and agriculture, or training in environmental technologies, it is often poor women and children . . . who suffer disproportionately higher health risks in the presence of environmental degradation."[30] *Heroes and Saints* documents these injustices and the protests against them, staging motherhood in ways that bring both a painful physicality and a surreal poetry to these issues of environmental racism, toxic poisoning, and ecological destruction.

In a linear series of two particularly compelling scenes, for example, Moraga imaginatively reconceives motherhood. In the first scene, Cerezita's mother watches over the newly made coffin of her granddaughter Evalina while Cerezita sleeps. She places a candle near Cerezita's head, kneels, and prays to her: "I can't pray no more to a God no tiene oídos. Where is my Dios, mija? I turn to you coz I got nobody left now. Give me a sign mi querida virgencita. Enséñame com aliviarnos del dolor que nos persigue en esta valle de lágrimas."[31] Cerezita's mother imaginatively recreates Cerezita as La Virgen, refusing to pray to a God who has simply watched over the deaths and bodily injuries of her children and grandchildren and instead praying to Cerezita for healing, comfort, and wisdom. Cerezita then takes on the role of the Virgin Mother herself: she opens her eyes, sees her mother praying to her, and accepts this new responsibility by saying, "Go to sleep now, 'amá. I'll watch over Evalina." The next morning, Cerezita ministers to her sister, Yolanda, whose baby, Evalina, has died from pesticide poisoning. Yolanda's breasts are so full of milk that she is in great pain. She cries, "Nobody told my body my baby is dead. I still hear her crying and my breasts bleed fucking milk. I remember the smell of her skin and they bleed again." Cerezita moves her *raite* and says, "Let me take the pain away. Your breasts, they're so heavy."[32] Yolanda opens her shirt, and Cerezita presses her face to Yolanda's breasts to nurse from her as the lights fade out. In the shocking viscerality of these moments, these two scenes of motherhood illuminate the devastating losses caused by toxic waste dumpings and environmental poisonings. Performing La Virgen to whom her mother prays and the baby her sister nurses, Cerezita re-creates herself as an active agent, witnessing and shouldering the burdens of her mother and relieving the pain of her sister.

In the final scene, Cerezita asks the children to shave her head and dress her as they begin the dangerous procession to the fields in protest. The stage directions read, "A brilliant beam of light has entered the room and washes over Cerezita. She is draped in the blue-starred veil of La Virgen de Guadalupe. . . . The raite is covered in a white altar cloth with the roses of Tepeyac imprinted upon it." Cerezita's own mother pushes her to the church where the protest will begin, and the people come to her, singing and bringing "pictures of their dead and deformed children in offering to la virgin."[33] In *Borderlands / La Frontera: The New Meztiza*, Gloria Anzaldúa reclaims La Virgen de Guadalupe, explaining that La Virgen originates in the Mesoamerican fertility and Earth goddesses and merges with the Christian saint, the Virgin Mary, becoming a symbol of protection and hope. "Because Guadalupe took upon herself the psychological and physical devastation of the conquered and oppressed *indio*," says Anzaldúa, "she is our spiritual, political, and psychological symbol . . . of our rebellion against the rich, upper and middleclass; against the subjugation of the poor and the *indio*." Anzaldúa further explains, "During the 1965 grape strike in Delano, California and in subsequent Chicano farmworkers' marches in Texas and other parts of the Southwest, [La Virgen's] image on banners heralded and united the farmworkers."[34] As La Virgen and symbol of Madre Tierra, Cerezita sustains the dispossessed, the women, the children, the poor, and the land itself.

Just as Rivera staged the impossible mother in *Marisol* when Lenny, a man, gives birth, here Moraga stages another impossible mother: Cerezita, a head without a body, becomes a mother, La Virgen and Madre Tierra, to whom the villagers sing, "Oh, María, madre mía!"[35] Like Harraway's cyborg, a "boundary creature" who moves between dualistic categories, Cerezita—a head without a body, a virgin yet a mother and a sexual being, a mother who cannot have a baby and who cannot touch the earth but who acts to save the earth and the children—resembles Anzaldúa's mestiza, a hybrid, third consciousness whose work is to "break down the subject-object duality that keeps her a prisoner" and who shows "how duality is transcended" through "a massive uprooting of dualistic thinking." This is the work of what Anzaldúa calls "morphogenesis," a revolutionary, "alchemical" transformation that deconstructs, questions, and transcends the polarities of dualism. "*Soy un amasamiento*," Anzaldúa writes, "I am an act of kneading, of uniting and joining that not only has produced both a creature of darkness and a creature of light, but also a creature that questions the definitions of light and dark and gives them new meanings."[36] Just as Catriona Sandilands argues that ecofeminism should call for a "direct confrontation with the bifurcating categories . . . that order the world in oppositional pairs,"[37] through Cerezita the play rejects dualistic thinking and stages a character whose bodily mutations empower her to move between binary polarities such as abled/disabled, self/other, culture/nature, male/female. Further, while Cerezita embodies the connections between women and the earth through her identification with Madre Tierra, she radically resists this alliance as a marker of submission to a patriarchal or Eurocentric society by reconceptualizing body/female/nature/other as active agent, subject, nonhierarchical partner, and embodied intentionality. Critiquing and displacing Eurocentric concepts evoked by "Mother Earth," the play stages a new respectful, reciprocal relationship to the earth and a connection to an indigenous goddess and Madre Tierra that is caught up in resistance, solidarity, community, and protection of the earth.

Both these plays throw into the foreground the deep structures of oppression in our culture that have framed the dualistic concepts in Western thought of the domination of nature, women, racial minorities, and the poor. Multiply displaced in her homeland as a Puerto Rican woman and unmoored through environmental apocalypse, Marisol cannot find her way home or her place in society; her dispossession and the earth's destruction are symbolized by images of the maternal that have become unhinged from their normative structures. The play, however, does not end in oppression but in resistance: though Marisol is gunned down and killed, she performs her own death and resurrection and returns to the stage. Wrenched from their own complacency, the people join the angels to fight the destruction of the Earth. Marisol describes a scene of "billions of poor, of homeless, of peaceful, of silent, of angry . . . fighting and fighting as no species has ever fought before . . . Oh God. What light. What possibilities. What hope." The stage bursts into light, "bright, bright light begins to shine directly into the audience's eyes," and the characters "seem to be turned into light."[38]

A victim of pesticide poisoning and the target of environmental racism, Cerezita, a bodiless head, nurtures her family, resists victimization, and reincarnates herself as La Virgen, taking on the symbols of Earth Goddesses, the Aztec fertility goddess *Tonantzin*, and Madre Tierra. As Cerezita moves into the fields with the corpse of her niece, a police helicopter rumbles overhead and guns them down. The people, El Pueblo, drop to the ground, then rise together and rush out to the vineyards, shouting, "Burn the fields! Enciendan los files!" The stage directions then read, "Moments later, there is the crackling of fire as a sharp red-orange glow spreads over the vineyard."[39] Like the bright light of the new millennium at the end of *Marisol*, the red glow of the fire signals destruction and resistance, solidarity and renewal of community, family, identity, motherhood, and the land. Both plays end in apocalypse, yet neither is an ending of apocalyptic despair. Rather, the deaths of Marisol and Cerezita are catalysts for urgent rebellion and restoration. The blinding light and fire signal a revitalized call to arms and a radical repositioning of victim and victimizer.

In *Marisol* the characters throw anything they can find—"rocks, sticks, screams"[40]—up into the heavens to join with the angels and to renew the desperate fight against universal ruin. In *Heroes and Saints*, the villagers raise their fists into the sky against the machine gun fire from the helicopters and charge into the fields to protest the "asesinos" (*assassins*) who have killed Cerezita, the babies, and the land. They fight, as Cerezita says, to be free: "Free to name this land *Madre*. Madre Tierra. Madre Sagrada. Madre . . . Libertad. The radiant red mother . . . rising."[41] They fight to have the freedom to have a new relationship with the earth, to rename the land "Madre" in ways that destabilize and displace hierarchical connotations of "Mother Earth," to restore health and vitality to the land and to the community, and to create a more democratic and ecologically sustainable world. Through the metaphors of maternity and the material-ecological implications of a poisoned Madre Tierra, these plays imagine alternatives to the "logic" of control and globalization and show how the theatre can be an voice for an ecofeminist vision of equality and a space of fertile, material, and embodied rebellions against environmental injustices.

Notes

1. Cherríe Moraga, *Heroes and Saints*, in *Heroes and Saints & Other Plays* (Albuquerque, NM: West End Press, 1994) and José Rivera, *Marisol*, rev. ed. (New York: Dramatists Play Service, 1999).
2. Karen Warren, "The Power and the Promise of Ecological Feminism," in *Ecological Feminist Philosophies*, ed. Karen Warren (Bloomington: Indiana University Press, 1996), 19.
3. Vandana Shiva, *Staying Alive: Women, Ecology and Development* (London: Zed Books, 1988).
4. Rosemary Radford Ruether, *Ecofeminism: Symbolic and Social Connections Between the Oppression of Women and the Domination of Nature* (Charlotte: University of North Carolina, 1991), "Introduction," 5. See also Ynestra King, "Ecofeminism and Feminist Theory," in *Reweaving the World: The Emergency of Ecofeminism*, ed. Irene Diamond and Gloria Fenman Orenstein (San Francisco: Sierra Club Books, 1990), 100–105; King, "The Ecology of Feminism and the Feminism of Ecology," in *Healing the Wounds: The Promise of Ecofeminism*, ed. Judith Plant (Philadelphia: New Society Publishers, 1989), 18–28; Rosemary Radford Ruether, ed. *Women Healing Earth: Third World Women on Ecology,*

Feminism, and Religion (Maryknoll, NY: Orbis, 1996); and Carolyn Merchant, *Earthcare: Women and the Environment* (New York: Routledge, 1995).

5. Val Plumwood, *Feminism and the Mastery of Nature* (London: Routledge, 1993), 32, 123. See also Karen Warren, *Ecofeminist Philosophy* (Lanham, MD: Rowman and Littlefield, 2000).
6. Catriona Sandilands, *The Good-Natured Feminist: Ecofeminism and the Quest for Democracy* (Minneapolis: University of Minnesota Press, 1999), 72.
7. Rivera, *Marisol*, 25, 22.
8. Frank Rich, "The Angel of No Hope Visits New York," *New York Times*, May 21, 1993, C3, http://www.nytimes.com/1993/05/21/theater/review-theater-the-angel-of-no-hope-visits-new-york.html (accessed January 1, 2015).
9. Rivera, *Marisol*, 9.
10. Rich, "The Angel of No Hope"; J. Chris Westgate, "Toward a Rhetoric of Sociospatial Theatre: José Rivera's *Marisol*," *Theatre Journal* 59 (2007): 21; Rivera, quoted in Lynn Jacobson, "An Interview with José Rivera," *Studies in American Drama, 1945–Present* 6, no. 1 (1991): 54.
11. Rivera, *Marisol*, 41.
12. Sheila Rabillard, "*Fen* and the Production of a Feminist Ecotheater," *Theater* 25:1 (1994): 63; Elaine Aston, "'A License to Kill': Caryl Churchill's Socialist-Feminist 'Ideas of Nature,' in *Performing Nature: Explorations in Ecology and the Arts*, ed. Gabriella Giannachi and Nigel Stewart (Oxford: Peter Lang, 2005), 166, 167.
13. Una Chaudhuri, "'There Must Be a Lot of Fish in That Lake': Toward an Ecological Theater," *Theater* 25:1 (1994): 23.
14. Rivera, *Marisol*, 18, 19.
15. Ibid., 16, 17.
16. Stacy Alaimo, *Undomesticated Ground: Recasting Nature as Feminist Space* (New York: Cornell University Press, 2000), 3.
17. Rivera, *Marisol*, 29, 38, 49.
18. Sandilands, *The Good-Natured Feminist*, 73.
19. Rivera, *Marisol*, 49, 51.
20. Donna Haraway, "A Manifesto for Cyborgs: Science, Technology, and Socialist Feminism in the 1980s," in *Feminism/Postmodernism*, ed. Linda Nicholson (New York: Routledge, 1991), 196.
21. Rivera, *Marisol*, 52, 53.
22. Ibid., 53.
23. Moraga, *Heroes and Saints*, 92.
24. Ibid., 94.
25. Bert O. States, *Great Reckonings in Little Rooms: On the Phenomenology of Theater* (Berkeley: University of California Press, 1985), 5, 34.
26. Cherrie Moraga, "Author's Notes," in *Heroes and Saints*, 89, 90.
27. According to Moraga, the bodiless character in Luis Valdéz's play *The Shrunken Head of Pancho Villa* (1964) inspired Moraga to create Cerezita. While Cerezita clearly is in dialogue with Valdéz's character, Moraga challenges Valdéz by empowering Cerezita, who explores her own sexuality, challenges patriarchal notions of Mother Earth, and becomes

a revolutionary hero (as Juan calls Cerezita in *Watsonville: Some Place Not Here* [1996], the sequel to *Heroes and Saints*).

28. Robert Bullard, ed., *The Quest for Environmental Justice: Human Rights and the Politics of Pollution* (San Francisco: Sierra Club Books, 2005), 4.
29. A few examples of mothers taking leadership against environmental destruction are: Lois Gibbs, who led the activism against hazardous wastes in Love Canal; Mothers of East Los Angeles (MELA) protesting hazardous waste dumping; the Chipko movement to protect trees in India; and Wangari Maathai's leadership of the Green Belt Movement in Kenya, which works to plant trees, combat deforestation, and stop soil erosion. See also chapter 1, "Nature is a Feminist Issue," in Warren's *Ecofeminist Philosophy*.
30. Yvonne Yarbro-Bejarano, *The Wounded Heart: Writing on Cherríe Moraga* (Austin: University of Texas Press, 2001), 64; Warren, *Ecofeminist Philosophy*, 177.
31. Moraga, *Heroes and Saints*, 137. Translation: Show me how to relieve us of the pain that follows us in this valley of tears.
32. Ibid., 137, 142, 143.
33. Ibid., 144, 148.
34. Gloria Anzaldúa, *Borderlands / La Frontera: The New Mestiza* (San Francisco: Aunt Lute, 1987), 52, 51.
35. Moraga, *Heroes and Saints*, 148.
36. Anzaldúa, *Borderlands*, 102, 103, 103.
37. Sandilands, *The Good-Natured Feminist*, 74.
38. Rivera, *Moraga*, 57, 57.
39. Moraga, *Heroes and Saints*, 149.
40. Rivera, *Marisol*, 57.
41. Moraga, *Heroes and Saints*, 148.

Making a Spectacle

Motherhood in Contemporary British Theatre and Performance

—JOZEFINA KOMPORALY

Maternal subjectivity and embodiment have consolidated as central themes in late-twentieth-century British drama and performance art and have continued to occupy an important position in the early years of the third millennium, appearing regularly in text-based theatre, radio drama, and live art and performance installation. In theatre, to give an example, the works featuring mothers or mothers-to-be cover a multitude of genres and approaches, from revivals of classics to foreign plays in translation and new writing for the stage. The trope of the maternal appears recurrently in works authored by both male and female artists, as well as in collaborative practice, and often appears alongside the investigation of other issues. For the purposes of this essay, I focus on plays and performances that center on a dedicated rather than incidental examination of mothers, motherhood, and mothering and that address the complex biological, emotional, political, and financial circumstances of maternity in the contemporary world.

The range of work to be discussed deliberately brings together a number of approaches, as the essay wishes to negotiate the boundaries between theatre and live art. *Glass Body: Reflecting on Becoming Transparent* (2006) and *My Glass Body* (2007), by Anna Furse (belonging to the latter category); *Once We Were Mothers* (2004), by Lisa Evans; and *Colder than Here* (2005), by Laura Wade (belonging to the former) are united by their investigation of a long-standing concerted effort on the part of the protagonists to carry out some sort of parental function, either in the present, past, or future. In this selection of plays and performances, the desire for becoming a biological mother sits alongside the trials and tribulations of practicing motherhood, and alongside the disruption of the maternal process (due to loss or bereavement) that gives way to grief and memory. In other words, the essay maps out the desire for connectivity in accord with a "matrixial" economy as theorized by Bracha Ettinger and charts the (fluid) shifts from maternal presence to maternal absence.

My reading of the positions and alternatives offered in the pieces discussed proposes an examination of the maternal as a venture targeting mainly the future, alongside the maternal as a form of day-to-day investment of labor situated in the present and the maternal as an encounter between different subjects (modeled on the psychoanalytic "I" and "non-I") that takes place beyond the here and now and that can include the past. In parallel with the above positions, and as a common denominator, I also wish to situate the treatment of the maternal in terms of the Butlerian performative—considering the maternal as "a kind of doing, an incessant activity performed" and as a "practice of improvisation"[1]—and to argue that the representation of mothering and of the desire for motherhood is often located in a discourse that spectacularizes the maternal body. Positioning the maternal as spectacle immediately suggests the existence of an external agent witnessing the performance and the prevalence of a certain power derived from the observant gaze. The essay acknowledges the loss of agency associated with being looked at; however, it also emphasizes the celebration of the maternal subject's desire to unleash its performative potential as a platform for consolidating or reclaiming agency. In this sense, I am not talking about the feminist empowerment associated with the female gaze (as a subversive reappropriation of Laura Mulvey's concept of the voyeuristic "male gaze") or about the Oedipal or phallic gaze, but paraphrase Bracha Ettinger's less oppositional concept of the "matrixial gaze" that opens up a space for connection and coexistence: the "matrixial borderspace" of transsubjectivity in which nonrelating entities come into a mutually transforming relationship.[2]

I am also indebted to Ettinger for the terms "resonance," "overlay," and "interweave," with which she titles her 2009 solo art exhibition at the Freud Museum in London. Like Ettinger, who emphasizes the ways in which her art practice resonates with the Freudian space of memory and migration, I wish to signal the convergences between an amazing body of work by women artists that deals with the theme of the maternal and an emerging cluster of theoretical and critical writings that respond to this work. Ettinger's concept of "overlay" is present in the intertextuality and shared lineage that runs through feminist work but also, more literally, in the technical and conceptual ways in which artists construct their pieces. Like Ettinger, artists such as Anna Furse incorporate found objects and tokens of memory into their performances. Most powerfully, Furse overlays scientific imagery of internal bodily structures onto the performing body, thus superimposing the inside and the outside (addressing the issue of copresence) and raising questions about documentation, witnessing, voyeurism, and spectatorship. Ettinger's artwork is an interweaving of temporalities, and the exhibition literally interweaves some of her pieces into the existing display at the Freud Museum, while responding to and commenting on that particular space. Women's writing on the maternal is an interwoven fabric, too: both as a body of work that is the result of and invitation for multiple internal dialogues and as individual pieces wherein the various component strands coexist and converge.

The last few years have witnessed a resurgence of academic interest in the treatment of the maternal across disciplines, and perhaps the most visible forum for discussion in the United Kingdom has been the research network Mapping Maternal Subjectivities, Identities and Ethics (MAMSIE), based at Birkbeck College, University of London, and initiated by Lisa Baraitser or Sigal Spigel. This platform can be considered as a UK equivalent to the pioneering Association for Research on Mothering (ARM, 1998–2010) and its successor the Motherhood Initiative for Research and Community Involvement (MIRCI) led by Andrea O'Reilly and operating out of the University of York in Toronto, Canada. This current organization houses the *Journal of the Motherhood Initiative* (formerly *The Journal of the Association for Research on Mothering*), Mother Outlaws, The International Mothers and Mothering Network (formerly IMN), Young Mothers and Empowerment Forum, and The Motherhood Studies Forum and is partnered with Demeter Press. MAMSIE also runs its own online publication (*Studies in the Maternal*, now in its seventh year) and organizes regular study days and events hosted by departments across the UK higher education spectrum. The group's landmark international conference "M(O)thertrouble" (Birkbeck College, University of London, May 30–31, 2009) attracted around a hundred scholars, with keynote speeches by high profile thinkers on the maternal, including the artist and psychoanalyst Bracha Ettinger and the philosopher Adriana Cavarero, timed to coincide with the opening of an exhibition of paintings at the Freud Museum by Ettinger.

In June 2015 Ettinger returned to London for another major international conference: "Motherhood and Creativity" hosted by London South Bank University, with Ettinger and Mary Kelly as guest speakers and Griselda Pollock as discussant. In addition, various alternative platforms have come to the fore in recent years, such as the *Mums and Babies Ensemble* (initiated by practicing mothers, performance-makers, and academics Duska Radosavljevic, Annie Rigby, and Lena Simic), which explores issues such as the value of female labor (at home and in the workplace), the politics of breastfeeding, and the drama of bringing forth new life.[3] In August–September 2015, the United Kingdom-based performance company Zoo Indigo recreated the journey of one of the duo's grandmothers, who at the end of World War II was expelled from her birthplace in Silesia after being raped by soldiers and walked 350 km to Germany with her two small children in tow. Zoo Indigo's contemporary performance act *No Woman's Land* reflects on this complex experience of being a mother—rooted in trauma and resilience—and the performers walked with their own life-size cardboard children, creating a documentary and a multimedia performance of the journey that had its first public airing in April 2016 at the Attenborough Arts Centre in Leicester. In the light of the ongoing refugee crisis this work-in-progress gains particular momentum and situates reflecting on motherhood—in conjunction with migration and the loss of belonging—as a key ethical responsibility of our age.

Research on the treatment of maternal representation in drama and performance is, I believe, part of this resurgence; and, as this collection of essays and the conference preceding it (at Mount Allison University in Canada) illustrates, there are multiple convergences between research conducted on both sides of the Atlantic. To demonstrate this transatlantic dialogue, I wish to reference in particular two contributions to the debate that my work resonates with, authored by Elaine Aston (UK) and Sara Freeman (US). Aston's article, "A Critical Step to the Side: Performing the Loss of the Mother," investigates the ways in which daughters evoke their mothers' memory in their performances and thus reinstate the maternal as subject.[4] The protagonists Aston discusses tell their own stories by telling the stories of their mothers, and therefore reenact their mothers and become agents of the maternal. Aston talks about a "stepping to the side" function as the daughters perform their mothers and posits the experience of being "beside" as a key component of being in the position to "think otherwise," a concept she borrows from Eve Sedgwick. In this way, for Aston, "thinking otherwise" connects to how performance can "think mother."[5] Building on Aston's work, Sara Freeman examines the interrelation between maternal absence and maternal presence in her as yet unpublished essay, "Absent Mother/Present Mother: Wertenbaker's *Credible Witness* and Kushner's *Homebody/Kabul*." Freeman argues that "the travels of mother and child cause encounters of alterity that ask for an opening of political and familial connections," as she examines these plays' connection of the geopolitical with the maternal.[6] It is this "interplay of maternal absence and maternal presence," as Freeman puts it, that in particular interests me as a potential framing device for my paper, and I intend to show that transformations between the two states are a staple of contemporary British drama exploring maternity.

My case studies in this essay include work by both relatively young (Laura Wade) and long-established (Lisa Evans, Anna Furse) figures on the British theatre and performance scene, writing as a result of an artistic commission or a mentoring platform (Evans for New Vic Theatre in Newcastle-under-Lyme, Wade on the Young Writers' Programme at the Royal Court) and generating work collaboratively with performance companies (Furse working with Athletes of the Heart). In several instances I note the recurrence of the trope of motherhood in the artist's career, especially for Anna Furse, who not only takes inspiration from personal experience but also masterminds a cluster of work, emerging over a decade, to explore the issue of maternal desire in conditions of reduced fertility. Furse's work includes an array of generic manifestations: from stage play (*Yerma's Eggs*, 2002) to children's theatre (*The Peach Child*, 2001), and from performance installation to radio drama (*Glass Body: Reflecting on Becoming Transparent*, 2006, and *My Glass Body*, 2007)—not to mention her *Essential Infertility Companion*, a comprehensive guide to available IVF treatments in the United Kingdom, published by medical publishers Thorsons in 1997 and since revised and reprinted.[7]

Motherhood appears in works by these artists as the central facet of the protagonists' identities and is discussed in conjunction with a number of connected issues: the medicalization of the female body in relation to the infertile (in Furse's term, "subfertile") and/or aging mother-to-be (Furse in *Glass Body: Reflecting on Becoming Transparent*, 2006, and *My Glass Body*, 2007; Evans in *Once We Were Mothers*, 2004), the impact of maladies or deviations from the norm (Down syndrome in Evans), motherhood in absentia (disappearing children in Evans), the denial of motherhood via infanticide (Evans), and, last but not least, the practice of motherhood in the final stages of life and preparation for maternal absence (Wade's *Colder than Here*, 2005). Moreover, the body has become constructed as spectacle in our digitalized environment, a place where—via the mediation of ultrasound—the evolution of the unborn baby can be visualized and hence spectated (Furse). Thus, artists document and interrogate performance in relation to the fetus appearing—on routine medical scans—in seeming isolation from the expectant mother, and I wish to juxtapose this strand to the recurrent trope of mothers themselves as performers: of an activity loosely defined as mothering, generally consisting of care.

For Evans's and Furse's protagonists, professional fulfilment has constituted the central preoccupation for years and, reminiscent of Claire Luckham's and

Timberlake Wertenbaker's similarly career-focused characters in *The Choice* (1992) and *The Break of Day* (1995), respectively, they postpone motherhood until its achievement is jeopardized by serious impediments. Unlike Luckham, who suggests termination when the baby in utero is diagnosed with Down syndrome, and Wertenbaker, who looks at failed IVF treatment and cross-continental adoption, both Evans and Furse wish to be positive about their protagonists' reproductive choices and chances, including giving birth despite the risk of fetal malformation (Evans) and the need for medical intervention to conceive (Furse). This shift from the rather gloomy prospects of late attempts at motherhood, often dominating the 1980s and 1990s, rightly marks the significant advances achieved in assisted reproductive technologies as well as in neonatal care, however, it equally signals the ongoing changes in the demography of motherhood. Women today, on the whole, have children later in life than did previous generations and often take the decision to mother despite economic pressures and/or while negotiating careers.[8]

Responding to the complex circumstances in which contemporary motherhood is exercised, both Evans and Furse underline the changing material conditions of motherhood and focus on debating the pitfalls of medical interference. Thus, in mapping the impact biotechnology has on human reproduction, on the one hand, and on the maternal subject, on the other, the playwrights dramatize views in alignment with Butler's claims in *Undoing Gender*. Clearly, neither Butler nor Furse or Evans intend to occupy a partisan position with regard to technology. Their interests lie in investigating the multiple implications of technology for those who utilize it and in making these often contradictory implications widely known: "Feminists who criticize technologies for effectively replacing the maternal body with a patriarchal apparatus must nevertheless contend with the enhanced autonomy that those technologies have provided for women. Feminists who embrace such technologies for the options they have produced nevertheless must come to terms with the uses to which those technologies can be put, ones that may well involve calculating the perfectability of the human sex selection."[9]

Unlike most plays where motherhood, past or present, is inherent from the outset, Furse concentrates on the journey toward becoming a mother in both her radio play and her performance installation. Since she starts from the premise of reduced fertility, she does not question the need for intervention, and she posits the dissociation of reproduction and sexual activity, claiming that "reproductive science tries not so much to cheat Nature as to set, opportunistically, the optimum conditions for a favourable result."[10] She has, however, reservations as to the precise manner and frequency of this practice. Asserting the need to be protective over the boundaries of the female body, Furse calls attention to the invasive nature of investigations into the interior, and she subtitles her piece *Reflecting on Being Transparent* precisely to posit the importance of the vulnerability of the female body in relation to medical gaze. The protagonist of *My Glass Body* talks about being "see-through,"[11] while *Glass Body* restages the early days of X-ray availability when people would dress up and have X-rays taken of their feet or hands to be sent to loved ones, delighted at becoming transparent, before the discovery of radiation dangers.

Furse wishes to make an ethical as well as political point by inviting her audience to consider their own position as gazing subjects, on the one hand, and potential objects for scientific scrutiny, on the other. Furse states that the technological advances that have made the visualization of the inside of the human body possible are often used beyond their immediate necessity, and a trend emerges toward a gratuitous spectatorship by the medical world and parents-to-be alike. According to the historian of the body Barbara Duden "the formation of the fetus is to a large extent the history of its visualization," and Furse endorses Duden's contention that it was visual culture that conditioned our obsession with the naturally invisible, gestating life within the womb.[12] For expectant parents, this visually underwritten connection brings about a so far unimaginable emotional relationship with their unborn babies, at times leading to "just for fun" uses of ultrasound examination. In the process of assisted reproduction, Furse claims that "women's bodies continue to provide spectacle for (professional) others": the "womb [emerges as] a barely lit stage," while the expectant mother finds herself perceived as "a mobile peepshow" as the medical profession "just can't stop looking, deeper and deeper."[13] This frivolous enjoyment of technology, however, is disempowering in Furse's view; women's bodies find themselves erased from view, as on scans the fetus appears dissociated from the mother and is granted an independent star status of sorts. Furse, like earlier commentators such as Rosalind Petchesky and Rosemary Betterton, interrogates the location of the mother's body when the fetus is visualized in this way.[14] She posits that the unborn baby unknowingly performs for the cameras when snapped in 3D/4D, whereas the mother is deliberately edited out of this performance: "The danger is that as the fetus becomes more visible, so do we as women potentially become more invisible."[15] In this way, the embodied connection between mother and fetus is torn apart, the mother's role in the reproductive process is curtailed, and her right to intimacy with her unborn baby is severely undermined.

Furse, of course, talks about what is often termed "other" or "not natural" mothers,[16] whose only path to parenthood is via assisted reproductive technology

(ART) such as in vitro fertilization (IVF). In this way, for Furse, the appropriateness of technology as such does not come under scrutiny; what is debated are the implications if it. Referencing the Butlerian view that "technology is a site of power in which the human is produced and reproduced,"[17] Furse divides her attention between addressing the use of technology and lamenting the circumstances that led to the very necessity for intervention. Like Lorca's Yerma, the protagonist of *My Glass Body* flagellates herself for not conforming to a traditional stereotype of womanhood by being a "waste of eggs, breast, womb" who is "measuring everything in menstrual cycles; spoonfuls of loss, all gone for nothing" and who blames herself for missed opportunity.[18] Furse endorses Emily Martin's views on the language used to describe menstruation as a loss or failure and Martin's claim that the female period "carries the idea of production gone awry, making products of no use, not to specification, unsaleable, wasted scrap."[19] Invoking the imagery of the Russian matryoshka dolls,[20] to refer to the biological fact of women being born with a lifetime of eggs, Furse puts forward the potential perpetuation of reproductive difficulties for future generations as well. Simultaneously, however, she also wishes to use the same imagery in a celebratory fashion when marking a successful gestation in *My Glass Body*: "Amazed that inside me my little matryoshka was busy becoming flesh and blood," or when having the performer pull a DNA-like string of beads from her mouth in *Glass Body*. Opposing, in Furse's terms, medically assisted "wide awake conception" to the traditional "made in the bed baby," both *Glass Body* and *My Glass Body* acknowledge the role of "chemical heaven" as a legitimate alternative route toward human reproduction. Neither piece elaborates, however, on the potential inherent in technology as far as the reproduction of non-heterosexual subjects is concerned, and there is negligible focus on the reproductive possibilities of those not in stable partnerships. Inspired by Furse's own experience, the agenda of *Glass Body* is to reiterate the maternal desire of the aging and/or less fertile heterosexual subject, and, as such, it constitutes a welcome intervention in the social and political negotiation of this particular aspect of human rights.

Glass Body is a piece that locates technology firmly in the realm of theatre. Furse, however, also consolidates this connection by bringing the performance installation *Glass Body* back into the sphere where medical experience takes place. The premiere of the piece took place at the Chelsea and Westminster Hospital in 2006, and the work has since been shown at London's Guy's and St Thomas' NHS Foundation Trust. Moreover, Furse's research has been scientifically mentored by one of the pioneers into 4-D imaging technology, Professor Stuart Campbell at Create Health. As a result, *Glass Body* incorporated cutting-edge medical imagery (of the developing fetus, among others) projected onto the performance space and the performer's body, and the audience was invited at the end of the twenty-minute performance to remain in the space and respond to the piece via writing, painting, and playing with an interactive computer program. Aside from science, *Glass Body* also references traditions in the visual arts, such as Rembrandt's celebrated painting of seventeenth-century anatomical lessons, thus blending scientific and artistic portrayals of the interior world of the human body. This duality is also marked by the financial endorsement of Athletes of the Heart's and Furse's work by both the Wellcome Trust and the Arts Council of England, making the simultaneous presentation of the body as an object of diagnostic scrutiny and site of sheer spectacle even more intertwined.

As opposed to *Glass Body*'s blending of technology, film projection, live performance, and especially composed sound by Graeme Miller in a visually enticing sensory and poetic narrative, its radio adaptation, *My Glass Body*, adjusts to the possibilities offered by the genre, to refocus onto sound, context, and strong performances. For this occasion—a commission by the BBC to launch *The Wire* series on Radio 3 in May 2007—Furse reconfigured the piece into a forty-minute radio play and included in the cast Jack Klaff, her own partner and father of their daughter born via IVF, thus perpetuating the personal connection. (In *Glass Body* she provided the narrative voice to Marie-Gabrielle Rotie's silent performance.) First-time writer for radio, Furse claims that she enjoyed the more personal note allowed by the medium and felt strangely comfortable in this new role.[21] Aided by Graeme Miller's score, she wanted to appeal to the imagination of the listeners, to help them conjure up their own visual imagery in response to the piece; and it is fitting that this open invitation to the listeners to create their own mental performances should mark the final stage in Furse's raft of projects on the topic of maternal desire against the odds.[22]

Unlike Furse's performance installation, which privileges liveness, Lisa Evans's work circulates in both print and staged versions, and it is strongly text-based. Evans's Ali in *Once We Were Mothers* resonates with Furse's protagonists in that she also considers motherhood relatively late in life, reinforcing a major societal trend.[23] Yet the play's focus is not on maternal desire but on the aftermath of birth. This is a play that examines not an "other" form of mothering but dealing with a child who is labeled "other" by societal norms. Ali is advised—by both the medical profession and her own mother—to consider letting someone else take over the responsibility of raising her disabled child. Ali's daughter, Flora, has Down syndrome and a serious heart condition and requires around-the-clock care, and initially Ali struggles with the lack of maternal love for this child who simply does not perform according to her family's expectations. Evans gives nuance to Ali's difficulties in relating to her new situation and focuses on her dilemma between giving her child up for adoption and the solution she eventually chooses, that of assuming her maternal role to the best of her abilities. This dilemma reflects current theoretical debates on motherhood—see Badinter's observations on the pressures women face to assume the role of the ideal mother in the twenty-first century—and is also in rhyme with preoccupations discussed in other studies included in this special issue. In the resolution of the plot, Ali finally opts for performing the daily routine of motherhood rather than continuing her career as a dancer, prioritizing the performance of maternal care and duty over professional ambition.

Instead of making the choice clear-cut (as it was, for instance, for Caryl Churchill's Thatcherite protagonist, Marlene in *Top Girls*, 1982) the play focuses on the gradual journey Ali traverses. Following an initial prospect of combining motherhood and career (as it is fairly typical for her generation), Ali fluctuates between continued professional success at the cost of guilt for maternal abandonment and full-time investment in motherhood with a long-term suspension of career ambitions. As she chooses the latter, motherhood *becomes* her career, and performing the social duty of the maternal takes the place of her ambitions as a dancer. In this way, following Butler, Ali's trajectory tests and confirms the claim that "the performative is not a singular act used by an already established subject, but one of the powerful and insidious ways in which subjects are called into social being."[24] Through Ali, Evans frames performing motherhood as a ritual practice. However, she also insists on delving beyond the mere repetitive nature of the performative, as Ali's emerging consciousness confirms the performative as "one of the influential rituals by which subjects are formed and reformulated."[25] Through Ali, Evans joins a timely debate on the ethics of care in relation to disability. According to Evans, the dilemma faced by Ali regarding career and motherhood is only one facet of the problem; it is parental, medical, and social responsibility regarding the non-able-bodied and -minded that crucially matters here. The fact that Ali's decision is critiqued by her mother signals a strong generational discord as far as the societal perception of disability and parental duty is concerned. While Ali's mother has every intention to continue with her own mothering style based on exclusion, Ali herself wishes to institute a form of maternal encounter based on acceptance, care, and concern.

Evans brings together three very different maternal pathways in *Once We Were Mothers*; thus the play itself operates as an illustration of Ettinger's "matrixial borderspace" of connection and coexistence.[26] Channeling Ettinger's 2009 London exhibition, the play provides an *interweave* of temporalities and is a platform of *resonance* with a rich body of maternal experience and dramatic literature. The play also offers an *overlay* of disparate geographical and political constructions of motherhood, juxtaposing contemporary middle-class Britain (via Ali) to displacement and civil war in the former Yugoslavia. In the latter strand, Evans points out the untenable nature of formerly common interethnic relationships (in this case Croatian and Bosnian) and posits the separation between mothers of one ethnicity and their children, supposedly of another, as the first stage in ethnic cleansing. The epitome of punishment for a woman captured by the enemy, however, is the total annihilation of her personal boundaries via the physical and emotional invasion of rape. Reminiscent of Furse's perception of the female body in the process of intrusive medical intervention, Evans depicts the utter denial of agency to her protagonist. As Butler argues, "Although we struggle for rights over our own bodies, the very bodies for which we struggle are not quite ever our own. The body has its invariably public dimension."[27]

Evans maps out the public takeover of Milena's body through the serial rape perpetrated upon her, indicating the institution of a shared ownership. While Furse's characters transform into objects of medical scrutiny rather than maintain their individuality as women, Evans's Milena ceases to be the person she used to be and becomes an emblem of her nation: one that needs to be annihilated/assimilated from the perspective of the invaders, and salvaged at all costs, from her own. It is this successful performance of another self—a self that does not allow itself to be in sensory communication with the exterior—that saves Milena's life and allows her to hold out until the end of the atrocities: "I have gone somewhere they will never reach me."[28] The invasion of her body, however, has left not only psychological marks but also a child, resulting from gang rape, that she cannot terminate. As she gives birth, abandoned and alone, Milena assumes the hardest task for a woman: to kill her newborn child in order to survive and forget. Unwilling to expose this child to the enduring hatred toward her violators—and, by extension, toward the child itself—Milena makes her decision based upon responsibilities not only as a parent and woman but also as an ethnic being. Instead of condemning the infant to a future of suffering, she punishes herself with the lifelong memory of infanticide. Loss in this case becomes a premise on which Milena's future can be rebuilt. Presence would have signified the persistence of humiliation and ultimately integration into another, colonial, community. Infanticide, for Milena, is not a criminal act but a reinforcement of her ethnic belonging, and it has a nation-building rather than a destructive effect. In Butler's words, "loss becomes condition and necessity for a certain sense of community, where community does not overcome the loss, where community *cannot* overcome the loss without losing the very sense of itself as a community."[29]

The route from being a mother to being childless is also problematized by Evans in the third strand of *Once We Were Mothers*. Unlike the two contemporary protagonists of the play, Kitty lives in the 1950s, in a peaceful Yorkshire setting, and her daughter Susannah is a teenager instead of being a baby. One day, however, she does not return home and the mystery of her whereabouts is never solved. From this moment onward Kitty's sole preoccupation is the recovery of her daughter, to the abandonment of her other duties, including her responsibilities to her younger daughter, Jeanette. Not only does she indirectly punish the latter for being the one who survived but she also accuses her of not having looked after her sister. In this sense, Kitty is oblivious to Jeanette's feelings of loneliness and potential guilt and fails to exercise her maternal function properly toward Jeanette, while proving to be a perfect mother to the missing Susannah. Thus, her inadequacy as a mother to the surviving daughter cancels out her wholehearted investment in her missed maternal opportunity. Kitty ceases to be an actual mother the moment of Susannah's disappearance, yet she repeatedly labels herself a housewife and mother, a typical role for her time and age.

Kitty's search for Susannah echoes the journeys charted by Freeman in her essay on Wertenbaker's and Kushner's "diasporic plays of maternal seeking."[30] But while Wertenbaker and Kushner focus on maternal searches in a foreign land and stage mother-child relationships notable for their complex capture of maternal and geographical politics, Evans's quest is carried out at a local level, within the confines of the domestic. The intensity with which Kitty experiences her maternal quest, however, is on par with that of Petra Karagy or Homebody, and although she does not travel elsewhere to confront foreign authorities, she exercises the same degree of rigor. Kitty in fact hardly leaves the house, just in case her daughter returns, and therefore her journey is first and foremost a quest of maternal expectation. Kitty refuses to contemplate the possibility of Susannah not returning, and hence closes down all avenues toward coming to terms with her loss. As Butler claims, "mourning has to do with agreeing to undergo a transformation (perhaps we should say submitting to a transformation)," and Kitty self-consciously denies herself access to the "transformative effect of loss."[31] In other words, she chooses not to perform in a particular way even if that route leads to resolution, and even if she is expected to perform that way by society. Kitty's reluctance to move on and allow grief to help her deal with facts simultaneously denies and offers her agency. It clearly restricts her to the role of an "expectant" rather than "practicing" mother where the absent child carries all the power, but it also consolidates her certainty in the appropriateness of her original maternal performance. Kitty does not question the reasons why Susannah did not come home and does not connect Susannah's disappearance with her own or her family's behavior. Consequently, the play was often viewed as a story of abduction rather than abandonment, and subsequent connections have been made with the widely publicized case of Madeleine McCann.[32] Evans claims that the storyline is rooted in fiction (as opposed to her immediate contact with Down syndrome babies and war refugees), being prompted by a moving account of a family destroyed by absence: "For my play I thought that the surviving daughter was the crucial one, the one who stays behind but who is receiving some appalling mothering."[33]

The concept of imminent absence via ceasing to be a mother is dramatized by Laura Wade in her studio play *Colder than Here*, directed by Abigail Morris and premiered at the Soho Theatre in London on February 3, 2005. Wade emerged as an explosive talent in British theatre in the mid-noughties, having two plays staged simultaneously at London's most prestigious venues and winning the Critics' Circle Theatre Award for Most Promising Playwright 2005 for *Breathing Corpses* and *Colder than Here*. These days, Wade is first and foremost associated with her latest play *Posh*, about an exclusive Oxford University dining club, staged at the Royal Court in 2010 and filmed by Lone Scherfig as *The Riot Club* (2014). By virtue of her present and earlier work, Wade belongs to a category of playwrights who privilege the single-authored play, yet she is also a practitioner commissioned by theatres and production companies to be involved with the production of her work (she notably wrote the script of *The Riot Club*, thus being responsible for the intermedial transfer of *Posh* from stage to screen).

On the whole, Wade's work is best described as text-centered and in this sense might feel closer to a lineage in dramatic literature than in performance, however, in terms of subject matter it endeavors to breathe fresh air into a seemingly conventional form. In *Colder than Here* the protagonists are a couple in their late fifties and their two twentysomething daughters. Myra, the mother, is dying of cancer and, aware of her imminent death, wishes not only to have a say in the organization of her own funeral but also, crucially, to make an attempt at rekindling the dormant bond between the members of her family. In this latter sense, I claim, Myra emerges as an epitome for Ettinger's concept of subjectivity as encounter. As Griselda Pollock, Ettinger's most vocal UK commentator, clarifies, according to Ettinger "we yearn or languish for a connectivity that moves at the shared borderlines without suspending them, that works across shared borderspaces without violating difference."[34]

Wade's play follows a trajectory from maternal presence to maternal absence, but unlike other plays where it is the child who is in a position of agency and departs—generally prompting the mother/parent to follow and seek—*Colder than Here* focuses on the mother's own imminent departure: from life and, hence, from her unfinished maternal project. Myra's is ultimately a death story, a cancer story to be precise, and, to dwell on Aston's observations on the daughters retelling their mothers' deaths through the medium of performance, the play operates "in the realm of what Eve Sedgwick, herself a cancer patient, describes as the difference between knowing and realizing: the difference between knowing and really knowing one is going to *die*."[35] In such circumstances, Sedgwick notes, "whatever else we know, we know there isn't time to bullshit."[36] And indeed Myra's acts are characterized by an acute sense of urgency: She wants to accomplish her maternal project.

The Bradleys epitomize, according to Wade, the contemporary "normal" family (two parents and two children) where each member pursues their own interests.[37] Myra has been happy with this arrangement in the past, but her diagnosis makes her revisit the importance of family: "There may come a time when you need to learn to talk to each other."[38] Thus Wade's play defines a theatrical space in which the postreproductive mother experiments with her final performative potential: the orchestration of death (via staging her own eco-friendly burial), on the one hand, and the (re)negotiation of family bonds by reconciling her husband and daughters, on the other. As Myra insists on preordering and decorating her biodegradable coffin herself, she wants, as it were, to test-drive her final exit; and her script, a Powerpoint presentation, contains all her funeral wishes. When she sends her family to check out potential burial sites she assumes the role of a director of sorts in shaping the forthcoming funeral show, but also in making them deal with harsh reality alongside engineering new human bonds. Her daughters initially resent being cast as understudies but accept the responsibility and learn to negotiate; and, being given the opportunity to make a decision on their mother's behalf, they indirectly join in the directorial process. Closing her play with a promising rehearsal, Wade makes sure Myra maintains her agency until the last minute. Rather than relinquish control as is generally the case with the terminally ill or those needing medical intervention, Wade's protagonist finds strength in sharing responsibility. Moreover, her successful directorial debut and pre-acting for a unique performance soon to come offer the same peace of mind to her loved ones, whose initial fear of Myra's seemingly morbid interest in the details of her own mortality has also transformed into a profound respect for Myra's choices and a deeper understanding of human nature.

Wade clarifies in a different context that "advances in medicine and palliative care mean more people now have the opportunity to plan their own deaths, and also plan for those who are left behind."[39] She notes, however, that this alters the operation of the grieving process altogether as grief needs to be occupied, and organizing the funeral was traditionally a major way of coming to terms with grief both publicly and privately. Butler argues that "what grief displays . . . is the thrall in which our relations with others hold us, in ways that we cannot always recount or explain, in ways that often interrupt the self-conscious account of ourselves we might try to provide, in ways that challenge the very notion of ourselves as autonomous and in control."[40] In this vein, Myra's husband reclaims his right to grief in order to reassert his long-term attachment to his wife as a gradual—rather than instant—journey toward separation. Alec states, "The funeral . . . isn't for you. It's for us. Maybe if you could leave us, maybe something to do. To be—To be occupied with. After you—People need something to do."[41] This comment puts Alec's attitude throughout the play in a fresh light: His generally passive stance, though clearly rooted in his inability to get involved emotionally, is also a reflection of his resentment at being denied his way of dealing with the loss of his wife. Because he is not consulted about his wife's funeral, he is left without a role in the performance of death so expertly engineered by Myra.

All of the above works tackle in some form the family as a unit of social organization, at a time when young writers in particular have tended to orient toward the "me and my mates" plays, addressing issues preoccupying young, unattached people.[42] The focus for Evans, Furse, and Wade is the exploration of the desire for connectivity via either the desire for or the practice of motherhood, and in most instances motherhood is also discussed in conjunction with fatherhood. Opening up the practice of parenthood to more than one gender, in alignment with anthropologist Sarah Blaffer Hrdy's 2009 views on breeding among humans as a "co-operative" practice, the playwrights and practitioners discussed in this essay make their mark on the rethinking of the maternal in and for the twenty-first century.[43] In Furse's radio play the female protagonist's journey toward maternity is accompanied by that of her supportive male partner's, replicating the artist's own experience, while Evans's Ali argues for the importance of paternal involvement in raising their child and succeeds in persuading her reluctant husband. Wade presents a buttoned-up, emotionally crippled father who gradually opens up toward his family, eventually requesting a chance for more involvement in the preparation of his wife's funeral. In keeping with the 1950s trend for fathers to be uninvolved in domestic life, Evans prevents Kitty's husband from appearing onstage, while she presents the Bosnian Tajib as an initially caring father and husband who, later on, experiences serious difficulties in coming to terms with the wartime invasion of his wife's body.

This essay has tried to show that motherhood, as dramatized by contemporary British authors and practitioners, has significant performative aspects. In several cases the protagonists' professional affiliation as artists has played an essential role in opting for maternity at the time and under the circumstances that they did and has also allowed them to experience a closer connection with their bodies. The association of motherhood and performance is manifold, ranging from access to empowerment to curtailed agency and an assumption of an altered/limited self. Wade's Myra is the epitome of someone who achieves a heightened sense of agency by allowing herself to accept the imminence of death and preparing for it as she sees fit: pre-acting for her final exit and directing the funeral proceedings. Furse's protagonists, on the other hand, experience an intrusion into their privacy due to the intensity of ART protocols and find themselves exposed to an unnecessary medical gaze that makes them lose agency (as it focuses solely on the spectacle of the gestating fetus). Evans intertwines three strands in which motherhood appears as a simultaneously joyful and heartbreaking experience. She examines the gradually improving maternal performance of Ali in opposition to Kitty's dwindling output. As Kitty laments her missing daughter, she neglects her surviving child, acting simultaneously as a "perfect" as well as an "inadequate" mother. Milena never fluctuated in terms of attachment to her children, yet she was forced to experiment with a performance of a new self in order to cope with the aftermath of rape. She survives the atrocities of civil war and paradoxically redeems herself by committing infanticide: thus she invests in loss rather than presence as her capital for the future. In terms of dramaturgy, the works examined equally cover a broad path: Writers continue with single-authored dramatic texts in which they put across strong views that often challenge expectations regarding subject matter (Evans, Wade), but equally, they collaborate with performance companies and incorporate an increasingly comprehensive blueprint for *mise-en-scène* into their scripts (such as Furse's layering of her pieces with multimedia elements including literary, artistic, and scientific imagery). Thus, the discussion of topical issues—informed by personal political convictions—intersects and challenges the formal boundaries between drama, theatre, and performance and is underpinned by an exploration of a new vocabulary, stemming from the practitioners' desire to expand the boundaries of dramaturgy and experimentation in performance.

Notes

1. Judith Butler, *Undoing Gender* (London: Routledge, 2004), 1.
2. Bracha L. Ettinger, *The Matrixial Borderspace*, ed. Brian Massumi (Minneapolis: University of Minnesota Press, 2006); Griselda Pollock, "One Painting Opens onto the Many: A Brief Encounter with the Matrixial-aesthetic Project of Bracha Ettinger," exhibition brochure *Bracha Ettinger: Resonance/Overlay/Interweave in the Freudian Space of Memory and Migration* (Leeds: Centre CATH Documents, 2009).

3. Cf. Radosavljevic, Duska, "Baby Boom," *Exeunt*, May 21, 2015. http://exeuntmagazine.com/features/baby-boom/ (accessed July 8, 2015).
4. Elaine Aston, "A Critical Step to the Side: Performing the Loss of the Mother," *Theatre Research International* 32, no. 2 (July 2007): 130–42.
5. Aston, "A Critical Step to the Side," 136.
6. Sara Freeman, "Absent Mother/Present Mother: Wertenbaker's *Credible Witness* and Kushner's *Homebody/Kabul*," *Journal of Dramatic Theory and Criticism* 30.2 (Spring 2016).
7. For a detailed discussion of *Yerma's Eggs*, see Jozefina Komporaly, *Staging Motherhood: British Women Playwrights from 1956 to the Present* (New York: Palgrave Macmillan, 2006), 155–65.
8. Cf. Karen Bamford and Sheila Rabillard, "Introduction: Rethinking the Maternal," *Theatre History Studies 2016: Volume 35*.
9. Judith Butler, *Undoing Gender*, 11.
10. Anna Furse, "Performing in a Glass: Reproduction, Technology, Performance and the Bio-Spectacular," in *Feminist Futures? Theatre, Performance, Theory*, ed. E. Aston and G. Harris (New York: Palgrave Macmillan, 2006), 149–68 (150).
11. Anna Furse, *Glass Body: Reflecting on Becoming Transparent* (performance installation, 2006).
12. Barbara Duden, *Disembodying Women: Perspectives on Pregnancy and the Unborn*, trans. Lee Hoinacki (Cambridge, MA: Harvard University Press, 1993), 92; Furse in Aston and Harris, *Feminist Futures?* 164.
13. Aston and Harris, *Feminist Futures?*, 158; Furse, "Performing in a Glass," 149–68.
14. Rosalind Petchesky, "Foetal Images: The Power of Visual Culture in the Politics of Representation," in *Reproductive Technologies: Gender, Motherhood and Medicine*, ed. Michelle Stanworth (Cambridge: Polity Press, 1987); Rosemary Betterton, *An Intimate Distance: Women, Artists and the Body* (London: Routledge, 1996), 113–19.
15. Furse in Aston and Harris, *Feminist Futures?*, 165.
16. Furse borrows the term "other mothers'" to describe those able to parent as a result of Assisted Reproductive Technology from Dion Farquhar. Cf. "(M)Other Discourses," in *The Gendered Cyborg*, ed. G. Kirkup, L. Janes, K. Woodward, K. and F. Hovenden (London and New York: Routledge, 2000), 209–20.
17. Judith Butler, *Undoing Gender*, 11.
18. Anna Furse, *My Glass Body* (BBC Radio Three, 2007).
19. Emily Martin, *The Woman in the Body: A Cultural Analysis of Reproduction* (Boston, MA: Beacon Press, 1992), 46.
20. A matryoshka doll or a Russian nested doll, also known as a stacking doll or Babooshka doll, is a set of dolls of decreasing sizes placed one inside the other. The term "matryoshka" derives from the Russian female first name "Matryona," traditionally associated with a robust woman. A set of matryoshkas consists of a wooden figure that can be pulled apart to reveal other nested figures inside one another, usually five or more. The shape is mostly cylindrical, rounded at the top for the head and tapered toward the bottom, but the dolls have no hands or feet. Traditionally the outer layer is a woman containing other figures that may be of either gender, generally ending in a baby that does not open.
21. Jozefina Komporaly, private conversation with Anna Furse, June 19, 2008.
22. A range of Furse's projects were brought together for a brief installation in March 2008

at the Bernie Grant Arts Centre in London, as part of the "The Gathering: Bodies and Memory" Festival curated by Gaylene Gould.

23. *Once We Were Mothers* was first performed on September 3, 2004, at the New Vic Theatre in Newcastle-under-Lyme, as a result of a long-standing collaboration between Evans and director Gwenda Hughes. The play was revived to great acclaim at the Orange Tree Theatre, Richmond, in November 2007.
24. Judith Butler, *Excitable Speech: A Politics of Performance* (London: Routledge, 1997), 159–60.
25. Ibid.
26. Cf. Ettinger, *Matrixial Borderspace*.
27. Judith Butler, *Precarious Life: The Powers of Mourning and Violence* (London: Verso, 2004), 26.
28. Lisa Evans, *Once We Were Mothers* (London: Oberon, 2004), 80.
29. Judith Butler, "Afterword" to *Loss: The Politics of Mourning*, ed. David L. Eng and David Kazanjan (Berkeley: University of California Press, 2003), 468.
30. Freeman, "Absent Mother/Present Mother," 21.
31. Butler, *Precarious Life*, 21.
32. Madeleine McCann, who was just under the age of four, disappeared from a holiday apartment in Portugal in May 2007. Despite one of the best-orchestrated search campaigns all over Europe and worldwide, she has not yet been found.
33. Jozefina Komporaly, private conversation with Lisa Evans, November 2007.
34. Griselda Pollock, "One Painting Opens onto the Many," 3.
35. Elaine Aston, "A Critical Step to the Side," 140; Eve Kosofsky Sedgwick, *Touching Feeling* (Durham, NC: Duke University Press, 2003), 174.
36. Sedgwick, *Touching Feeling*, 149.
37. Aleks Sierz, "Interview with Laura Wade," *Theatre Voice* (February 16, 2006) http://www.theatrevoice.com/listen_now/player/?audioID=380 (accessed July 18, 2008).
38. Laura Wade, *Colder Than Here* (London: Oberon Books, 2005), 23.
39. Lyn Gardner, "Death Becomes Her: Interview with Laura Wade," *The Guardian*, February 2, 2005.
40. Butler, *Precarious Life*, 23.
41. Wade, *Colder Than Here*, 92.
42. Aleks Sierz, "'Me and My Mates': The State of English Playwriting," *New Theatre Quarterly*, no. 20 (2004): 79–83.
43. Cf. Sarah Blaffer Hrdy, *Mothers and Others: The Evolutionary Origins of Mutual Understanding* (Cambridge, MA: Harvard University Press, 2009). Karen Bamford and Sheila Rabillard, "Introduction: Rethinking the Maternal," *Theatre History Studies 2016: Volume 35*.

Un/Natural Motherhood in Marina Carr's *The Mai*, *Portia Couglan*, and *By the Bog of Cats* . . .

—KARIN MARESH

> I don't think the world should assume that we are all natural mothers. And it does. . . . The relationship between parent and child is so difficult and so complex. There's every emotion there. We mostly only acknowledge the good ones. If we were allowed to talk about the other ones, maybe it would alleviate them in some way.
>
> MARINA CARR

As Karen Bamford and Sheila Rabillard note in their introduction to this collection of essays, the mother-daughter bond that was deemed "too difficult" to stage by women playwrights at the height of second-wave feminism in the 1980s has become more common in the plays of the past quarter century.[1] This is especially true of Irish drama, most notably through the work of Marina Carr. The mothers in Carr's plays remain as depressed and tormented as their predecessors; however, they suffer for different reasons. Whereas the mothers of early-twentieth-century Irish drama suffered the deaths of their children, often to the nationalist cause, the mothers in Carr's plays suffer because they defy the core concepts of essential motherhood that have defined motherhood in Ireland for so long. They are selfish, rather than self-less; they are often ambivalent about rather than accepting of motherhood and marriage; they are openly sexual rather than chaste; they are damaged from maternal abuse or neglect; and they harbor violent tendencies that result in abuse, suicides, and filicide.

In short, the women of Carr's *The Mai* (1994), *Portia Coughlan* (1996), and *By the Bog of Cats . . .* (1998) are "unnatural" mothers who suffer because they are women for whom the ability to mother does not come naturally, or because they mother their children in ways that contradict the patriarchal model of essential motherhood entrenched in Irish culture.

Self-sacrificing mothers, whose needs and desires are always secondary to those of their children and any male characters, can be found in numerous Irish plays of the early twentieth century. Often these women are depicted as suffering martyrs, or "Moaning Mammies," as defined by Áine McCarthy in her study of Irish mothers in twentieth-century Irish fiction (97).[2] For example, J. M. Synge's *Riders to the Sea* (1904) depicts a mother of the Aran Islands who loses all six of her sons to the treacherous sea. In the end, she is left, along with her two daughters, to keen for her sons: "They're all gone now, and there isn't anything more the sea can do to me."[3] In Lady Augusta Gregory's *Gaol Gate* (1906) a mother mourns the death of her son wrongly accused by the state, and, calling upon nationalistic stirrings, declares her son's baby boy lucky in being able to boast of such an honorable father who remained loyal to his countrymen even in the face of death. The suffering, self-sacrificing mother is also represented in Sean O'Casey's *Juno and the Paycock* (1924) through the characters of Juno and Mrs. Tancred. Both women lose their sons to the Irish Civil War, and the saintly Juno endures the antics of her drunkard husband and the unplanned pregnancy of her unwed daughter. The mothers in these plays are devoted to their children—especially their sons—and do not question their essential categorization as woman/mother. They are mothers first and individuals second.

In fact, mothers present in much of twentieth-century Irish drama, with only a few exceptions, are, as Diane Stubbings argues, "merely apparent" and contained within the male character(s)' story.[4] This reflection of the social positioning for women in Irish society—women who are "rendered invisible, or when visible . . . [are] seen one-dimensionally,"[5] as Patricia Kennedy notes in *Maternity in Ireland*—continues in Irish drama through most of the century. They are characters who are the result of the idealization of motherhood by the Catholic Church in Ireland, especially during the mid-twentieth century when, according to Clare O'Hagan, the Church urged women to act "as patriarchal gatekeepers, promoting motherhood and family ideologies."[6] The ideal woman during this period, according to the Church, was neither "feminist nor flapper,"[7] as Maryann Valiulis argues. Rather she was a "self-sacrificing *mother* whose world was bound by the confines of her home, a woman who was pure, modest, who valued traditional culture . . . who inculcated these virtues in her daughters and nationalist ideology in her sons" (my emphasis).[8] Since the ideology of essential motherhood ingrained in Irish society promoted the idea of all women as potential mothers whose life and domestic responsibilities must be protected, it is mothers, rather than single or "childless" women, who the Irish Church and government lauded as ideal women. Of course, women who became mothers outside the sanctity of traditional marriage were never, despite their status as mothers, considered ideal women.

Nowhere is Ireland's construction and preservation of an essential and ideal vision of motherhood more apparent than in the Irish Constitution, which was ratified in 1937. In Article 41 of the Constitution, the family unit is described as the "natural primary and fundamental unit group of Society"[9] and women/ mothers[10] are singled out for their specific purpose within that unit. Section 2 of Article 41 states that Ireland "recognizes that by her life within the home, woman gives to the State a support without which the common good cannot be achieved,"[11] and that, therefore, the government must "endeavor to ensure that mothers shall not be obliged by economic necessity to engage in labour to the neglect of their duties in the home."[12] In practice this meant that married women in Ireland for much of the twentieth century were barred from working in the civil service and many other professions precisely because of their potential to become mothers. Ireland's promotion of essential motherhood, which, Patrice Diquinzo notes, "construes women's motherhood as natural and inevitable,"[13] affected every facet of the Irish woman's life throughout much of the twentieth century. Women who did not live up to the ideal image of motherhood were considered aberrant and unnatural and faced social stigmatization.

In her groundbreaking study on motherhood, *Of Woman Born*, Adrienne Rich critiques the institution of motherhood, which she believes affects all women, regardless of their actual parental status, since all women are viewed as potential mothers. Women who, whether by choice or biological reasons, do not have children lose part of their identity as women; they are negatively termed "barren" or "childless." Mothering is so enmeshed in the female identity that the lack of it necessarily means a woman becomes less of a woman within a patriarchal culture such as Ireland. The same is not true for men; Rich notes that the term "'nonfather' does not exist in any realm of social categories."[14] The institution of motherhood in a patriarchal culture, as in Ireland, establishes essential motherhood as the norm. The ideology of essential motherhood asserts that women, rather than men, are psychologically and physically predisposed to the nurturing behavior associated with mothering; that women, in fact, *need* to be mothers in order to achieve happiness and emotional stability. According to Diquinzo, essential motherhood "requires women's exclusive and selfless attention to and care of children based on women's psychological and emotional capacities for empathy, awareness of the needs of others, and self-sacrifice."[15] Therefore, women who have no desire to be mothers, or who are ambivalent about mothering their children, are deemed unnatural or even "deviant or deficient as women."[16]

A 2010 study of motherhood by *Irish Times* journalist Victoria White offers a very different remembrance of a mid-twentieth-century mother, providing a clear contrast with the "official" belief throughout the last century that Irish women primarily achieved happiness through motherhood. In her provocatively titled *Mother Ireland: Why Ireland Hates Motherhood*, White, a mother of four, states, "I don't know why I'm so interested in children. I had, after all, a mother who told me often when I was a child—that she didn't like children. This may well be at the heart of it; I still feel the outrage of a child at that comment."[17] Also important to White's study is her assertion that there needs to be a loosening of the antiessentialist drive—to borrow from Elaine Aston—that has conditioned Irish women to view career as their singular goal, while childcare (and anything associated with it) is to be avoided or remain secondary or even tertiary in their lives. The result of the drive to equalize and get beyond gender[18] in the workforce is that motherhood in Ireland has "little value outside the home"[19] and that women who mother are valued only for the successes they achieve in their nondomestic careers. Thus while legally women continue to be defined as "potential mothers," the social expectations for Irish women have shifted as the Irish economy grew during the 1990s and second-wave feminist groups fought against the oppressions of the patriarchal Irish state. In the opening epigraph to this essay, Carr notes that motherhood may not be natural for *all* women. Her comment begs the questions: What of those women for whom the ability and desire to mother does *not* come naturally? What of the women who are ambivalent about mothering, or become violent toward their children and themselves in part because of their ambivalence? Through the use of metaphor, myth, and fantasy Carr's plays address the complicated position of motherhood in a country that, for economic reasons, needs women to put career before family (clearly a more antiessentialist perspective) while simultaneously maintaining the legal and social expectations that women should become mothers and are better equipped than men to parent (an essentialist perspective).

Motherhood has been a topic central to Carr's writing since she first began her career as a working playwright. In fact, Carr's absurdist play *Low in the Dark* (1989) is one of the first plays in Irish history to deal directly with motherhood and childbirth, weaving in discussion and images of childbirth, female reproductive organs, breastfeeding, abortion, and menopause. It is also in *Low in the Dark* that Carr began to present an antiessentialist view of motherhood, challenging the idea of the "natural" mother. One of the central characters, Bender, is a woman focused on and proud of her ability to reproduce: "As soon as I get my figure back I'll have another and then another, because I am fertile!"[20] However, Bender is as likely to kiss and hold her babies as she is to hit her pregnant belly or throw her child. She also has difficulty maintaining a relationship with her adult children. The bond between mother and child in this play, if it ever existed, has been severed and cannot be mended. One of the original actors in *Low in the Dark*, Sarahjane Scaife, has noted that mothers in Carr's work "cannot seem to provide any real sustenance for their offspring: it seems to be part of the human condition that they are unable to help alleviate the suffering of the children that they have been instrumental in creating."[21] Even a mother like Bender who has the desire to create, nurture, and care for her children is incapable of actually doing so.

Representations of these "bad" mothers, as defined by the ideology of essential motherhood—women who, according to Andrea O'Reilly, "by choice or circumstance, are not the selfless and tireless nurturers of idealized motherhood"[22]—continue through Carr's subsequent works. As a result, some critics, such as Christina Hunt Mahony, argue that Carr's women are "too much lovers to be effective mothers,"[23] too focused on the needs of the men in their lives and clinging to the illusion of romance. All three heroines in Carr's unofficial "midlands trilogy"[24]—*The Mai, Portia Coughlan*, and *By the Bog of Cats . . .*—also allow their despair to consume them, eventually taking their own lives. They are, Mahony contends, "failed mothers" because they abnegate their parenting responsibilities.[25] The implication is that Carr's women are defective because they lack the ability to fully nurture their children and because they selfishly protect their individuality, including their own needs and desires.

The first of Carr's plays in the unofficial trilogy, *The Mai*, brings together four generations of women: the Mai, who is the central character, her grandmother, her two aunts, her two sisters, and her eldest daughter, Millie, who also serves as the play's narrator and from whose perspective the Mai's story is told. As in the plays discussed in Elaine Aston's article, "A Critical Step to the Side: Performing the Loss of the Mother," *The Mai* is a play in which a daughter "performs the loss of the mother."[26] Fourteen years after her mother's suicide, Millie continues to relive the painful memories of her mother's life and death. The daughter mourning the loss of her mother in this play is omnipresent on the stage, watching her memories play out before her and interjecting periodically with relevant or anecdotal stories, as well as occasionally becoming drawn into the action of her recollections as her sixteen-year-old self. She is a figure who is teetering "along the fringe of the world,"[27] who cannot escape the trauma of her childhood (and one wonders if she ever will) and must instead succumb to the haunting images of her mother's final year.

None of the mothers present in *The Mai* adheres to the patriarchal ideal of "good" mothering. This fact is exemplified in Millie's mother, the Mai, a forty-year-old woman who is more focused on Robert, the philandering husband who abandoned her, than she is on her four children. The play opens with a reunion between Robert and the Mai following Robert's voluntary five-year absence from his wife and children. What at first is a romantic, physically charged union devolves into bitterness, more affairs, and finally the Mai's suicide. Her obsession with Robert manifested itself in her struggle to save up money to build an extravagant house on a prime piece of land she hoped would, and eventually did, bring Robert home to her, even leaving her children to do so. As Millie relays, the summer before her father returned the Mai left her children in the care of a friend, "a dressmaker with ten children of her own,"[28] and took a summer job at a hairdresser's shop in England in order to make some extra money. Millie describes how she and her siblings "sat down to dinner in shifts and slept eight to a room" that summer "while The Mai swept up the curls of Arab royalty."[29] More significant for Millie is the jealousy she felt about the friendship that developed between the Mai and a young client at the shop. The Mai would write to Millie of the young client, detailing "how they played ring-a-ring-a-rosy, of the songs she taught her, of a shopping spree they went on together."[30] It is clear that the Mai is not void of the nurturing characteristics required of "natural" mothers, as evidenced by her interactions with the young Arab princess. In later scenes she also talks of collecting her own children from school, doing their laundry, and preparing their meals; in so doing, she fulfills many of the responsibilities expected of the traditional Irish mother. However, Carr literally creates a visual representation of the Mai's lack of focus on her children. Millie is the only one of the Mai's four children to appear onstage—the children are always in bed, at school, or at the movies—and the interaction between Millie and her mother is limited to only a few exchanges. The Mai's identity is utterly consumed by Robert, leaving her children, especially Millie, wanting more from their mother.

The thirty-year-old version of Millie who narrates the play tells of her own experience as a single mother to a five-year-old son. Like the generations of women before her, she refuses to eschew her new role as mother when her son is born. She states that she "thought of having him adopted but would not part with him when the time came."[31] Yet the residual effects of her past trauma color her relationship with her son. She admits that he is already "watchful and expects far too little of me, something I must have taught him unknown to myself,"[32] something that the Mai taught her.

Grandma Fraochlán, the oldest of the women at one hundred years of age, is the matriarch of the family and receives much of the blame from the other characters for the family's unhappiness. As does White's study of contemporary motherhood, Grandma Fraochlán's presence suggests that mothers of past generations had as much difficulty adhering to the societal expectations of motherhood as do those in the current generation. Grandma Fraochlán's daughter Julie accuses her of having had "little time for her children except to tear strips off us when we got in her way. All her energy went into"[33] her husband, a trait passed on to the Mai. After her husband's death, Grandma Fraochlán's despair consumed her, making her even less involved in her children's lives. Julie claims that she prevented her mother from committing suicide multiple times and asserts that it was she who "brought myself up and all the others" while her mother stayed "at the window pinin' for the nine-fingered fisherman,"[34] just as the Mai stands at the window of her Owl Lake home waiting for her Robert to return. Grandma Fraochlán readily admits that her love for her beloved nine-fingered fisherman made her a neglectful mother. She knows she "was a useless mother"[35] who would have thrown her seven children "down the slopes of hell for one more night with the nine-fingered fisherman."[36] She tells her daughters that there are "two types of people in the world . . . them as puts their children first and them as puts their lover first and . . . the nine-fingered fisherman and meself belongs ta the latter of these."[37] She also suggests that parents who are lovers "is not parents at all, not enough love left over,"[38] a statement that supports Mahoney's assertion that Carr's women are too much lovers to be good mothers. In spite of these statements of "unmotherly feelin'"[39] toward her children, Grandma Fraochlán worries that she failed her children and still grieves the loss of her daughter, Ellen, the Mai's mother. In other words, her guilt causes her to recognize that her way of mothering may have hurt her children and grandchildren, but she refuses to apologize for being the only kind of mother she was capable of being.

Grandma Fraochlán's behavior and inability to be a "good" mother is explained in part by her unconventional childhood. Her own mother was "an absolute nut" of a woman who insisted her child refer to her as The Duchess and said her father was the Sultan of Spain: "I believed her and watched on the cliffs every day for the Sultan of Spain. And at the end of every summer the Sultan would not have arrived."[40] A single mother in turn-of-the-century Ireland, The Duchess endured the stigma of rearing a "bastard" by clinging to the fantasy she created of her heroic Sultan. Years later, Grandma Fraochlán forced her own unwed and pregnant daughter, Ellen, to marry the father of her child in order to avoid a similar scandal. Ellen, who worshipped her mother and wanted to please her, endured a loveless marriage to the man, who spent most of his time working in England, visiting just long enough over the summer months to impregnate her three more times. In an attempt to alleviate Ellen's emotional pain, Grandma Fraochlán "belittled" Ellen's husband and filled her head with impossible hope about all that she could have been. That is "what killed her," Julie claims, "not childbirth, no, her spirit was broken"[41] by her mother's feeble and misguided attempts to care for her daughter. Grandma Fraochlán's inability to mother affected her grandchildren, too. The Mai and her sisters, who Grandma Fraochlán raised after Ellen's death, believe that their grandmother didn't prepare them for life; rather she filled their heads with the same stories and "too much hope . . . in things to come."[42]

In *Portia Coughlan*, Carr presents an even greater challenge to idealized notions of motherhood. According to Melissa Sihra, the main character in *Portia* "contrasts radically with passive and idealized images of femininity which present woman variously as symbols of nation, the maternal and the domestic."[43] Portia is anything but maternal and domestic. She is depressed and haunted by her twin brother's suicide fifteen years prior to the start of the play, and she spends her days drinking and wandering along the river of her childhood rather than passing her "day like any normal woman."[44] She has affairs and is very free with her sexuality, which is contrary to a primary goal of essential motherhood, that is, linking women's sexuality with motherhood; that, as Diquinzo states, "women value sexual activity and pleasure primarily as a means to motherhood rather than as ends in themselves."[45] Portia is too caught up in the memories of her brother to find pleasure in her marriage or her affairs, and she certainly does not connect her sexual activity with motherhood. Portia also has difficulty remembering to pick up her children from school and often leaves them to fend for themselves: "Your home is a mess, your children is motherless,"[46] her mother tells her. Even her closest friend, Stacia, acknowledges that Portia's kids are "in an awful state," that "they're not minded, exceptin' what Raphael does, and they're very violent and destructive,"[47] suggesting Portia's lack of mothering skills is damaging her children. Portia's youngest, four-year-old Quintin, is particularly affected by his mother's ambivalence toward him. Stacia, who often transports Portia's kids to and from school, states that Quintin "was bawlin' his eyes out" because he did not want to go to school and had to be dragged "from the car into the classroom."[48] Portia, who Carr notes is "*barely listening*" to this information, simply judges Quintin to be "fierce difficult"[49] for displaying such behavior. Portia's husband, Raphael, long believed he could woo Portia into becoming a "natural" mother, that her maternal instinct—which he assumes is an essential aspect of her womanhood—would eventually allow her to manifest the qualities necessary to mother her children. Stacia, too, hopes that Portia may soon "take charge of"[50] her children.

The hauntings of the past that inform and invade *The Mai* are even more potent in *Portia Coughlan* and represented by the division of the stage picture between the reality of the domestic setting and the fantastic, mythical Belmont River where the ghost of Portia's brother, Gabriel, lingers, waiting for his sister to join him and beckoning to her with his angelic voice. While she lives, Portia is never able to fully traverse the boundary between herself and her brother's ghost—he disappears whenever she runs to the river to find him—just as she is unable to fully occupy space in reality. Like the heroines of *The Mai* and *By the Bog of Cats . . .* , Portia is on the fringe of her world, in limbo between life and death and unable to find happiness in a world that has always expected her to be something other than what she is; and, like the Mai, Portia also commits suicide by drowning in the body of water to which her soul is tied. The nonlinear structure of *Portia Coughlan* prevents a melodramatic reading of Portia's suicide, since we see her drowned body at the beginning of the second act only to see a live Portia interacting with family and friends in the moments leading up to her death in the third act. Frank McGuinness has rightfully likened Portia to the "ghosts of Japanese theatre"[51] who are doomed to live, die, and then to come back to relive their suffering. We know Portia's fate as the final act begins, that she will (has) die(d) a death that will bring her no peace and, in effect, sense that we are watching another of Carr's ghosts wrestling with the conflict between past and present.

As is the case in *The Mai*, examples of "bad" mothering abound throughout multiple generations in *Portia*. Portia's mother, Marianne, who Portia describes as weak, married into a family headed by the controlling matriarch Blaize Scully. Blaize, who endured years of sometimes-public abuse from her philandering husband, took out her anger on Marianne and her grandchildren. When Marianne first married her husband, Sly, and moved into the Scully household, Blaize routinely banished Marianne and her twins to their room: "Six o'clock on summer evenin's, sent to the room, the sun shinin' as if it was midday, because ya couldn't bear to share your kitchen with a Joyce."[52] Sly, who continues to be controlled by his now eighty-year-old mother, did nothing to protect his wife from the emotional and psychological abuse Blaize routinely inflicted upon her. Marianne's only outlet was her children and it was at them that she directed her rage. Years later Marianne still seems unable to fully love her daughter. In the penultimate scene she and Portia engage in one of their many arguments. Enraged by Portia's assertion that their mother's rage "was nothin' compared with" her "feeble attempts to love"[53] her children, Marriane declares that she loved her son more than she did Portia and wishes Portia had never been born. Shortly after this outburst, Marianne pathetically attempts to connect with Portia by presenting her with a new dress for her birthday. Even when mothers are present in Carr's plays—when there is no loss of the mother tormenting the daughter—they often have difficulty maintaining relationships with their children. Portia is unable to bond with her sons, but she is one in a line of women who, because of abuse, neglect, and unrealistic expectations, are incapable of fostering nurturing relationships with their children.

Since *Portia Coughlan* critiques the idealization of motherhood, it is noteworthy that Carr wrote the play on a commission from Ireland's National Maternity Hospital to celebrate the organization's centenary. Rather than offering a celebration of motherhood in all its positive, and traditional, forms, *Portia* presents characters for whom mothering is not instinctual, or natural, and for whom their identity as "normal" women is questioned. Portia admits she *wants* to be "a natural mother, mindin' me children, playin' with them, doin' all the things a mother is supposed to do,"[54] but, she confesses to her husband, she keeps her distance from them for fear of hurting them: "When I look at my sons, Raphael, I see knives and accidents and terrible mutilations. Their toys is weapons for me to hurt them with, givin' them a bath is a place where I could drown them. And I have to run from them and lock myself away for fear I cause these terrible things to happen. Quintin is safest when I'm nowhere near him, so teach him to stop whingin' for me for fear I dash his head against a wall or fling him through a window."[55] Portia's violent tendencies are a result of several things. Violence, both threatened and actual, and rage run through the veins of all the characters in Carr's play; the dysfunctional relationships between mothers and their children in the world of *Portia* is genetic and, thus, unavoidable. Portia is also clearly lost without her twin brother and living in a home with a man she cannot abide. Part of the reason for her failure to remain rooted in reality, and to connect with her children, is a result of her inability to disentangle herself from Gabriel. (The two siblings shared an incestuous relationship as children and planned to escape their suffocating environment through death together. Only Gabriel succeeded in the initial suicide attempt.) However, and most importantly for this essay, Portia has been thwarted by the societal expectations of a young Irish woman. She wanted to attend college, but her father demanded she stay home and marry the wealthy Raphael. She married at seventeen and bore three children even though she "never wanted sons nor daughters"[56] and now finds she is unable to love them because she has no more love to give. She has lost and given up so much in her life, and her children serve only as reminders of that fact. The violent thoughts that consume Portia when she is near her children are a direct result of this. In fact, the ambivalence she feels about her children and her abnegation of the motherly duties expected of her are Portia's way of keeping her children safe from all the violent acts she fears she may do. As she tells her mother, "My sons'll be fine for if I do nothin' else I leave them alone and no mark is better than a black one."[57]

The violent acts Portia imagines are realized in Carr's *By the Bog of Cats . . .* (1998), an adaptation and contemporized version of the Medea myth. The play is a mixture of fantasy and realism and meshes the grotesque image of filicide with a betrayal and abandonment by the mother. Of the three plays discussed in this essay, *By the Bog of Cats . . .* is the most linear—there are no narrators interjecting in the dialogue with direct audience addresses or disruptions of time sequence—yet it provides the most concrete connections between reality and the afterlife in the form of ghosts interacting with the living. From the opening moments when a Ghost Fancier[58] appears onstage with Hester Swane, the main character, saying he has come "ghoulin' for a woman be the name of Hester Swane,"[59] we are aware of not only the play's form of fantastic reality but also the death awaiting Hester at the play's end. Hester is Carr's reincarnation of Medea. She is a tinker, or traveler by birth, an aspect of her identity that automatically positions her as an outsider within her community. As in the Greek myth, Hester is thrown aside by her lover of sixteen years, Carthage Kilbride, for a younger, respectable woman, and she is asked to leave the Bog of Cats, the only home she has ever known. As if these sacrifices are not enough, Carthage accuses Hester of being a delinquent mother and threatens to take custody of their daughter, Josie. Unlike Euripides's Medea, Hester avenges Carthage's treatment of her first by refusing to leave the Bog of Cats, and then, upon realizing there is no chance Carthage will return to her, by burning their home and Carthage's livestock. After she has destroyed the material effects of their life together, Hester turns to thoughts of suicide. However, the thought of leaving Josie behind, as Hester's mother had done to her, is too much to bear; thus Hester kills Josie and then goes "into a death dance"[60] with the mystical ghost fancier that ends with a knife plunged in Hester's heart. As gruesome as Hester's actions are, the crime of filicide is committed not out of revenge for a wrong done to Hester but to break the cycle of abandonment begun by Hester's mother, Josie Swane, and perpetuated by Carthage. The loss of the mother first performed by Millie in *The Mai*, a performance that Millie seems unable to stop reliving, is ended once and for all in a violent yet loving action by Hester in *By the Bog of Cats . . .*

The most prevalent theme running through the play is the importance of the bond between mother and daughter, which marks a significant change from Irish drama such as Synge's *Riders to the Sea* and O'Casey's *Juno and the Paycock*, where relationships between women are always circumvented by the playwright's focus on the father-son relationships, or the women's relationships to the men in their lives. The women in *By the Bog of Cats* . . . are more concerned with either losing their children or having been abandoned by their mothers than they are about their husbands or fathers. In act 1, Hester admits to her confidant, Monica (a woman whose own son died an early death), that her "life doesn't hang together without"[61] Carthage, a statement that belies what is really at the heart of her suffering. Later in the play, Hester confesses that her mother's abandonment of her is the real cause of her grief, and Hester's belief that her mother will return, rather than her love for Carthage, is the reason she refuses to leave the Bog of Cats. She admits, "There's a longin' in me for her that won't quell this while gone";[62] this is further manifest in the fact that Hester names her only daughter after her mother.

The immediacy of Hester's situation and relationship with Carthage appears to be what drives Hester to commit her crimes, yet Carr craftily champions the imprint of the mother over that of the husband. This is further made clear by Carr's inclusion of another plot element from *Medea*. Just as Medea murdered her brother, so too does Hester, though once again for different reasons. Medea's crime is motivated by her attempts to help Jason steal away from her homeland. Hester, on the other hand, is motivated by jealousy for her brother's relationship with their mother, a jealousy that exists because Josie Swane left Hester to begin a new family elsewhere, a new family that included Hester's brother, Joseph Swane. When Joseph's ghost appears to Hester in the final act of the play, she confesses that she killed him not for money, as he believes, but because he was named for their mother, and because he was "an arrogant git" who "wouldn't shut up talkin' about . . . [Josie Swane] as if she wasn't"[63] also Hester's mother. Years after Josie Swane's abandonment of her, Hester continues to blame herself for her mother leaving: "Was it somethin' I done on her? I was seven, same as me daughter Josie, seven, and there isn't anythin' in this wide world Josie could do that'd make me walk away from her."[64]

Ironically, Hester has longed her entire life for the return of a mother who everyone says was mad and far from being a "good" mother. Xavier Cassidy, father to Carthage's new bride, reminds Hester of the times he brought food and water to Josie Swane's caravan so the young Hester wouldn't starve. He and his mother also helped care for Hester when Josie would disappear on one of her many jaunts: "Times I'd walk by that caravan and there'd be ne'er a sign of this mother of yours. She'd go off for days with anywan who'd buy her a drink. . . . And you, you'd be chained to the door of the caravan with maybe a dirty nappy on ya if ya were lucky."[65] The mystical Catwoman, akin to the seers in ancient Greek drama, tells Hester that she began to turn against Josie Swane when Josie, wanting to signify the connection between her child and the natural world, left the newborn Hester in a swan's lair amid the snow and ice for three successive nights. All three nights Catwoman snuck Hester back to her own home—and then "brung ya back to the lair before she'd come lookin' for ya in the mornin'"[66]—so Hester wouldn't die of exposure. The ghost of Joseph Swane also confirms Josie Swane's selfish nature. Although he describes Josie Swane as a "gentle" woman, he admits to Hester that their mother denied Hester's existence—"she told . . . [our father] you were dead, that ya died at birth . . . that ya were born with your heart all wrong."[67] He reminds Hester that Josie Swane also abandoned him and their father, that she "hung around for no wan."[68] Like Portia, Josie Swane became bitter when the expectations of motherhood confined her, and she either could not or refused to live up to them. Although traumatized by her mother's abandonment of her, Hester might have incurred further and more violent abuse at the hands of her mother had Josie remained a settled woman—which contrasts with her traveler identity—in the Bog of Cats. "Ya were lucky she left ya,"[69] Catwoman tells Hester.

The theme of abandonment by the mother is also a key to understanding the character Caroline Cassidy, Carthage's new bride. Caroline desperately longs for her mother who died while Caroline was still a child and left her with a trove of dreams and fantasies but no sense of reality. Her mother used to "describe for me my weddin' day. Of how she'd be there with a big hat on her and so proud. And the weddin' was goin' to be in this big ballroom with a fountain of mermaids in the middle."[70] Caroline's actual wedding day is far from the idyllic image her mother painted for her, in part because of her mother's absence. She has her mother's wedding tablecloth and silver, but they do not take the place of her mother. Although Olive Cassidy did not deliberately abandon her daughter, as Josie Swane did Hester, she allowed her grief for the accidental death of her son to overwhelm her and hasten her own death. Xavier Cassidy, who Hester says is responsible for his son's death, claims his wife died of "spite" against him, that she effectively stopped living after the event. Olive harbored such devotion for her son, a characteristic of essential motherhood, that it undermined her very health.

Carthage's mother, Mrs. Kilbride, is the ultimate example in any of Carr's plays of a mother's adoration and devotion to her child gone awry. She meddles in all of Carthage's affairs and treats her son as a surrogate husband. At his wedding she wears "*what looks extremely like a wedding dress, white, a white hat, with a bit of veil trailing off it, white shoes . . .*," and tells all assembled "that if Carthage will be as good a son to Caroline as he's been a husband to me then she'll have no complaints."[71] Her dominant influence over her son even bordered on incest after the death of her husband. At the wedding she announces that Carthage "used come into the bed to sleep beside me for fear I would be lonely. Often I woke from a deep slumber and his two arms would be around me, a small leg thrown over me in sleep."[72] Mrs. Kilbride revels in her "marriage" to Carthage and reminds her son that she is his mother and "won't be goin' away. Ever."[73] She is a woman for whom motherhood has meant selfish consumption of her son rather than selfless love and self-sacrifice, and that will not end with her son's marriage to another woman.

Hester's relationship with her daughter, Josie, is the only truly positive, relatively healthy mother-child bond depicted in these plays. Hester—who occasionally leaves Josie to fend for herself, who is candidly open about her sexual relations with Carthage, and who can be verbally cruel to her daughter—is as close to a "natural" mother of any of Carr's heroines. She is devoted to Josie and always relents after verbally lashing the child. Yet she questions what she can offer her. In the final scene of the play, Hester says to Josie, "Don't ya want to be with your Daddy and grow up big and lovely and full of advantages they tell me I have not the power to give ya?,"[74] implying the love of a mother for her daughter is not enough of an advantage. Carthage has money and property after his marriage to Caroline and can provide material advantages for Josie. Josie responds that she'd always be "hopin' and waitin' and prayin'"[75] for her mother to return if Hester left. Still intent on committing suicide, Hester pushes Josie away, as her mother did to her, but the more she pushes the more frantic Josie becomes. Unable to bear causing Josie the same kind of pain her mother caused her, Hester makes the decision to kill Josie, telling her daughter's limp body, "It's because ya wanted to come."[76] The cycle of abandonment is finally ended in that one, violent act. Shortly after Josie's death, the ghost fancier, unseen by the other characters onstage, leads Hester in a death dance that ends in Hester's death by means of the same knife that killed Josie. Hester's final words—"Mam–Mam–"[77]—echo Josie's final words as Hester slits her throat, symbolizing the bond between mother and daughter.

Hester Swane challenges the idea that there is only one kind of "natural" mother—the idealized, essential matriarch. Hester is in many respects a "bad" or "unnatural" mother. She is selfish and is very focused on her own personal demons. Committing filicide is the most obvious example of Hester's "bad" mothering. However, hers is simply a different way of mothering, one that involves her in the care of her child but does not necessitate a complete destruction or sacrifice of her identity. *By the Bog of Cats . . .* is also one of the first of Carr's plays to represent truly affectionate, caring moments between a mother and her child onstage. Unlike the Mai, who, when she shares moments with her daughter, remains solely focused on her own trauma (i.e., her marriage to Robert), Hester is always concerned for Josie's welfare, making sure she is fed, clothed properly, and washed, which is more than her mother did for her. Josie and Hester's first scene together is one in which their love and affection for one another is manifest. They playfully tease one another with mock insults while Josie impersonates her grandmother. Hester then inquires as to whether Josie has had breakfast and if she brushed her teeth, to which Josie replies, "Why do I always have to wash my teeth? . . . What do I need teeth for anyway?"[78] Hester good-naturedly retorts, "Ya need them for snarlin' at people when smilin' doesn't work any more. G'wan in and wash them now."[79] In contrast to Hester's loving care of her "beautiful child"[80] is the treatment of Josie by Mrs. Kilbride, who refers to her granddaughter as a "bastard," a "coward," and a "pussy baby."[81]

The complexities of motherhood represented in these plays call into question the validity of the idealized image of essential motherhood perpetuated throughout twentieth-century Ireland and demonstrate that there are many kinds and ways of mothering. The "unnatural" or "bad" mothers in Carr's plays are, in fact, women who are set up to fail because the idealization of Irish motherhood is symbolic and is in reality impossible to achieve. For them, the role of mother is but one part of their identity, one that is not necessarily required for them to find happiness and fulfillment and one that brings some of them more misery than good.

Notes

Epigraph. Marina Carr, quoted in Melissa Sihra, "The House of Woman and the Plays of Marina Carr," *Women in Irish Drama: A Century of Authorship and Representation*, ed. Melissa Sihra (Basingstoke, England: Palgrave Macmillan, 2007), 211.

1. Karen Bamford and Sheila Rabillard, "Introduction: Rethinking the Maternal," *Theatre History Studies 2016: Volume 35*.
2. Áine McCarthy, "'Oh Mother Where Art Thou?': Irish Mothers and Irish Fiction in the Twentieth Century," in *Motherhood in Ireland: Creation and Context*, ed. Patricia Kennedy (Douglas Village, Cork: Mercier Press, 2004), 97.
3. J. M. Synge, *Riders to the Sea: The Playboy of the Western World and Other Plays*, ed. Ann Saddlemyer et al. (Oxford: Oxford University Press, 1995), 11.
4. Diane Stubbings, *Anglo-Irish Modernism and the Maternal: From Yeats to Joyce* (New York: Palgrave, 2000), 115.
5. Patricia Kennedy, *Maternity in Ireland: A Woman-Centered Perspective* (Dublin: Liffey Press, 2002), 7.
6. Clare O'Hagan, "Ideologies of Motherhood and Single Mothers," *Single Motherhood in 20th Century Ireland: Cultural, Historical and Social Essays*, ed. María de la Cinta

Ramblado-Minero and Auxiliadora Perez-Vides (Lewiston, NY: Edwin Mellen P, 2006), 69.

7. Maryann Valiulis, "Neither Feminist Nor Flapper: The Ecclesiastical Construction of the Ideal Irish Woman," in *Chattel, Servant or Citizen? Women's Status in Church, State and Society*, ed. Mary O'Dowd and Sabine Wichert (Belfast: Institute of Irish Studies, 1995), 178.
8. Valiulis, "Neither Feminist Nor Flapper," 178.
9. *Bunreacht Na hÉireann/Constitution of Ireland*, July 1, 1937, last modified 2012: 160, https://www.constitution.ie/Documents/Bhunreacht_na_hEireann_web.pdf.
10. The Constitution of Ireland uses the terms "mother" and "woman" interchangeably, thus supporting the argument that all women in Irish society are believed to be potential mothers.
11. *Constitution of Ireland*, 162.
12. *Constitution of Ireland*, 162.
13. Patrice Diquinzo, *The Impossibility of Motherhood: Feminism, Individualism, and the Problem of Mothering* (New York & London: Routledge, 1999), xiii.
14. Adrienne Rich, *Of Woman Born: Motherhood as Experience and Institution* (New York: Norton & Company, 1976), 11. The connotation of the term "father" is also significantly different from that of "mother." To *father* a child a man needs only to provide sperm to create the child. To *mother* implies raising and nurturing a child.
15. Diquinzo, *The Impossibility of Motherhood*, xiii.
16. Ibid., xiii.
17. Victoria White, excerpt from *Mother Ireland: Why Ireland Hates Motherhood* (London, 2010), quoted in "Fear and Loathing: What's Our Problem with Mothers and Children?" *The Irish Times*, October 9, 2010, http://www.irishtimes.com/newspaper/weekend/2010/1009/1224280689839.html.
18. Elaine Aston, "A Critical Step to the Side: Performing the Loss of the Mother," *Theatre Research International* 32, no. 2 (2007): 131.
19. Breda O'Brien, "Motherhood Still Holds Little Value Outside the Home," *The Irish Times*, October 30, 2010, http://www.irishtimes.com/newspaper/opinion/2010/1030/1224282315751.html.
20. Marina Carr, *Low in the Dark* in *Marina Carr: Plays One* (London: Faber and Faber, 1999), 10.
21. Sarahjane Scaife, "Mutual Beginings: Marina Carr's *Low in the Dark*," in *The Theatre of Marina Carr: "Before Rules Was Made,"* ed. Cathy Leeney and Anna McMullan (Dublin: Carysfort Press, 2003), 11.
22. Andrea O'Reilly, *Rocking the Cradle: Thoughts on Feminism, Motherhood and the Possibility of Empowered Mothering* (Toronto, ON: Demeter Press, 2006), 13.
23. Christina Hunt Mahony, *Contemporary Irish Literature: Transforming Tradition* (New York: St. Martin's Press, 1998), 192.
24. The setting for all three of these plays is the Irish midlands, where Carr was raised and which she considers "the crossroads between the worlds" (Marina Carr, "Afterward," in *Portia Coughlan, The Dazzling Dark*, ed. Frank McGuinness [London: Faber and Faber, 1996], 311).
25. Christina Hunt Mahony, *Contemporary Irish Literature*, 192.
26. Aston, 130.

27. Marina Carr, *The Mai* in *Marina Carr: Plays One* (London: Faber and Faber, 1999), 184.
28. Carr, *The Mai*, 152.
29. Ibid., 152.
30. Ibid., 153.
31. Ibid., 164.
32. Ibid., 164.
33. Ibid., 145.
34. Ibid., 141.
35. Ibid., 182.
36. Ibid., 182.
37. Ibid., 182.
38. Ibid., 144.
39. Ibid., 182.
40. Ibid., 169.
41. Ibid., 146.
42. Ibid., 163.
43. Melissa Sihra, "The House of Woman and the Plays of Marina Carr," 210.
44. Marina Carr, *Portia Coughlan* in *Marina Carr: Plays One* (London: Faber and Faber, 1999), 211.
45. Diquinzo, *The Impossibility of Motherhood*, xiii.
46. Marina Carr, *Portia Coughlan*, 248.
47. Ibid., 244.
48. Ibid., 204.
49. Ibid., 204.
50. Ibid., 244.
51. Frank McGuinness, "Introduction: Masks," in *The Dazzling Dark: New Irish Plays*, ed. Frank McGuinness (London and Boston: Faber and Faber, 1996), ix.
52. Marina Carr, *Portia Coughlan*, 216.
53. Ibid., 249.
54. Ibid., 233.
55. Ibid., 233.
56. Ibid., 221.
57. Ibid., 210.
58. M. K. Martinovich describes the Ghost Fancier as "an Irish Grim Reaper" who is suggestive of "the dead living among us, a mainstay of Irish folk tradition" (M. K. Martinovich, "The Mythical and the Macabre: The Study of Greeks and Ghosts in the Shaping of the American premiere of *By the Bog of Cats . . .*, in *The Theatre of Marina Carr: "Before Rules was Made,"* ed. Cathy Leeney and Anna McMullin [Dublin, Ireland: Carysfort Press, 2003], 121).
59. Marina Carr, *By the Bog of Cats . . .* in *Marina Carr: Plays One* (London: Faber and Faber Ltd., 1999), 266.
60. Ibid., 341.
61. Ibid., 269.
62. Ibid., 275.
63. Ibid., 319.
64. Ibid., 319.

65. Ibid., 295.
66. Ibid., 275.
67. Ibid., 320.
68. Ibid., 320.
69. Ibid., 276.
70. Ibid., 336.
71. Ibid., 311.
72. Ibid., 310.
73. Ibid., 282.
74. Ibid., 338.
75. Ibid., 338.
76. Ibid., 339.
77. Ibid., 341.
78. Ibid., 286.
79. Ibid., 286.
80. Ibid., 327.
81. Ibid., 277–79.

Flying Babies and Pregnant Men

Staging Motherhood in Marina Carr's *Low in the Dark*

—JENNIFER DOUGLAS

One of the most prominent Irish playwrights today, Marina Carr writes about women's lives in flux: women who have endured abuse, women who struggle in unhappy marriages, and even women who choose to kill themselves or their children. Her plays, spanning from the late 1980s through the present, begin with Beckettian absurdity and transition into the realms of myth and tragedy. *Low in the Dark* (1989), a play based on short, comedic episodes with mothers and children, introduces an innovative genre-bending style, which draws on Samuel Beckett's nonlinear form but with attention to the female body and gender identity.

Since Marina Carr wrote *Low in the Dark*, in 1989, motherhood has become even more complicated, biologically, socially, and technologically. Reproductive technologies have made in vitro fertilization possible at much older maternal ages, making multiple births more common and more extreme: *Jon and Kate Plus Eight*, the "Octomom," and *19 Kids and Counting* exemplify our cultural obsession with multiples and large families. As a culture, we crave the schadenfreude of watching parents struggle while six preschoolers overwhelm them. The increasing attention to surrogates, gay parents, and celebrity moms creates a dizzying array of pregnancy spectacle that emphasizes the burgeoning body during pregnancy and its rapid shrinking in the frenzy to reach pre-baby weight. Even pregnant men have made the news: Oprah made famous the transgender man whose female reproductive system made it possible to successfully carry and give birth to a baby. Pregnancy has taken on such different significations as to resist definition after the sperm fertilizes the egg: It is viewed simultaneously as a right and a privilege, a sacred bodily responsibility and a physical blight, a way to begin a family and a way to redefine the nuclear family as we have known it. Although women are feted for their own reproductive choices, once pregnancy begins, the pressure to perform pregnancy correctly and to make the *right* choices can quickly transform education into indoctrination. As Elisabeth Badinter writes, "la mère écologique" (the natural mother) can become an oppressively narrow view of motherhood that calls for strict maternal behaviors, such as breastfeeding for a prescribed length of time.[1]

Low in the Dark engages with Eve Kosofsky Sedgwick's concept of *beside* insofar as motherhood becomes an array of behaviors, roles, discourses, and bodies that cannot be easily contained within a dualistic essentialist or antiessentialist paradigm. The play circles around, teases out, and bounces between radically different depictions of motherhood, from older mothers to young mothers, from female mothers to male mothers, and from dedicated mothers to ambivalent mothers. Each of these representations evokes cultural stereotypes around mothering by displaying maternal bodies prominently, citing gender norms for raising children, and foregrounding the tensions between *la femme et la mère* (woman and mother). By not focusing on one specific mother character or version, the play becomes literally that—a playful space that allows for critique and affect without linearity or hierarchy.[2]

Carr's particular Irish context frames some of the issues in the play, but contraception, abortion, and other reproductive issues transcend Ireland and reflect struggles in other Western countries with similar religious underpinnings. It is worthwhile to remember the specific conflicts around access to birth control, abortion, and sex education that inform Ireland in 1989.[3] These conflicts resonate with the return to controversial forms of abstinence education and certain Christian groups' emphasis on preserving virginity, both issues that have shaped US culture in recent years. That is, Carr's choice of topics has not faded into the cultural landscape but has become even more pronounced and divisive since the time the play was first performed. Because of the nonlinear, episodic style of the play, multiple versions of motherhood can coexist and interact without privileging one viewpoint, one maternal body, or one maternal role. At the same time, it's clear that the humor and satire take aim at the divide between "woman" and "mother," between fertility and femininity, between biological motherhood and maternal acts. All of these dualisms exist, rather, *beside* each other, in Sedgwick's terms, such that they are constantly in dialogue and constantly intertwined. Sedgwick fittingly compares the spatial tensions of *beside* to siblings sharing a bed: not necessarily "egalitarian." Rather, she writes, "*Beside* comprises a wide range of desiring, identifying, representing, repelling, paralleling, differentiating, rivaling, leaning, twisting, mimicking, withdrawing, attracting, aggressing, warping, and other relations."[4] *Low in the Dark* embodies all these actions, both corporeally and discursively. The play builds up and tears down conceptions of motherhood as easily as the characters build walls and knit scarves onstage.

Although Carr addresses some aspects of motherhood and femininity from a specifically Irish context, she also engages with the debates around motherhood that have dominated Western culture in the last century. Susan E. Chase articulates the vastly disparate ways that motherhood has been regarded: "At different times, in different contexts, and from differing social locations, feminists have treated motherhood as an oppressive *and* an empowering experience, a source of alienation from *and* connection to their bodies, a form of work that is enervating *and* rewarding; a relationship that constrains women's autonomy *and* invites their personal growth; a cause for distance from *and* a bridge to other women; a motivator of conservative *and* progressive political action."[5] *Low* brings together many of these contradictions in a satirical way to illustrate the conflicting cultural expectations for mothers' attitudes, behaviors, and bodies.

By staging motherhood as a continuous performance that can both reinforce and resist societal conventions of gender, *Low* showcases motherhood as a performative role that combines the phenomenological materiality of the body and the semiotics of discourse. While some aspects of *Low* foreground the body, this attention to the physical is embedded in gendered language that both confirms and undermines bodily representation.[6] Carr subverts stereotypes through a humorous combination of excessive pregnancies and gendered language, the mutability and threat of the pregnant body, the cultural expectations for being the ideal mother, and the tensions between fertility and femininity. In essence, *Low* disrupts traditional gender roles and discourses that valorize motherhood as a natural, intuitive part of being a woman. At the same time, the play questions the typical dichotomy between the sexualized female body and the maternal, nonsexualized female body. Kelly Oliver calls the maternal body the "body without borders" because of the way that the maternal body splits into the mother and the baby, thus seeming to spread out and diverge. Oliver's phrase becomes literal in *Low* because of the ubiquity and visibility of pregnant bodies and babies.[7] These pregnant bodies become a source of obvious humor and satire, but they also foreground the responsibilities of being a "good" woman, including the conflation of fertility and femininity based on the display of the reproductive body. By representing pregnancy in excessive, unusual ways, Carr reinforces that "normal" motherhood does not exist in any one incarnation.

The Mutable Maternal Body Onstage

Sedgwick's notion of *beside* takes on literal dimensions with the rigidly gendered layout of the set. One side of the stage is the men's area, consisting of "tyres, rims, unfinished walls and blocks strewn about." On the other side of the stage, the women's area consists of a "bizarre bathroom: bath, toilet and shower," which are full of babies.[8] The set reproduces the gendered spaces of the home only to break down these barriers through maternal bodies, behaviors, and words associated with both male and female characters. Although these stage areas establish where male and female characters will normally be, they exist in order to call attention to gender conventions rather than to enforce them. The deliberate artifice of the stage design prompts the viewer to grapple with these radically different sites associated with masculine and feminine behavior, especially since motherhood becomes a communal activity based on both biology and behavior.[9] Within the women's area, the bathroom becomes the focal point for the birth and care of babies, thus conflating the scene of birth and excretion to emphasize the abjection of the birthing process and to initiate a trend toward the grotesque maternal body in the play. Emphasizing the home as birthing place also reinforces the woman's traditional role in Irish national identity to reproduce and guard the domestic sphere.[10] Susan Cannon Harris writes that Irish women have been expected to exhibit sexual purity, produce children, and take care of the domestic sphere as a "shrine to national identity." In contemporary culture, the return of the "maternal instinct" in our discourse points to the fact that motherhood retains a central role in our ideals of stability and family. Although the maternal instinct has been lauded as the inevitable mammalian cascade of hormones and derided as too simplistic for human mothers, the uneasy relationship between *maternal* and *instinct* emerges in this farcical set design.[11] This staging satirizes women's roles by upsetting the sanctity of the home and the reproductive process.

The mother and daughter pair, Bender and Binder, argue frequently about motherhood and mother-child relationships, revealing that conventions of femininity and mothering often become conflated in gendered language or stereotypical statements. Even their names sound like testaments of female suffering and motherhood as subjection: "bend her" and "bind her." Bender, a fifty-something woman, is the most prolific mother in the play, giving birth to babies (represented by dolls) and continuing to nurse them in multiple scenes, despite the fact that she is past the age when most women experience menopause. Her daughter Binder, a twenty-something woman, both resents her mother's fertility and tries to emulate it by nursing the babies and having a child of her own. Binder's fluctuating attitude illustrates the different views of motherhood as control over one's body versus motherhood as subjection of one's body. She also highlights the cultural expectations regarding the ability of older women to have children and perform mothering roles at a time when their bodies may naturally be past childbearing, and she shows that technology has changed the boundaries of childbearing beyond what we could have predicted twenty years ago. Her fascination with the babies evinces the culturally and religiously engrained view of motherhood as women's highest goal, but her interactions with the babies undermine the idea of maternal instinct as a natural response of new mothers.

Bender and Binder's attitudes are juxtaposed with their maternal bodies to subvert essentialized notions of motherhood while also attesting to the return of stringent mothering practices such as exclusive breastfeeding. The appearance of these breastfeeding mothers and the constant feeding of numerous babies is the most farcical, outrageous display of the maternal body in the play. This staging brings to light cultural uneasiness about eroticism and the maternal body while dramatizing the frenzy and chaos around adapting to newborns. As Rosi Braidotti argues, the changing bodies of pregnant and nursing women are threatening because of their lack of borders and constant flux; she claims that the maternal body even has monstrous connotations because it is "morphologically dubious" in its ability to change. Breastfeeding is particularly dubious because breasts fluctuate between their sexual and reproductive functions, thus prompting viewers to shift between the mother/lover distinction. This split between maternity and sexuality is an unhealthy one, according to Mary Rogers and Susan Chase, because mothers who display their sexuality are deemed morally suspicious and unhealthy. Breastfeeding is viewed as an unerotic activity that is disconnected from pleasure or sexuality. They write, "Culturally de-eroticizing breastfeeding breasts means that overall women's breasts properly belong to someone else, namely, men and children." Since the sexual aspect of breasts usually belongs to the male cultural domain of arousal, breasts are either objects of desire or objects for feeding. By contrast, Rogers and Chase enter the debate around the many functions of the maternal body by arguing that breastfeeding does not need to be desexualized completely; rather, the maternal body can retain sexual attractiveness and the mother can experience erotic feelings in that maternal function. Bender and Binder depict the extremes of maternal behavior in their constant nursing while also asserting their sexual identities overtly, such that these roles are constantly *beside* each other. When they breastfeed and primp themselves for dates in the same scene, they juxtapose their maternal and sexual roles in ways that undermine the distinction between them.[12]

In the original production of the play, the costuming emphasized the conflation of sexuality and maternity to make the maternal body unavoidably visible onstage. To visualize the scene, I draw on Sarahjane Scaife's description of the first production: "There were dozens of babies, made up of wrapped, stuffed cotton, with different colour codes. In the bath, Bender was constantly dropping babies and feeding them, and demanding more. Both Bender and myself [Binder] had fantastic John Paul Gaultier style boned costumes with cone shaped 'boobs,' Madonna style. The 'boobs' unzipped to reveal babies' faces on them. We were constantly unzipping them to feed the babies."[13] By making breasts the obvious visual focus, these costumes tempt the audience to stare at women's chests and transgress the boundary between sexual desire and maternal function. Similar to their inspiration in Madonna, the Material Girl, these costumes accentuate the breasts in a sexual but slightly unusual way by making them conical and by painting babies' faces on them. While most people may avoid staring at breastfeeding women in public, these costumes invite and practically demand that the audience participate in that kind of staring. The costumes, then, sexualize breastfeeding while also making it a frantic, never-ending activity that likely depicts the endless cycle of feedings that many women experience. The babies are unavoidably present, and the women are perpetually linked to their maternal, breastfeeding roles, emphasizing the grotesque connotation of the maternal body as "open, protruding, irregular, secreting, multiple, and changing."[14] They also convey the sense that breastfeeding, while beneficial, is exhausting and continuous and that cultural discourse has now returned to breastfeeding as an obligation of motherhood (*la mère* écologique) and stigmatizes women who don't or can't nurse.

At the same time, continually nursing and throwing babies produces a wonderful scene of physical comedy, with different-colored babies flying through the air like banana cream pies and women nursing from cone-shaped breasts. The maternal body becomes a mutable, fluid site with unnatural breasts and, later, male pregnancies. Both biological function and maternal behaviors pass from women to men such that motherhood is literally beside itself; neither sex can claim sole responsibility or blame for mothering. In *Low* every serious conflict about mothering and femininity becomes a means of satirizing itself, especially as words and bodies come into tension with each other. As Anna McMullan writes, "*Low in the Dark* refuses to idealize the role of mother in relation to female identity."[15] Even further, *Low* refuses to limit the role of mother to female identity or to land on one definitive model for mothers. Each character resists being a type by fluctuating through the spectrum of positive and negative aspects of pregnancy and raising children.

Speaking the Language of Fertility and Femininity

In addition to the physicality of the characters, the dialogue of the play exposes the characters' views of their own sexuality, their capacity to be desirable, and their skills as mothers. Together, the physical comedy and verbal role-play produce a kind of grotesque, farcical humor that attempts to surprise and even disorient the audience. The element of surprise and unconventionality makes the action onstage unfamiliar to the audience, such that the audience might be able to see various kinds of gendered expectations for mothers and children. This carnivalesque quality unsettles norms and encourages play in order to enter the essentialist/antiessentialist dialectic and create a space of critique. Alongside grotesque depictions of maternal bodies as a "violation of harmony, symmetry, and proportion" and the "macabre," the black humor of the dialogue highlights language's carnivalesque quality. Carr emphasizes the power of words to inscribe gender traits into impressionable children, builds her humor around conventions of mothering, and in later plays will transform these parenting structures into tragedies.[16]

The mother-daughter antagonism between Bender and Binder centers on tension between sexual freedom, maternal responsibility, and familial roles. Bender and Binder's interactions range from comparing their bodies to competing for men, and their conversations about their babies' fathers dismantles the nuclear family as the only mechanism for raising children. Shortly after Bender gives birth onstage, Binder helps her compose a letter to the absentee father of the baby. Even though this effort represents a collaborative approach to forming a family, their constant disagreements throughout the scene reinforce an overall mother-daughter antagonism, thus undermining the stability of their family structure. This scene capitalizes on the features of a one-night stand: Bender cannot remember the man's name, occupation, or address, which certainly does not bespeak a commitment from her or him. Bender's sexual freedom challenges the virginal, virtuous expectations for women by positioning sexuality outside of a monogamous, marital relationship, but her actions don't glorify her sexual choices either. Bender writes to the father because of social expectation, exclaiming, "I'd better write to him. Get out the pen and paper!" In the process of writing the letter, they address whether Bender knows which night she conceived, whether she cried at conceiving ("women always cry when they conceive"), and whether she can even identify the father of the child. She thus positions motherhood as triggering some biological and emotional reaction, like crying, but also as being divorced from institutional attachments or familial ties. This scene addresses stereotypes only to subvert and ridicule them; in this case, the letter implicates the mother as well as the father in an apathetic stance toward the child. The letter is a farce, as seen by the fact that the two women cannot decide on the child's gender or say anything for certain about the father. They begin like this:

BENDER: My dearest . . . My dearest? My dearest man, I am writing to tell you that you have another son . . .
BINDER: Daughter!
BENDER: That you have another child. It was a difficult birth but . . .
BINDER: It wasn't!

The letter cannot even be sent and is ultimately a futile exercise, but Bender is completely unconcerned. Although we usually associate this kind of letter with locating the deadbeat dad after a one-night stand, here the deadbeat mom is equally to blame for not knowing or caring about the history of the father. The letter also tacitly admits the existence of father's rights with a half-hearted attempt to inform the father, but falls short of full acknowledgment of such rights because Bender does not know his identity.[17]

Building on these unconventional relationship patterns, the play also highlights the characters' disagreement over reproductive technology. The science of fertility, exemplified in the birth control pill, has been a controversial issue in Irish, Roman Catholic belief and in current debates over abstinence-based sex education. In act 1, scene 5, Bender and Binder orchestrate the feeding of the enormous pile of babies, leading to some tensions about the appropriate number of children. When Bender accuses Binder of jealousy for not having any babies, Binder tells her to go on the pill. At the time of the play's premiere, the Health and Family Planning Bill of 1985 in Ireland had finally allowed condoms and spermicides to be sold by regional health boards and clinics to anyone over eighteen without a prescription. This bill marked the first time in Ireland that condoms were available without a prescription. The Health and Family Planning Act of 1979 had legalized contraception (including the pill, IUDs, spermicide, and condoms) with a doctor's prescription, with the stipulation that it should be used for "bona fide family planning purposes," meaning for married couples only. The availability of these contraceptives in this limited way did not address the needs of unmarried women, nor did it negate the Catholic Church's official anti–birth control stance. Although the pill has become seemingly ubiquitous today, distribution over the counter is still unavailable in the United States, and many women still lack access. Badinter points out that the pill has decreased in popularity under recent cultural mores because women fear gaining weight, getting cancer, and even becoming infertile. The trend toward being "natural" and the fear of chemicals has made birth control less attractive to the generation of women it is designed to help. Both in Ireland and current Western culture, the question of taking the pill, then, is not a throwaway comic line but a controversial issue for many Generation X and Millennial women.[18]

In other scenes, Bender and Binder continue to critique the gender roles surrounding childbirth as well as the medicalization of the birthing process. After giving birth silently early in the play, Bender goes into the throes of childbirth again, and this time Binder jumps into a role play, donning a hat and tails in order to play the part of an insensitive, 1950s-style sitcom father at his child's birth. This role play re-creates the time when fathers were uninvolved in the birthing process, were kept out of the delivery room, and were depicted as ignorant of what to do during labor. While Bender writhes and screams "Epiduuraaal!" the man (aka Binder) asks whether dinner is ready and where his slippers are. He ineptly pats her head while the baby is being born and then rushes out of the room holding the new baby boy. The specific references to epidurals enter into current debate between those who advocate no medication during childbirth and those who embrace medication for making the experience more comfortable. In this scene, Bender's cries for an epidural go unanswered and she gives birth to the baby in the bathtub before the man carries it away. This violent birth scene presents one model of ineffective relationships between men and women, but it does so in such a grotesquely comical way that the audience would probably laugh rather than cry at the man's ineptitude, partly because this "man" is a woman in disguise. In effect, this scene enacts the debate over pain medication in childbirth and the fear of having inadequate support during that time. This father's ignorant behavior foreshadows several of Carr's other plays in which the father's absence or conflict with the mother makes the child an accessory to parental problems.[19]

Whereas Bender and Binder role-play around an actual birthing process, they also dispute the relationship between fertility and femininity with an earthy, grotesque language that enacts the fraught relationship between the reproductive female body and its sexual attractiveness. Pregnancy confirms fertility and seemingly enhances femininity, but, ironically, it also changes the mother's body in ways that often reduce the sense of femininity (if femininity is defined by limited norms of erotic attractiveness). In the first scene, mother and daughter start to fight by hurling pregnancy-related insults at each other. Bender begins, "There's plenty where she came from . . . as soon as I get my figure back I'll have another and then another, because I am fertile!" She articulates the cultural expectation that women be both fertile and able to transform their bodies back to prepregnancy shape. In our current popular culture, we are constantly inundated with celebrities whose pregnancies and weight loss are excessively chronicled (e.g., Halle Berry, Victoria Beckham, Gisele Bündchen). Anyone who still exhibits any baby weight three months postpartum is subject to ridicule and intense scrutiny. The ability to transform one's body postpregnancy reads as an empowering or self-validating ability even though postpartum weight loss may not rest entirely in the woman's control and may cause significant anxiety. Binder jabs back:

BINDER: I had a dream last night your uterus fell out.
BENDER: I dreamt your ovaries exploded!
BINDER: At least I have ovaries and eggs, lots of eggs, much more than you because I'm young. I'm in my prime.
BENDER: I've had my fair share of eggs . . ..

Binder clings to youth as her main advantage, although neither woman is afraid to reference her good store of eggs. Their bluntness in using correct anatomical terms—even scientific terms—conflicts with the more archaic content of the insult, namely, that reproduction alone determines a woman's worth and that the reproductive capacity supersedes personal identity. Their anatomical references also relate to the medical discourse around fertility that emphasizes restrictive gender roles, which position women as passive in sexual interactions and fertility as a measure of personal success. Emily Martin, who analyzes medical discourse about reproductive anatomy, finds that eggs are described as passive and waiting for fertilization in contrast to the active sperm on a journey or mission to fertilize the egg. Likewise, eggs are portrayed as degenerating over time and even wasted if not used, while sperm are seen as endlessly replenishing even though billions of them are "wasted" in nonreproductive sexual activity. Menstruation is often described as shedding or "expelling" blood or "denuding" the uterus because of a *failure* to reproduce rather than as a cleansing activity for the body to renew itself. This language of passivity and failure simultaneously positions the woman's body as a passive receptacle at the same time that nonpregnancy becomes a failure to perform reproduction correctly. This medical language emphasizes the paradox of embodiment: The presentness and opaqueness of the body make it unavoidably lived while also inexplicable; it exists and yet is beside itself in operating largely outside conscious control. Although Bender and Binder value their bodies enough to claim their eggs as assets, they do so at each other's expense by emphasizing that the aging eggs will inevitably deteriorate before they can be used.[20]

Bender and Binder's knowledge of their own reproductive systems and cycles, however, highlights the *lack* of sex education historically available to women in Ireland and many other countries. Sex education continues to be at the center of debate around religious and ideological beliefs about sexual activity. A survey conducted in Dublin in 1983, six years before the play, revealed that 62 out of 112 girls "had no knowledge of their own fertility and its relation to the menstrual cycle, and twelve had only a rough idea." In 1984, the Women's Right to Choose Campaign in Dublin wrote, "All women are sexually oppressed in Ireland. We are oppressed because we have little chance to understand and define our sexuality on our own terms, or to express it in ways we have freely chosen." This statement demonstrates the vehemence of resistance about the place of women's sexuality in Irish society, and the play addresses these same issues from the angle of satire and humor. Reality shows such as *16 and Pregnant* and *Teen Mom* cast a spotlight on teenage moms by deglamorizing teen motherhood while creating a tabloid following of their latest mishaps. By making pregnancy an object of satire, the play reinforces the fact that women's reproductive choices have been severely limited, and even now the issue of appropriate maternal age, behavior, and bodies continues to attract media coverage.[21]

In contrast to the lack of reproductive knowledge exhibited by many Irish girls, Carr hyperbolically represents reproduction and women's knowledge of their own bodies. Mother and daughter not only taunt each other verbally but also physically compete to have babies, thus valorizing the idea of being Miss Reproductive. They engage in reproductive competition because of Bender's seemingly boundless fertility and Binder's resentment of the continuous baby birthing. Their dialogue enacts the tensions around female fertility: Does motherhood make a woman more womanly? Do youth and fertility define femininity? By presenting dichotomous ideas about pregnancy beside each other, Carr engages them to show their prevalence and also reinvigorates the discussion around the "appropriate" amount of fertility.

Another possible response to these questions comes later in the play, when Binder criticizes Bender for continuing to have babies, and Bender defends her decision by calling herself an artist: "I am an artist, a *bloody* genius in fact! Show me the art that is life! You can travel the whole world and nowhere, nowhere will you find it except in the big stretch-marked belly of a woman." The pregnant body has emerged as a cultural symbol that's valorized while discourse also demands that women erase the marks of pregnancy by removing signs of stretch marks and losing weight. We simultaneously want to display pregnancy while concealing its effects and disconnecting it from its source in menstruation. The epithet "bloody" ironically alludes to the impurity of women's blood because of its links to menstruation or the loss of virginity. Even though the maternal body exists on a cycle of blood that is continually in preparation, this blood becomes an object of disgust when made public. In the Irish context, Harris argues that for Irish nationalism in the earlier part of the twentieth century, the woman's body had to be seen as pure and idealized, thus the need to hide the reality of menstrual blood. She explains, "It was the intense investment in the image of the ideal and inviolable female body that made nationalist audiences so sensitive to representations of Irish women [in Synge and Yeats]." By claiming that the maternal body is in fact an art form, and that it combines art and life better than other art forms, Bender attempts to raise pregnancy from a biological act to an artistic one that recognizes different facets and consequences of maternal identity.[22]

Pregnancies eventually translate into parent-child conflicts, as Bender and Binder viciously demonstrate. When verbal sparring between them becomes actual blows, these fights enact the conflict between a young woman in her reproductive prime and an older woman who may be more sexually experienced. Similar in content to their first verbal fight about fertility, this time a literal wrestling match occurs when the two women compete for the same man. This fight, which is a comical physical battle onstage, prefigures the tragic violence in Carr's later plays such as *Ariel*, in which a mother-daughter fight becomes a brutal stabbing. In this scene, they are comparing their bodies and trying to prove whose physique is superior for attracting men. Binder resents her mother's competition for a man, leading to this exchange:

BINDER: [. . .] You knew he preferred me so you had to move in! Hadn't you?
BENDER: Preferred you! The croaky little voice of you with your ostrich eyes and your pancake diddies!
BINDER: (*whispers*) Menopause, men o pause, men . . . o . . . pause!
BENDER: Stop it! (*Starts hitting her.*)
BINDER: Menopause, hot flush, empty womb.

In one sentence, Bender compares her daughter to a frog, an ostrich, and a pancake. This barrage of insults turns Binder's body into a monstrous conglomeration that negates any sense of sexual attractiveness by defeminizing her body. While Bender claims to be fertile and continues to exhibit fertility, Binder latches onto the sensitive subject of aging and the loss of that fertility in order to torment her mother. By focusing on menopause, Binder supports the conventional view that menopause is the end of a woman's useful life, and even is a form of castration. At the advent of hormone replacement therapy, menopause was pathologized as a disease that could be treated by keeping women feminine through estrogen such that these hormones were presented as a remedy for failing female bodies. Similar to the discourse surrounding childbirth and birth control, the medical language around menopause can be presented as both reclaiming and poisoning the female body. In the case of hormone replacement therapy, as with many medical treatments, long-range effects may prove more harmful than the short-term benefits of the treatment; this therapy has proven dangerous for the risk of uterine cancer, but millions of women have already taken these hormones to stave off effects of menopause.[23]

This conflict between two women also concentrates on issues of pride and juxtaposes desirability and fertility so that the two cannot be wholly separated. Both women want to achieve these ends, and they will not let their mother-daughter bond stand in the way, even if it means wrestling each other for superiority. In later plays, such as *The Mai*, mother-daughter relationships also become entangled in the mother's romantic battles such that passing advice or conveying affection is not idealized or essentialized. Fiona Becket observes, "In Carr, then, the effects of the transmission of knowledge through matrilineal channels (underpinned by the mother-daughter model) is both a central feature of women's relationships in her recent plays *and* a target for devastating irony." Becket's comments emphasize that the exchange of knowledge tends to occur in women's circles, and especially from mother to daughter. While this sharing of advice often represents a tangible bond between mother and daughter, advice can also become cloying and stifling.[24]

Bringing Home the Baby: The Perils of Raising Children

In addition to many conversations and disputes about the maternal body, the issues of raising children also take center stage, both from the perspective of good parenting behavior and the gender traits inscribed into the children. In the first scene of the play, Bender miraculously gives birth silently and then launches into an argument with Binder over the sex of the baby, the care of the baby, and the number of babies Bender has had. Within this dialogue, the two women keep disputing the sex of the baby and the gendered traits associated with the baby. Binder initially says, "babies are always boys," but throughout the conversation they both change their minds several times about the sex of the baby. Although the sex of a child would seem to be physically obvious, Carr makes it ambiguous and contested by having the characters reclassify the baby repeatedly. Biological determinacy bows to the view that socialization and interpellation into the dominant gender ideology will have more effect on the baby's life. If gender is a performative category, this scene invokes Judith Butler's claim that the original "It's a girl" sets in motion a lifetime of being inscribed within normative behaviors, both sexual and gendered. The play explicitly tackles the subject of raising children and gendering them through the language of naming and labeling; it also addresses the sense that there are multiple influences on the child's life in addition to the biological mother.[25]

The fact that the two women cannot decide on the baby's sex seems at first like a farcical joke, but it leads to the larger process of inscribing the rules of gendered behavior into a child's body. For example, Binder starts breastfeeding the baby and claims, "She sucks like a man," to which Bender says, "She'll have luck so!" In this case, the strength of sucking carries several connotations. First, sucking connotes oral sex, but to say "she sucks like a man" seems unusual. More likely, to compliment a woman for this skill, it would be more typical to say "she sucks like a pro" (that is, a professional in the sex business—a prostitute). In this line, Carr displays a trend that continues throughout the play of combining two clichés in unexpected ways to reveal how gendered expectations cling to these clichés even when they are fragmented. We might expect "Take it like a man!," but not "she sucks like a man." Nevertheless, in this scene, sucking becomes a gendered trait and a measure of future success. For a female baby to suck like a man means that she acquires masculine traits such as being vigorous, ambitious, and strong, despite the fact that sucking itself is a female trait in this context. Only a few lines later, when the baby is deemed male, Bender tells Binder to "put him in the shower and give him a doll." When Binder protests, "They're for the girl-babies," Bender says, "Well then give him a train and give his mother a drink!" This common division between gendered toys again highlights the extent to which parents often socialize their children in specifically gendered ways by giving them gender-specific toys.[26]

Furthermore, the drinking mother blatantly ignores the health threats of nursing or pregnant mothers consuming alcohol. Although most would agree that mothers should be aware of how their behavior affects their children, this example enters into the debate about the relative importance of the mother's needs and the child's needs. If the idea of maternal instinct has reentered cultural discourse, as Badinter argues, then good mothering is defined according to "la mère écologique"—supposedly natural practices that prevent toxicity in the environment or otherwise from harming the child. Badinter recounts debates about BPA in bottles, disposable diapers, and the superiority of breastfeeding in order to explain why the concepts of "woman" and "mother" are so contentious. She asserts, "L'environnement, les pression socials, l'itinéraire psychologique semblent toujour peser plus lourd que la faible voix de 'notre mère Nature'"(Environment, social pressure, and the psychological agenda always seem to outweigh the faint voice of Mother Nature). In other words, the idea of motherhood as a natural category lives in tension with environmental, social, and psychological pressures to perform motherhood in specific, narrowly accepted ways. In Sedgwick's terms, these roles of woman and mother are *beside* each other, such that they repel, mimic, attract, aggress on, and warp each other; that is, they coexist uneasily rather than harmoniously. Susan Bordo argues that mothers' subjectivity is often diminished or ignored in favor of the child's subjectivity, thus diminishing the mother to a mere incubator or maternal function. She writes, "The essence of the pregnant woman, by contrast [to the fetus], is her biological, purely mechanical role in preserving the life of another." Because of this viewpoint, courts have sometimes ignored the bodily integrity of the mother or her individual rights to order medical procedures that would preserve the fetus against the mother's wishes. This is not an argument in favor of abortion, Bordo stresses, but rather an argument that recognizes the importance of the woman's subjectivity in controlling what happens to her body. Mothers in this play seek to control their fertility but seem frantically unable to cope with the bodily consequences of breastfeeding and childcare.[27]

In addition to the overwhelming number of female pregnancies, presenting pregnant male characters foreshadows the medical advancements in surrogacy and alternative forms of pregnancy: most notably, a transgender man, Thomas Beatie, who was born with female anatomy has given birth to two children while legally male and married to a woman.[28] When Bone—a male character—becomes pregnant while also impregnating Binder, their conversations and use of props extend motherhood across both sexes: they alternate knitting while baking buns for each other, they role play about who is the "father" of Bone's child, and they argue about who should have been taking the pill to prevent these pregnancies. The cross-dressing of Bone and Baxter, the other male character, along with their role playing and pregnancies, remove mothering from the female realm, thus temporarily severing the dualism between "woman" and "mother." During his pregnancy, Bone's conversations with Baxter about parenting reinforce common gender stereotypes about socializing girls. Earlier, Bender labeled her babies according to occupations and planned their lives in prescriptive ways, but here Bone and Baxter are seemingly scripting the details of a daughter's gestures and attitudes. Their plans again draw on gendered expectations for girls' sexual behavior, like "how to put lipstick on," "how to flutter the eyelids," "how to say no, when she means yes, and yes when she means no." Both men accept and want to encourage these flirtatious and stereotypical female behaviors, which are often used as justification for assaults when women are "asking for it." This lighthearted scene carries sinister undertones of endangering a daughter by teaching her behavior that would be misinterpreted, but that emphasis on teaching children stereotypical traits is precisely the point. This scene is an extreme example of the way that all parents model gendered behavior, explicitly or implicitly; moreover, this function rests not only with mothers but also with those who assume an authoritative or mothering role and exert influence over the child. At the same time, the idea that parents are solely responsible for a child's gender or sexual identity is a fallacy as well. These particularly egregious examples caricature parenting behaviors in order to make more subtle behaviors noticeable.[29]

This conversation allows men to enter the realm of mothering but confirms that all kinds of mothers risk the stigma of bad mothering. More importantly, though, these scenes of raising children enter into the discourse of maternal guilt and the cultural impulse to blame the mother for all the children's faults. Chase describes the development of the "institution of motherhood" as an outgrowth of the Victorian expectation for women to be completely selfless and self-sacrificing in raising children, whose constant happiness is of utmost importance. In Badinter's terms, the return of the maternal instinct risks a resurgence of the essentialistic view of motherhood that discourages women from accepting a range of physical and emotional experiences. This discourse has often demonized mothers who work outside the home or those whose children face physical, emotional, or psychological problems. At the same time, the play acknowledges the importance of socialization in shaping the child's gender identity and the mother's important role in that process.[30]

Raising a child, however, begins with the decision whether or not to keep the pregnancy, thus bringing abortion into the mix of parenting issues. After Bone becomes pregnant, he soon admits that he's thinking about an abortion because he has "a right to choose," to which Baxter replies, "There's a life inside of you! A destiny, all its own." Again, Bordo's assertion that women are viewed as living incubators without subjectivity comes into play in the debate over the mother's rights versus the fetus's rights. As of 2015, abortion was still illegal in Ireland except in cases in which the mother's life is at risk due to suicide or physical illness, and only twenty-six abortions were carried out in Irish hospitals during 2014. In the United States the legality and availability of abortions continues to be debated, sometimes with violent means, and some individual prolife activists have murdered abortion providers. Bone and Baxter rehearse some of the most conventional positions on abortion, perhaps alluding to the idea that men tend to be more active in the antiabortion movement than in the proabortion movement. Because these statements come from a pregnant man and his male friend, they not only take abortion out of the normal realm of a "women's issue" but also defamiliarize clichéd arguments. In particular, the play undermines the idea that a baby has "a destiny, all its own," since Bender, for example, labels all her children according to their future professions (Doctor, Pope) and raises them accordingly. Having a destiny of one's own also depends on the gender assigned and how that gender is encouraged or enforced, so the idea of a self-determining destiny seems more and more remote. The play simultaneously questions whether (pregnant) men can take opposite positions on abortion, whether women can ever completely control their bodies, and whether babies can eventually shape their own destinies.[31]

From the issue of abortion, the play then broadens the discussion of birth to discuss a "successful" birth as a kind of abortion. The most Beckettian moment in the play, a conversation about the birthing process, emphasizes that the hardships of life begin with birth and blames the mother for this pain. This moment also transforms the earlier conversation about babies having a "destiny all their own" into a pessimistic consideration of a painful existence. Bone admits,

BONE: I was a natural birth. From paradise I came, through the chink, to this galaxy of grief. I'll never forget it and I'll never forgive her for it. Purged from the womb, jostled down the long passage, umbilical cord around me neck, the grunting, the groaning, the blood, the shit, the piss, and the first scream, there was no point of return. A rough start to a rough journey I tell you. I wouldn't wish life on my worst enemy, I'll have an abortion.

BAXTER: We're all abortions, some later than others, that's all.

This passage, more than any other, resonates with Beckett's "birth through shit" mantra and his bleak view of the "accursed progenitor" who brings us into the world. Moreover, passages like this one in *Low* point to the sardonic, haunting quality in Carr's work and prefigure the tragic situations that characters face in her later plays.[32]

In *Woman and Scarecrow* (2008), for instance, the woman on her deathbed bargains with the incarnation of Death, who is also the embodiment of her desires and disappointed hopes. Scarecrow admonishes her for not leaving her husband when she had a chance and for not pursuing happiness for herself. At the same time, Scarecrow accuses her of having eight children for selfish reasons: because Woman needed to own these children in order to validate herself. Woman admits, "Yes, I used them. They were my little soldiers. I was the fortress. And how they protected me from terrors imagined and terrors real, my soothers, my buffers to fortune. And I'm sure I've damaged them in some vital, irreparable way, but I have also loved them with a hopeless, enchanted love." Although Woman seems concerned about what will happen to her children after she dies, she spends more time contemplating whether she should have left her husband for the lover who gave her the diamond ring or the six-foot-four lover with the crocodile boots. This protracted death scene presents children as one facet of the woman's life that is intertwined with the troubled relationship she has with her husband and that she approaches with mixed motivations. Rather than motherhood becoming an autonomous role that subsumes all others, motherhood is rather *beside* other roles in a constantly shifting interplay.[33]

The maternal ambivalence in *Low* becomes tragic violence in future plays as Carr depicts mothers who kill themselves and sometimes even kill their children. In later plays, the maternal body becomes a living tableau, both actor and acted upon. Motivation is never simple: If Carr's plays demonstrate one thing, it is that being a mother is but one facet of personhood that only magnifies tensions in other areas of life. Romantic relationships, sibling rivalries, and conflict with the older generation all intensify when children are involved. In B*y the Bog of Cats . . .* , Hester Swayne kills her only daughter to prevent their separation when Hester's lover marries a younger, wealthier woman; in *On Raftery's Hill*, the family's cycle of incest and abuse collapses mothers, daughters, and sisters into a single generation. These plays cannot be read simply as a condemnation of mothers or as monolithic constructions of motherhood. The beauty of these characters lies in the ways that they continually seek to renegotiate their identities amid painful circumstances. The fact that their choices so often lead to violence against themselves and others illustrates tragedy as the grief of being beside oneself: separated mentally, emotionally, and physically from everyday existence and acting in a state of altered consciousness.[34]

Carr creates a picture of the maternal body that transcends women but also reminds us how tightly fertility and femininity are intertwined. Through conversations, arguments, and role playing, the characters enact the tensions surrounding "la mère écologique" and the volatile relationship between woman and mother existing *beside* each other. The patriarchal and religious structure of

Ireland and larger Western culture comes under fire for denying women knowledge of their own bodies and power to use their sexuality as they wish. The play's depiction of raising children likewise invokes the predominant attitude of blaming the mother while also exposing the broader cultural and familial influences on the child's gender development. This brilliantly satirical work anticipates the conflicts that become more tragic in Carr's later plays, when women in oppressive situations sometimes resort to suicide or murder, even murdering their children. Whether writing in this comedic, absurd mode or crossing into tragedy, Carr in her plays peels back the layers of motherhood to lay bare the underlying contradictions that permeate our culture.

Notes

1. Elisabeth Badinter, *Le Conflit: la Femme et la Mère* (Paris: Flammarions, 2010).
2. Eve Kosofky Sedgwick, *Touching Feeling: Affect, Pedagogy, Performativity* (Durham: Duke University Press, 2003).
3. At the time of the play's premier, the Irish Health and Family Planning Bill of 1985 had finally allowed the "distribution of condoms by regional health boards and clinics, and allowed anyone over 18 to get them without a prescription" (Richard B. Finnegan and James L. Wiles, *Women and Public Policy in Ireland: A Documentary History 1922–1997* [Dublin, Ireland: Irish Academic Press, 2005], 214). This bill marked the first time in Ireland that condoms were available without a prescription. Although the birth control pill was legally available, it could be prescribed only to married couples, and it was not condoned by the Catholic Church as a family planning method. Legal battles around abortion centered on whether the mother's life was at risk, primarily because of suicide. A 1983 constitutional amendment placed the mother's life and fetus's life on equal footing, thus negating the mother's right to an abortion. Following this amendment, in 1988 the Irish Supreme Court ruled it illegal to distribute any abortion information in Ireland, including advertisements for English abortion clinics. See Irish Family Planning Association, "Abortion in Ireland: Legal Timeline," *Irish Family Planning Association*, accessed September 3, 2015, https://ifpa.ie/Hot-Topics/Abortion/Abortion-in-Ireland-Timeline. Following these rulings, in a famous 1992 case, a fourteen-year-old rape victim, known as X, was allowed to travel to England for an abortion because she threatened suicide. Statistics suggest that annually between six thousand and seven thousand Irish women travel to England for an abortion. See Patrick Kenny, "Irish Pro-Lifers: The Road Ahead," *Human Life Review* 31, no. 4 (2005): 72–78, and Siobhan Mullaly, "Debating Reproductive Rights in Ireland," *Human Rights Quarterly* 27 (2005): 78–104.
4. Sedgwick, *Touching Feeling*, 8.
5. Susan E. Chase, "Motherhood and Feminism," in *Mothers and Children: Feminist Analyses and Personal Narratives*, ed. Susan E. Chase and Mary F. Rogers (New Brunswick, NJ: Rutgers University Press, 2001), 3–20, 19.
6. Maria Kurdi explains, "Underscoring the social constructedness, performativity and

inherent ambiguity of the most widely accepted gender roles, the unfolding chain of reversals [in *Low*] shows the 'normal' in the cracked mirror of gender divisions." If mirrors are a central part of constructing self-identity, the metaphor of the cracked mirror shows that images of gender identities may be skewed and false from the start, thus questioning the arbitrary nature of gender divisions. A cracked mirror may also duplicate an image, suggesting a kind of reproduction, such as the plethora of babies onstage. See Maria Kurdi, "Alternative Articulations of Female Subjectivity and Gender Relations in Contemporary Irish Women's Plays: The Example of Marina Carr," in *Codes and Masks: Aspects of Identity in Contemporary Irish Plays in an Intercultural Context* (New York: Peter Lang, 2000), 59–72, 60.

7. Kelly Oliver, *Subjectivity without Subjects: From Abject Fathers to Desiring Mothers* (Lanham, MD: Rowman and Littlefield Publishers, Inc., 1998), 61.
8. Marina Carr, *Low in the Dark*, in *Marina Carr: Plays* (New York: Faber and Faber, 1999), 1–100, 5.
9. Matthew Winston, "Black Humor: To Weep with Laughing," *Black Humor: Critical Essays*, ed. Alan R. Pratt (New York: Garland Publishing, Inc., 1993), 249–68, 266. Winston's article is about the strategies of black humor. The comment I cite pertains to the form of the drama, but I believe it applies equally well to the stage design, since it doesn't conform to a realistic or naturalistic box set and is both humorous and puzzling at the same time.
10. Throughout the play, references to baking and exchanging buns intertwine the domestic sphere and the pregnant body by making the pregnant body an oven for ever-burgeoning babies.
11. Susan Cannon, *Gender and Modern Irish Drama* (Bloomington: Indiana University Press, 2002), 68. Badinter recounts the recent history of "maternal instinct" as dependent on establishing skin-to-skin contact between mother and newborn within six hours after birth ("qu'elles ont seize heurs après l'accouchements pour établir un contact 'peau à peau' avec leur nouveau-né"), or, later, arising through breastfeeding initiating a cascade of hormones (71–80).
12. Rosi Braidotti, *Nomadic Subjects* (New York: Columbia University Press, 1994), 64; Susan E. Chase and Mary F. Rogers, "Mothers, Sexuality, and Eros," in *Mothers and Children: Feminist Analyses and Personal Narratives*, ed. Susan E. Chase and Mary F. Rogers (New Brunswick, NJ: Rutgers University Press, 2001), 115–34, 125.
13. Sarahjane Scaife, "Mutual Beginnings: Marina Carr's *Low in the Dark*," in *The Theatre of Marina Carr: "Before Rules Was Made,"* ed. Cathy Leeney and Anna McMullan (Dublin: Carysfort Press, 2003), 1–16, 10.
14. Mary Russo, *The Female Grotesque: Risk, Excess, and Modernity* (New York: Routledge, 1995), 8.
15. Anna McMullan, "Gender, Authorship and Performance in Selected Plays by Contemporary Irish Women Playwrights: Mary Elizabeth Burke-Kennedy, Marie Jones, Marina Carr, Emma Donoghue," in *Theatre Stuff: Critical Essays on Contemporary Irish Theatre*, ed. Eamonn Jordan (Dublin: Carysfort Press, 2000), 34–46, 42.
16. John R. Clark, *The Modern Satiric Grotesque* (Lexington: University Press of Kentucky, 1991), 19; Winston, "Black Humor," 260.
17. Carr, *Low*, 11–14.

18. See Irish Family Planning Association, "Ireland's Sexual and Reproductive Health History," *Irish Family Planning Association*, https://www.ifpa.ie/node/82 (accessed September 3, 2015). Badinter's full quote about the decrease in women using the birth control pill reads, "Entre 2003 et 2006, les ventes de plaquettes ont baissé d 65 à 63 millions: 'peur de grosser, refus de la chimie sont les principaux griefs' des trentenaires. Les unes invoquent les risques de cancer, d'autres un possible dérèglement hormonal, d'autres enfin la crainte de la stérilité" (55).
19. Carr, *Low*, 15–16.
20. Ibid., 10–11; Emily Martin, "The Egg and the Sperm: How Science Has Constructed a Romance Based on Stereotypical Male-Female Roles," *Signs* 16, no. 3 (1991): 485–501, 486.
21. Jenny Beale, *Women in Ireland: Voices of Change* (Bloomington: Indiana University Press, 1987), 85, 87.
22. Carr, *Low*, 51–52, emphasis mine; Harris, *Gender*, 11.
23. Carr, *Low*, 78; Marina Carr, *Ariel* (Loughcrew, Ireland: Gallery Books, 2002); Anne Fausto-Sterling, *Sexing the Body: Gender Politics and the Construction of Sexuality* (New York: Basic Books, 2000), 170.
24. Fiona Becket, "A Theatrical Matrilineage?: Problems of the Familial in the Drama of Teresa Deevy and Marina Carr," in *Ireland in Proximity: History, Gender, Space* (New York and London: Routledge, 1999), 80–93, 90.
25. Judith Butler, *Bodies that Matter: On the Discursive Limits of "Sex"* (New York and London: Routledge, 1993).
26. Carr, *Low*, 9–10. For an example of research on toys and gender, see Eileen Wood, Serge Desmarais, and Sara Gugula, "The Impact on Parenting Experience of Gender Stereotyped Toy Play of Children," *Sex Roles* 47 (2002): 39–49. In this study, children played individually with their fathers, their mothers, and nonparents, using an assortment of traditionally masculine and feminine toys. The study concluded that even though parents sometimes disagreed with traditional categorizations of some toys, they still followed stereotypes when playing with their children.
27. Badinter, *Le Conflit*, 83; Susan Bordo, *Unbearable Weight: Feminism, Western Culture, and the Body* (Berkeley: University of California Press, 1993), 72–76, 79.
28. When this story broke in 2008, Beatie was asked to explain why he did not remain a lesbian woman instead of becoming legally male. He replied, "Sexuality is completely different than your gender. I felt more comfortable being the male gender" ("It's My Right").
29. Carr, *Low*, 47, 61–62, 69. They consistently try on women's clothing and role play common relationship scenarios, such as who should be the primary breadwinner, what kind of dresses are most attractive, and what makes a good lover. Bender differentiates between her babies in terms of social roles: the Black Sheep, the Doctor, the President, and the Pope babies, all traditionally male professions. Only the Black Sheep in this list exists as an outcast; the other children have highly prestigious, important careers ahead of them in medicine, politics, and the Church. In Catholic Ireland, being the Pope is hypothetically the highest calling for any person; even having a priest in the family might be the hope of many parents. Anthony Daniels, for example, claims that "within living memory it was the ambition of every family to have one son or daughter enter the Church." Bender favors the Pope and wants him to be fed as much as possible so that he

will be healthy and fat, and so that he will take care of her when she is old. See Anthony Daniels, "The New Ireland," *National Review* 57, no. 8 (2005): 27–28.

30. Susan E. Chase, "The Institution and Experience of Motherhood," in *Mothers and Children: Feminist Analyses and Personal Narratives*, ed. Susan E. Chase and Mary F. Rogers (New Brunswick, NJ: Rutgers University Press, 2001), 60–78.
31. Carr, *Low*, 79; See Irish Family Planning Association, "Abortion in Ireland." In the United States, many of the most violent shootings of abortion doctors and bombings of abortion clinics have been carried out by men in conservative prolife organizations. See "Apologists for Murder," *Time*, August 15, 1994, 39.
32. Carr, *Low*, 80; Samuel Beckett, *Endgame* (New York: Grove Press, 1958), 9.
33. Marina Carr, *Woman and Scarecrow* (Oldcastle: Gallery Press, 2006), 66.
34. Marina Carr, *By the Bog of Cats . . .*, in *Marina Carr: Plays* (New York: Faber and Faber, 1999), 257–341; Marina Carr, *On Raftery's Hill* (New York: Dramatist's Play Service, 2002).

Mothers, Daughters, Identity, and Impossibilities

—RHONA JUSTICE-MALLOY

In her disturbingly misogynistic book *Oh, NO! I've Become MY MOTHER*, author Sandra Reishus promises the reader, "You are not doomed to become your mother. You can change the script and live happily ever after, not by asking 'What would mom want me to do?' but rather 'What's best for me?'" The back cover declares, "Escape your mother's emotional grip and make your life your own. You love your mom—you just don't want to be her." In her introduction, Reishus describes what she has coined "the mom gene" as those "similarities, traits, and qualities passed from mother to daughter." All depression, sadness, confusion, and failure can be blamed on the "mom gene," and there is no greater insult than a partner remarking on the fact that you have "become" your mother. The introduction promises tactics to locate your "mom gene" and eradicate it, effectively removing your mother's influence from your life and thus allowing you to live up to your full potential. The reader is encouraged to think of mom as a spider, and daughter is caught in her web: "It's all about separation, separation, separation and once you learn about her web and start to disconnect from your mother's personal issues and live your own life, you've got the cards stacked in your favor." Reishus celebrates the fact that in today's society it is entirely appropriate to ridicule mom, making her the butt of jokes and laughing about her behavior with your friends. With regard to mother-daughter relationships, mothers are categorized in the following niches: absent, critical, drama queen, helpless, intrusive, and jealous.[1]

It would seem that it is necessary for a daughter to resolve mom issues (and that these are always and already mom issues is a given) before she can work on her personal issues and identity. This resolution must always include some value of separation. There is the overarching trope throughout popular self-help literature that mother must be distanced to some degree. In her book *Lives Together/Worlds Apart: Mothers and Daughters in Popular Culture*, Suzanna Danuta Walters convincingly makes the argument that "the dominant contemporary discourses—stressing struggle and separation as well as the importance of mother/child bonding in infancy—have emerged out of a variety of cultural, political, and psychological discourses, [and] these discourses themselves grew out of substantive shifts and contradictions in the social fabric. The shift to discourses centered on a relationship *constructed in conflict* has its origins both in social shifts as well as in the cultural practices that developed alongside and within those structural changes. To define this relationship *psychologically* and within terms of a simple dichotomy (bond/separate) is therefore not 'natural' but actually quite contrived."[2] We would do well to keep this in mind in a study of mother-daughter relationships, especially as they are portrayed on the contemporary stage.

One of many titles in the self-help genre, *Mama Drama* has a subtitle that describes mom as "The One Woman Who Can Push Your Buttons, Make You Cry, and Drive You Crazy." Certainly moms have earned this right as they "ought to know how to push our buttons—they were the ones who installed them." The author opines that the relationship between a mother and her adult daughter is something to be tolerated as "there is nothing like a visit from the mother to push your buttons. To say the least, it's an endurance test dodging the bullets of guilt, criticism and control."[3] It would seem that the best way to negotiate the mother-daughter relationship is by eliminating it, or at least distancing it as far as possible from everyday influence.

These publications about mothers and daughters begin with the assumption that the mother-daughter relationship is problematic and that the source of the difficulty resides in the mother and her "mothering" techniques. In *Daughters and Mothers: Making it Work*, the authors offer strategies for both parties to negotiate a truce. They promise that as a daughter you'll learn how to:

- Stop blaming your mother and become the architect of your life
- Recognize and harness your authentic power and personal strengths
- Identify and abolish negative habits from childhood
- Appreciate your mother's unique life experience

As a mother you'll learn how to:

- Stop feeling guilty for what you did wrong
- Appreciate your daughter's uniqueness instead of judging her
- Support your daughter without stifling her
- Renew your dreams and goals outside of your role as mother[4]

It is interesting to note that the agenda for the daughter insinuates the necessity to undo the effects of faulty mothering while acknowledging that mom's mistakes are simply the product of her "unique life experience." On the other hand, mom will learn to acknowledge and accept her mistakes and amend them by not judging or stifling her daughter, the implied message being that these are the natural and negative attributes of mothering. Finally, mom will learn to redirect her energy from her role as mother to that of a person who, by the choice of being a parent, or more specifically a mother, has put aside her identity, dreams, and goals. These authors promise to lead mom to a *truly* authentic and fulfilling identity independent of her relationship with her daughter. From this narrow survey of popular literature some through lines can be traced.

First, popular culture assumes that the relationship between a mother and her daughter is by necessity problematic. Mothers harm their daughters by being either too close or too distant, and this proximity is always determined by the mother alone. There is no mention of a daughter's shared responsibility for the intimacy of the relationship. Indeed, intimacy and proximity are to be overcome, as separation is necessary if one is to realize authentic identity. A book by psychologist and therapist Evelyn Bassoff, *Mothers and Daughters: Loving and Letting Go*, exemplifies this unfortunate resonance: "In order to realize the full possibilities of her individual life . . . the middle-aged mother must not only separate from her adolescent daughter, she must also complete her separation from her aging mother. It is, after all, only as mothers and daughters grow apart, that each becomes a full woman."[5] How sad to think that women must separate themselves from arguably the most influential entity of their lives in order to realize autonomy.

For all the *Glass Menageries*, *The Effect of Gamma Rays on Man-in-the-Moon Marigolds*, and *'night Mothers*, which problematize the mother and mothering, there are contemporary playwrights who are turning the dialogue from mothering to the concept of "daughtering." That I felt the need to put "daughtering" in quotes, and not mothering, attests to the fact that this is a novel notion. Susanna Walters writes, "As long as no concept of 'daughtering' remains, 'mothering' lives under the extraordinary burden of being the active member in a relationship in which she is semantically overburdened."[6]

In the two plays I examine in this essay, *Memory House*, by Kathleen Tolan,[7] and *Well*, by Lisa Kron,[8] mothers are confronted by daughters who are seeking attention, affection, and answers. While the category of "mother" has been subject to scrutiny in many plays, these plays offer an opportunity to examine the mother-daughter relationship specifically as it relates to issues of self, identity, and desire. The conflict at the heart of each play is the tension between what the daughter wants from the mother, what she needs from the mother, and what the mother desires to give her child, all of which ultimately define what "mother" is. The disconnect between these objectives provides conflict and drives the action of each play. In her book *Mothering the Self: Mothers, Daughters, and Subjects*, Steph Lawler makes the observation, "Knowledge around selfhood and subjectivity, around being a daughter, around being a mother, are interlinked, drawing upon each other to produce a set of seemingly intractable truths around the person, the mother, and the daughter."[9] Through their exploration of the individual roles of "mother" and "daughter" across adoption and illness, *Well* and *Memory House* refute the tropes of self-help books with observations of the mother-daughter relationship defined not by facile pop psychology or even quasi-Freudian notions of mothering found in classic American dramas but by newly mutual acts of storytelling that allow integration of the self and representations of "mother" on the stage.

The Impossibility of Origins

The frame of Kathleen's Tolan's play *Memory House* is the everyday distractions of grocery shopping, kitchen work, or travel in the car that diffuse the questions a child might ask her mother to open weighty discussions. Like characters in a play by Chekov who politely use the words "would you mind" to mediate the harshness of an impossible request or to mitigate an unspeakable sadness, so too the inevitable questions that daughters pose to their unsuspecting mothers play out through mediated negotiations. These questions that deserve but don't always receive truthful answers are best posed when at least one of the participants is otherwise engaged. It is a blessing to be able to keep your eyes on the road when you are asked, "Mom, how old were you when you first had sex?" or "Mom, did you smoke pot in high school . . . college?" *Memory House* is a difficult and intriguing two-person play in which a daughter asks some very important questions and a mother answers those questions as truthfully as she can. I use this play to examine issues of identity and transnational adoption and what I call the "impossibility of origins."

It is New Year's Eve in Maggie's New York City apartment. Maggie is in her fifties, divorced, a professional-dancer-turned-secretary. Her job is not challenging or fulfilling, and neither is it especially unpleasant. As Maggie tells her daughter, "I love my job. I do. You don't understand that's part of the deal with an office job, you go home and complain. That's the deal." Maggie's literal action throughout the 120-minute play is to make and bake a blueberry pie, and this is the action that mediates and makes possible the difficult questions and dialogue that are the essential actions of the play. Her daughter, Katia, was adopted when she was six from an orphanage in Russia by Maggie and her husband (now her ex-husband), a distinguished college professor. This evening Katia has come from her father's apartment across town where she has just completed her application to her "first-choice" university. The application includes a writing assignment called the "Memory House" in which the applicant is asked to write about her memories and the place she stores them. But Katia laments, "I have to write about a fucking memory house and how the fuck can I do that if I don't remember anything."[10] Ironically Katia had not demonstrated much interest in her past or the box of mementos from the orphanage in Russia that Maggie has kept for her over the years. At this moment, Katia's essay is actually complete and stored in her computer but she cannot bring herself to print it out. Somehow doing so would end the process of integration, signal acceptance of her past and her identity as an adult and a daughter, and demand recognition of the realization that she feels she needs to leave Maggie and pursue her own life.

This integration is always complex but even more so when the child is a transnational adoptee. As the playwright explained, "Katia does have these very tiny, and crucial, and important memories. But she's afraid that if she allows autonomy Maggie will suffer."[11] So then, the action of the play on the face of it is for Maggie to bake a pie and Katia to construct a childhood narrative that leads to autonomy with the least amount of discomfort and the most optimistic possibility of repair. This process necessarily falls on the shoulders of the mother. In *Mothering the Self*, Lawler discusses the power of story to define the mother-daughter conundrum: "Although this point may sound an obvious one, I make it because so many analyses of the mother-daughter relationship collapse the mother's story into that of the daughter: the daughter is seen as possessing a privileged insight into the relationship, and her account is seen as giving a 'true' representation of the mother. . . . The daughter must struggle against the mother's influence if she is to achieve 'autonomy.'"[12]

Katia's parents took her to visit Russian immigrant friends, read Russian stories to her, and attempted to sustain her cultural and national heritage, yet Katia laments, "They're not my customs. It's not my language. . . . They're not my dolls, painted eggs, songs."[13] Katia routinely rejects the artifacts of origin Maggie has assembled for her. The tasks of writing the essay and going through the box of mementos exacerbate Katia's already uneasy relationship with her parents, especially Maggie, and her search for an authentic identity and origin.

In her essay "Adoption Narratives, Trauma, and Origins," Margaret Homans discusses the idea of birth culture, which is constructed through the knowledge that allows the individual to "know and fix one's origin," and the unique dilemma of children of transnational adoption where children are placed outside of their birth communities. Often in such situations adoptive parents "construct narratives of the adoption trips or first encounter . . . told in place of birth stories, and in the case of transnational or transethnic adoption, parents construct a simulacrum of the 'birth culture' by providing same-race role models and incorporating into family life cultural fragments (holidays, food, clothing) that are supposed to be authentic but are, inevitably, translated and hybridized."[14] Faced with the task of discovering and fixing her own origins (both authentic and hybridized) for the scrutiny of strangers, Katia has become nearly incapacitated socially and scholastically. She has stopped going out and meeting with friends and put off applying for college. Her mother and father are concerned, yet they each approach the challenge in different ways. Her father suggests she return to Russia to seek knowledge of her deceased birth mother. He advises she address the intellectual and political issues of transnational adoption. His contextual approach, which Katia describes as "ripping children off from their bleeding countries," is cerebral and objective. Maggie, the dancer, responds more intuitively: "You came from here. From me."[15] Throughout the play Katia makes remarks denigrating Maggie's role as the "adoptive" mother. Katia establishes Maggie within the dynamic of the bad/adoptive mother and the good/birth mother. She lashes out at Maggie declaring, "You stole me." Ultimately the dead birth mother is a martyr, while the adoptive mother is a thief. And though well-intentioned, Katia's father encourages her to find her context, her origins, and her "good" mother.

This tension between the adoptive birth culture and the authentic identity proves the impossibility of origins that Homans discusses in her essay. She writes that the adopted, from Oedipus on, are convinced that there is an origin that is attainable. She adds "narratives of adoption are best understood not as about the unearthing of the veridical past, nor yet again about revealing the past . . . but about the creation of something new."[16] Indeed this is exactly what occurs as Katia goes through the artifacts in the memory box Maggie has saved for her. The box contains a video of Katia playing at the orphanage, a girl's (Katia's) party dress, a stuffed teddy bear, court adoption papers, and an audio cassette tape of the director of the orphanage speaking in Russian as the translator explains how Katia came to the orphanage, brought by her grandmother after the death of Katia's mother and abandonment by her father.

In a conversation with the playwright I discovered that the relationship between Maggie and Katia and their testy conversation this New Year's Eve is the daughter's attempt to learn how Maggie will accept her declaration of independence. Although Katia initially reads as a rather spoiled, ungrateful teenager who ridicules her mother's life, job, and past choices, Tolan encouraged a deeper, more complicated exploration of the play. She explains that Katia is in the process, though painfully, of integrating into a whole, healthy woman. She is about to leave home, she is retrieving tiny but crucial bits of childhood memories, and she is constructing a context for her life, and in the process Maggie's story of identity is frustratingly collapsed into her daughter's.[17] Maggie does not seem to understand this need of Katia's. She says, "You know, I would like context too . . . I'm serious. I mean, culture, god. I mean, being a mutt from Minneapolis, being a lapsed Catholic, well, I'm so not attached to any of that. It means nothing to me." Katia replies, "Well good for you. You have that luxury. You know where you came from."[18] While Katia's response seems snotty and selfish, Tolan explains the tension created by Katia's integration: "She desires to somehow merge her ancient past and less ancient past, to come together fully and wholly, and yet at the end of this process she has to have Maggie's acceptance of that whole self. Katia's two major concerns are that Maggie would not accept the Katia who has finally been brought into context but also that Maggie might not survive Katia's autonomy."[19] Throughout the play Katia applies a series of tests and jabs. She criticizes Maggie for giving up her career as a dancer to become a secretary, she accuses Maggie of being a homebody, she blames Maggie for "stealing" her from the orphanage, and most hurtfully she accuses Maggie of smothering her. She says in a particularly tense moment near the end of the play, "I come home and you're sitting there on the couch or you're kind of slumped over drooling on the pillow and your face is like this old dog who looks really strange cuz he's like had a mild stroke while I was out, but he perks up anyway cuz his beloved master has come home, that's all he cares about, he's completely dependent on her for his life and his love for his master is going to eat me it's going to devour me."[20] In her attempt to separate herself from her mother, Katia struggles to create herself from a past she cannot remember, and she is unwilling to accept the life Maggie tried to create for her. She interrogates Maggie in an attempt to explain her isolation and find a connection between her present self and the six-year-old Russian girl she barely remembers.

When Lawler discusses the construction of identity in children, she emphasizes the importance of stories and narratives. She writes, "Narrative is an ontological category: it structures our being, as we tell stories to ourselves and to others about our selves, our being, our place in the scheme of things. Lives are understood through being 'emplotted.' But personal narratives cannot be seen in isolation; they are linked with social narratives which also tell stories about individuals and their place in the world."[21] And so it seems by the end of the play, Katia comes to the understanding that what she searches for cannot ultimately be found. There is not, for any of us, an unmediated access to our identity, our origins, our selves. These things do not reside somewhere in the past waiting to be reclaimed. It is not so much that Katia recovers her origins in the box or through the essay as she creates them in the present, for the present. Through the uneasy practice of repetition, of listening to the tapes, interrogating Maggie, accessing memories, Katia comes to an origin that is more comfortably settled in the present. She writes in the essay, "A memory house is a construct originating in the Middle Ages. The idea is if you visualize a house and you imagine putting facts and ideas in specific nooks and crannies in the house, you can always go there to get them. The visualization helps you to remember. I find it hard to visualize a house. I find it hard to decide to remember."[22] But, ultimately she does remember, and construct, and write, and recite something, perhaps not exactly historical, but something that allows her to complete the application with the knowledge that both she and Maggie will survive this time of breaking away and moving to the next chapter of experience. As she puts on her coat to go to the post office, Katia pauses to give Maggie a very heartfelt thank you. Katia has found a way, with Maggie's help, of integrating the many aspects, real and imagined, of her origins.

Identity, Chronic Illness, and the Impossibility of Intention

Lisa Kron's loosely autobiographical play *Well* is difficult to synopsize or describe. *Backstage* compared it to a "postmodern Pirandello."[23] Let it suffice to say that established theatrical conventions are routinely demolished in this play. The demarcations between the real, the performed, the really performed, and the performed reality of the play are vague, more a series of layers than lines. Performance artist Lisa Kron has rented a theatre, hired actors, and even brought her mother along to enact, as she reads from a note card, "a multicharacter theatrical exploration of issues of health and illness both in the individual and in a community."[24] There are several social issues addressed in the play, including race relations and integration, but in this essay I want to address the topic of chronic illness, identity, and the impossibility of intent in this particular mother-daughter relationship. Kron performed the role she had written for herself in the first production. Subsequent productions have had an actress playing Lisa just as an actress eventually plays Ann, her mother. Kron the author scripted an onstage Lisa who has scripted an "intended play" that during the course of the evening will completely unravel, and this is the source of the tension and conflict of the work. The impossibility of her intended play is mirrored by the impossibility of intention in chronic illness, which by its nature robs the individuals of the ability to view their illness as a mere interruption of their life chronology or, being chronic, denies them the opportunity to plan for recovery or the intention to achieve wellness.

First, though, some backstory. Lisa and her mother have shared a mysterious illness they call the "allergies." She explains, "These days her condition would probably be labeled chronic fatigue syndrome or fibromyalgia." Lisa's mother, Ann, has suffered her entire life with excruciating pain, discomfort, and debilitating fatigue. Lisa suffered for a period of time, but after an extended stay in the Henrotin Hospital's allergy unit in Chicago, she recovered and eventually found a healthy and energetic life as an actress in New York. The question of Lisa's play is, "Why are some people sick for years and years and other people are sick for a while and then they get better? Why is that? What is the difference between those people?"[25] The implicit, underlying question Lisa poses is what is the nature of their differences. Why did Lisa get well while Ann did not, and is this difference a result of Lisa's separation from her mother or rather separation from her mother's identity as a chronically ill parent? In this essay, I argue the latter.

In the book *Good Days, Bad Days: The Self in Chronic Illness and Time* Kathy Charmaz addresses issues of illness as time marker and how chronic illness forces questions of identity. She discusses the idea that chronically ill people mark the illnesses of their lives as divided periods of time. These markers can also give meaning to notions of self and identity. "Chronically ill men and women divide their lives into periods of illness and no illness, crisis and quiescence, flare-ups and remissions, rigid regimens and convalescence. Illness scores and marks events, and sets boundaries between events."[26] Lisa describes her extended family as keeping time by chronologizing their illnesses. She tells the audience, "For instance, people in my family often say things like, 'Now, I know for a fact that the warranty's not up on that dishwasher. I got it the winter I had congestive heart failure seven times.'"[27]

Charmaz also points out that chronic illness takes up a lot of time and that this immersion in constant crisis can overtake people. It is as if the illness overtakes self. "The markers of such a chronology pile upon one another in such swift succession that they blur together. Moreover, the markers may pose such an assault on one's sense of self that they lie beyond one's ability to take them fully into account." Ann's days are marked by good allergy days and bad ones. Lisa's illness chronology is marked by one catastrophic reaction to wheat in the allergy unit. Lisa's illness is defined as an interruption, though a defining one, and it does not rob her of the ability to create intentions for her life. She makes plans, she recovers, she becomes well. But for Ann, recovery is not a possible outcome. All she can hope for is regaining the last plateau: a "good allergy day." Over time, illness becomes an accepted state of life. "What began as an alien reality, after months or years, may come to feel natural, unalterable. . . . What may once have devastated someone can become a path to developing confidence, competence, and compassion."[28] This is exactly what happened to Ann when she became president of the West Side Neighborhood Association in West Lansing, Michigan, in 1968. Unlike the City of Lansing and the real estate community that believed the neighborhood was sick and going to die, Ann strongly believed that through integration the community could be healed. She spends the next seven years working for the wellness of her community, depleting what few physical resources she has. She tells the audience, "Those years I did the Neighborhood Association—it was so hard. Every day. That kind of fatigue—not fatigue—there should be another word. It's like some sort of irresistible voice calling you all day just to close your eyes. Just give in and close your eyes. And I worked so hard, I had to work so hard to fight it. Even when I was sleeping, I was dreaming I was trying to stay awake." Moreover, Lisa acknowledges her mother as a role model and brags, "My mother is a fantastically energetic person trapped in an utterly exhausted body." Later she laments, "She doesn't make any sense at all as a character. . . . She doesn't! My mother is so sick and she's so well! Explain that to me."[29]

Toward the end of the performance, as Lisa's intended play is reduced to chaos with scenes randomly being cut and the hired performers about to walk off the stage in frustration, Lisa finally expresses the crux of her fears regarding her mother and the possibility of their shared identity: "I see her in that almost comatose state in that chair—just to raise her arm a little or turn her head makes her gasp in pain, and I get angry. She can't walk. She can't move. The moaning—the moaning drives me crazy. What is the difference between that body and mine? What thin membrane separates us, really? I look at her in that state and I feel like I'm going to drown."[30] In *Good Days, Bad Days* Charmaz acknowledges that faced with chronic illness, as Lisa is in relation to her mother, identity questioning means: "1) acknowledging the identifications of self in the present, 2) composing past identity with that of the present, and 3) wondering what identity one will have in the future."[31]

It would be easy to accept the belief that the key to both women finding a comfortable way to coexist in a healthy relationship is, as quoted in the introduction of this essay, "separation, separation, separation." Indeed Lisa talks about how she needed to physically distance herself from her mother. Moving to New York, finding a partner, taking therapy, escaping, as she says, "to the land of healthy people—people who have chosen strength and love and sex and attractive clothes and organic foods and Target over Kmart even if it costs a little more—and when I come back here I want to scream: 'I'm NOT LIKE YOU!'" Yet both women talk about earlier times when their identities were intertwined. In a particularly moving monologue addressed to the audience, Ann confesses, "She is like an amazing star to me—my daughter. But I . . . I don't even know how to say it. It's like we were one thing. Or we were rooted in the same place and she kept growing which was the most wonderful thing. To see her branch off and to have a life so different, and to have all that energy that I couldn't even imagine. But I guess I never questioned that we were starting from the same place."[32] Lisa echoes this sentiment in the dialogue below.

At the end of the play, the stage is shared by Ann and Lisa only, and it becomes the arena of a final act of desire and construction of identity. Lisa finally confronts Ann with the question "WHY CAN'T YOU MAKE YOURSELF WELL?!" Lisa seems in this moment to be accusing Ann of choosing chronic illness, yet it is clear throughout that Ann doesn't intend to be ill any more than she can intend her recovery:

> ANN. You have seen me struggle for years.
> LISA. I know. I have.
> ANN. Then what are you saying?
> LISA. I was sick, too. And I got better.
> ANN. And I am so grateful for that. But we are not the same person.
> LISA. But we were, Mom. We were entwined. And that was good in a lot of ways. I mean, I understand why those actors fell in love with you—there is no place better, safer, warmer, than right up against you. That is just true. But in order to get better, I had to grow in a different direction.
> ANN. Of course. You went into the Unit and you got better.
> LISA. No, Mom. No.

> ANN. So what you're saying is—what?
> LISA. I think I was sick because you were sick, Mom. I think I watched you and took for granted that was how one lives in the world. And then I went away and learned I didn't have to be like that. And I'm sorry, Mom, because I didn't intend to say any of that//here—
> JAYNE. (*suddenly breaking character*). Lisa, stop. I'm sorry. (*To the audience.*) I'm so sorry. I know this is very jarring. But—I need to stop being Ann Kron right now.[33]

In this moment, Jayne Howdyshell, the performer, steps in to mediate the seeming impasse between mother and daughter. Up to this moment in the play it would be easy to apply the concepts discussed in the introduction of this essay about mother-daughter relationships and the construction of identity. These relationships include conflict, rejection, damage, and ultimately separation if the daughter is ever to fully realize authentic identity. Such a reading of the play could work, and indeed it may be the one the onstage Lisa believes to be the truth of her "planned" performance, but here in the last moments of the play, Lisa Kron, the playwright, brilliantly introduces a mediator who offers a more complex and satisfying alternate reading. Jayne tells Lisa that her take on Ann's identity and their relationship is too small and trite. She tells Lisa, "You've drawn a line down the middle of this play and made sure that we see that you're on one side and your mother's on the other. But, Lisa, you can't just separate out the things you don't understand" (84). I think that what Jayne is offering is a shift from escaping mothering to embracing daughtering. Rather than separation, she offers integration. Jayne hands Lisa a speech Ann had written years earlier for a neighborhood meeting. "You wrote this play where your mother's onstage with you. So—Here she is. Let her in." Jayne exits; Lisa reads: "This is the purpose of integration. This is what integration means. It means weaving into the whole even the parts that are uncomfortable or don't seem to fit. Even the parts that are complicated and painful. What is more worthy of our time and love than that?"[34] In this final moment, not in Lisa's words or the action of her intended play but, ironically and appropriately, in Ann's words (this speech really was delivered by Ann in Lansing), we are offered an alternative approach to community and personal identity that encourages thoughtful acceptance.

Conclusion

In both of these plays there certainly is conflict between mothers and daughters; there are desires and there are obstacles. But what has changed regarding the usual tactics for staging mothers in the history of dramatic literature is that both of these playwrights offer resolutions based on integration rather than separation. Although intentions are not always realized, in the face of popular psychology books on daughters troubled by their mothers, impossibilities are recognized as opportunities rather than as obstacles. Katia does not realize a perfectly accurate or authentic birth origin, but she does learn to respect and acknowledge Maggie's contribution to the process. Lisa does not ultimately perform her planned, intended play, but she does come to a better understanding of her mother's failure to achieve health. In both plays, emphasis is shifted from rejecting mothers to taking some responsibility in effective daughtering: choosing acceptance and integration over separation, however uneasy this truce may seem.

Notes

1. Sandra Reishus, *"Oh, NO! I've Become My Mother": How to Outwit the "Mom Gene" and Have the Life YOU Want* (New York: McGraw Hill, 2006), back cover, ix, 5, table of contents.
2. Susanna Dunuta Walters, *Lives Together/Worlds Apart: Mothers and Daughters in Popular Culture* (Berkeley: University of California Press, 1994), 12.
3. Denise McGregor, *Mama Drama: Making Peace with the One Woman Who Can Push Your Buttons, Make You Cry, and Drive You Crazy* (New York: St. Martin's Griffin, 1998), 1.
4. Dorothy Firman and Julie Firman, *Daughters and Mothers: Making It Work* (New York: Continuum, 1989), back cover.
5. Evelyn Bassoff, *Mothers and Daughter: Loving and Letting Go* (New York: Penguin, 1988), 215; quoted in Reishus, 193.
6. Walters, *Lives Together/Worlds Apart*, 10.
7. Kathleen Tolan, *Memory House* (Playwrights Horizons, Dramatists Play Services, 2005).
8. Lisa Kron, *Well* (Woodstock, IL: Dramatic Publishing Company, 2007).
9. Steph Lawler, *Mothering the Self: Mothers, Daughters, Subjects* (Boulder, CO: NetLibrary, http://umiss.edu/record=b2345981, 2001).
10. Tolan, *Memory House*, 20; 27.
11. Rhona Justice-Malloy, interview with Kathleen Tolan, July 2008.
12. Lawler, *Mothering the Self*, 24.
13. Tolan, *Memory House*, 36.

14. Margaret Homans, *Adoption Narratives, Trauma, and Origins* (Ohio State University, http//muse.ihu.edu/journals/narrative/v014/14.1homans.html, 2006), 1.
15. Tolan, *Memory House*, 54; 59.
16. Homans, *Adoption Narratives, Trauma, and Origins*, 4.
17. Justice-Malloy interview with Tolan.
18. Tolan, *Memory House*, 77.
19. Justice-Malloy interview with Tolan.
20. Tolan, *Memory House*, 77.
21. Lawler, *Mothering the Self*, 13.
22. Tolan, *Memory House*, 86.
23. Leonard Jacobs, Backstage: The Actor's Resource, http://www.backstage.com/ bso/esearch/ article_display.jsp?vnu_content_id=1002275734 (accessed March 31, 2006).
24. Kron, *Well*, 16.
25. Ibid., 14; 11.
26. Kathy Charmaz, *Good Days, Bad Days: The Self in Chronic Illness and Time* (New Brunswick, NJ: Rutgers University Press, 1997), 198.
27. Kron, *Well*, 13.
28. Charmaz, *Good Days, Bad Days*, 199; 5.
29. Kron, *Well*, 71; 84.
30. Ibid., 75.
31. Charmaz, *Good Days, Bad Days*, 101.
32. Kron, *Well*, 71.
33. Ibid., 81–82.
34. Ibid., 84–85.

"She Was Always Sad"

Remembering Mother in Caryl Churchill's *Not Enough Oxygen* and *A Number*

—MARGARET SAVILONIS

In her book *Lives Together, Worlds Apart: Mothers and Daughters in Popular Culture*, Suzanna Danuta Walters claims that "popular images both reflect and construct; they both *reproduce* existing mainstream ideologies and help *produce* those very ideologies."[1] Although focused on popular discourses about mother-daughter relationships, Walters's observation extends to the social production of familiar images, ranging from mother as self-sacrificing nurturer[2] to mother as destructive force,[3] that contribute to cultural definitions of motherhood that do not adequately reflect many women's lived experiences. In several of her plays from the 1970s to the present, Caryl Churchill examines such representations in various ways. In *Top Girls* (1982), for example, she questions symbolic representations of mothers in literature and art by employing them, putting characters such as Chaucer's patient Griselda and Brueghel's Dull Gret onstage. Additionally, she subverts stereotypes with characters such as Marlene and Joyce in *Top Girls* and Betty, Lin, Victoria, and even Edward in *Cloud 9* (1979)[4] by presenting mothers as individuals who actively negotiate the social, political, and economic challenges of motherhood rather than as supporting characters who merely act upon, or in relation to, their children. Yet two of Churchill's most complex examinations of the intersections of gender and power as they relate to cultural constructions of mothers, motherhood, and mothering come from *Not*

Not Not Not Not Enough Oxygen (1971) and *A Number* (2002), plays in which mothers are conspicuously absent.

Not Enough Oxygen and *A Number* are, on one level, domestic dramas, depictions of family crises playing out between fathers and sons within the home, so the absence of the maternal figure is difficult to ignore, particularly because of the small casts (three characters in *Not Enough Oxygen* and four in *A Number*, in which each scene is a father-son two-hander). Yet though the action of both plays is set within the private sector of the home, Churchill enables the family structure to function metaphorically as a microcosmic representation of the social structure by drawing attention to external forces such as environmental crises, government regulations, and scientific interventions into the processes of reproduction, all of which significantly affect familial relationships. As Churchill has noted, her writing is influenced by "a tradition of looking at the larger context of groups of people. It doesn't mean you don't look at families or individuals within that, but you are also looking at bigger things."[5] Among the "bigger things" Churchill explores in both of these plays is the way in which ideas about maternity are culturally constructed, and the lack of mothers' active participation in the conversations highlights the challenges women face in shaping those constructions. According to Shari L. Thurer, "Just as the practice of mothering has veered widely within the mores of different epochs, so has the status of mothers. . . . As men realized their contribution to procreation and seized control . . . the mother has been dehumanized, that is, either wildly idealized . . . or degraded."[6] Because the mothers in these plays exist only as disembodied characters (never there but also never *not* there) who feature in the stories of their husbands and sons, their physical absence simultaneously exposes and enacts the process of dehumanization, as "mother" is constructed solely through memory and myth.

Originally broadcast on BBC 3 in 1971, *Not Not Not Not Not Enough Oxygen* is a radio play set in 2010, offering a bleak vision of a future in which severe environmental crises affect the planet and its population; there is not enough oxygen or water, and grass is a precious commodity, cordoned off in the park, a little patch just visible over the heads of the people in the perpetually swarming crowd. In this nightmarish world, nature is not merely subordinate to technology—faster elevators, larger televisions, oxygen spray—but overcome by it, a barely lingering victim on the verge of obsolescence. The dystopian setting, with its uncomfortably close parallels to contemporary society despite its science-fiction trappings, is marked by loss and absence. For although the world is paralyzingly overcrowded, there is, paradoxically, a loss of community that is punctuated on the individual level by the absence of family, especially the absence of mothers.

The action takes place in a "room in a tower block" in "the Londons," where sixty-year-old Mick and his thirty-year-old girlfriend Vivian await the arrival of Mick's son Claude, a nineteen-year-old celebrity whom Mick hasn't seen for five years.[7] Mick and Vivian's tense anticipation at the beginning of the play is exacerbated by the environment, a space that reflects Michel Foucault's description of the "*enclosure*" demanded by discipline, "a place heterogeneous to all others and closed in upon itself,"[8] and the cramped quarters both shape and reflect the characters' physical and emotional containment. Mick and Vivian have virtually no physical contact with the outside world, for the towers provide not only living quarters but also shops, and they refuse to go outdoors, in part because they are afraid of encountering the "fanatics," people who engage in violent acts of protest. High above the street, their view obstructed by blinding haze and suffocating fumes that force them to keep the window closed, Mick and Vivian rely primarily on the television to keep them connected to the outside world. In fact, the television has been Mick's only physical link to his son for years; he admits to Vivian that when he is alone, he often kisses Claude's image on the screen. From his memories and what he sees on television, Mick has created an image of Claude that offers hope in a hopeless environment.

Claude, literally Mick's fair-haired boy, represents salvation for Mick and Vivian. With class divisions amplified by the limited resources, Claude's wealth affords him options and opportunities that are not available to average people, and Mick's plan for a better future—moving out of the towers and into a cottage in the park—depends entirely on his son's willingness to share his fortune. Claude's status as a revered entity is highlighted by the fact that he was "one of the last children born in the Londons,"[9] his birth made possible by the purchase of a special license granting Mick and his second wife permission to have a child, for Mick already had a son from his previous marriage. Although few details are provided, it is clear that at some point Mick's relationship with his second wife and son disintegrated, for when Claude was fourteen years old, his mother "brought him [to Mick's apartment] to say goodbye" as he was preparing to go to college in Africa.[10] Thus, though Mick invested financially in Claude's government-sanctioned birth and seems to be interested in following his son's achievements, his claim that "father and son counts even today" is not entirely persuasive, in part because Mick's technologically mediated affections verge on idolatry, especially when he likens himself to the "thousands of little girls [who] must do the same," kissing Claude in secret, longing for a connection to him.[11] For Mick, Claude is, in effect, an object, a personality rather than a person.

So, too, is Claude's mother, Mick's unnamed former wife. Although she never appears in the play, her presence looms over the action, not only as a subject of conversation but also as an implicit part of Claude, who, according to Mick, has his mother's eyes. Of course, Mick is present in Claude as well, and Mick asserts a kind of ownership over Claude when he remarks, "He gets his looks from me. His mother had a certain brightness but not so much the shape of feature."[12] Mick's tendency to position himself in opposition to Claude's mother is established at the very first mention of her, when he says, "[Claude] can give me all the money he likes and be sure I'll make good use of it. Not like his mother, who won't take a pound from him. Say nothing about her."[13] Mick's declaration establishes a dichotomy, and his command to Vivian to refrain from mentioning his former wife in Claude's presence suggests that he does not want to put himself into relief against her when he finally gets to see his son.

Furthermore, Mick's desire to excise Claude's mother from the conversation draws attention to the constitutive power of speech, and his efforts to control, and ideally eradicate altogether, the image of his absent former wife reveal his need to keep discomforting truths at bay. Mick's desire to edit the past through silence is mirrored by his desire to shut out the present, literally, as each time Vivian opens the window during the course of the play, Mick orders her to close it. Eventually the audience learns that Mick has kept several significant details about his life hidden from Vivian, who knows nothing, for example, about his first marriage and his older son, hearing about them for the first time when Claude makes his visit. When Claude asks Mick if he has heard from Alexander, Vivian asks, "Who? Alexander who? I don't know who Alexander—," and is cut off by Claude's response: "My half-brother."[14] Confronted by the unexpected encroachment of a past he has been trying to negate through silence, Mick jumps in, attempting to downplay the significance of the omission by offering a rushed rejoinder, saying, "Yes I have an older son, much older. By my first marriage, which I have just mentioned, I think."[15] Thus, Mick's history unfolds bit by bit over the course of the play, as he is forced, incrementally, to acknowledge various people who exist outside of his hermetically sealed enclosure. Mick's penchant for evasion and omission consequently leads the audience to question the veracity of his opinions, opening a space for alternative readings of the voiceless characters Mick constructs through dialogue.

Additionally, the fact that Mick's sons, Claude and Alexander, are both named, but neither wife/mother is named exposes the process of dehumanization; the absence of the women's names makes their physical absence even more pronounced and draws attention to the ways in which they are stripped of their individuality. Because these women are defined exclusively by their roles, and Claude's mother is always referred to as Claude's mother, never as Mick's wife, there is a disquieting sense of anonymity and distance. Claude's mother, however, occupies the peculiar position of one who is at the mercy of others—needing government permission to have a child; having no literal voice in the world of the play; remaining nameless; her identity inextricably linked to her role as mother—but who, nevertheless, manages to define herself by literally relinquishing her legal identity, burning her identification cards and giving up her assigned room to fend for herself in what Mick calls the "jungle" outside the Londons,[16] a decision that affects not only her but also Mick and Claude, albeit in markedly different ways.

Significantly, it is Claude who recounts the details of his mother's recent departure, introducing her into the conversation almost immediately upon arriving at Mick's room, forcing Mick to confront both the past and the present. Suddenly the question of what the child "got" from each parent goes beyond physical attributes, as Claude's outlook on existence in this horrific world seems to be informed by his mother's choices and philosophies, which Mick and Vivian consider to be radical:

> Claude: You hear from mother?
> Mick: Hear from your mother? Now and then.
> Claude: She's gone off, hasn't she? Gave up all her gave up all her things. Not that she had much, she was never—Tried to give her—when I first earned—but she wouldn't. February she wrote me she'd formally relinquished her room, burnt her cards, just gone. So many do.
> Vivian: Not many in the normal normal way only fanatics—
> Claude: That's what she is of course if you call them that.
> Mick: I never did understand your mother. She was always sad about one thing or another. I used to turn the news off, it upset her so much. Twenty years ago. The news is very much worse now and it must have turned her mind, poor woman . . .[17]

By making his mother a topic of conversation, Claude has thwarted Mick's desire to remain silent about her. As a result, Mick tries to control Claude's mother's presence by offering a patronizing description of her. Yet the idea that his former wife was too frail to cope with the pain of the world is actually challenged by her actions. As Geraldine Cousin suggests, Claude's mother's decision to abandon the chaotic and stifling society in which she lived is one of the "hopeful elements" in the piece.[18] What Mick suggests is weakness reads, instead, as strength, because Claude's mother had the courage to challenge the status quo rather than continue to lose her humanity in an increasingly inhumane culture. Furthermore, Claude's response to Vivian's use of the popular pejorative "fanatic" to describe his mother (and others like her) serves as counterpoint to Mick and Vivian's fear of those who challenge the system, hinting at his ideological kinship with his mother and raising questions about the detrimental effects of the compliance exhibited by Mick and Vivian.

The link between conformity and inhumanity continues to emerge as Claude tells a story about his half-brother, Alexander. Out of touch with his eldest son, whom he describes as "always too full of ideals," Mick is caught off guard by Claude's question, "Do you not know then about the baby?" Claude goes on to tell Mick that Alexander's wife "wouldn't have another abortion though [they] hadn't got exemption," so the couple "kept moving country to country to avoid the regulations" until their child was born. In the end, however, the couple "changed their minds" and killed the baby because it was not a licensed child, and they wanted to "clear their conscience." They were sentenced to five years for "evading abortion," but the sentence was suspended because the child was dead.[19]

Claude's story resonates in several ways. First, it reveals the extent to which the processes of reproduction are controlled by the government; human life is being contained and apportioned just like the grass, the oxygen, and the wildlife. And though the regulations have psychological and emotional repercussions for both parents, women suffer especial physical constraints and interventions. Additionally, the fact that Alexander and his wife killed their child as a way to "clear their conscience" for breaking the law serves as an extreme example of the ways in which inhumanity has become institutionalized, in part because familial relationships are subordinate to fealty to the state. And though Vivian notes it is "fanatic to kill a baby," Alexander and his wife seem to have abandoned their attempt to risk life outside the system, choosing instead to carry out their penance as "doctors to one of the epidemic areas."[20] Furthermore, Vivian and Mick's responses to the story illustrate the different ways in which they, too, have adapted to the system. Vivian's choices are predicated on fear, for even though she admits wanting a baby of her own, she says, "I've never dared never dared evade the regulations," her stuttering speech pattern indicating the depth of her anxiety. Mick, however, seems less concerned with the repercussions of breaking the rules, focusing instead on finding ways to work within the system. For while Vivian expresses dismay over the baby's murder, Mick seems befuddled by his son's efforts at evading the laws since with "all his mother's money Alexander could have bought a licence [sic]."[21] Juxtaposed with Mick's pragmatism, Vivian's dread, and Alexander and his wife's capitulation, Claude's mother's idealism becomes increasingly admirable, and her pursuit of her ideals seems increasingly courageous.

Additionally, because Claude's stark portrait of the world outside Mick's room offers details about people Mick actually knows, rather than the nameless "fanatics" that he and Vivian hear about on the television, Mick is forced to confront reality directly. Indeed, over the course of the play, it becomes progressively difficult for Mick to turn a blind eye to the problems inherent in the system, in part because Claude serves as a corporeal ambassador from the outside world, and Mick cannot simply tune out what he doesn't want to see or hear. For example, as Claude elaborates on Alexander's experience, Mick says, "I would rather not have known about it, Claude," to which Claude replies, "I'd rather you did know about it."[22] Thus, though he longed to see Claude because he hoped their meeting would result in the realization of his dream, Mick finds that Claude's presence, instead, challenges his fantasies. Claude, no longer the teen idol singing on television but a disenchanted youth who is looking for a way to make sense of his life, insists on making that which is absent present.

Claude's story also serves as the springboard for the revelation of his plan to follow in his mother's footsteps, though the exact nature of the path he intends to take is somewhat ambiguous. His alignment with his mother starts to become clear when the topic shifts to Mick's dream of a life in the park as an escape from the hell of the towers. Claude says, "Be better off with my mother walking about. Still open country some places. Risk is you starve of course like most people," suggesting that he sees his mother's decision to escape the enclosure as a positive course of action despite its dangers.[23] Yet Mick has no desire to take that step, demonstrated by his report that he refused his former wife's invitation to go with her and "end [their] lives together."[24] Thus, when Claude reveals that he has given away all of his money because he is preparing to make his own exit, Mick feels betrayed. He tries to persuade Claude that there is no need to engage in radical acts, saying: "Do you think no one was starving then? In the sixties, seventies, eighties? Do you think there weren't any wars when I was a young man? You're not the first person to see horrors. We learnt to watch them without feeling a thing. We could see pictures of starving children and still eat our dinner while we watched. That's what we need to survive. Your mother was no good at it so her mind went and she's gone off to die in a jungle gnawing a leaf or some nonsense."[25] Here again, Mick sets himself up in opposition to Claude's mother, his tone now more derisive than patronizing, in an effort to convince his son to reconsider his decision. Yet Mick's definition of survival is acquiescence and acceptance; his wife, on the other hand, could not inure herself to the horrors and took action. Thus, Churchill posits a challenge to traditional notions of power, as Claude's mother's embracing of anonymity reflects Claudine Hermann's idea that "physical or mental, man's space is a space of domination, hierarchy and conquest, a sprawling, showy space, a *full* space . . .. Woman, on the other hand, has long since learned to respect not only the physical and mental space of others, but space for its own sake, *empty* space . . .. The *void* is for her, then, a respectable value."[26] Stepping into the void, a conscious and deliberate act, confers power onto a woman who, heretofore, has been made powerless by existing social structures, her absence hinting at the potential for establishing alternative cultures beyond the boundaries of the established order.

Thus, it is through her very absence that Claude's mother is rendered both individual and iconic. Embracing the void grants her autonomy, allowing her to define herself by refusing the boundaries of the established order. At the same time, however, her absence takes on symbolic weight, for Churchill does not dispose of mythologizing in this play; rather she employs Claude's mother's absence to lay bare the process of mythologizing and, in doing so, allows the audience to regard that process with a critical eye. Because Mick and Claude do the work of creating Claude's mother's identity through dialogue, the audience, in order to reach its own conclusions about her character, must consider not only what is said but also what is not said, not only what is present but also what is missing. Mick's rote dismissals of his wife's sadness play into the stereotype that women allow their emotions to interfere with rational thinking, and by writing off his former wife as one whose mind has "turned," he suggests that feeling is a handicap. Yet Mick's detached approach to the world is off-putting, and through the juxtaposition, the value of empathy becomes clear. Claude's mother's sensitivity, her refusal to continue to look at "pictures of starving children and still eat [her] dinner," seems to be a necessary antidote to this society's ills.[27] As Amelia Howe Kritzer notes, "The play warns against the tendency to concentrate on personal relationships and individual concerns, while ignoring global dangers and the fate of others besides oneself."[28]

Yet Churchill does not set forth this warning via an oversimplified male/female dichotomy, even though Mick and Claude's mother are positioned as ideological opposites throughout the play. Nor does she offer unquestioning veneration of the absent mother, which would merely perpetuate the problematic mythology of the idealized mother. For though Claude clearly admires his mother, he does not romanticize her, in part because he does not dwell in the past the way Mick does. Furthermore, because Claude has aligned himself with his mother, Churchill suggests that the capacity for empathy is not by any means limited to women. Rather, the play seems to reflect Françoise d'Eaubonne's claim, "The only change capable of saving the world today is that of the 'great reversal' of male power which is represented . . . by this mortal industrial expansion. Not 'matriarchy,' to be sure, nor 'power-to-the-women,' but destruction of power by women. And finally, the end of the tunnel: egalitarian management of a world to be reborn."[29] Claude represents a move toward that rebirth, and his emergence as an active participant in the quest for change, shaped by his rejection of his father's singular focus on self-preservation and his adoption of his mother's willingness to sacrifice, is linked directly to his mother's absence.

Claude's declaration of his intentions, however, implies that his sacrifice may be more final than his mother's. For as Vivian becomes increasingly frightened of Claude, saying, "Mick don't you see see how he looks how he looks at you? Don't you see why why he's come he's a fanatic Mick come to kill us kill kill kill us come to kill us,"[30] Claude reassures them that he is "Not going to kill anyone else," the word "else" hanging heavily in the air, suggesting that his own life may very well be at stake. He goes on to say, "Just came to see my father. Thought he'd be glad afterwards that he saw me once more first. Not happening till this evening so there's been the day to fill with last things. You've nothing to be frightened of," his calm demeanor contrasting sharply with Mick's response.[31] And though the details of Claude's plans are left unsaid, it is clear that he believes this is the last time he will ever see his father.

Mick certainly feels that finality, and his initial reaction to the impending loss reveals a vulnerability that has been hitherto unseen. He tries to persuade Claude not to leave, saying, "Even with everything the way it is and getting worse you could be happy at times. There are always moments."[32] Yet this plea is unfortunately rooted in Mick's unwillingness to admit that his current way of life in untenable. His inability to relinquish his fantasy is symbolized by his final attempt at detaining Claude. Early in the play, before Claude arrives, Vivian gets very excited because she believes she has seen a small bird outside the window, leading Mick to ponder the fact that his son "can't have seen a sparrow" since he is not yet twenty. According to Mick, birds were still around in the eighties, "before elimination," but now they are scarce.[33] Though he never actually sees the bird, Mick clearly wants to believe in its existence, and he calls upon this seemingly impossible sighting to try to detain Claude a little longer. Claude, however, is nonplussed, his reply, "Must have been nice for you," punctuating the distance between them. Yet Mick presses on, saying, "It must still be about somewhere. If you keep your eyes open."[34] Claude, however, as Mick has already noted, has his mother's eyes, and his sights are set on a different horizon.

At first, Claude's exit incites Mick and Vivian to action, albeit limited action. Driven to open the window to try to keep Claude in view, the two quickly abandon their pursuit, unable to handle the encroachment of the smoke from the ever-increasing, ever-closer fires that are raging in the Londons. As he did at the beginning of the play, Mick orders Vivian to close the window and spray her oxygen, a symbolic gesture of erasure, eliminating any lingering traces of Claude's visit. As the play draws to a close, Mick's detachment resurfaces, emphasized by his suggestion to Vivian to turn on the television because he thinks Claude's "death might get a mention."[35] Mick, embedded in the system, continues to live his safely mediated, though hollow, life.

Maternal absence similarly informs the action of *A Number*, originally produced at the Royal Court Theatre in 2002. The play features four characters played by two actors: Salter, "a man in his early sixties," and three of his sons, Bernard (B1), aged 40; Bernard (B2), aged 35; and Michael Black, also 35.[36] As with *Not Enough Oxygen*, there is a science-fiction feeling to the piece, which comes mainly through the fact that Salter's son B1 has been cloned. Otherwise, the world in which the characters exist is virtually undistinguishable from the present. The setting is loosely defined; Churchill offers no exact time or place, other than that the scenes all take place "where Salter lives."[37] The play consists of five scenes in which Salter meets with his sons. The first four scenes present alternating meetings with B2 and B1, and the last is with Michael Black, whom Salter is meeting for the first time, having just recently learned of his existence, as well as the existence of eighteen others. Salter's wife, B1's mother, never appears onstage, yet she figures in several conversations, her absence becoming increasingly pronounced over the course of the play.

The play raises questions about identity, the "key question" being, according to critic Lyn Gardner in her review of the 2002 Royal Court production, "from what [does] the essential core of self [derive]: from nature or nurture, genetic inheritance or environmental circumstance?"[38] Familial relationships are central to the plot, though the nature of those relationships is difficult to ascertain beyond the immediate moment of each scene, for the details of the Bernards's upbringing, revealed over the course of the first four scenes through their memories and Salter's, are inconsistent and contradictory. As a result, Salter's relationship with the two sons he has raised, to varying degrees, is most clearly defined in his scene-by-scene interactions with them. Because Salter's wife never appears in the play, her relationship to B1 and B2 is mediated exclusively through memory and storytelling, making determining the effects of her presence (and absence) particularly complicated. Additionally, the details of Michael Black's upbringing are not addressed at all. Thus, though questions about the effects of environmental circumstance on identity are undoubtedly relevant, as the markedly different personalities of Salter's sons indicates, Churchill's script provides no clear or easy answers to this philosophical inquiry.

In *A Number*, the absence of the nameless mother is even more pronounced than it is in *Not Enough Oxygen*, precisely because her son B1 has virtually no memory of her, and B2 discovers that what he believed about his mother was never true at all. As a result, her identity is controlled almost exclusively by Salter, who constructs, and reconstructs, the image of his dead wife as it suits his purposes. In the opening scene, Salter and B2's conversation reveals the crisis at the center of the play: B2 has been informed that he is one of "a number" of men who are replications of an "original" human being, and he wants Salter to provide him with answers about this news. As the conversation unfolds, Salter reluctantly admits that he was, in fact, involved in the decision to produce a clone of his son, claiming that his child had died and that he wanted to replace that child. It is here that the myth of mother first emerges. B2 has always believed that his mother died in childbirth, but Salter, having to contend with the exposition of the cloning, now changes that story, telling B2 that his mother and his "original" died in a car crash when the boy was four years old. Yet in scene 2, Salter is confronted by B1, his older, more hostile, "original" son, whom he has not seen in over thirty years. The validity of Salter's story from scene 1 is thus immediately undermined, for B1 is alive and well and showing up to challenge Salter about his decision to send him away and have a copy made in his place. B1's presence introduces new questions for the audience, not the least of which is the question of whether Salter's wife, too, may still be alive.

Indeed, everything Salter says is called into question as scene 2 unfolds. Like B1 and B2, the audience is in the vulnerable position of relying on Salter to provide answers, and just as B1 and B2 discover that they have been (and continue to be) misled, so does the audience. Over the course of the second scene, it becomes clear that Salter reveals only what he feels is necessary for him to maintain order; equally clear is that he is adept at lying. Thus, his diversionary tactics, which in scene 1 seemed innocuous to some extent, become increasingly suspect as the action of the play progresses. He speaks in short, often incomplete, sentences, his clipped phrases hanging as he waits for his sons to fill in the gaps. In fact, Salter's claim that B1 had died as a child is actually initiated not by Salter but by B2 in the first scene of the play:

> B2: Some time before I was born there was
> Salter: another son, yes, a first
> B2: who what, who died
> Salter: who died, yes
> B2: and you wanted to replace him
> Salter: I wanted

B2: instead of just having another child you wanted
Salter: because your mother was dead too
B2: but she died when I was born, I thought she
Salter: well I'm telling you what happened.
B2: So what happened?
Salter: So they'd been killed in a carcrash, and
B2: my mother and this
Salter: carcrash
B2: when was this? how old was the child, was he
Salter: four, he was four[39]

Churchill's choice to eschew punctuation and capitalization creates the impression that the lines are fluid, as one speaker completes the other's sentences, and contributes to the improvisational feeling of Salter's story. Salter's hedging initially suggests he feels guilty about lying to his son, and his pronouncement that he is telling B2 "what happened" indicates that he is offering his son the facts that he had previously withheld, though his repetition of the word "carcrash" signals a hesitancy that foreshadows the subsequent revelation that this story is also a fabrication.

Furthermore, much of Salter's dialogue, especially in the first half of the play, is devoted to denials. Sometimes his denials are definitive, such as when he is confronted by B1 in scene 2:

B1: You know when I used to be shouting.
Salter: No.
B1: When I was there in the dark. I'd be shouting.
Salter: No.[40]

Here, Salter's responses, set off from B1's sentences with full stops, are not presented as part of B1's thought process but as a direct challenge to that thought process. As the scene progresses, however, Salter's denials become less assertive; he continues to try to challenge B1's memories, but he does so in a way that mirrors the halting speech pattern he had in scene 1:

B1: could you hear me shouting?
Salter: no I don't
B1: no
Salter: no I don't think this happened in quite the
B1: what?
Salter: because I'd
B1: again and again and again, every night I'd be

Salter: no
B1: so you didn't hear?
Salter: no but you can't have
B1: yes I was shouting, are you telling me you didn't
Salter: no of course I didn't
B1: you didn't
Salter: no[41]

The incomplete nature of Salter's sentences in the second half of scene 2 creates the impression that he is, once again, slightly off guard and needs to appease his son by providing plausible answers without revealing anything that will damage his own reputation. Ultimately, Salter deflects B1's challenge by saying, "Of course sometimes everyone who's had children will tell you sometimes you put them to bed and they want another story and you say goodnight now and go away and they call out once or twice and you say no go to sleep now and they might call out again and they go to sleep."[42] Thus, he shuts down B1's questioning with a generalization that is neither a denial nor an affirmation of B1's recollection.

This pattern of hedging and denying continues throughout the play, as Salter creates a history for himself and his sons through a process of dismantling and rearrangement, changing the details of his story several times, so much so that it seems as if he has no investment in the "truth" of that history. As a result, the constitutive power of language in *A Number* is paradoxically rooted in negation. Salter's anonymous wife, without a name, not even "wife," but always "mother," is malleable; her identity is dictated by the story Salter chooses to tell. She has no voice, and she has no control over her legacy, in any sense of the word. Furthermore, for much of the play, Salter avoids talking about his wife in detail, which, ironically, makes her absence that much more striking.

Her absence is, in fact, central to the conflict in scene 2. When confronting Salter, B1 reveals his intensely bitter feelings about what he perceived to be his parents' disaffection, feelings that clearly have had detrimental effects on his personality. For example, some of B1's hostility stems from his memories of being left alone in the dark, calling out for help, but receiving no comfort from either parent. He claims that his mother would "be there but she wouldn't help stop anything."[43] Salter questions the veracity of B1's memories, as B1 was "maybe two" when his mother died, making it difficult for Salter to believe that B1 could remember something from such a young age.[44] Yet Salter, focused on maintaining his own innocence, never tries to change B1's perception about his mother. In fact, Salter offers no information about B1's mother in this scene other than the brief mention of her death.

B2's understanding of his mother, as well as himself in relation to his mother (and father), is complicated in different ways. Having believed throughout his life that his mother died when she gave birth to him, he is now, at age thirty-five, discovering that she was already dead before he was born. In scene 3, B2 tells Salter that B1 has found him and confronted him, and B2 has been frightened by the experience. Looking for answers about the things that B1 has told him, B2 presses Salter for more details about his mother. The longest description of her occurs here, at the center of the play, in the middle of the middle scene, and the structural foregrounding of her absence suggests that despite Salter's best efforts, he cannot effectively contain her. Yet, even though Salter offers the most detailed characterization of his wife in this conversation, the picture of her is still fuzzy and, as a result, somewhat suspect. She is reduced to her emotional state, much as Mick's "always sad" former wife is in *Not Enough Oxygen*. Describing his wife, Salter says,

> Salter: Your mother, the thing a thing about your mother was that she wasn't very happy, she wasn't a very happy person at all, I don't mean there were sometimes days she wasn't happy or I did things that made her not happy I did of course, she was always not happy, often cheerful and
> B2: she killed herself.[45]

Here, again, Salter's story is more evasive than definitive; his circuitous speech—repeated words, seeming contradictions, and focus on abstractions rather than concrete details—reads as stalling, though whether it is because he is not sure where he wants to take the story or because it is difficult for him to tell the truth is unclear. By offering a generalization about his wife's emotional state, he allows his son to draw the inference that this malaise resulted in suicide. Critically, it is B2 who speaks the words "she killed herself"; though Salter eventually provides details about the manner of suicide, he allows his son to introduce the subject. Furthermore, Salter's wife's vague unhappiness is amplified by Salter's emotional detachment, both in his recollection of the event and his characterization of his relationship with his wife and the then two-year-old B1 at the time the death occurred; he tells B2 that he thinks he was off "having a drink" when his wife threw herself under a subway train, and he cannot remember "where the boy was" when it happened.[46]

This account of Salter's wife's death, though ultimately as unverifiable as all of the other versions Salter offers, casts her in a different light; she is no longer the unfortunate mother who died in childbirth or the unwitting victim of a car accident, but the arbiter of her own fate. As a result, her absence takes on a new dimension, as the deliberateness of suicide introduces the question of abandonment into her relationship with her sons, and the extremity of her choice, if one can believe what Salter says at this point, becomes her clearest statement. B2 drops the subject of his mother entirely after struggling to get his head around the idea that "she was already always" dead, and she is not mentioned for the remainder of the scene.[47] In fact, after this point in the play, Salter's wife is never mentioned again, a detail that ultimately serves to make maternal absence even more pronounced.

Interestingly, once Salter presents this version of the family history, he begins to own up to his own shortcomings, even admitting by scene 4 that B1's memories of being abandoned are valid: "Sometimes I was there, I'd sit and listen to you or I'd not be in any condition to hear you. . . . Sometimes I'd go out and leave you."[48] Yet Salter's sudden desire to take responsibility for his actions shifts dramatically from a plaintive effort at making amends with B2 at the end of scene 3 to a vitriolic attack on B1 in scene 4. Additionally, Salter's hedging, halting one-liners give way to lengthy speeches, his brutishness embodied in his language not only in content but also in form. The violence of his language mirrors the increasing violence of the play, for B1 visits Salter in scene 4 with the express purpose of telling him that he has killed B2. Thus, to some extent, Salter's outrage is understandable, yet the audience cannot help but wonder, as it witnesses Salter's cruelty firsthand, how Salter's treatment of his son has contributed to B1's destructive, antisocial behavior, as well as how the lack of a maternal figure has affected him.

Once Salter is finally willing to be more forthright about the events leading up to the proliferation of copies of his son, he tells B1, "I'll tell you a thought, I could have killed you and I didn't . . .. I spared you though you were this disgusting thing by then . . .. I remembered what you'd been like at the beginning and I spared you, I didn't want a different one, I wanted that again because you were perfect just like that and I loved you."[49] By this point in the play, the issue of cloning has become subsidiary to the drive behind it. Salter's attitude toward his children, his wife, and human life in general is increasingly revealed to be callous, despite all his talk about love. Salter's choices suggest that people have become commodities, capable of being exchanged, disposable, from the "dead ones" that failed to materialize from the "test tubes the dishes" to the biological child that Salter, in effect, threw away.[50] Thus, both mother and children have been dehumanized by the replication of the original child, as they become objects that are manipulated by Salter and the vaguely identified scientists and doctors who engineered the replication. Yet perhaps the most critical element of the dramatization of this process of dehumanization is the gradual revelation of the inhumane behavior that both fosters and is fostered by it.

Salter's inhumanity is markedly different from the inhumanity of the characters in *Not Enough Oxygen*, however. For while Mick and Vivian lose their humanity by failing to engage with the world around them, Salter loses his by feeding his unquenchable need to control everything and everyone he can. His quest for power takes shape not only in the details of his participation in the co-option of the processes of reproduction but also in his interaction with other people. By scene 5, both B1 and B2 are dead, so Salter seeks out one of B1's clones, though what he wants from this man, Michael Black, is not entirely clear. What is clear is that Michael is a disappointment. Salter keeps pressing Michael to tell him something about himself, but Michael always talks about himself in relation to other people, a point that irritates Salter.

> Salter: I was hoping I don't know something more personal something from deep inside your life. If that's not intrusive.
> Michael: Maybe what maybe my wife's ears?
> Salter: Yes?
> Michael: Because last night we were watching the news and I thought what beautiful and slightly odd ears she's got. . . . They're always there but you know how you suddenly notice and noticing that, I mean the way I love her, felt very felt what you said something deep inside. Or the children obviously, I could talk about, is this the sort of thing?
> Salter: It's not quite
> Michael: No
> Salter: Because you're just describing other people or
> Michael: Yes
> Salter: Not yourself
> Michael: But it's people I love so
> Salter: It's not what I'm looking for.[51]

Salter wants something individual, separate from others, but Michael understands himself in relation to others.

Furthermore, Michael relishes sameness in a way that Salter does not. Responding to Salter's heated dismissal of things that are "unifuckingversal,"[52] Michael blithely notes, "We've got ninety-nine percent the same genes as any other person. We've got ninety percent the same as a chimpanzee. We've got thirty percent the same as a lettuce. Does that cheer you up at all? I love about the lettuce. It makes me feel I belong."[53] Additionally, unlike Salter, Michael is not obsessed with perfection, as his admiration of his wife's "slightly odd" ears implies, and he finds joy in things that Salter finds mundane:

> Michael: The world's a mess of course. But you can't help, a sunny morning, leaves turning, off to the park with the baby, you can't help feeling wonderful can you?
> Salter: Can't you?
> Michael: Well that's how I seem to be.[54]

Thus, it is in this final scene that Churchill offers a brief glimmer of hope for humanity in *A Number*. Michael Black is the least tormented character in the play; in fact, the play ends with Salter asking Michael, "And you're happy you say are you? You like your life?" to which Michael replies, "I do yes, sorry."[55] While it is possible to read Michael as naively oblivious to the problems of the world around him, it is also possible to read his understanding of himself in relation to other people as a positive sign.

In *Not Enough Oxygen* and *A Number*, Churchill critiques the ways in which prevailing power structures strip individuals of their humanity by constructing environments that undermine the productive power of community. By leaving maternal bodies offstage, Churchill points to a gap that needs to be filled. On one level, she takes advantage of common cultural assumptions by strategically employing the stereotype of mothers as nurturers. Because the fathers in these plays are almost completely devoid of the impulse to nurture, maternal absence symbolizes a lack of empathy in the dystopian worlds of the plays. For although Salter admits that he made a concerted effort to do things differently "the second time round," such as sleeping "very lightly with the door open,"[56] his interaction with his sons and Michael Black over the course of the play suggests that his self-serving behavior is so firmly embedded that it overrides the small gestures he makes. B2 acknowledges this point in scene 3:

> B2. I'm not saying you weren't horrible.
> Salter: Couldn't I not have been?
> B2: Apparently not.
> Salter: If I'd tried harder.
> B2: But someone like you couldn't have tried harder. What does it mean? If you'd tried harder you'd have been different from what you were like and you weren't . . .[57]

Salter's attempts to be more empathetic ultimately fail because, in the end, he is trying to improve his performance rather than changing his perspective.

Similarly, in *Not Enough Oxygen*, even though Mick tries to connect with Claude, his effort is short-lived, and he regresses to detachment almost as soon as his son departs. Mick and Salter both display a philosophy of individualism that is rooted strictly in personal concerns,[58] resulting in an inability to nurture, the detrimental effects of which are amplified by the lack of maternal presence.

At the same time, however, Churchill undermines those same assumptions and calls into question the idea that nurturing is exclusively the province of mothers. According to Sarah Blaffer Hrdy, "Nurture, in our species, is more nearly an art form passed down from mothers or others to subsequent generations. Contrary to the notion of a 'maternal instinct,' a person's responsiveness to the needs of infants is to a large degree acquired through experience—through both the experience of nurturing and the experience of being nurtured. . . . Both males and females start out with an innate capacity for empathy with others and for nurture, but past experiences along with proximate cues are critically important for the development and expression of nurturing responses."[59] Both Claude and Michael Black embody this idea that experience and "proximate cues" have allowed them to develop and express nurturing responses. For example, although Claude's decision to relinquish his material possessions and leave the Londons may seem like a kind of abandonment, as Mick seems to believe, it is possible to see his choice as one that signals his desire to assist others. For though he seems to recognize the futility of his actions, as when he notes that he's "given what [he] can but five million pounds goes in a day,"[60] Claude's dedication to his cause, inspired in part by his mother's choices, reveals the strength of his impulse to do whatever he can to have a positive impact on the rapidly dwindling world. Even more pronounced is Michael Black's penchant for nurturing in *A Number*. As he talks about being a father, he apologizes to Salter for not having any photographs, noting, "there's no need for photographs is there if you see someone all the time,"[61] suggesting his active engagement in family life, a point that is further enhanced by his references to taking the children to the park on sunny mornings and his interpretation of Salter's request to talk about "something from deep inside" as an opportunity to talk about his love for his family. And though the audience does not learn the details of Black's upbringing, the fact that Salter was not the person responsible for rearing him allows the audience to consider the possibility that nurture may indeed trump nature.

In many ways, *Not Enough Oxygen* and *A Number* serve as cautionary tales, offering reflections on the dangers of societies in which competition supersedes coalition with potentially devastating consequences. Simultaneously, however, they are plays about possibility, offering glimmers of hope in the actions of characters who reject the established order and seek to effect change, even in the face of almost certain defeat. Locating the action of the plays within the domestic sphere emphasizes the personal repercussions of accepting dehumanizing sociopolitical and environmental conditions, reminding the audience that the "big picture" is ultimately composed of countless small ones and that individuals are responsible for not only themselves but also one another. Furthermore, by putting ideas about family at the center of each play, and by making mothers who never physically appear in the plays the subject of conversations that drive the central conflicts, Churchill raises questions about the ways in which mothers and ideas about mothering both shape and are shaped by existing social structures. As Janelle Reinelt suggests in her analysis of Churchill's *Softcops* (1984), "The absence of women [in the play] is not an accident: *Softcops* is about patriarchal culture and its power relations. The absence of women makes this clear. . . . Women do not have to be represented on the stage for a gender critique to take place or for a feminist politic to underlie the dramaturgy."[62] Similarly, the absence of mothers in *Not Enough Oxygen* and *A Number* introduces an opportunity for critical reflection, the structural choices of her scripts simultaneously honoring empathy, nurturing, and comforting and questioning the impulse to attribute those qualities to mothers alone.

Notes

1. Suzanna Danuta Walters, *Lives Together, Worlds Apart: Mothers and Daughters in Popular Culture* (Berkeley: University of California Press, 1992), 11.
2. The quality of nurturing can be positive, of course. It is, however, one that has specific gendered associations that mark it as a "feminine" quality that can be detrimental when used as a standard by which to judge women, as well as in its exclusion of men. The problem is not the impulse to nurture but the ways in which the term has come to have a connotation that establishes an ideal to which not all women aspire.
3. These iconic representations (i.e., Madonna/Medea) are firmly embedded in the Western cultural consciousness, a fact that ultimately points to the power of and problems with the images of mothers that have been constructed by various forms of media. For discussions of these iconic/archetypal images, see, for example, Shari L. Thurer, *The Myths of Motherhood: How Culture Reinvents the Good Mother* (New York: Penguin, 1994); Mary Anne Ferguson, *Images of Women in Literature*, 4th ed. (Boston: Houghton Mifflin, 1986); and Maxine L. Margolis, *Mothers and Such: Views of American Women and Why They Changed* (Berkeley: University of California Press, 1984). Walters chooses the terms "maternal sacrifice" and "mother-blame" to label these categories (*Lives Together*, 18).
4. Caryl Churchill, *Cloud 9*, in *Plays: One* (New York: Routledge, 1985). In *Cloud 9*, Edward's inclination to nurture dramatizes the potential for mothering to be an activity that is not

delimited by gender or biology. In act 1, young Edward is often caught playing with his sister's doll, and when he is scolded for doing so, he explains to his parents, Clive and Betty, that he is "minding" Vicky's doll for her, rather than "playing" with her, since he has been reprimanded for playing with the doll in the past. The next time he is caught with the doll, however, Edward protests giving her up, saying, "She's not Victoria's doll, she's my doll. She doesn't love Victoria and Victoria doesn't love her. Victoria never even plays with her" (275), a scenario that foreshadows Victoria's nontraditional performance of her maternal role in act 2 of the play. As an adult, Edward assumes the duties of homemaker after he moves in with Victoria, her lover Lin, and the women's respective children. Describing his living situation to his former lover, Gerry, Edward says, "I'm on the dole. I am working, though. I do housework. . . . They [Lin and Vic] go out to work and I look after the kids" (315). Thus, Edward's desire to nurture is liberating for both him and Victoria, and both are freed from their socially defined roles through their adoption of a reimagined notion of family.

5. Caryl Churchill, interview by Kathleen Betsko and Rachel Koenig, *Interviews with Contemporary Women Playwrights*, ed. Kathleen Betsko and Rachel Koenig (New York: Beech Tree, 1987), 78.
6. Thurer, *Myths of Motherhood*, xxvi.
7. Caryl Churchill, "Not Not Not Not Not Enough Oxygen," *Not Not Not Not Not Enough Oxygen and Other Plays*, ed. Terry Gifford and Gill Round (Essex: Longman Group UK, 1993), 24.
8. Michel Foucault, *Discipline & Punish: The Birth of the Prison* (1975), trans. Alan Sheridan (1977), 2nd ed. (New York: Vintage, 1995), 141.
9. Churchill, "Not Enough," 38.
10. Ibid., 27.
11. Ibid.
12. Ibid.
13. Ibid., 26.
14. Ibid., 35.
15. Ibid.
16. Ibid., 38.
17. Ibid., 34.
18. Geraldine Cousin, *Churchill the Playwright* (London: Methuen, 1989), 75.
19. Churchill, "Not Enough," 35–36.
20. Ibid., 36.
21. Ibid.
22. Ibid., 35.
23. Ibid., 37.
24. Ibid., 38.
25. Ibid., 38–39.
26. Claudine Hermann, "Women in Space and Time" (1976), trans. Marilyn R. Schuster, in *New French Feminisms: An Anthology*, ed. Elaine Marks and Isabelle de Courtivron (New York: Schocken, 1981), 169.
27. Churchill, "Not Enough," 38.
28. Amelia Howe Kritzer, *The Plays of Caryl Churchill: Theatre of Empowerment* (London: Macmillan, 1991), 31.

29. Francoise de Eaubonne, *Le Feminisme ou la Mort* (1974), trans. Betty Schmitz, in *New French Feminisms: An Anthology*, ed. Elaine Marks and Isabelle de Courtivron (New York: Schocken, 1981), 67.
30. Churchill, "Not Enough," 39.
31. Ibid., 40.
32. Ibid.
33. Ibid., 30.
34. Ibid., 41.
35. Ibid., 42.
36. Caryl Churchill, *A Number* (New York: Theatre Communications Group, 2002), 7.
37. Ibid.
38. Lyn Gardner, review of *A Number* by Caryl Churchill, Royal Court, London, 2002, *The Guardian*, September 27, 2002, http://www.guardian.co.uk/stage/2002/sep/27/theatre.artsfeatures1 (accessed June 12, 2009).
39. Churchill, *A Number*, 20.
40. Ibid., 31.
41. Ibid., 33.
42. Ibid., 34.
43. Ibid., 32.
44. Ibid., 31.
45. Ibid., 40.
46. Ibid., 41.
47. Ibid.
48. Ibid., 51.
49. Ibid.
50. Ibid., 26.
51. Ibid., 58.
52. Ibid., 61.
53. Ibid., 62.
54. Ibid., 56.
55. Ibid., 62.
56. Ibid., 61.
57. Ibid., 44.
58. In "Studies of Individualism-Collectivism: Effects on Cooperation in Groups" (*Academy of Management Journal* 38, no.1 [February 1995]: 153), John A. Wagner III and Michael K. Moch define individualism as "the condition in which personal interests are accorded greater importance than are the needs of groups. Individualists look after themselves and tend to ignore group interests if they conflict with personal desires. The opposite of individualism, collectivism, occurs when the demands and interests of groups take precedence over the desires and needs of individuals."
59. Sarah Blaffer Hrdy, *Mothers and Others: The Evolutionary Origins of Mutual Understanding* (Cambridge, MA: Belknap, 2009), 290.
60. Churchill, "Not Enough," 37.
61. Churchill, *A Number*, 55.
62. Janelle Reinelt, *After Brecht: British Epic Theater* (Ann Arbor: University of Michigan Press, 1994), 96.

"Who Let in One of Them Mothers?"

Maternal Perversity on the American Musical Stage

—JENNIFER WORTH

The musical is often hailed as a place within the American theatre where women are given voice, both literally and metaphorically. D. A. Miller of Columbia University is quick to note that although both women and men have their places on the stage, "the female performer will always enjoy the advantage of also being thought to represent the stage, as its sign, its celebrant, its essence, and its glory."[1] It must be equally recognized, however, that in most cases, those celebrated voices are not really their own but rather the ventriloquisms of male creators, built around conventional, heteronormative romance and leaving a particularly narrow range of female representations: dewy ingénues, femmes fatales, comically sexual sidekicks, and feisty, but typically sexless, older women.

While these sorts of characters have historically been very frequently, if not well, represented in musicals, mothers, the subject of the present interrogation, are noticeable more for their absence. Where they do emerge, their relationship to their children is not a plot point, and they are often limited to brief appearances in order to give sage advice to the young lovers, or simply to figure as vague background figures of approval or censure. Typically, when a character is *primarily defined* by her status as a mother, she is given a marginal role and correspondingly little stage time. This is not to say that motherwork, which encompasses a variety of tasks including physical care and protection as well as what Steph Lawler in her book *Mothering the Self* refers to as the "emotional management" of another, has no place on musical stages.[2] But motherwork can be performed by anyone, for anyone. When granted more than an advisory role, female characters who perform motherwork become slightly more complex but often lose their role as mother and resurface as caretakers of other sorts, like the aunts of *Oklahoma!* and *Mame* or the doting governess-cum-stepmother found in *The Sound of Music*. In such cases, motherwork is welcome, even celebrated. But actual mothers are rare, and when they do exist, they typically fill the stage with their fascinating perversity.

The "Star Mother"

It seems that any discussion of the treatment of mothers in musicals must begin with *Gypsy*'s Momma Rose, even though their presence, however slight, goes back much further, at least to Kern and Hammerstein's *Show Boat* in 1927.[3] Miller himself uses Momma Rose as the model for his trope of what he calls the "Star Mother" in the third section of his long essay *Place for Us*. Miller reports that *Gypsy* was his first experience of musical theatre, which, as a boy, he saw in the company of (naturally) his mother. He makes clear that his enchantment was complex and polymorphous but was largely due to the performance of its charismatic star Ethel Merman as Momma Rose, whose story of endlessly deferred desire mirrored his own.[4]

The Star Mother is that Broadway creation combining aspects of culturally acceptable feminine power—that is, primarily glamour, beauty, and a great, balcony-reaching belt—in an overt display allowing gay male spectators to enjoy "the thrills of femininity become their own."[5] Rather than wanting to possess her, they wish to *be* her. While I have no objection to Miller's contention that the musical offers a secret subtextual haven for gays, even as it masquerades as a celebration of heteronormative romance, I must ask: At whose expense?

There is no question that the Star Mother represents a kind of power, but she is still the object of (in this case gay) male fantasy, to be colonized, projected upon, desired, but denied her own subjectivity. She is created and displayed in order to be worshipped and appropriated for *his* pleasure. Moreover, Miller makes few distinctions in doling out his Star Mother label—for him, the Star Mother seems to be any adult female who takes center stage (Momma Rose, Mame, Charity, Dolly, Fanny, etc.), regardless of her relationship—biological or otherwise—to children. But as I've already mentioned, there are significant differences in their representation, and Miller's broad brush interpretation has repercussions not only for mothers but also for all women. If we equate the vague idea of "nurturing" with "mothering," we risk the erasure of the material conditions and representations of real mothers, when the truth is that the standards for real mothers and others who do motherwork—especially those from whom it is not expected—are vastly different, and it's rarely to the advantage of real mothers.

Miller seems trapped in an oedipal nightmare, wherein any woman with power (however fleeting or illusory it may be) is transformed to a mother: his own.[6] And that's exactly the point: Here we have the *idea of Mother*, rather than any reality of mothers or mothering. The Star Mother is an ultimately unproductive—I might even say abortive—trope when discussing mothers in/and American musical theatre, because the abstraction once again leads to a privileging of the child's (in Miller's formulation, the gay male spectator's) subjectivity, displacing mothers from their own stories. As ever, we want mothering, without the trouble of Mother.

This erasure of Mother is curious, because the entire musical system overtly defines women *in relation to* other figures (primarily male figures), forbidding them to stand alone, even when they stand center stage. And yet more than any other, the role of "mother" is based primarily on her relationship to another: the child. Of course, in the formula for the traditional musical, which, generally speaking, relies on the reconciliation of two disparate groups (be they farmers and ranchers or whatever else) through marriage, the ultimate symbol of that reconciliation—the child that embodies it—is only implied.

There are a small number of musicals, however, wherein mothers *qua* mothers take on a primary role, and it is to these minority figures that I turn in order to explore questions of displacement of female subjectivity and a deep sense of mother-fear in the American musical, through the interrogation of two musicals that share a surprising number of traits, even though they are divided by almost half a century: *Gypsy* (1959) and *Grey Gardens* (2006). In both of these musicals, mothers share the stage with their children, specifically, their daughters, and the mother-daughter bond replaces the traditional romantic relationship at the center of the story. In 1977, Adrienne Rich declared that the story of mothers and daughters was "the great unwritten story," and perhaps that's just as well, for rather than celebrating it, in musical theatre this bond is pathologized, characterized by competition and aggression as much as by love and nurturance.[7]

The Shows

I am interested in representations of biological mothers, and coincidentally (or perhaps not), the subjects of both of the musicals under inspection are based on real mother-daughter pairs. *Gypsy: A Musical Fable*, by Arthur Laurents (book), Jule Styne (music), and Stephen Sondheim (lyrics), was "suggested by" the memoirs of burlesque star Gypsy Rose Lee, and recounts the relationship between a hard-driving stage mother and her reluctant performing daughters in the waning years of vaudeville. The story—and Momma Rose herself—captivated audiences from its debut in 1959 and has since seen four Broadway revivals: in 1974, 1989, 2003, and 2008. All five of the women to embody Rose on Broadway have been nominated for Tony Awards; four have won.

Grey Gardens, too, has some basis in reality. The collaborative effort of Doug Wright (book), Scott Frankel (music), and Michael Korie (lyrics), *Grey Gardens* is a musical reimagining the 1975 Maysles brothers' documentary of the same title, which is as well known for its cult status among gay men—a category that includes the creators of the musical—as for the eccentric pair of women it features. The film details the mental, emotional, physical, and financial decay of Kennedy cousins Edith Bouvier Beale and her adult daughter "Little Edie" in their moldering East Hampton estate.

While only the briefest summary of *Gypsy* is necessary, *Grey Gardens* warrants a bit more synopsis. The heavily fictionalized first act is set in 1941, at the zenith of the Beales's wealth and social power. Little Edie, a debutante and dancer known as "Body Beautiful Beale," is about to publicly announce her engagement to Joe Kennedy. As preparations for the society-pages event progress, the production reveals Edith's desire for a singing career stunted by her strained, patrician marriage, and the tensions between mother and daughter for male recognition. Before the act is over, Edith has been informed that her husband, expected to attend the party, has left the country to obtain a quickie divorce, and Little Edie is jilted by her fiancé for a reputation unbefitting an aspiring politician's wife. The second act, which borrows heavily—at times word-for-word—from the documentary, leaps forward to 1973 to find the women trapped by squalor and the weight of their shattered dreams, with Little Edie now mothering—both physically tending to and emotionally managing—the bedridden Big Edie. One is hardly surprised to read in nearly every review the musical's blatant, camp appeal to what the *New York Times*'s Ben Brantley characterized as "the gay-bait thrills of women in extreme states of glamour and grotesqueness, preferably at the same time." *Grey Gardens* opened on Broadway in 2006 after an extended off-Broadway run and earned both of its leading ladies accolades and Tony Awards.[8]

Queer Mothers

While the actresses are lauded for their skillful portrayals, and the characters may be idolized as Star Mothers by gay spectators, as women and mothers they are generally perceived as monstrous or freakish. Why pathologize a strong bond between women? Is there lesbian anxiety surrounding these relationships because a mother-daughter bond can be more powerful than that of spouses? Stacy Wolf has already unpacked the lesbian subtexts of *Gypsy* in her study of midcentury musical stars, but there are suggestions of lesbian desire in both shows.[9]

Even though there are important heteronormative relationships in each show, they are subordinated to other, less socially valued bonds. Momma Rose's household is a mockery of domesticity: The peregrinating Hovick tribe includes Rose, her daughters, her lover Herbie (whose proposals of marriage are always being put off for the sake of the girls' career), a number of "stolen" boys who perform as a chorus, and a menagerie of animals. While the mother-daughter attachment is also primary in *Grey Gardens*, Edith, whose husband never appears onstage, has two other decidedly "queer" relationships. The first, in act 1, is with George Gould Strong, her live-in accompanist and "soulmate," with whom she shares everything but a sexual relationship. In the second act she uses the same term for a local teenage boy who she calls "the Marble Faun," after Hawthorne's romance, acting both maternal and coquettish toward him, much to Little Edie's dismay.[10]

But it is to their daughters that the mothers are first and foremost committed, and each musical includes an emblematic song sung by the pair, with lyrics that hint at a quasi-romantic or even sexual relationship. After Louise explodes with frustration at being forced to (inadequately) fill her sister's shoes, Rose wheedles her into the rousing "Together Wherever We Go," which not only reinforces their emotional commitment to one another but also includes vaguely sexualized lyrics about "sleeping cheaper together."[11] Even more explicit is *Grey Gardens*' "Two Peas in a Pod," a charming diegetic duet that was "the very first song" Little Edie learned from her mother, and the one she uses to beguile her mother out of a foul mood. Like "Together," "Two Peas" serves to bolster the relationship and mend hurt feelings, but, as the title implies, it also foregrounds the commitment of mother and daughter: they are "A permanent team" that "stick[s] together like a cushion and pins."[12] As the two slip into a familiar song-and-dance routine, their song, meant for a male/female romantic duo, makes clear reference to a marital and even a sexual relationship with the promise of babies. This is not to say that the characters were conceived of or performed as either explicitly or implicitly lesbian, but that cultural discomfort with them and their relationships may be based in a distrust of intimate female relationships that trump, or perversely mimic, heteronormative behavior, as when Louise gifts her mother with a mink and invites her to a party, or when Edith and Little Edie jealously squabble over Jerry's motives for helping them.

Even as they deeply love their mothers, each daughter chafes under her mother's single-minded attentions, and each sees the solution in heterosexual marriage, for either the mother or the daughter: Louise wistfully fantasizes about her life "If Momma Was Married," and Little Edie knows that "new worlds await / Beyond the garden gate" . . . as long as she escapes her mother by marrying Joe Kennedy.[13] It is understood, by both the characters and the audience, that the marital bond would—and *should*—replace the mother-daughter bond. But it doesn't; the mothers divorce, and the daughters never marry.

Many, including Clum, Doty, Miller, Most, Savran, and Wolf, have written of the inherent queerness of the musical form, and certainly "queer," figured as "productively different," has proved a useful lens for many who deviate from sex/gender norms. But musical mothers don't seem to benefit, presumably because they have preempted the possibility of queer power by following the traditional path to marriage and motherhood.

The Maternal Subject

Of course, problems with mother (and daughters) go beyond gay male appropriation or fear of lesbian desire to broader cultural notions of acceptable behavior for mothers. It is no coincidence that both Rose and Big Edie are, or, rather, *want to be*, performers. To some degree, this is attributable to the well-established fact that many musicals are self-referential: about the business of putting on shows, the lives of performers, and so on, but it is important that their career aspirations are performance-based. They don't want to be stenographers, or plumbers, or president of the United States; what they want is the spotlight. And as Miller points out, as women, the stage is their birthright. But motherhood throws a wrench in the works for two reasons: the relegation of mothers to the private sphere, and the problem of maternal desire.

If mothers are figured as the arbiters of morals and protectors of children, and the stage (or the performing life) is inherently immoral—or even simply amoral—then a mother who performs, or encourages her child to do so, brings with her a severe internal conflict from the outset. Sally Bowles sums up the position of mothers toward "life upon the wicked stage" in *Cabaret*: in short, "Don't Tell Mama." *Gypsy* establishes the divide immediately, with its opening line by "Uncle Jocko," the emcee of a kiddy show: "Everybody—SHUT UP! . . . All mothers—out. (*To his assistant*) Georgie, I don't want them in the wings, I don't want them in the theatre, I want them OUT!" And Rose just as quickly breaches it by remaining in the theatre to coach her girls. Jocko bellows, "Who let in one of them mothers?"[14] A mother's place is in her home, and not on or even near the stage, that most public of venues. For both Rose and Edith, to have a place as a woman and a role in the public sphere as an actress or singer is *incompatible* with her position as a mother. This means, in essence, that upon becoming a mother, a character in effect *ceases* to be a woman and thus must surrender her "easy, almost automatic access" to the stage and its privileges.[15]

Drama of any sort hinges on desire: someone wants something. However, since motherness is by definition "built on responsiveness, on meeting [others'] needs, on relationality," mothers necessarily have less room to exercise their needs and desires.[16] It follows that if the someone doing the wanting is a mother, she will be read as deeply flawed, if not an utter failure. Mothers are free to desire only on behalf of their child/ren—and, as *Gypsy* and *Grey Gardens* amply demonstrate, sometimes not even then. But both Big Edie and Rose want for themselves, quite desperately, the stardom they can never have. The very desires that make them interesting as individuals make them inadequate, even perverse, as mothers. Because they insist on trying to have it all, they are doomed to failure at just about everything. Within the musicals, Rose is referred to as a "pioneer woman without a frontier" and Edith as "an actress without a stage."[17] Neither is given the chance to be the subject—the star—of anything, not even her own life.

Both musicals foreground the professional aspirations of the mothers in question, even as they frustrate them. *Grey Gardens* opens on Edith in the thick of preparations for the only sort of concert her husband will allow: a parlor recital for friends and family. Her love of performing and her self-dramatizing nature are as apparent as her power struggles with her beautiful daughter, who also wants a life on the stage as a dancer or actress. Although Edith never sings professionally, she continues to harbor memories of her glorious singing voice and the career she might have had, repeating her stories over and over, as if to make them true. The references to Rose's frustrated past are legion; it is her thwarted desire that fuels her quest to conquer one vaudeville circuit after the next—albeit vicariously, through her daughters. In her famous eleven o'clock number, Rose cries, "Don't I get a dream for myself?" She's a mother, so she doesn't. Their frustrated desires take them to the breaking point. Edith's deluded senescence is perhaps less dramatic than Rose's show-stopping "Turn," in which she finally admits that her legacy is merely "scrapbooks full of [her] in the background," but it is no less humbling.[18]

Even Miller ultimately seems to recognize the impossibility of being both Star and (literal) Mother; his reading of Rose in her final song both infantilizes and re-sexes her, turning her into a boy like he was, fearful and needy of her (his) own mother. "In a word, 'Rose's Turn' turns Rose into a boy, any one of the million male child wannabes grown pale and puny in their basement prisons."[19] Even at her most desperate and electrifying, Rose forfeits her own identity—both woman *and* mother—to that of her male spectators.

Not only do Rose and Edith fail as women performers, but they are further punished through the perversion of their female identity. Both women practice the patriarchal tradition of naming their children after themselves: Little Edie is so graced from birth, and Louise is christened "Rose Louise" when she is reborn as a pretty adolescent girl, after years in boy-drag playing second fiddle to her sister June. Additionally, Rose and Edith become crones: acid-tongued, given to meddling, and either neuter or, inappropriately, grotesquely sexual. Whereas in *Grey Gardens*' second act, Mary Louise Wilson's Edith lounged half undressed, making lascivious comments to and about their teenage neighbor, Merman's notoriously sexless affect reinforced the Momma at the expense of the Rose. In the 2003 revival of *Gypsy*, a smoldering Bernadette Peters was given a mixed bouquet of praise and derision for her clearly sexual interpretation of the role, and 2008's Rose, Patti LuPone, was characterized as a "sexual succubus."[20]

With this denial of their appropriately feminine sexuality comes the denial of the very currency of the musical: romantic love. Edith's marriage is revealed early on to be a sham; while Edith spends most of her time in the Hamptons with her gay accompanist, her philandering husband remains in the city, "working" as much as possible. And although Rose has a romantic companion and potential husband in Herbie, he is eventually driven away by Rose's relentless quest for stardom, even if it's only vicariously, at a third-rate Wichita burlesque.

Their daughters suffer, too. As it is currently conceived, the goal of all motherwork is the successful individuation of the child, which, in classic Freudian psychoanalytical theory, requires the metaphorical death of the mother (which the mother herself is supposed to facilitate) through the child's rejection of her.[21] Both musicals demonstrate this theory. Edith and Rose are inadequately subservient to the needs of their daughters, and neither does what they are culturally tasked with: Edith must ensure that Little Edie marries well, and Rose must provide Louise (and her sister) a stable domestic environment. As a result, Little Edie is trapped in the family manse, desperate for marriage and escape, but utterly unable to separate—physically or psychically—from her mother. Louise achieves some level of triumph as she takes her own place as a woman (and a sexual commodity), but not a wife or mother: the show ends with her departure for a fabulous party not in the company of a beau, but of Rose. She may have captured the spotlight, but Momma is still her shadow. Mother and daughter remain two peas trapped in a pod; together, wherever they go.

The impossibility of sufficient individuation in such a case was rendered with startling clarity in the 2008 production of *Grey Gardens*: Christine Ebersole plays Edith in the first act, and now-middle-aged Little Edie in the second. Her remarkable performance in this double role literally embodies the dilemma of the mother-daughter pairs under discussion here: as they struggle against each other to claim the privileges of the stage/subjectivity, they are in essence fighting to inhabit the self-same body. Little wonder there are clashes. And little wonder, too, that these women are perceived as pathological: they are purposefully conceived that way.

Both of these mother-daughter relationships are set before the rise of second-wave feminism, even though one is a product of the early twenty-first century. Two other 2000s musicals involving mothers, *The Light in the Piazza* and *Hairspray*, set in 1953 and 1962, respectively, hew to the same model of acceptable motherhood. *The Light in the Piazza*, which is very much about the relationship between an overprotective mother and her adult daughter, doesn't include performance, or any career aspirations, as a goal for either Margaret Johnson or her daughter Clara, thus removing the major obstacle to "successful" mothering. *Hairspray* is slightly more complicated. Desire for public performance and attendant fame is a crucial part of the story, and both mother Edna Turnblad and daughter Tracy achieve it, without lasting damage to their relationship or identities. While this might seem to undercut my argument, I contend that the Turnblads are able to avoid sharing the Beales' and Hovicks's fate because the mother, Edna, was conceived, played, and recognized as a drag role. By contrast, the Turnblads' nemeses, the scheming Velma and Amber Von Tussle (both played by/as women), display pathologies in their relationship and characterizations similar to those found in *Gypsy* and *Grey Gardens*. These examples are in no way an exhaustive catalog, but the fact that twenty-first-century writers, librettists, and composers would turn to stories of tyrannical mothers and their cowed daughters as attractive, marketable material indicates how far women, and particularly mothers, have yet to go.

A New Model of Motherhood

Miller asserts that "the Broadway musical is the unique genre of mass culture to be elaborated in the name of the mother." It may *invoke* the mother—but only occasionally, and never in a way that entails her ultimate triumph or success, either in her motherwork or her self-actualization. To some degree musicals are cultural products that allow (a very small number of) real women, like those who play Momma Rose and Edith, access to public life, fame, and even some measure of profit as the real stars of the musical stage, but in fact, as Miller goes on to describe, the stage's "utopia of female preeminence" is paid for not just by the lack of preeminence elsewhere but also by the narrow range of representations wherein that success is permitted.[22]

In case we need a reminder: representation is *not* sufficient. There is no denying the complexity of the mother-daughter bond, or the issues of identification and independence that are unique to this relationship. But given that well over 60 percent of Broadway spectators are women, and that the vast majority of women *do* become mothers, it is all the more striking that more positive, or at least less universally damning, representations haven't appeared.[23] And of course, the mothers represented on the musical stage represent a very thin sliver of what motherhood has ever looked like. But that even these mothers—who might be considered the most privileged of the lot—are given such a raw deal makes me long for new models of musical motherhood, perhaps even some written, composed, or produced by actual mothers.

One such example is *Mamma Mia!* Two years after its London premiere, this "jukebox musical" based on the songs of ABBA opened on Broadway just weeks after September 11, 2001, to immediate commercial success. Excoriated as "bland, hokey, corny, stilted, self-conscious and—let's not mince words—square" by the *New York Times*'s lead theatre critic, it has nonetheless been enthusiastically embraced by audiences in more than a dozen countries around the world during its now-over fifteen-year run.[24] In 2008, a film version was released that was also critically panned as a "mindless, hedonistic assault on coherence": "How on earth could it not . . . be . . . shit?" Regardless, the box office was strong, and the film earned more than 609 million dollars worldwide, making it one of the top 100 highest-grossing films ever made.[25]

Mamma Mia! shares a number of important features with both *Gypsy* and *Grey Gardens*, including a nontraditional household with a central mother-daughter relationship, a focus on marriage, and a mother's love and desire for performing. However, despite high stakes and hurt feelings, mother Donna, daughter Sophie, and their relationship all thrive. Raised by Donna on a Greek island, Sophie is about to be married to her fiancé, Sky. Unbeknownst to her mother, she invites three of her mother's former lovers, one of whom may be her biological father, to the wedding. Over the course of two days, Donna reunites with her best friends, with whom she had enjoyed a spectacular singing career as Donna and the Dynamos, and gets reacquainted with the men from her past. Sophie quickly kindles warm, caring relationships with all three men, and Donna realizes that she still has deep feelings—which are deeply reciprocated—for her old lover Sam. In an unconventional twist on what is otherwise a rather conventional (if fanciful) plot, the wedding that was planned for Sophie and Sky happily becomes a wedding for Donna and Sam, while the young couple decides to leave the island and see the world together before marrying.

While the story is peppered with conflict and emotional confusion, Donna is able to succeed in every way that Rose and Edith cannot. She meets with success in her professional life, both as the lead singer of a pop group and as the owner of a taverna. She is portrayed as mature but sufficiently youthful and attractive that her encore performance with the Dynamos is an occasion for pride and pleasure, rather than shame. Her sexuality is neither perverted nor maligned (although she reports that her mother disowned her when she became pregnant out of wedlock), and she is even rewarded with love and marriage to a man who has long carried a torch for her. Moreover, her daughter is offered the support of not one, but three father figures, the promise of her own successful union, and the unfettered chance to explore the wider world, away from her mother.

There are several possible reasons for this significant change of perspective on musical motherhood. First, *Mamma Mia!*, unlike the other two shows, is an entirely fictional creation (loosely borrowed from the 1968 film *Buona Sera, Mrs. Campbell*), free from the need to observe biographical or historical necessities; indeed, *Mamma Mia!*'s contemporary setting and characters don't chronologically jibe with the Dynamos' disco-era past. But the fact that the story is set in the present day, with its significantly different social and sexual mores, especially those that govern women's behavior, is significant. Lastly, it is certainly more than a coincidence that *Mamma Mia!*, although built around songs created by ABBA's Benny Andersson and Bjorn Ulvaeus, was written, directed, and coproduced by women. Catherine Johnson, Phyllida Lloyd, and Judy Craymer not only brought *Mamma Mia!* to the stage but also were the creative team behind the film.

The ultimate purpose is not to argue that *Mamma Mia!* is a better or more important musical than either *Grey Gardens* or *Gypsy*, which is generally recognized as *the* great American musical, but to point out how the conventions of musical theatre serve to marginalize and pathologize mothers (and by extension, all women) for merely attempting to carve out an identity for themselves.

Furthermore, I hope to advocate for the inclusion of mothers as creative forces and for use of the stage as a place to fantasize about new models of motherhood in order to produce more productive, woman- and mother-friendly images, rather than relying on older ones that fuse maternal subjectivity with maternal perversity. The realities of mothers' lives offstage undoubtedly affect their representations onstage, and I am left hopeful that ongoing changes in the larger culture will bring more defensible models of musical motherhood, and that those will do their part, in turn, to permit real-life mothers more subjectivity.

Notes

1. D. A. Miller, *Place for Us: Essay on the Broadway Musical* (Cambridge: Harvard University Press, 1998), 7.
2. Steph Lawler, *Mothering the Self: Mothers, Daughters, Subjects* (London: Routledge, 2000), 132.
3. Arthur Laurents and Stephen Sondheim, *Gypsy: A Musical Suggested by the Memoirs of Gypsy Rose Lee* (New York: Theatre Communications Group, 1994), 5. The title of this essay is taken from the musical *Gypsy*.
4. Miller, *Place for Us*, 69.
5. Ibid., 90. The use of a belt or chest voice often reaching into the lower range is common for mothers (and Star Mothers, for that matter), whereas ingénues are typically written for soprano voices.
6. Ibid., 110. "We are allowed to recognize how all our need and veneration must transform the star, no matter what role she plays, into the familiar figure that every woman becomes once we bury thus our desperate, adoring faces in her skirts."
7. Adrienne Rich, *Of Woman Born: Tenth Anniversary Edition* (New York: Norton, 1986), 225.
8. Ben Brantley, "Whatever Happened to Little Edie?" *New York Times*, March 8, 2006. Fascination with this pair isn't limited to the musical stage; in the spring of 2009, HBO premiered an unrelated film, also called *Grey Gardens*, about the Beales. Starring Jessica Lange and Drew Barrymore, the telefilm was also greeted with critical laurels and popular acclaim. In 2015, a restored version of the Maysles' film was rereleased to mark its fortieth anniversary, while comedians Fred Armisen and Bill Hader dedicated the first episode of their IFC parody series *Documentary Now!* to a spoof of *Grey Gardens* titled "Sandy Passage."
9. See Stacy Wolf's chapter "Ethel Merman" in *A Problem Like Maria: Gender and Sexuality in the American Musical* (Ann Arbor: University of Michigan Press, 2002), 89–130, for a full discussion of *Gypsy* and Merman's queerness.
10. Doug Wright, Scott Frankel, and Michael Korie, *Grey Gardens: The Complete Book and Lyrics of the Broadway Musical* (New York: Applause, 2007), 55–57, 113–25.
11. Laurents and Sondheim, *Gypsy*, 67.
12. Wright, Frankel, and Korie, *Grey Gardens*, 51.

13. Ibid., 34.
14. Laurents and Sondheim, *Gypsy*, 3. "Life upon the wicked stage" is a quote from Show Boat.
15. Miller, *Place for Us*, 117.
16. Lawler, *Mothering the Self*, 171.
17. Laurents and Sondheim, *Gypsy* 16; Wright, Frankel, and Korie, *Grey Gardens*, 48.
18. Laurents and Sondheim, *Gypsy*, 106–7.
19. Miller, *Place for Us*, 118–19.
20. Ben Brantley, "Curtain Up! It's Patti's Turn at *Gypsy*," *New York Times*, March 28, 2008. Patti LuPone starred in the 2008–2009 Broadway run, joining Ethel Merman (1959–61), Angela Lansbury (1974–75), Tyne Daly (1989–1991), and Bernadette Peters (2003–04). Of course, the body types of the women who have played Rose have undoubtedly played a role in their interpretations, as well as the understandings of Rose's sexuality (or lack thereof) by their respective audiences, but generally speaking, Rose Hovick has *not* been played by willowy sexpots. The 2015 London revival of *Gypsy*—the first West End production in forty years—starred the diminutive, mumsy Imelda Staunton as Momma Rose.
21. See Julia Kristeva's "Motherhood According to Bellini" in *Desire in Language* (New York: Columbia University Press, 1980), 237–70; and "Stabat Mater" in *Tales of Love* (New York: Columbia University Press, 1987), 234–64, for a reassessment of Freud's theories of mother-child dynamics and individuation.
22. Miller, *Place for Us*, 83, 89.
23. The Broadway League, "Demographics of the Broadway Audience Report," for 2005–2006, 2006–2007, 2007–2008, and 2008–2009 seasons. These indicate that women purchased 62 percent, 64 percent, 66 percent, and 66 percent of tickets sold, respectively.
24. Ben Brantley, "Mom Had a Trio (And a Band, Too)," *New York Times*, October 19, 2001. *Mamma Mia!* closed on September 12, 2015, just shy of 5,760 performances.
25. A. O. Scott. "Does Your Mother Know You Sing ABBA Tunes?" *New York Times*, July 18, 2008; Box Office Mojo, "All Time Worldwide Box Office Grosses."

Decolonizing Motherhood

Images of Mothering in First Nations Theatre

—ANN HAUGO

> Performance can describe, through the fulsome, hopeful, radically humanist gesture of the utopian performative, how social relationships might change. I go to see performances anticipating transformative experiences, ones that will let me see a sliver of a vision, let me feel for a moment in my body and my soul what the world might be like were some form of social justice or progressive social change or consistent act of real, human love even partially accomplished. The performatives I'm engaging here aren't iterations of what *is* but transformative doings of what if. This kind of hope represents an opening up, rather than a closing down, of consciousness of the past and the future in the present.
>
> JILL DOLAN, *UTOPIA IN PERFORMANCE: FINDING HOPE AT THE THEATER*, 2005

I first saw a production written by Marie Clements nearly fifteen years ago, a staged reading of *Now Look What You Made Me Do*, a text that even as a staged reading I could only describe as kaleidoscopic, a collage of images and relationships, tied together with a central narrative enacted by a mixed-blood female character seeking agency, power, a center. Then as now, I feel that to write a narrative that interprets, theorizes, or explicates a theme or direction in Clements's work serves mostly to reduce her work, to force that collage of themes and images into a false stability, molded into my own narrative frame. Reid Gilbert, who has written several articles on Clements's plays, offers a reading of Clements's work that stems from his concept of "sheer theatricality," a method that "denaturalizes reception" through avoiding a reading that begins with the stabilizing impulse of marking genre, avoiding the static codes of reception. Gilbert's process allows for refraction and reflection, grounded in the idea of the mise-en-abyme, the between-mirrors effect, the idea of an image reflected endlessly through or onto mirrors placed opposite each other, an infinite cache of images. Gilbert attempts a Lacanian-Derridean turn with sheer theatricality, "suggesting a kind of 'writing' whose text is constructed through a coining of physical and sensory 'graphemes,'" graphemes that he specifies as composing a "physical and sensory language carried in bodies, sound and apparatus." "Such writing," Gilbert continues, "remains dynamic, resisting unitary meaning: as it undulates in and out of various genres and in and out of the various responses of spectators, it exposes its own hybridity, its dialogism. More important, it also harkens far back for citation. By moving to a place before calligraphy and even before orality, it moves to a space without imperial signification."[1]

Like Gilbert, I am fascinated by the multiple trajectories of meaning and the complex readings that Clements's dramaturgy produces, built by a web of image citations, reflecting and accumulating from scene to scene. My interest, however, resides not only in that astounding complexity but also in the political contexts for her work, in all its layers of meaning and images: feminist and indigenous, a liberating and transformative poetics that makes theatre into ceremony—not a New Age, let's-all-feel-good-and-dance-in-a-circle ceremony but a ceremony of communal power, often *women's* communal power, that transcends the material limitations placed on her characters in daily life. It is this merging of a precise political vision and a postmodern practice that fuels my interest in her plays. Although her subject matter is often dark or troubling—domestic violence in *Now Look What You Made Me Do*, the death and destruction wreaked by uranium mining and atomic bombs in *Burning Vision*, or the serial murders of Native women in Vancouver's skid row in *The Unnatural and Accidental Women*, for example—her plays enact the militant optimism that Dolan describes in the opening epigraph.[2] In Clements's work, this manifests as an authorial standpoint from which women (and sometimes men) regain their agency, restored to a vital mobility from which they can move into a new future and, sometimes, amend the past. Since many of her characters are indigenous, that restoration of agency often means that her characters confront and overcome obstacles that have their roots in gendered colonialism.

The powerhouse play that confronts gendered colonialism is undoubtedly her *The Unnatural and Accidental Women*, which premiered at the Firehall Arts Center in Vancouver, British Columbia, on November 2, 2000. On that same day, an interview with Vancouver barber Gilbert Paul Jordan appeared in the *Vancouver Sun*, and according to the *Globe and Mail*, Jordan on that night for the second time in a week violated a court order that prohibited him from drinking with women or in public bars.[3] The coincidence seems something out of a movie plot, as it was the women killed by Jordan who inspired Clements to write the play. At least eight women, most of them First Nations women, are believed to have died at the hands of Jordan, the "boozing barber." His MO: coaxing or forcing women to drink large quantities of alcohol and assaulting them once they had passed out or died. His first victim died in 1965—Ivy Rose Oswald, an English-born switchboard operator, and the only one of his eight presumed victims who was not Aboriginal.[4] He was finally convicted and sentenced to fifteen years in prison for the death of Vanessa Lynn Buckner, who died in a Vancouver hotel room at the age of twenty-seven, her blood alcohol level reading .91. Jordan presumably fled the hotel room and waited an hour before calling the authorities. Charged with first-degree murder, he was convicted on manslaughter charges and sentenced to fifteen years in prison; that sentence was lessened to nine years on appeal, with parole available after six.

And so, when the Firehall staged *Unnatural and Accidental Women* in 2000, Jordan was in fact out of prison. In news accounts about the alleged murders and the one that did finally send him to prison, Jordan's dysfunctional life, erratic behavior, and flagrant lack of remorse became the focus. The press attention on Jordan and the continued marginalization of the women who became his victims mobilized Clements, who has written that she originally wasn't interested in writing about the case: "What changed my mind was that there were three pages dedicated to this loser murderer but only a paragraph and a picture describing each woman he had victimized, their last known whereabouts, where they ended up—which was in hotel rooms, dying alone. They had no story as far as the world was concerned other than what Jordan had done to them. I started writing because I was angry. . . . I looked into these paragraphs and their pictures, images started appearing, and I followed them into words."[5] The characters that Clements created are built from the biographies of the victims, women living on Vancouver's Skid Row, some of them prostitutes, all of them marginalized by poverty and the residue of colonial policies. Despite the fact that her mission was to rescue the women's stories—to privilege their lives in a way that they had not been privileged in life—Clements's characters are not one-dimensional heroic victims. They are "perfectly imperfect," Clements notes, as she describes how actors have brought such "guts and beauty" to the play: "We know these women from the inside out. They are our sisters, our mothers, our aunts, and maybe parts of ourselves. They lived, had dreams, were perfectly imperfect, and loved like any other human being."[6]

Among the imperfections of Clements's characters are troubling images of motherhood, troubling because the images on one level are all stories of failed mothering—women who have seemingly abandoned their children and headed to Vancouver, like too many of the women, perhaps, who we see on the streets today, drug-addicted, turning tricks, homeless, while in cultural stereotypes of "these women"—especially if they are women of color—their abandoned children form the tragic backdrop to the story, presumed forgotten by the errant, unfit mothers. Clements is deeper than this, of course. In this play, her mothers fight their own positioning, they mourn their lost children or lost selves, and their longing to escape Skid Row becomes connected to dreams of their children. In telling this story, Clements becomes historical materialist. Rooting the women's stories in Vancouver's history, she embeds their exploitation at the beginning of the twenty-first century in the colonial and capitalist relations that produced and sustain contemporary Vancouver and its Skid Row, while at the same time constructing lovable, multidimensional, and spirited characters.

Clements is one of several contemporary Native playwrights who have tackled images of Native mothering in their plays. This article begins an exploration of that work, using Clements's play as a starting point, a navigational tool, perhaps. In this colonial world in which Native women are still seen by at least some segments of the population as, in activist Sharon Powell's observation, "better dead than pregnant,"[7] in what ways does Native women's theatre and performance grapple with colonial narratives about mothering? Several other plays, both published and unpublished, by Native women of the United States and Canada stage mothers and mothering relationships. Among them is Vera Manuel's *The Strength of Indian Women*, which provides a window into the lives of several women survivors of residential schools, zeroing in on three generations—grandmother, mother, daughter—on the day of the youngest woman's puberty ceremony, when all the older women gather and begin to finally share their stories about residential school. *Red Mother*, by Muriel Miguel (who, incidentally, originated the role of Aunt Shadie in Clements's play), takes the audience member on a historical journey, back through two centuries of colonization and war. Adapted from Brecht's *Mother Courage and Her Children*, the play is, according to Miguel, about capitulation, about what a mother can sacrifice in order to survive. Daughter Murielle Borst, who directed a performance at the National Museum of the American Indian, wrote, "'Red Mother' is about not the noble mothers, but the failed ones. Their spirits linger and cannot rest due to the deaths of their children, or because of abuse for which they have never made amends. These women exist, whether we like it or not. Native women and native people everywhere have been dehumanized. Our survival over the years is the result not only of our nobility, but of our fallible humanity. Thus, 'Red Mother' is also about the responsibilities of motherhood and the consequences of failure."[8] The plays mentioned here were chosen particularly for their staging of mothering relationships, so this sampling is not meant to be representative of all Native plays. It is, however, one facet of the decolonial potential of Native women's theatre, in this case, through the specific ways that key plays restage Native motherhood. Together, these plays adopt a conscious strategy in which historical roots of family dysfunction are exposed and articulated to colonial policies and mother-characters become archetypal figures of strength. Clements's *The Unnatural and Accidental Women* accomplishes this through a reclamation of motherwork by her indigenous characters.

In *Conquest: Sexual Violence and American Indian Genocide*, Andrea Smith explores the implications of Native women's reproductive capacities in light of historical and ongoing efforts by colonial governments to gain access to Native lands and resources. In short, Smith argues that as the site even of potential reproduction, Native women are cast as "pollutants," the vessel that would threaten colonial dominance by continuing—even expanding—the colonized population. This of course contrasts markedly with the role of mothering or "motherwork" in traditional cultures. Lisa Udel posits that in contemporary colonial relations in North America, Native women's motherwork has taken on a political connotation and has been embraced as a form of activism.[9]

The concept of motherwork was first coined by Patricia Hill Collins to provide a foundation for theorizing about the reproductive labor of racial ethnic women, a reproductive labor "that challenges social constructions of work and family as separate spheres, of male and female gender roles as similarly dichotomized, and of the search for autonomy as the guiding human quest."[10] Motherwork becomes for Collins a way of articulating a reproductive labor that does not fit Western feminist theories built—whether consciously or unconsciously—through discourses that privilege individual autonomy. Motherwork takes on a collective quality, as it "goes beyond ensuring the survival of one's own biological children or those of one's family. This type of motherwork recognizes that individual survival, empowerment, and identity require group survival, empowerment, and identity."[11] Significantly for my application of Collins's concept, she reaches to Native poet/theorist Marilou Awiakta, who describes in "Grandmother" the power of mothering connections in her own world: "But from the presence of her arms I also feel the stern, beautiful power that flows from all the Grandmothers, as it flows from our mountains themselves. It says, 'Dry your tears. Get up. Do for yourselves or do without. Work for the day to come.'"[12] For Awiakta, the embrace of her own grandmother connects her to the women of her nation and to her world and place in it. At once nurturing and powerful, it activates her, speaks to her to be active in her world. To summarize

Udel, in the indigenous rooting of the concept, motherwork makes women sacred, places them at the center of movements for cultural persistence, and in many cultures, necessitates their being leaders. Their power, of course, is mediated by colonial intrusions upon traditional beliefs and practices, and in many cultures, the political roles women play have diminished under colonialism. In activist and recovery movements in North America, the role of mothers in the culture is often retrieved or validated.[13] In the twentieth and twenty-first centuries, as those movements have become increasingly pan-Indian, motherwork extends beyond the boundaries of each individual culture; it becomes interpreted and acted on as a wider intertribal imperative. Udel quotes Yet Si Blue (Janet McCloud), the Tulalip activist and elder, "It is going to be the job of Native women to begin teaching other women what their roles are. Women have to turn life around, because if they don't, all of future life is threatened and endangered. I don't care what kind of women they are, they are going to have to worry more about the changes that are taking place on this Mother Earth that will affect us all."[14]

Reclaiming motherwork

Through writing, Indigenous women identify the poisons that threaten to destroy us. To promote survival we must name our enemies.
ELIZABETH ARCHULETA, "'I GIVE YOU BACK': INDIGENOUS WOMEN WRITING TO SURVIVE," 2006.

Elizabeth Archuleta begins a discussion of the activist potential of writing by deferring to the observation of Scott Lyons (Ojibwe) that literary production was itself often the scene of violence against indigenous peoples, a point that theatre scholars would do well to remember as we review the three centuries of plays in the United States and Canada that contain Native characters, or perhaps better put, *mis*representations of Native peoples. What could be more insidiously violent than misrepresenting—and thereby broadcasting on stages and screens—the most basic of kinship relationships, the family unit? In historical representations of Native women in film, theatre, and literature, we find an echo of that "pollution" discourse that Andrea Smith describes. The two prominent images of Native women—the princess and the "squaw"—replicate the larger culture's fear of Native women's reproductive capacities. The character who reproduces—and does so often—is the squaw. Often oversexed with many children, the squaw is the bad Indian of the good Indian/bad Indian female binary, the counterpart to the male Indian savage, she is "lustful, immoral, unfeeling, and dirty."[15] She is also typically a mother and is depicted as a particularly ineffective one: Her children have been produced as a result of that overzealous sexual appetite, and their upbringing has been haphazard at best at the hands of an unfeeling and immoral mother. The Indian Princess, though sexualized in most representations, often remains "pure," does not reproduce, and therefore produces no more little indigenous bodies that might one day grow up and challenge the colonial system. The historical record, of course, is different. History tells us that Lady Rebecca Rolfe did have a child, for example, but the mythic capital of that is far less powerful than the mythic capital of her rescue of John Smith. (Rolfe was known to her own people by the name Matoaka and is known mythically as Pocahontas, not her real name; the name Lady Rebecca Rolfe is historically more appropriate to the period in which she bore the child, and the child is usually associated with Lady Rebecca, not "Pocahontas.") In pictorial and literary representation, "Pocahontas" remains prematernal, her body a site of potential sexuality, not realized sexuality.

This inherited representational context for Native women characters onstage might be considered to be one of the enemies against which Clements's text "writes," and it is intimately related to the stereotypes of Native women that circulate throughout popular culture today, affecting not just our literatures but also our daily interactions. For all of Jordan's real Native victims were seemingly regarded by not just the press but also the coroner's office and the police force as throwaway victims. Native women living on Vancouver's Skid Row, they were assumed to be prostitutes, drug addicts, and alcoholics, dying "unnatural" but "accidental" deaths by alcohol poisoning, drinking themselves to death. Three of Jordan's victims were even found in his own barbershop, dead by alcohol poisoning, yet no charges for those deaths were brought against him. The publicity material for the Canadian television series *Exhibit A: Secrets of Forensic Science* is telling. Advertising a past episode of the series that focused on the Gilbert Paul Jordan case, it reads, "Coincidentally they were all native and alcoholics, so it is some time before an astute pathologist questions the staggeringly high blood alcohol levels."[16] Importantly, however, the press coverage of the women also un-mothers them, disconnecting them from families and lives that they had before becoming Jordan's victims, isolated by static reports of their deaths despite the families outside the city that missed them.

While I would describe *Unnatural and Accidental Women* as decidedly non-narrative, there is a central narrative through which the collage is woven. That is the story of Rebecca, described as a thirty-year old mixed-blood writer "searching for the end of a story."[17] Rebecca's story locates the lives of the women in Vancouver's history, as she struggles to understand what brought and held her mother here. Rebecca's "story" is a doubled one, as she is both character and author, writing a narrative that becomes part of the play itself. The ending that Rebecca searches for, at least initially, is her mother, who left Rebecca and her father years earlier. Following her mother's trail through the hotels and bars of Vancouver's Lower East Side will eventually lead her to cross paths with the Barber himself. Although Rebecca will not discover this until near the end of the play—in a scene when daughter and spirit mother reunite to end the Barber's killing spree—her mother has become one of his victims.

In the structure of the play itself, act 1 reveals the histories of ten women to us, while Rebecca's own story gradually unfolds in her narration. Each woman is identified by name, date of death, age, and the coroner's report on her death—deliberately sterile, impersonal announcements that recall the minor reporting on the lives and deaths of Jordan's real-life victims in the Vancouver papers. With just one exception, the dismissive fact reporting comes only after complete scenes have built a biographical context for each woman. This article is most interested in four of the women whose identities as mothers or daughters figure prominently in their characterization: Aunt Shadie, Rebecca, Verna, and Valerie.

Aunt Shadie appears at the top of the play, emerging nude from a pile of leaves, calling Rebecca's name. Her character name is Rita Louise James, reported to have died in 1978. The name used throughout the play, "Aunt Shadie," recalls the last woman who is known to have died in Jordan's company, Edna Marie Shade, an Aboriginal prostitute who was found in a Vancouver hotel room in November 1987.[18] Her name of course also plays on the idea of a "shade" as ghost or spirit. In the character descriptions, Clements writes that Aunt Shadie is "Native," embodying "mother qualities of strength, humour, love, patience."[19] Through Aunt Shadie calling Rebecca's name and through a somewhat disembodied relationship as Rebecca and Aunt Shadie together tell the history of the founding of Vancouver in the opening scene, we learn—or at least surmise—that they are mother and daughter. While Aunt Shadie as spirit can see and interact with Rebecca, influencing her actions, Rebecca is unaware of Aunt Shadie's presence until the final moments of the play yet aware as the action progresses that she draws closer to her.

Of the mother figures in the play, Valerie appears next, in a scene set in the Clifton Hotel. We grow to know Valerie through two scenes in which her only physical scene partner is a talking dresser. About developing the characters, Clements has said that she tried to picture them in their rooms, tried to understand what needs Jordan seemed to be able to fulfill for each of the women.[20] In Valerie's scenes, the offering becomes embodied in and through the animated dresser. Initially motivated by sexual lust, the dresser comments on Valerie's breasts as she adjusts them in the dresser's mirror: "Nice set." The scene is filled with nearly violent sexual banter, as the dresser becomes part john, part adversary, reinforcing Valerie's sexual objectification both through her own concern with her body and in the dresser's sexualized language and treatment of her body. It offers her red lingerie and then (after a man's face begins to appear in the mirror) aggressively grabs a breast after teasing her down to a drawer. As if fighting the dresser's desire to trap her in her own objectification, Valerie fights back, but her own words continue to define her as sexualized. Trapping its hand in the drawer, Valerie makes it tell her that she still has great tits, and then as if needing to reinforce the thought, tells the dresser, "I had two sons, you know . . . and I still have great tits."[21]

Valerie's first scene ends in an all-out fight with the dresser, rolling on the floor, which is where we find her next, after several other scenes, both she and the dresser trying to put themselves together after either a fight or violent sex—or both—and still sparring verbally. The dresser then offers Valerie something else. From inside a drawer, the voices of Valerie's boys emerge—Evan and Tommy, ages eight and five, respectively. Evan is sarcastic, older, wiser, and hardened to his mother's absence, refusing to believe that his mother will come home and interrupting her lines about "working" and substituting "drinking." On the other hand, Tommy is hopeful and eager to let his mother in on what he's been doing, telling her first that he's become a good dancer, even better than Evan, and then asking her directly when she will come home. Valerie tells them that she can still picture them in her head, that she wants to come home: "I'm gonna get this job and soon. . . . Maybe I could take a couple days off . . . working. And we could get together. . . . Just me and my two little men." The connection fades as the boys both ask, "Mom?" as if they can't hear her any longer. Crawling closer, Valerie responds, "Yeah, I'm listening. I'm right here. I'M RIGHT HERE." On the final note of her desperation, the dresser attacks Valerie, pummeling her to the ground until she is almost unconscious. Then as if to deliberately torture her, it opens a drawer again, letting little Tommy's voice out, "Mommy?" Valerie wakes, crawls again toward the dresser—now both the means of her torture and death and the site of her son's voice. "I'm coming . . . I'm coming." The dresser attacks again and knocks her unconscious with her head now on "the Tommy drawer," unable to fend off the hand as it begins to grope her body.[22]

The layering of images in this scene is classically Clements—surreal, poignant, laden with meaning. Gilbert uses this scene to illustrate his point about sheer theatricality, arguing that Clements's writing in this scene (and others) resists simple translations of meaning, rendering readers unable to "fix" or stabilize a meaning for the scene, instead reading the scene by "picking up their 'rhythms,' textures, and wave lengths: those invisible—those 'sheer'—nuances which Clements stipulates and which, it appears, the scriptless audience can, in fact, 'read.'" I agree with Gilbert's argument here, noting that often the scenes' internal "meaning" only begins a play of meaning as each scene, each image, refracts and reflects images and rhythms from other scenes. To interpret this scene requires negotiating its multiple meanings.

For Valerie, on the one hand, the dresser is a violent john, the scenes playing out the possible scene between Jordan and victim, at times straightforwardly violent. But the dresser also speaks to Valerie's deepest desires, asking it in one instance to validate her, to bear witness to her great tits, unaffected by childbearing. At the same time, the dresser embodies the children she has left behind, and in her exchanges with it in this scene, we see played out a mother thinking of her children in her last minutes on earth, a hope that will be reflected also in Verna's scenes, multiplying and layering the investment in the maternal. Valerie's desire to hear and see her children again liberates her depiction from the stereotype of poverty-level, dismissive mothers—and especially mothers of color. Her *inability* to mother is depicted as cut off by a cycle of addiction and poverty, a cycle that at some level she recognizes her immersion in. This perfectly imperfect mother still longs to connect, still hopes that one day she can, and in her mind, she still hears her sons' voices as she sees death approaching. She dies, then, not as an imperfect mother who has abandoned or forgotten her children; for audiences, Valerie's final dying image is that of an estranged mother craving a lost connection to her children so deeply that she crawls back to the instrument of torture—the dresser—because she identifies her children within it. Clements's character thus breaks the colonial bonds of representation, becomes vital, no longer the static two-line death reporting in the Vancouver papers but a woman—a mother—who is tragic and fallible, yes, but also resilient enough to argue with her oppressor (whether the dresser, a john, or Gilbert), hopeful enough to imagine reaching her children, and desperate enough to make promises that she probably can't keep.

Verna appears in one traditional scene and weaves in and around other scenes, following around the stage a toy airplane she has purchased for her son. Placed just before Valerie's first scene with the dresser, Verna's first scene is shorter than Valerie's, occurring in a transitional phase in act 1 in which the deaths of the women occur faster, building a momentum that will lead not to a final scene of conflict or dramatic tension at the end of the act but to a moment of confident unity. In performance, Valerie's and Verna's scenes weave back and forth, building a collage of fragmented or interrupted motherhood. Verna is on the phone, arguing with someone who seems to have trouble believing her—she's bought a gift for a "him," for a birthday, and she asks that the conversant bring "him" to meet her.[23] Fondling a bottle, she seems to be trying to decide between the bottle and the toy. The stage directions tell us that her ex-husband is on the phone, but in performance, the conversation is less specific than this. To the airplane she holds in her hand, she says, "My son'll like you. Almost spent my whole skinny cheque. I hope he likes you. I hope he likes me. I hope he's not mad. My son has a temper just like his mother."[24] Like the dresser in Valerie's scenes, the airplane animates Verna's longing for her child. From her dialogue, we learn that Verna works a wage job of some sort, and later, in act 2, we learn that she has been sobering up. Presumably for Verna, her death at the Barber's hands occurs right at a momentous change in her life, and in that sense, her story stages the hope that might have been Valerie's—a more legitimate job, sobriety, the moment when she can return home and resume being a mother, all of it hard-won through bitter determination and coming with more than a little anxiety about what might happen at the reunion with the children.

Verna's demise is less graphic than Valerie's. Following the airplane through the "hotel," she stops outside Room 315, where she hears a man's voice—the Barber's, repeating the line that becomes ritualized by its repetition in this act, "Can I get you a drink?" In the script, the voice is a sound effect, disembodied. For Verna's character, the lines represent the lure that Jordan may have had for one of the women, competing with the buzz of the toy airplane that represents home, a child, the life that she would like to escape back to. A man dressed as an airplane pilot seats her, offers her a drink, and the toy airplane crashes to the ground, followed by the impersonal reporting of her death: "Verna Deborah Gregory, 38. Died September 25, 1986 with a 0.63 blood-alcohol reading. Gregory's death was ruled 'accidental as a result of acute alcohol poisoning.'"[25]

Less specific than Valerie's story, Verna's motivations will become clearer in act 2. As the young Violet questions why Verna remains so angry, Verna bites out, "Because I'm dead and I'm still thirsty." In Clements's hands, Verna's thirst becomes metaphorical, a key to understanding what makes Verna feel empty inside, those things that in fact might drive her *to* drink. To Violet, who questions, "Thirsty?," Verna angrily explains, "THIRSTY, you fuckin' parrot. I'm thirsty for . . . for . . . my kids, my man. I'm thirsty, thirsty, thirsty, THIR-sty, THIRSTY, dehydrated, dry, parched, thirsty." As Violet grows quiet and hurt, Verna becomes more sheepish, realizing she has hurt or scared Violet. Her anger, she says, "is the only way I know how to get from here . . . to there."[26] She is not the alcoholic Native woman who simply drank herself to death here, as the reporting might lead one to believe. Here, Verna is three-dimensional, leaving behind a life with potential, caught in a moment of weakness within a day of great hope, the day that she would see her son again, the day that she would deliver the toy airplane that she desperately hoped he would love.

At the end of act 1, all of the Barber's "victims" organize, led by Aunt Shadie, who calls them together. Beginning in his barbershop, Aunt Shadie calls to the spirits of three women who the Barber has killed in the shop—Penny, Patsy, and Marilyn. It is in this final collage of act 1 that Aunt Shadie's purpose in the story becomes clear. The mother image in the play, her role now surpasses that of being only the mother for whom Rebecca searches. She is the spirit who will lead the women to help Rebecca overcome the Barber, ending his killing spree and in the process presumably saving Rebecca's life. Now, having crossed over, she also appears centered in her culture, as she leads the women in song not just in English but in Cree. Bits and pieces of Aunt Shadie's identity that were revealed earlier come cascading together, as her role as cultural motherworker becomes clearer. From her suitcases earlier, Cree words tumble out, and as she "rises" from rummaging in the suitcases, the stage directions tell us, the suitcases grow heavier. This is "baggage" perhaps, but perhaps not negatively so. Those bags contain not simply her past but her roots. In conversation with Rose, the switchboard operator who greets each of the women as they cross over to the other side, Aunt Shadie recalls her mother's rabbit fur mitts, days spent on the trapline, the skill and endurance of her young body. She carries her mother's strength with her, her mother's endurance and fortitude, all of which she will call upon in act 2 as she brings the women together to face the Barber and, in the end, save her own daughter's life. In death, she is able to transcend the pull of the city, to root herself in a cultural and familial identity. The "city" comes to represent not just the decadence of drugs, sex, and poverty but also a site of colonial intrusion, the drugs, sex, and poverty being not the static "condition" of these women but the colonial residue that separates them from home, family, tribe, and self. In death, as spirits on another plane, still "here" and able to enact change, Aunt Shadie through her song—in her original language—mobilizes them into action.

The song weaves over and under the remaining "scenes" in act 1, as one by one, the remaining women—Violet, Brenda, and Verna—die and cross over, joining the song, while the women killed earlier rise and join Aunt Shadie in song. The youngest of the women, Violet, is met by Aunt Shadie, who tells Violet that she should stay with her rather than following the others into the bar because "You're too young." When Rose greets her, she hugs her so hard that Violet exclaims, "She's squishing me." "Hugging—Squishing. It's all the same thing," Aunt Shadie tells her. "Love."[27] The moment interestingly echoes Awiakta's grandmother's hug, the arms that connected her to not just her grandmother but all of the grandmothers, to her world and her culture. Violet is both the youngest in age of the women, dying at age twenty-seven, and in the chronology, the most recent of the deaths, dying on October 12, 1987, the same date as real-life Vanessa Lee Buckner, and at the same blood-alcohol level, .91. Her introduction at the end of act 1 reveals her positioning among the characters. In the action of the play, both in act 1 and act 2, Violet is mothered, rather than becoming the motherer, as most of the women do. She is consequently in some ways parallel to Rebecca: young, lost, needing guidance.

As the song builds and the scene becomes focused, the older women gather in the bar, closing in on Rebecca, Ron (a young man who will become Rebecca's love interest in act 2), and the Barber, although the latter three characters are unaware of their presence. The women have become spirits—and clearly, Aunt Shadie and Rose have been so throughout the play—and their ability to affect the actions of the mortal characters becomes clear in these final moments. Coming together through the words of the song, Verna plants Rebecca's wallet on the Barber's table, the action that will set the events of act 2 into motion.

Act 2 begins with a rather different comedic tone, opening in Rebecca's apartment the morning after the scene in the bar. The spirit women have gathered here: Mavis, Verna, Valerie, and in a later scene, Violet. Aunt Shadie will momentarily "phone in" from another location, where she and Rose are beginning to set a large table for tea. The convention begun in act 1 continues here, the women able to affect Rebecca's actions while Rebecca is mostly unaware of their presence. As Rebecca wakes, hungover, stumbling through the apartment, she interacts unknowingly with the women, stepping on Verna's foot and calling out once when she thinks she hears something. But they are, for the most part, invisible to her, their action weaving through her own, as she stumbles back to the bathroom, takes a pee, discovers her horrible morning-after look in the mirror, and continues to stumble back to her bed. The women's dialogue is antie-like,[28] and indeed, in the ceremony that closes act 1, they invoke each other as sisters. Now, they bicker with each other, half-teasing the unknowing Rebecca, and interacting with each other as if they have known each other—and Rebecca—for a long time. Trickster-like, they tease and prod, their humor scatological. Mavis pinches Ron's ass, they comment like children on the stink he creates in the bathroom, and they debate the size of a Canadian Mountie's dick relative to that of his horse.

The premise here is one that has become if not common, then at least frequent in the work of some Native theatre artists—the staging of a spirit world that exists simultaneously with the mortal world and that can affect our own, often playfully and sometimes with great gravity. Tomson Highway's *Rez Sisters* and *Dry Lips Oughta Move to Kapuskasing* both employ the convention, as Nanabush shape-shifts into various characters, affecting the action while most of the other characters remain blissfully unaware. In Highway's plays, the only characters who seem to recognize the trickster's presence are those who are somehow "touched." In *Rez Sisters*, this is Zhaboonigan Peterson, who is mentally challenged and has survived a brutal rape, and in increments throughout the play, Marie Adele Starblanket, as she begins to edge closer to death, to becoming spirit herself. Monique Mojica's *Princess Pocahontas and the Blue Spots* employs a similar convention. As Contemporary Woman #1 continues on her search, she is accompanied by Spirit Sister, the characters described by Mojica as inhabiting "parallel worlds of time and space."[29] In this play, Contemporary Woman #1 begins to inch closer to Spirit Sister as she grows closer to an understanding of her own place in this world, as the Spirit Sister functions as a guide and in some ways a cultural compass.

To call this "convention," however, is to perhaps oversimplify or dismiss the cultural roots for the choices that these Indigenous playwrights make. In a roundtable discussion at a conference sponsored by the Native American Women Playwright's Archive, several playwrights, including Mojica, discussed—among many other qualities that distinguish Native theatre—this practice of staging the spirit world, of finding a literal or theoretical way to grapple with it. Mojica began, "I try to write different voices, spirit voices, and . . . how to write that so that it comes close to representing what you hear, see, or experience is something."[30]

In *Unnatural and Accidental Women*, the spirit women's agency propels the outcome of the play. Far from tertiary to the action, they lead it. They guide Rebecca to her final action, confronting the Barber in his shop. They don trappers' clothing, invoking the strength of Aunt Shadie's mother and grandmothers. They lead Rebecca to the spot where he has hidden their braids, and in his death scene, it is Aunt Shadie's hand that guides Rebecca's, as Rebecca brings the knife to the Barber's throat. In these final moments, Rebecca at last "sees" and feels the presence of the women, as she and Aunt Shadie greet each other, Aunt Shadie speaking her name. This is conscious, deliberate action by the spirits, its source and reasoning—a mother's relationship to and responsibility for her child, along with the place of women on the earth—defined by the mothers—Valerie and Verna—in beautiful poetry in a scene Clements titles "She Sleeps

Like a Rock." Their words weave through Rebecca's as she describes her own heaviness, wherein "the only language we have to know has molded from the earth—its tears and blood, its laughter and love—gone solid. . .. I hold it in my heart, it keeps me attached to the gravity of a perfect knowing."

> Valerie: A mother opens the heart of her child and places her rock inside the flesh. Inside, so no one—no man, no ugliness, will ever place its grabby hands on it.
>
> Verna: A mother buries its knowledge inside the child. Kiss-ageeta-ooma. It drops inside the eternity of blood and earth. Kiss-ageeta-ooma. I love you, silly face.
>
> Valerie: A mother opens the heart of her child and places her rock inside the flesh. A growing child takes a rock from the earth it walked from and places it in a leather pouch and hangs it around her neck. A woman walks heavy.[31]

The outcome of the action in this play can thus be understood in part as a hopeful act of motherwork, as playwright Clements leads us to imagine a world in which these women may not escape their own fate at Jordan's hands but save their daughters, reaching from the spirit world to aid a daughter in connecting with her mother, escaping from Jordan, and ending his life, rather than the other way around. Tellingly, the Barber's death is not the final scene of the play. Once Rebecca has returned the braids to each woman and embraced her mother, she begins to walk away, her journey complete, as the spirit women "sit down to a beautiful a la The Last Supper,"[32] their work complete. For now.

Notes

1. Reid Gilbert, "Marie Clement's *The Unnatural and Accidental Women*: Denaturalizing Genre," *Theatre Research in Canada* 42, no. 1–2 (2003): 125–46.
2. Jill Dolan, *Utopia in Performance: Finding Hope at the Theater* (Ann Arbor: University of Michigan Press, 2005), 141.
3. Ginny Ratsoy and James Hoffman, eds., *Playing the Pacific Province: An Anthology of British Columbia Plays, 1967–2000* (Toronto: Playwrights Canada Press, 2001), 473; and Kim Lunman, "Crown Wants Booze Killer Kept in Jail; Man Linked to Women's Deaths not Obeying; Court Orders, Prosecutor Contends," *Globe and Mail*, November 29, 2000: A13.
4. The number is "at least" eight, in part, because Jordan himself estimated that he was with about two hundred women a year, as addicted to the predation and sex, it seems, as to the alcohol.
5. Marie Clements, "In the End You Are Made Accountable," *Theatre and AutoBiography: Writing and Performing Lives in Theory and Practice*, ed. Sherrill Grace and Jerry Wasserman (Vancouver: Talonbooks, 2006), 329.
6. Ibid., 330.
7. Quoted in Andrea Smith, *Conquest: Sexual Violence and American Indian Genocide*

(Durham, NC: Duke University Press, 2015), 80. Smith borrows Powell's phrase for the title of her fourth chapter, "Better Dead Than Pregnant: The Colonization of Native Womens' Reproductive Health."

8. Carol Anne Douglas, "Spiderwoman's *Red Mother*," *Off Our Backs* (n.p., 2008), May 21, 2009.
9. Lisa J. Udel, "Revision and Resistance: The Politics of Native Women's Motherwork," *Frontiers* 22, no. 2 (2001), 43.
10. Patricia Hill Collins, "Shifting the Center: Race, Class and Feminist Theorizing about Motherhood," *Mothering: Ideology, Experience, and Agency*, ed. Evelyn Nakano Glenn, Grace Chang, Linda Renney Forcey (New York: Routledge, 1994), 47.
11. Ibid.
12. Ibid., 47–48.
13. Udel, "Revision and Resistance: The Politics of Native Women's Motherwork," 43–45.
14. Ibid., 44.
15. Elizabeth Archuleta, "'I Give You Back': Indigenous Women Writing to Survive," *Studies in American Indian Literature* 18, no. 4 (Winter 2006): 92.
16. "Exhibit A: Secrets of Forensic Science," *Kensington Communications*, May 21, 2009.
17. Marie Clements, *The Unnatural and Accidental Women* (Vancouver: Talonbooks, 2005). All references to the play are to the Talonbooks edition (2005), 5.
18. Brian Hutchinson, "Dead Women, Judges, Left in His Wake: At Least 8 Women Have Died of Alcohol Poisoning while with Sexual Predator," *National Post*, August 13, 2004, A3.
19. Clements, "In the End You Are Made Accountable," 5.
20. Ibid.
21. Clements, *Unnatural and Accidental Women*, 2005, 30.
22. Ibid., 48–51.
23. Ibid., 47.
24. Ibid., 54.
25. Ibid., 62.
26. Ibid., 92–3.
27. Ibid., 64.
28. In an indigenous family, you're more likely to be called an "antie," not an auntie.
29. Monique Mojica, *Princess Pocahontas and the Blue Spots*, in *Princess Pocahontas and the Blue Spots: Two* Plays (Toronto: Women's Press, 1991), 55.
30. "NAWPA Authors' Roundtable," *Native American Women Playwrights' Archive*, March 19, 1999. Miami University of Ohio. http://spec.lib.miamioh.edu/home/nawpa/ (accessed March 11, 1993).
31. Ibid., 83–4.
32. Clements, "In the End You Are Made Accountable," 126.

Part III

ESSAYS FROM THE CONFERENCE

The Robert A. Schanke Award-Winning Essay

Whispers from a Silent Past

Inspiration and Memory in Natasha Trethewey's *Native Guard*

—CHANDRA OWENBY HOPKINS

The Angel of History must look just so. His face is turned towards the past. Where we see the appearance of a chain of events, he sees one single catastrophe, which unceasingly piles rubble on top of rubble and hurls it before his feet.
WALTER BENJAMIN, *ON THE CONCEPT OF HISTORY*

Some names shall deck the page of history as it is written on stone.
Some will not.
NATASHA TRETHEWEY, *NATIVE GUARD*

As part of the National Civil War Project, in the fall of 2014 the Alliance Theatre in Atlanta, Georgia, partnered with former US Poet Laureate Natasha Trethewey to stage her Pulitzer Prize–winning collection of poetry, *Native Guard*.[1] Inspired by her youth as the child of a then-illegal marriage between her black mother and white father, Trethewey fuses autobiography with historical meditation on a Civil War soldier's experiences in the first African American Union troop. *Native Guard* has been called "a play, a poetry reading, an art installation, a film, a diorama and an immersive experience for the audience."[2] "Theatrical installation" may come closest to defining Trethewey's stage work, which defies traditional categorization. Trethewey was born on the hundredth anniversary of the

Civil War's end, and her poetry in performance offers a wellspring for reshaping interactions in the contemporary southern United States.

Employing Walter Benjamin's image of the angel of history as an analytical touchstone, I engage the tension at play in the first full staging of *Native Guard* at the Alliance Theatre between personal and collective history, text and stage.[3] Similarly, I draw on Hans-Thies Lehmann's exploration of postdramatic theatre to parse the transition of poetic voice to fixed historical subjectivity when adapted for the stage despite multivalent staging techniques. Moving from historical event to author, performer, and audience, I ask: How might Trethewey's poetry-in-production work allow theatre scholars to reconsider the foundational dialectic of text-based theatre and its alchemical move from page to stage? What new categories for praxis and study are mobilized by theatrical installations that blend fact and fiction, hybridizing the individual and communal histories of race in the United States? From these questions, I propose that even as the stage performance uses the exact text from Trethewey's poems with words spoken, sung, and projected, including the beautifully sparse dedication, "For my mother, in memory," the performance is fundamentally multivocal and in this aural plurality the power of historical question and discovery is unleashed.[4] What start as Trethewey's painful personal reflections become echoes of a larger history of unwitnessed lives and forgotten deaths. In the fusion of poetry and play Trethewey's *Native Guard* offers a new medium for discovering the shared history that relentlessly shapes the present of the American South.

To understand this new approach to historical performativity, I first consider the source text of *Native Guard*, and then I examine Trethewey's fusion of familial memory with Southern history and the affective power of that collision in the Alliance Theatre's production. Three conflicts drive Trethewey's elegiac collection: race and the American South, the death of her mother, and what Trethewey calls the "historical amnesia" that has haunted the unmemorialized yet unforgotten black Union soldiers of the Louisiana Native Guards.[5] The collection begins with an opening poem, "Theories of Time and Space," and follows with parts one and three, which are primarily centered on Trethewey's life, and a middle section of four poems from a black Union soldier's imagined journal entries. Like the soldier she channels, Trethewey was born in the Deep South in Gulfport, Mississippi, on April 26, 1966, to Eric Trethewey and Gwendolyn Ann Turnbough. Trethewey's birth came one year before the US Supreme Court struck down antimiscegenation laws in *Loving v. Virginia*; her birth certificate, which lists her mother's race as "colored" and her father's as "Canadian," echoes the criminalized ontology to which she was born.[6]

Trethewey weaves the dangerous aftermath of her parent's union in haunting terms within a collective Southern history scarred by war. She marks her own past, remembering the pejorative names she was called as a child and that the Ku Klux Klan burned a cross in her family's yard. She binds the stories of these personal traumas to a larger Civil War history—including the experiences of a black soldier guarding Confederate prisoners of war at Fort Massachusetts on Ship Island, Mississippi. Her poetry creates original monuments that work to redress absences in history, a direct and defiant response to the overt Southern memorialization of the Confederacy to the extent that, as Trethewey has stated, "You might think the South actually won the war."[7] While Trethewey explores her experiences of being an outsider yet native of the South and the skewed relationship to the Civil War she grew up within, she problematizes the desire to sentence the South as the only site of erasure and willful forgetting. Trethewey asserts, especially her titular poem "Native Guard," that denial, amnesia, and willful rejection was not confined to the Confederacy. In the Alliance Theatre production the poem "Native Guard" was performed by actor Thomas Neal Antwon Ghant, who entered the theatre with the audience and sat in the house with his blue Union soldier's jacket draped over his arm, casual and calm, as if he were another audience member.[8] Ghant shared his reaction to this staging, commenting: "Since I was seated with the audience throughout the opening half of the show, I found a rare opportunity to get a hand on the pulse of the audience on what I call 'ground level.' I would USE that to charge my approach to the poetry each night."[9] Ghant began his performance of "The Native Guard" character from his position in the audience and later, from the stage, he shared the following:

> *June 1863*
> Some names shall deck the page of history
> as it is written on stone. Some will not.
> Yesterday, word came of colored troops, dead
> on the battlefield at Port Hudson; how
> General Banks was heard to say *I have*
> *no dead there*, and left them, unclaimed.[10]

The corporeality of performance connects present actor and audience bodies to those bodies condemned to disintegrate without burial. Their forgotten lives and unmemorialized war deaths are tied to their largely absent existence in our nation's memory of the Civil War.[11] Contemporary theatre that challenges text as the modus operandi of performance has, as Lehmann asserts, "the power to question and destabilize the spectator's construction of identity and the 'other.'"[12] Trethewey's text in performance troubles the discreet categories of audience and performer, dead ancestors and living descendants, via her contextualization of her life within a larger Southern and US history. Through performance and the deliberate intention to create a shared theatre event including, for example, Ghant's provocative "ground level" process, traditional categories of temporal identities ("now" verses "then") and performative agents ("actor" verses "spectator") are dismantled.

Working with the National Civil War Project, noted choreographer Liz Lerman comments on this sesquicentennial of the war's end: "Every anniversary is an opportunity to reflect. Our Civil War was 150 years ago: What does it still mean? What is the aftermath? Where is the damage?"[13] The damage of the war is articulated explicitly through Trethewey's imagined black Union soldier's journal entries that when brought to the stage become a shared journey to understand the violent transformation of not only the war but also the ontological movement from enslaved to free, or what Saidiya Hartman has called "the burden of transformation."[14] To this end, Trethewey makes clear the connection between past historical trauma and present corporeality through the aftermath of the war in her own life and how it influenced her personal experiences as a multiracial child in the Deep South. This enduring legacy is made clear through performance. From the fundamental transition of what is read to what is heard from multiple voices on the stage, the performance shifts the personal, poetic voice of Trethewey's collection to the shared space of audience and performer, resulting in what Lehmann calls the "total text" of the theatre, a cocreated text forged jointly between actor and spectator. Interestingly, this performance of lived and imagined personal and national histories further illuminates the failure of words to capture experience and preserve memory. The death of Trethewey's mother and Trethewey's inability as a writer to understand that loss in words becomes a personal microcosm in performance of the larger failure of language to adequately honor historical trauma. January LaVoy, who narrated the performance in the role of "the Poet," used Trethewey's words to guide the audience through a performance that routinely questions the assumption that progress toward racial and social equity has been finished in the United States:

> The brochure in my room calls this
> *living history*. The brass plate on the door reads
> *Prissy's Room*. A window frames
> the river's crawl toward the Gulf. In my dream,
> the ghost of history lies down beside me,
> rolls over, pins me beneath a heavy arm.[15]

Sleeping in "Prissy's Room," the character of "the Poet" notices the unsettling repetitive cycle of race and history, and in her recognition she is joined with Benjamin's angel, who questions the "appearance of a chain of events" and sees instead the crushing weight of the "rubble-heap" before us.[16]

While other writers, such as playwright Suzan-Lori Parks, abstract the personal and interlace it with historical figures that loom large in America's collective consciousness, Trethewey grounds the failure of history to capture the truth of experience in the absolutely personal loss of her mother. Trethewey's experience of her murder at the hands of her mother's second husband is evoked in "Myth," the tenth poem of *Native Guard*: "I was asleep while you were dying. / It's as if you slipped through some rift, a hollow / I make between my slumber and my waking, / the Erebus I keep you in, still trying / not to let go. You'll be dead again tomorrow, / but in dreams you live."[17] Onstage, LaVoy finished these words, folded a small piece of paper she held in her hand, and walked downstage toward the audience to move a round rock and place the paper beneath it in the sand. She rested her hand reverentially on the top of the rock and paused with her gaze to the ground before standing again, transforming the rock to headstone and the stage to shared cemetery through her movement. Localized in the loss of the maternal figure on the page, on the stage the poet's personal grief spirals out into a collective loss of forgotten ancestors from the bloodiest war in US history; the performance, akin to the Southern Crescent train, winds its way through scrubby backwoods and port city alike in a shared Southern terrain of the past and present onstage and in the audience.

In the migration from page to stage and stage to audience, the greatest efficacy of the performance is its ability to create a transtemporal space that is inhabited and shared between performer and spectator, history and present. Lehmann urges: "Theatre means the collectively spent and used up lifetime in the collectively breathed air of that space in which the performing *and* the spectating take place."[18] Upon entering the collective space of *Native Guard*, each audience member was handed an approximately four-by-two-inch brown cardboard memory tag that had been stamped with a typewriter-like font that read "Remember." The tag also bore a small brass safety pin that audience members were encouraged to use to attach their tag to the raw burlap that wrapped the theatre's walls. The night I saw the performance, tags had been hung across the walls, a great many of them creeping across the back wall of the stage. The set was open to the modified three-quarter thrust architecture of the Alliance's black box theatre with sand, rocks, thin wooden panels, and a shallow pool of water evoking an exterior that was a suggestive, yet neither Georgia nor

Mississippi, setting.[19] The largest concentration of sand was against the back wall of the space, which meant that when the audience moved to hang their memory tags, their feet sunk in and transformed the stage floor's surface into one reminiscent of a sandy shore before the tide washes away the echoes of human traffic. The design of the theatre space, including the audience seating, theatre walls, and open stage areas, reinforced the collectivity of shared experience between not only performer and spectator, as Lehmann articulates, but also actors and audience members as belonging to the same communities, including Atlanta, the South, and the United States.

To complement the open set, the traditional theatre audience seating had also been intentionally changed to include the spectators in the world of the performance. Chairs—dining room, kitchen, desk, and porch—unified only through their wooden materiality formed the audience seating and evoked something not of home or comfort but of the angel's uncanny pile-up of shared history. The chairs alone sparked a mental dialogue born of the fusion of the material and immaterial: "Didn't my grandmother have a lattice-backed chair like that once? The seat was small and hard like this one." Invited to sit in chairs that plausibly, presumably, were once in someone else's home and to "write a *name*, a *moment*, or an *idea* that you feel needs to be memorialized" and pin them to the theatre's walls, the audience became cocreator in the total text of *Native Guard*.[20] Rather than feeling comforted by sitting in someone's old chair or reading the walls of memories that included phrases such as "Remember butterscotch," "Remember July 4th, the first time he said he loved me," and the names, birth, and death dates of others, the performance space made manifest the impermanence of meaning and impossibility of memory, or what whispers from Trethewey's text: "That home-going road's always full of holes."[21] The prompt to add memories to the physical walls of the theatre materialized the evocative power of the performance to catalyze memory and affect the audience. While the performers never removed and read the memory tags onstage, the audience's shared memories became the physical backdrop for the action onstage, making an explicit and reciprocal bond between audience imprint on the space and the space's impact on the audience.

On the night I participated in the performance, Atlanta as troubled homeplace was central in the audience/performer discussion that followed the show. For what the Alliance titled "Act 2," audience members were given a drink ticket with their programs before the show and encouraged in the curtain speech and printed program to stay after the performance and "gather with a complimentary beverage to share your experience of the piece."[22] *Native Guard* director and Alliance Artistic Director Susan V. Booth explained in her program note to the audience: "Rather than bending the poetry to fit the theatrical form, we must figure out how to bend the theatrical form to serve the poetry. Act 1 is our attempt. In Act 2, we're hoping you'll tell us how we did."[23] I was corrected when I asked a staff member I assumed to be the House Manager about the "talkback" after the show: "It's not a talkback, it's a conversation." While the goal of act 2 was to create an open conversation, a different community member of Atlanta in the arts, academia, local government, or business moderated the dialogue each night as a "Guest Speaker." Audience members were asked by the guest speaker to speak up and state their name and where they were from before sharing their comment or question. The cast, including the vocalist and jazz pianist who provided preshow and transition music throughout the performance, changed out of costume and sat together in the bank of seats on the left side of the house among the audience.

Audience comments mirrored Trethewey's journey to understand her home, including shock over the fact that as middle-aged Atlantans they could remember that the film *Gone with the Wind* was watched in public school history courses as a factual account of the Civil War. This baffling treatment of shared history was discussed as laughable yet equally damaging in the perpetuation of a lie born from the justification of slavery as "good for them." These memories underscored the onstage performance of Trethewey's nineteenth poem, "Southern History," that preceded the conversation:

> *Before the war, they were happy*, he said,
> quoting our textbook. (This was senior-year
> history class.) *The slaves were clothed, fed,*
> *and better off under a master's care.*
> I watched the words blur on the page. No one
> raised a hand, disagreed. Not even me.[24]

Echoing Trethewey, perhaps the most repeated phrase during the audience conversation was, "I can remember." Inspired by a performance born of personal and collective histories, the audience moved away from typical talkback questions such as how long the cast rehearsed or how they went about creating their characters and instead engaged fully in a shared dialogue that was much more focused on one another as spectator witnesses than on the actors' process to create "the play."

If act 1 brought the lost histories of black Union soldiers' lives and deaths to audience awareness, the generative power of *Native Guard* to reach beyond the page and stage to create change came in act 2. Armed with complimentary cups of wine, soda, or water, black and white audience members spoke up and articulated the space between intention and reality in their attempts to live peacefully in the same phoenix city that was nearly obliterated as it fell to Union General Sherman following the 1864 Battle of Jonesborough. When I asked Booth why "the production team created the 'Act II' audience conversation part of the evening," she replied: "What we *didn't* want to create was a didactic post show discussion in which experts told us what we'd just seen. The notion was to create a shared space in which act one was a prompt and act two was a dialogue—and that both had equal weight and equal pride of place."[25] The ability of the audience to talk honestly about race and class relations and their own gaps in knowledge and understanding was best articulated by Ghant, the actor who embodied the memory of the Union solider. He shared, "I felt most nights the audience was on board with me and the Native Guards [sic] journey, because I think all of us could relate to a certain level of betrayal in the things we believe. How do we deal with that?"[26] As the onstage channel for Trethewey's imagined words of the Native Guard, Ghant made it his goal to not create a solitary character or "one GUY" but to bring to the audience "more like a spiritual representation of the Guard."[27] By creating a collective representation of many men rather than a singular Civil War–era character, Ghant's acting process took up the larger goal of dismantling "us" versus "them" categorical definitions that Trethewey engages in her writing on the Native Guard.

After *Native Guard* closed on October 19, 2014, I asked the Patron Services Manager of the Alliance, Shana Orr, what became of the memory tags that audience members had attached to the walls of the theatre. I was told, "Our props manager has them in storage."[28] It is uncertain whether the tags will stay stacked on a rarely touched shelf in props storage or whether they will be shared and displayed through the Atlanta History Center, as I was told they would be after act 2 concluded the night I participated in *Native Guard*. As tiny phenomenological emblems of the performance apparatus itself, the tags, like the pages of the Native Guard's journal, link us to ancestors both remembered and forgotten. Staging the living present of racial identity in the South *in dialogue with* the Civil War past, rather than restaging an attempt at authentic Civil War–era characters, offers the most dialectic for change and challenge in the contemporary Deep South in which Trethewey, Ghant, Booth, and the audience of *Native Guard* all live. Out of the sea of spoken and written vows of "I remember," *Native Guard* becomes a cocreated text or what Booth calls "poetry in motion," offering a template for creating community-based theatre events that engage the audience in a space not to watch quietly and leave on separate paths but to articulate together a new understanding of living peacefully one hundred and fifty years after the American Civil War.[29]

Figure 1. "For my mother" dedication with January LaVoy as the character of the Narrator in the September 26–October 19, 2014, Alliance Theatre production of *Native Guard*. Photo by Greg Mooney. Courtesy of the Alliance Theatre.

Figure 2. Thomas Neal Antwon Ghant as the character of the Native Guard in the Alliance Theatre's *Native Guard*. Photo by Greg Mooney. Courtesy of the Alliance Theatre.

Figure 3. January LaVoy in the Alliance Theatre's *Native Guard*. Photo by Greg Mooney. Courtesy of the Alliance Theatre.

Figure 4. Vocalist Nicole Banks Long in the audience of the Alliance Theatre's *Native Guard*. Photo by Greg Mooney. Courtesy of the Alliance Theatre.

Figure 5. January LaVoy in the Alliance Theatre's *Native Guard*, with set design by Anne Patterson and projection design by Adam Larsen. Photo by Greg Mooney. Courtesy of the Alliance Theatre.

Figure 6. "Southern History" moment with January LaVoy in the Alliance Theatre's *Native Guard*. Photo by Greg Mooney. Courtesy of the Alliance Theatre.

Figure 7. Thomas Neal Antwon Ghant in the Alliance Theatre's *Native Guard*. Photo by Greg Mooney. Courtesy of the Alliance Theatre.

Notes

This paper is the Robert A. Schanke Award-Winning Essay, as presented at the annual Mid-America Theatre Conference, March 2015, in Kansas City.

1. Natasha Trethewey, *Native Guard* (New York: Houghton Mifflin Harcourt, 2006). Epigraph quote on page 28. Before making it to Alliance's Hertz Stage, *Native Guard* was first developed as a stage performance with support from the Playwriting Center of Theater Emory at Emory University, where Trethewey is the Robert W. Woodruff Professor of English and Creative Writing. The world premiere was part of the National Civil War Project, which involved the development of twelve original theatrical pieces, four of these works being completed through partnerships between higher education institutions and professional theatres, including Emory and the Alliance; Harvard and the American Repertory Theater; George Washington University and Arena Stage; and the University of Maryland's Clarice Smith Performing Arts Center and Center Stage.
2. Collin Kelley, "Theatre Review: 'Native Guard' at Alliance Theatre," *Atlanta INtown*, October 7, 2014.
3. Walter Benjamin, *On the Concept of History* (New York: Classic Books America, 2009), 11.
4. See photograph 1 in Image Appendix following text. All images courtesy of the Alliance Theatre.
5. Charles McGrath, "New Laureate Looks Deep Into Memory," *New York Times*, June 6, 2012.
6. Ibid.
7. Deborah Solomon, "Native Daughter: Questions for Natasha Trethewey," *New York Times Magazine*, May 13, 2007.
8. See photograph 2 in Image Appendix following text.
9. Neal Ghant, "Thoughts on Native Guard." E-mail to author, February 8, 2015. Capitalization in original.
10. Trethewey, "Native Guard," 28. Italics in original.
11. For an excellent examination of how race historically shaped the ways in which America remembered its Civil War, see David W. Blight, *Race and Reunion: The Civil War in American Memory* (Cambridge: Harvard University Press, 2001).
12. Hans-Thies Lehmann, *Postdramatic Theatre*, trans. Karen Jürs-Munby (New York: Routledge, 2006), 5.
13. "About the National Civil War Project," *National Civil War Project*. n.d. Web. http://www.civilwarproject.org (accessed January 8, 2015).
14. Saidiya Hartman, *Scenes of Subjection: Terror, Slavery, and Self-Making in Nineteenth-Century America* (New York: Oxford University Press, 1997), 132.
15. Trethewey, "Pilgrimage," 20. See photograph 3 in Image Appendix following text.
16. Benjamin, Walter, *On the Concept of History* (New York: Classic Books America, 2009), 11.
17. Trethewey, "Myth," 14.
18. Lehmann, *Postdramatic Theatre*, 17. Italics in original. See photograph 4 in Image Appendix following text.

19. See photograph 5 in Image Appendix following text.
20. "Remember," *Native Guard* Program. n.d., 18. Italics in original.
21. Trethewey, "Graveyard Blues," 8.
22. "Native Guard Act 2," *Native Guard* Program. n.d., 17.
23. Susan V. Booth, "Between Us," *Native Guard* Program. n.d., 7.
24. Trethewey, "Southern History," 38. See photograph 6 in Image Appendix following text.
25. Susan V. Booth, "Act II of Native Guard," E-mail to author. February 4, 2015.
26. Neal Ghant, "Thoughts on Native Guard," E-mail to author. February 8, 2015. See photograph 7 in Image Appendix following text.
27. Ibid. Ghant, Neal. "Thoughts on Native Guard."
28. Shana Orr, "Memory Tags Question," E-mail to Author. February 7, 2015.
29. Booth, "Between Us," *Native Guard* Program. n.d., 7.

Keynote Address Delivered at the Mid-America Theatre Conference

En Ser Inspirado | *On Being Inspired*

—IRMA MAYORGA

Nudge a Mexican and she or he will break out with a story.
GLORIA ANZALDÚA, *BORDERLANDS/LA FRONTERA: THE NEW MESTIZA*

Above all else, it is about leaving a mark that I existed: I was here. I was hungry. I was defeated. I was happy. I was sad. I was in love. I was afraid. I was hopeful. I had an idea and I had a good purpose and that's why I made works of art.
FELIX GONZALEZ-TORRES

I want to open up my thoughts with three points of genealogy. A preface of a sort, if you will.

First genealogical point of order.

This is not my first visit to the Mid-America Theatre Conference (MATC); however, it is only my second time attending. My first visit to the MATC was over twenty years ago. The conference was held right here in Kansas City, Missouri. The Mid-America Theatre Conference was enjoying its eighth annual convening. That year, prescient in its planning, MATC also held a "Mini-festival of Plays for Young Audiences." About ten of my undergraduate student peers and I, along with our professor, Dr. Kaarin Johnston, had piled into vans and driven down from St. Joseph, Minnesota (north of the Twin Cities) to present a play in the festival. I was not an actor in our group; I was the show's costume designer. But Dr. Johnston strongly believed that I—a designer—should come to the conference nonetheless, that I should see in motion a conference dedicated to thinking on theatre. To further entice me, she dangled before me the allure of the conference's keynote speaker. In 1988, the keynote speech was delivered by the esteemed theatre historian Oscar G. Brockett. She knew this would get me in the van, because she knew I was a Brockett *fangirl*. I may have been a designer, who had started off with the intention of becoming an actor—but through it all, I adored the stories and tales found in Brockett's *History of the Theater*. Admitting this, I have now fully owned my life-long theatre nerdiness outright. And even though we were presenting, we also had to complete our theatre history homework for class the following week, so I had in tow Brockett's fifth edition. And when Oscar G. Brockett took the podium for his keynote, I listened with his landmark book clutched in my hands, mesmerized and starstruck.

I have no idea what Dr. Brockett said that day. And that's okay. However, I do remember being inspirited by the liveness of being in the same room with him, of putting a face and body to the person who had written all those pages of stories about theatre's history. When he finished speaking to a mob of what seemed like raging theatre history fans (probably just his colleagues congratulating him afterward) gathered around him, Dr. Johnston urged me to go have Dr. Brockett sign my copy of *History of the Theater*. I may have been an ardent fangirl, but I was also shy. When his groupies dissipated I approached him, and he gladly and cheerfully signed my book, which I have always treasured.

At that time, I could never have imagined that I, like Dr. Brockett, would also one day obtain my doctoral degree in theatre studies from Stanford. When I was last here in Kansas City for MATC, I was a young Mexican American woman attending a small liberal arts school, trying to make a bit of my own history by becoming the first person in my *familia*'s entire existence to graduate from college. The enormity of returning to MATC, having obtained that goal, suffuses my thoughts as I speak from this podium.

Second genealogical point of order.

Fangirl, and yet, I am not a theatre historian by training or degree. However, to do my work as a woman of color, Mexican American, Chicana-positioned theatre artist-cum-scholar, I always find myself digging in history. Usually, I'm foraging through archives in which me and my fellow Latina/o as well as other people of color theatremakers—most especially women of color—are absent or thoroughly inhumed. To prepare for today, I went digging once again.

I asked theatre historian and MATC conference coordinator Elizabeth Osborne if I could obtain a list of past MATC keynote speakers. Beth, along with instrumental help from Henry Bial and many members, generated a history of past speakers. The illustrious names that have addressed this body are a credit to past organizers. However, this excavation also revealed what I had suspected: the number of women of color theatremakers or scholars who have received this slot of keynote primetime are less than few: they are two, myself and one other. I raise this genealogical point of order not to chastise MATC, especially in a room where I can look out and meet eyes with good colleagues whom I consider friends, whom I respect and admire. In this I want to be clear: I am humbled to address you. However, it is significant to mark the history of this moment for myself and for you, who serve as critical witnesses to the second woman of color ever to address this body. Yet this sort of under-representation, this dogged absence is commonplace for US American theatre and academia. However, we are in the midst of a monumental demographic shift that has been, in the words of Sam Cooke, "a long time coming."

I am not only the second woman of color to offer an MATC keynote address but also, interestingly, the second Latina. The first Latina was the *estimada* Cuban American theatre artist Maria Irene Fornés. She delivered her keynote in 1995, right here in Kansas City. Playwright, theatre designer, and director Maria Irene Fornés has been a profound force within US theatre. Moreover, she is also one of the most significant figures in *US Latina/o theatre history*. In her now legendary Hispanic Playwrights-in-Residence Laboratory of the 1980s, Fornés nurtured a large number of the leading US Latina/o playwrights writing today. Fornés's instruction launched the careers of among others Milcha Sanchez-Scott, who wrote the play *Roosters*, Los Angeles's Josefina López, who wrote the play *Real Women Have Curves*, Texas Mexican playwright Octavio Solis, who wrote the Pulitzer Prize–nominated play *Lydia*, and Cuban American playwright Nilo Cruz, who was awarded the 2003 Pulitzer for his play *Anna in the Tropics*. My own playwriting teacher, Chicana dramatist, director, and landmark feminist Cherríe Moraga, also studied with Fornés. I have never taken it lightly that my playwriting genealogy tracks through Moraga directly back to Fornés, and today I come to yet another welcome intersection with her legacy.

I know that in your good hands, when we look back upon the next thirty-six years of MATC, its keynote history will reflect a plethora of women of color keynote speakers.

Final genealogical point of order.

One of my first gigs as a working designer was for a summer season at a performing arts school in Fargo, North Dakota, which hired me to design costumes for *The Music Man*. When I called home to San Antonio to tell my parents about my paying job, my father was of course happy. On the phone he replied that he knew a little bit about Fargo. "How, Dad?" I asked. My family had never lived there. "Well, mi'ja," he replied, "I used to pick the sugar beets up there in the summers." My father is a first generation US citizen. He had traveled up to Fargo and other Midwest points as a boy and teenager with my undocumented Mexican grandparents. They were migrant farmworkers who earned their living by working their way up from Texas along the spine of the Mississippi River, timing their migrant path to the clock set by crop rotation. He was proud of me because against the odds, in the mere span of one generation, he had enabled his daughter to return to the Midwest as something other than a manual laborer. My father's story and the stories of the many Mexican American people who are working their way to a better life in this country—such as the many Latina/o workers I've seen here in the hotel serving us, cleaning up after us—were the stories that first inspired me as a playwright. Mexican Americans make up 64 percent of all Latina/os in the United States.[1] This is a significant number, especially if you consider that the next largest Latina/o group, Puerto Ricans, comprise only 9 percent of the US Latina/o population, Cuban Americans only 3.7 percent.[2] 2010 US Census data have charted that since the year 2000 the US Latina/o population has increased to more than twice its size in one of every four counties in the United States. In the first decade of our present century, the Midwest experienced a staggering 49-percent increase in its Latina/o population.[3] In Nebraska, Kansas, and Illinois "at least 20% of the public school kindergarten population" are Latina/o.[4] While the Latina/o population has grown across the United States, the most significant increases have occurred in the South and here, in the Midwest, Mid-America.[5]

Introduction

Working with the concept of inspiration as a starting point has been akin to grappling with irascible, slippery concepts and theoretical ideas such as theatricality, performative, performativity—words and ideas so alluring in the depth of their applicability and descriptive force, and yet at the same time, often elusive in the success of their deployment; words now ubiquitous in describing and characterizing the work that theatre does as well as the investigations of its scholarship, and yet, as equally misunderstood, misused, or maligned.

"No"—I reply to my Facebook feed whenever a list-type post gets tacked onto it claiming that I will find inspiration if I click through—"that is not inspiring" . . . at least not to me. There's the rub about reaching the state or condition of being inspired: It manifests differently for every person. Even for oneself, it's highly conditional, highly temporal: What proved stirring at one time for a certain project or need may not be the object, idea, event, or experience that serves to activate you once more.

Like this year's conference description, I too turned to the *Oxford English Dictionary* to more thoroughly investigate the definition of inspiration. I sought exactitude to help me consider the term's denotative and connotative senses, its semantic depth. If inspiration is, as the *OED* notes, "The action of inspiring; the fact or condition of being inspired; a breathing or infusion into the mind or soul,"[6] then what I believe I am called upon to do today is to furnish an idea, a purpose for your mind that seeks to create what the *OED* goes on to describes as an "awakening, or creation of some feeling or impulse, *esp. of an exalted kind*."[7]

To fulfill this purpose, to undertake infusing an idea into your soul, I decided to come before you today as a storyteller, with some stories in hand, and in this, I consider myself a storyteller of two means: I tell stories as a theatre practitioner—as a playwright, director, designer, and dramaturg. I also fashion narratives as a scholar, drawing together theory and research to tell *cuentos* (stories) about important events that in turn hope to provide exquisite reckonings of those events and their wider implications—be it examining performances in formal spaces such as stagehouses, or performances in everyday spaces, *tu sabes*, like at the *taquería* up on the corner, or in your Tía Leticia's backyard, or to the east of us, over in the streets of Ferguson, Missouri.

Crafting these stories creates a running conversation between my artistic work and my scholarship. Thinking about theatre and performance in a sustained, scholarly manner that attempts to fathom the revelations and revolutions of its form, function, meaning, or purpose inevitably gives shape to the kind of theatre I desire to make. Conversely, making theatre deeply informs my thinking and critical writing about it. I often think of these two activities, these two modalities of storytelling, as two sides of the same coin or as a Möbius strip, an infinity loop of felicitous transitions between creative and critical activity.

As my preface makes no bones about articulating, I also arrive to this task of infusion as a Latina theatremaker. The stories I have pulled forward for this afternoon provide a testimony from my point of view as a woman of color in theatre at our contemporary moment. They will speak to the intersections of race, gender, and theatre in an effort to offer some mechanical coordinates as well as some affective textures that describe the personal stakes at hand for a woman of color—micro-details that can get lost in books, journal articles, blog posts, lists, canons, binders. This archive of microhistories I have accumulated as a Latina theatremaker is the singular topic no one else who has come before this body has offered (excepting perhaps Maria Irene Fornés, twenty years ago). And, when you think about it, my Latina perspective is rarely, if ever, heard in US theatre in total. Let's be clear, one Quiara Algería Hudes Pultizer Prize, as tremendously edifying as that accomplishment was for *mi gente*, does not a cohesive narrative of Latina theatre artists make nor Latina/o lives describe.

To achieve a state of being inspired, alchemy must occur. I cannot hand it to you, divine it for you. However, I can attempt the feat by breathing into this room, hopefully awakening your mind, hopefully kindling a purpose in your heart that concerns us all, not just me, a racially marked woman in this room. So I offer three short stories that I believe aptly describe some of my negotiations with theatre. They are stories of failure, fulfillment, and futurity that seek to incite you to obtain the condition of being inspired by race: its permutations, its demographics, its discourse, its aesthetic languages, its complexities, and its grace.

Primera Historia: Inspirator

As a theatre major in college I participated in nearly every facet of theatremaking offered to me. And yet, eager as I was, I passed on the two areas that I now participate in most actively as an artist. I passed on taking class in or trying my hand at playwriting or directing. Truth be told, I did not possess the self-confidence to attempt these endeavors. So ominous were they in my mind, so mysteriously complex, I feared trying my hand at them. Moreover, it was a gendered fear because from what I observed, saw produced on the stage at theatres nearby in the Twin Cities or in touring shows that came to my campus, in the vast majority, it was men who wrote plays, and it was men who directed them. And, in that, it was European or Euro-American white men who wrote and directed plays. And still, devoted to theatre of all kinds, I loved the plays that they wrote, bought them all, read them all, knew them all.

There's also a racial factor that contributed to my shying away from playwriting. The theatre I took in also never reflected my community or family, the ethnic-racial textures of my life, and from what I could observe, it did not want or need them. If the theatre had wanted my Latina stories, thought them valuable, surely I would have seen them staged, openly, proudly, prolifically—there at the Guthrie, which I attended regularly in college or at the Jungle Theater in Minneapolis, a theatre whose early work I admired deeply. And given this modeling, as a young Latina, it never once occurred to me that the stories of my Mexican American, Texas grown, military traveling family desperately trying to conceal the secret of my father's lifelong alcoholism were important, were the stuff of theatre.[8] Decades later, I can still see this thought at work in my own students of color as they look for themselves in the overweening whiteness of theatre productions, companies, or plays that appear on our stages, in their course syllabi.

So how, one wonders, does one think to try playwriting when, as a young woman of color, you've been charged to protect family secrets like alcoholism and deep poverty, which *beg* your silence not your pen, when the art form that you pour your life into, that you are attempting to ply your trade from, propounds that it's "reflecting the human condition" but only does so with EuroAmerican or European stories—how can you think of playwriting when the whole endeavor functions as if *you do not exist*!

To approach playwriting as a woman, much less as a woman of color, I had to meet an inspirator, that is, someone who inspirits, which means to animate, cheer, encourage, someone who incites you *to do something*.[9] I needed someone to acknowledge and then dispel the cultural conscriptions of my internalized misogyny and inspirit my mind with the notion that (1) I was allowed to write down my stories, (2) my Texas Mexican family, culture, and history were worth writing down, and (3) not only that, but I could write plays if I chose to do so. For me, it wasn't a matter of going out and finding a topic to write a play about—it wasn't about generating inspiration. Rather, it was a matter of extirpating the gendered and racialized beliefs that my stories were unimportant because they didn't look like those I saw rendered on a wide variety of stages. As capable as I may have been as a younger woman, and I was fairly capable—or so I've been told—I simply couldn't do this for myself because as a young Latina, despite college or fortitude, I remained culturally conditioned to be humble, demure, accommodating, inconspicuous, not take up too much space in the room, the ever-present cultural conscriptions that often prevent Latinas from achieving subjecthood altogether.[10]

Latina playwright Cherríe Moraga became my inspirator. I wrote my first play in one of the playwriting courses that she teaches at Stanford. I wrote the play alongside the coursework of my doctoral studies, alongside the theory class I took that term with the late Charles Lyons and the directing class I had with the curmudgeonly but caring Carl Weber. The playwriting class became a place where theory inspirited my dramatic imagination on the page along with heavy doses of my visual acuity as a designer.

As Stanford's playwright-in-residence, I believe Cherríe Moraga sits waiting for young, self-silencing Latina/os to come along so that she can enliven our tongues and turn us into writers—some of whom become playwrights. We've made it to Stanford, so she assumes we possess some intelligence; that's a good starting point. But she also knows the cultural constraints we must surmount as well. What her instruction of tough love and kick ass hopes to do is inform us that we are the writers, the storytellers, the scribes our Latina/o communities await. Novel, poem, or play, painting or song—it does not matter. Write down your stories, not for the academy, "*para nosotros, for us*!" begs Cherríe. And, she insisted that our stories didn't have to subscribe themselves to Aristotelian form; they didn't have to subscribe to anyone's strictures. Write the story in the way that you know our community will delight in it, attach to it, savor it; that's the framework you should use, because you are the one who knows your community best—not Aristotle. I believe this is why hundreds of students of color have flocked to her classes and workshops over the last twenty years: Because Cherríe Moraga refuses to subscribe to a thoroughly Western conception of dramatic form, and even if your play eventually arrives to that dramaturgical form, first and foremost, she asks you to bring the cultural specificity of your racial or ethnic, gendered, sexual, cultural identity to your writing—what you heard on the street, porch, or cul-de-sac growing up. Lay out your painful secrets, which *are* the stuff of drama.

I was thirty years old. I had worked in the theatre professionally for nine years. When Cherríe Moraga inspirited me with the command, "Go, write!" I rushed to the task with zeal, and it changed the course of my life.

Segunda Historia

They have a tradition at the O'Neill National Playwrights Conference. On the night that the workshop production of your play opens, you get to pin the program for your show onto one of the large wooden beams in the historic cottage the conference uses as a bar at their Waterford, Connecticut, compound. There is great fanfare for the pinning. Everyone in the company crowds into the small bar. The artistic director makes a short speech, congratulates you and your collaborators. Then, you stand upon a chair to reach the beam overhead, and you tack your program alongside the many that litter these rafters, their jagged corners hanging down like rows of pennants strung across the room. The program for my play *Cascarones*, a play about history, conquest, and a Mexican American family living in Texas, a play that I began in the classroom of Cherríe Moraga, hangs there now amid programs tacked up by Lanford Wilson, David Henry Hwang, John Guare, Wendy Wasserstein, Kia Corthron, and August Wilson.

When my play *Cascarones*—a title drawn from a treasured Eastertime tradition in South Texas that involves dyed eggs and confetti—was selected to participate at the O'Neill Playwrights Conference in the summer of 2003, it was an extraordinary year for the conference. For the first time, the blind submission process had selected works by seven female playwrights for participation in its hallowed summer workshop. This included myself, the first Mexican American playwright in the conference's history, and African American playwright Sherry Shephard-Massat. Paula Vogel paid a short visit to the conference that year, and she was delighted by this surprising turnabout of gender. To celebrate, she took us all out for a drink at the bar Eugene O'Neill used to frequent in search of *his* inspiration. When we arrived, she threw open the bar's door and proclaimed to the cave-like room, "Gene, we're here!"

Arriving at the O'Neill to develop my work should have been a vital and productive experience for me as a playwright—and I don't wish to diminish the necessity of this legendary play development institution, one of the last places where as a playwright you don't need a well-connected agent to get your play into the hands of an artistic director. It's a selection process in which you can, as I did, simply slip your script into the mail, sending it off with nothing but its artistic merits. However, the story of my participation at the O'Neill helps to describe how theatre's upper echelons have been inherently structured to aid the creative activities and spectatorial experiences of theatremakers and audiences who are white, a charge that theatremakers and companies (upper echelon or community troupes) time after time attempt to either dismiss, deny, or, even worse, justify. As we bemoan the loss of audiences and grasp at new ideas to fill houses, it behooves those of us committed to ensuring that theatre remains an integral part of our cultural landscape to remember always that we are in the midst of a monumental demographic shift and that no true "new audience" will be garnered without first marking and then dismantling this enduring, racialized bias in US theatre.

When the O'Neill National Playwrights Conference selects a play for its workshop, all sorts of preparations go into motion for the playwright. You are advised to offer a director and a dramaturg who might be a good fit for your project's workshop. And, you begin working with a casting agent to secure actors for your show.

As a very new and, at the time, Texas-based playwright, I couldn't offer a director of national acclaim; rather, I trusted the auspices of the O'Neill's reach to locate an appropriate, talented, and culturally competent collaborator.[11] I asked for a dramaturg who was versed in not only structural composition but also the representational strategies of feminist theatre *and* Latina/o theatre that my play employed. My play was non-naturalistic, jumped backward in time to visit different historical eras, and had the theatrical construction of Latina/o actors portraying white historical figures. My play depended on familiarity with Mexican American cultural rituals such as breaking piñatas as well as exploring the ideology embedded in cartography. And also, here and there, the play made references to some particulars of auto mechanics. The O'Neill selection committee had navigated all these ideas in their choice to select my work; now I needed a creative team of theatre artists who were *culturally competent*, just as all the other plays selected to participate would receive directors and dramaturgs who were culturally competent to animate their projects.

To its credit, the O'Neill may have been eager and ready to nurture a play about Latina/os by a Latina/o playwright in 2003, but structurally and administratively, it wasn't prepared to meet the specific needs of producing a Latina/o play. The most difficult part of bringing my play into the O'Neill turned out to be its casting process. The O'Neill Theater's longtime casting agency, whose network of actors covered only New York City, could not offer possible Latina/o actors, because the agency had no catalog of Latina/o equity actors to pull from. Even though it was 2003, I repeat, *the casting agency had no need to maintain a roster of Latina/o equity actors*.[12] In fact, the agency asked me to scurry up actors from any connections I had, "that'd be a help." Well, I replied, I knew trained, talented Latina and Latino actors in Los Angeles—they had done a workshop reading for me, with Chay Yew, now artistic director of Victory Gardens Theater, serving as consulting dramaturg. "Nope," the agent replied, "can't use them.

No money to fly them in." Essentially, the entire pool of Latina/o equity actors from California was out.[13]

Tomó mucho tiempo (it took a long time), but the casting agency brought together good folks for my cast—all from New York. And yet, despite my cast's best efforts, I did not hear my play, which is the whole purpose of the O'Neill workshop experience, that and featuring it in front of possible New York producers—but that's another story.

Latinidad, or pan-Latino/a solidarity, is tricky. It's a constant negotiation that seeks to forge community between different Latina/o ethnic identities while honoring the differences between us. But here's the thing about Latina/os: We may be gathered under the political efficacy of term like *Latinidad*, but we also have distinctive ethnic and national origin proclivities. You can see it in the way we dance or the foods we make. You can hear it in the way we speak English, and you can hear it in the *accentos* of our Spanish. And when you hear those differences on the stage, in your play about Texas, you cannot hear your play—only the distinct differences.

When you are born and raised in Washington Heights with a national and cultural heritage from the Dominican Republic, your ethnic identity, your *manera de ser* (way of being), your deportment in total is fundamentally different than, say, a cowboy-boot-wearing, western-twang-wielding, Spanglish-speaking Hispano born and raised in Santa Fe, New Mexico. It was difficult to watch my earnest, excited, definitely New York Latina/o actors take the stage at the O'Neill. All the way there, and I couldn't see my play—nor could the audience.

Unfortunately, my director, although very well intentioned and with an exquisite directorial pedigree, did not fully understand the play's Latina/o cultural coordinates nor the identic geography the play attempts to map, just as it attempts to map the history of the Grand Canyon. My O'Neill-assigned dramaturg, befuddled by the history-jumping structure, felt it best to recede, leave the feminist work alone rather than muddle about in unknown territory. So, when opening night came for my play, I was a mess.

It didn't help that as I sat in the audience, watching my play sink like a stone, it was happening in the same theatre that had seen the triumph of August Wilson's *Ma Rainey's Black Bottom*. I sat among decidedly older, white, wealthy, summering New Englanders on the edge of the Long Island Sound. I could hear their disappointment with the play. Why shouldn't they be disappointed? I was terribly disappointed—and I cared far more than they did. But we were disappointed for far different reasons—me for aesthetics, them for discomfort. After muttering snipes about the use of Spanish, admonishing the non-naturalistic structure, and complaining about the acting quality, many left at intermission.

I don't blame them. I wanted to leave too, but I couldn't—after the show, I had to go pin my program on the beam in the compound's bar, next to all the others, next to August Wilson's.

So, you're probably wondering, *oye*, Mayorga, *dónde está la inspiración* in this *pinche* depressing story? Pues, don't you remember, I mentioned failure when I began. Inspiration drawn from lessons about race and gender often isn't delivered in a neat package; it comes in shards, pieces you have to pluck at to stir the awakening in your heart, to infuse you with purpose.

I believe only one other person in the whole theatre got it that night, only one other person had the cultural competency to understood what was happening at this moment in American theatre history, when the first play by a Mexican American woman ever to grace the O'Neill Conference's stage was unfolding as a disaster, and that person was African American hip-hop theatre scholar and director Daniel Banks. I had just met him the year before; we were new friends. Now, here he was in residence at the O'Neill as a Directing Fellow. And he told me that my play was breathtaking and important and that's why it was at the O'Neill in the first place, *production be damned!* And he sat by me in the audience, also watching the stage, hearing the audience, letting me clench his forearm with displeasure and pain as we watched the mess that had been made.

This past summer my play *Cascarones* had its world premiere in Santa Fe, New Mexico. It was coproduced by Daniel Banks and Adam McKinney's company DNAWorks in conjunction with a small, intrepid Latina/o theatre company called Teatro Paraguas. It featured an all Latina/o cast of Mexican American actors from the Southwest. It was staged in a small theatre space that allowed the epic dimensions of the play's non-naturalistic storytelling to shine forth. The audience was composed of a wide variety of classes and races: white Santa Feans, Mexican Americans and Chicana/os, Native peoples, African Americans. The audience was majority young. And over and over again after the show, I heard from them about how the play could be their family's story. They saw, truly saw, something of themselves onstage. Daniel never, never forgot *Cascarones*. I had put *Cascarones* in a drawer, so devastating was my time in one of the zeniths of US theatre, because when you hear folks in the audience, older, white monied people, slight your work—my response wasn't one of "*I'll show you!*" My response was one of resignation, of retreating to the cultural self-policing of silence—*see, see what happens when you take up too much space in the room!* My other response was to move on, next project.

But Daniel, as I like to characterize it, kept *Cascarones* in his back pocket. Daniel did not move on. Daniel was inspirited by my work so that when he made the move to Santa Fe, after learning about his new Southwest community, after partaking in its currents and cadences, after gaining the cultural competency needed to direct Latina/o work, he phoned me one day and said, it's time, my company is in place, I am going to fully produce your play because it needs to be done. Daniel knows, as I do, that it's an incredible, incredible thing in this country when a Mexican American woman's play receives a full production. Maybe in 2003, a US audience wasn't ready to hear talk about the complications of the United States-Mexico border and reckonings with structural racism, allegations against the construction of history. But as Daniel tends to say, our times finally caught up with my play.

Historia Final: A Latina/o Theatre Commons or Inspired by Willful Neglect

If you want to make a human being a monster, deny them, at the cultural level, any reflection of themselves.
JUNOT DÍAZ

I am standing in the lobby of the Jackie Liebergott Black Box Theatre at Emerson College's Paramount Center, located in downtown Boston. I am stretched out long, arms thrust in front of me, in order to lay my hand on the forearm of award-winning Nuyorican playwright Migdalia Cruz. If you identify as Nuyorican, in case the term is unknown to you (we are in the Midwest after all), you are marking your experience in the Puerto Rican diaspora. You call Manhattan, Queens, Brooklyn, or the Bronx, or New York State in general, home. *Tu sabes*, like JLo and Lin-Manuel Miranda—both Nuyoricans—do. Along with me in the Liebergott's lobby, about fifteen other US Latina/o theatre artists or scholars are also trying to gently but firmly lay a hand on Migdalia as well.

Migdalia Cruz serves as a stand in for theatre artist Maria Irene Fornés, who cannot join us in Boston due to her advanced age and declining health. As one of Fornés's most devoted students, Migdalia functions as both Fornés's surrogate and also represents herself. Like those of us around her, Migdalia also stands with her body outstretched. She has her hand placed on the arm of legendary Chicano theatre playwright and director Luis Valdez. Yes! That Luis Valdez, the migrant farmworker turned theatre artist who in the mid-1960s worked alongside Chicano civil rights leaders César Chávez and Dolores Huerta. Yes!

That Luis Valdez, who used theatre as a political tool to help farmworkers see how their subjugation as laborers was linked to the capitalist, structural racism that California growers wielded in order to exploit their labor and thereby reap heftier profits. Yes! I cannot believe that I had the occasion to perform a movement exercise with folks like Luis Valdez and Migdalia Cruz.

Luis and Migdalia are at the center of our scrum of about seventy or so jumbled bodies comprising US Latina/o theatre artists and theatre scholars participating in an unusually visceral exercise whereby we are articulating our individual theatrical origins, our mentorship genealogy, and therefore, the connectivity between us within the larger historical context of US Latina/o theatre. We are rendering our history somatically. The exercise demonstrates that, as a group, we are deeply interconnected. Community inspirits us, and just as equally, we have been purposed to this action by lack and the willful neglect on the part of American theatre.

There were about eighty of us Latina/o playwrights, directors, designers, dramaturgs, actors, producers, and scholars who were invited to gather in Boston for three days at the end of October 2013. Our purpose was no less than to try to divine how to change the course of history for US theatre. We didn't arrive with any straightforward idea of how we were going to achieve this, but we were all in agreement that it needed to be done: for us as Latina/o theatremakers, and indeed, more so for Latina women, and more expansively on our horizon, we wanted to create a sea change for all people of color and minoritarian voices in the theatre. We were taking three days out of our lives to sit down with one another and map out our next action. It was a simple and yet audacious idea.

As Latina/o theatre artists and scholars, we were done with waiting for mainstream, community, educational, or regional theatrical producing organizations in the United States to "find" us, "discover" our work, or meagerly feature it every two to five years in their seasons, if at all. We were fed up with our productions being waylaid in the mire of developmental residencies that never culminated in main-stage premieres and yet also generated grant monies when it came time to go begging to foundations, the body of our work and our material bodies serving as diversity checkmarks to snag funding. This group was equally as impatient with the criticism, often heaped upon our work, that because a play had some Spanish or Spanglish, it was charged with being difficult. This group was also tired of having to abandon or awkwardly translate all our cultural symbols so that they were withered to assimilated pap that the white-dominant audiences of leading theatres could easily maneuver themselves around and digest. But in the end, this group was for the most part done with the willful neglect of US theatre for work created by US Latina/o theatremakers.

As one of our convening's cofacilitator, Kinan Valdez, son of Luis Valdez and now artistic director of *El Teatro Campsino* in California, reminded us in his welcoming, our Boston meeting was historic because it was the first meeting of its kind for US Latina/o theatre artists in over twenty-five years and also the first "of this century, of this millennium."[14] The fact of a crisp new century excited us all with its possibility. The last, large-scale national meeting of Latina/o theatre artists took place in 1986 under the auspices of the now defunct TENAZ (T-E-N-A-Z) Festival[15]—a Chicana/o theatre endeavor.[16] TENAZ festivals were held in California and the Southwest beginning in the early 1970s. We were gathered in Boston to discuss the decline of this heyday, even as we sought to forge something new.

Our meeting, which came to be called the Latina/o Theatre Commons National Convening, was the brainchild of Latina playwright Karen Zacarias, based in Washington, DC. Seventeen months earlier, in May 2012, Karen had brought together a group of eight Latina/o playwrights to Washington, DC, under the auspices of her residency with the American Voices New Play Institute and the group HowlRound, then housed at the Arena Stage. As Zacarias recalls: "My instinct was that it was time for Latina/o artists to discuss and design a viable, energetic, sustainable, inclusive 'something' that would serve a wide band of Latina/o artists nationally."[17] Zacarias was not alone; her instincts had picked up on a nationwide feeling among Latina/o playwrights and directors that had been simmering, I would say, since the late 1990s into the first decade of the 2000s. These eight Latina/o playwrights formulated the bold idea to widen their conversation and convene a gathering of one hundred Latina/o theatre artists in order to think on what to do to take the destiny of Latina/o theatremaking back into our own hands. HowlRound agreed to help facilitate the gathering.

A brief sidebar. You may be asking yourself, what is HowlRound? Begun about five years ago, HowlRound is an organization dedicated to creating a nationwide commons for theatremakers. As HowlRound's website explains: "It's a simple idea really. A commons is a place to share the resources you have and take the resources you need . . .. Access and engagement are our highest values, and everyone, yes *everyone*, has something to contribute to the learning, the making, and the sharing of art."[18] There's no time here to expand; however, if you are invested in the future of US theatre, you should be plugged into and finding inspiration in the information and knowledge platforms shared on HowlRound's website and blogs.[19]

Over the course of three days in Boston, with the wisdom of the incredible talent collected among us (including too many award-winning playwrights to name, along with a MacArthur "genius" grant winner), we posed and reposed three guiding questions to stimulate our conversation: "Why are we here? How did we get here? Where are we going?"[20] They were simple questions that led to difficult and revealing conversations. As Latina/o theatre artists and scholars, we had never had the opportunity to sit down together, discuss our dreams and visions of the future, or think aloud. As the days came to reveal, our ideas about future actions were uniquely situated by our personal experiences, by our racial identifications, by our genders, and by the dynamics of other nodes of identity such as sexuality and class. We often diverged drastically in terms of our goals, and we were often unable to find alignment. In effect, our intimate conversations readily educed the vast diversity that is collected under the umbrella term "Latina/o." But we sat there, talked, ate, thought, reflected, danced, and returned each day for three days to figure it all out.

At the close of our convening, we unanimously decided to form a commons of our own—a commons of Latina/o theatre artists, producers, designers, and scholars. We created a strategic vision based on goals of advocacy, art-making, meeting together, and scholarship. In these goals, we are committed to a deliberate effort to insert US Latina/o works into existing networks of US theatre-making. If you want to read about the convening, we commissioned a narrative report, written by theatre historian and convening participant Dr. Brian Herrera of Princeton University. You can obtain the report by visiting HowlRound's website and download it for free, *and* you should also order hard copies for your institution's library to make sure your students have access to it and to ensure that it sits in the archives of your institution.

Throughout the month of October 2014, the Los Angeles Theater Center in association with the Latina/o Theatre Commons organized a festival of Latina/o theatre of epic proportions. Entitled "Encuentro 2014" (Encounter 2014), the festival focused on presenting full productions of plays by Latina/o theatre companies or ensembles. As Steven Leigh Morris noted in his *LA Weekly* story about the festival: "There were more entries than this column has space to describe. With the range of aesthetics, and the caliber of performance, Encuentro 2014 made its case that Latino theater cannot be ignored in any serious discussion of how the United States is evolving."[21] With the Los Angeles Theater Center complex functioning as lead organizer and home base in downtown LA and under the artistic directorship of José Luis Valenzuela, this month-long festival brought together more than nineteen Latina/o theatre companies. Over 150 US Latina/o theatre artists—ages eighteen into their seventies, from the United States as well as Puerto Rico—presented productions that offered a startling constellation of aesthetics, representational strategies, and stories that described the lives of US Latina/os. To make the festival a reality, organizers raised one million dollars in funding in the short span of less than a year—an extraordinary feat for any theatremaking in the United States at this time. Each morning following the day's very full schedule of performances, Latina/o artists, producers, scholars, and audience members gathered together to discuss the previous day's work, to hear ourselves reflect. Every evening after the last performance, the festival held a dance party with a DJ spinning and a Los Angeles–based band singing us into the night because we know how to throw a party.

On the flight here to Kansas City, I finished reading the last of fifty new, as of yet unproduced or unpremiered, Latina/o plays. I began this task in January as a member of the selection committee for the Latina/o Theatre Commons next bold dream. We will hold our Carnaval of Latina/o Theatre at DePaul University, in Chicago, this coming July. For this festival, we will present staged readings of eight new plays selected from submissions by over one hundred Latina/o playwrights who answered our call for new work. As a scholar, the opportunity to read the new works of Latina/o theatremakers is a boon. As a playwright and director, I am amazed by the ferocity of the storytelling I've found. Stories in these plays discuss immigration, assimilation, diaspora, incarceration, masculinity, sexuality, religion, drug cartels, mixed-race heritages, racial discrimination, cultural schisms, bilingualism, violence against women, the United States-Mexico border, the legacy of Cuban exiles; the plays vigorously delve into the most pressing issues we as a nation face today. Some works have transposed Shakespeare and Chekhov into Latina/o contexts. Some offer musicals about important aspects of Latina/o history; one featured a singing Thurgood Marshall. Some are in English. Some are in Spanish. Some dance to the intense and clever rhythms of Spanglish. I find it interesting that as market forces have pushed many mainstream theatres to search for small cast plays, almost none of these plays are interested in that form, calling instead for five to fifteen actors or characters to dramatize their epic stories and the extensive social spheres that are characteristic of Latina/o family and community structures. Some plays have employed ravishing dramaturgy; others have been boring or poorly formed or misogynistic or crass. But I'm up for it all, this plethora of new Latina/o work—and these are just the plays we received. I'm sure there are hundreds of others that weren't submitted, out there, sitting in drawers.

A common concern that is voiced all too often by mainstream theatres is that there are no Latina/o works to be found or, equally as insulting, no plays of merit. Producers, theatre companies, theatre departments alike commonly cite lack as a reason Latina/o voices are absent from US stages. By curating work on our own terms, selecting works we believe are outstanding, our Carnaval seeks to disprove this claim. And we're quite direct in our redress. The Carnaval will provide each playwright we select with workshop time in Chicago, a Chicago-based director as collaborator, a culturally competent dramaturg, and Latina/o actors. Artistic directors and literary managers from all sizes of theatres across the country have been invited to our festival to come consider the work. We hope to inspirit these invitees, infuse them with the idea to produce these new plays that *we* have determined are important. They may or may not be inspirited—we are up for that. But the larger point is, as journalist Steven Leigh Morris surmised, we refuse to be ignored or neglected. To do so amounts to short-changing the future of theatremaking in the United States overall.

Epilogue

Right now, there is a paucity of students of color in theatre departments. I hear about it at each professional theatre conference I attend. And yet, just as our regional theatres do, departments wonder why, wonder how to engage students of color—even as they continue to offer year after year of seasons filled with play titles that signal to these students, I cannot see you, *you do not exist*! There will always be a few students, like my younger self, that find a home in a theatre department despite the fact that I didn't see a more direct reflection of myself there. But continuing to place the study of theatre made by people of color at the margins of the curriculums we offer—*as theatre departments have stubbornly continued to do*—cannot hold. And as student-of-color populations become ever more predominant in our classrooms, just from the sheer magnitude of the demographic shift I have cited, these students will demand their visibility. Rightly so, they will not let this center hold. And as I've learned in the past ten years, white students who position themselves as staunch allies, taking personal responsibility in the checking of privileges, who practice overt, consistent actions that foment diversity will not let it hold.

I want to inspire you to not only move the margins to the center but also, perhaps like HowlRound has done, like the Latina/o Theatre Commons has done, think on dismantling the center entirely to build something anew that better serves the future that quickly approaches. I hope that I've proffered thoughts that inspire you to a task—"*of the exalted kind*"—that ensures that the breadth of Latina/o theatre, African American theatre, Asian American theatre (the second-fastest growing population in the United States), and plays by women stand as necessary study in the very core of your department's curriculum. If our mission as educators is to prepare our students, inspirit them to be the most sophisticated, visionary thinkers and artists we can yield, anything short of this pedagogical ethos—in the face of the United States' demographic future—drastically underprepares them for the currents they will have to navigate in their lifetime as theatre artists and, more importantly, as people.

Notes

This article is the Keynote Address delivered at the Mid-America Theatre Conference, on March 21, 2015, in Kansas City, Missouri. In my title "En Ser Inspirado | *On Being Inspired*," I am reversing common practices of italicization whereby the English would be in nonitalic text and the Spanish words would be italicized. Here, it is a specific choice to reverse this practice and italicize the English.

1. Brown, Anna, and Eileen Patten, "Statistical Portrait of Hispanics in the United States 2012," Hispanic Trends, Pew Research Center, April 29, 2014. http://www.pewhispanic.org/2014/04/29/statistical-portrait-of-hispanics-in-the-united-states-2012/#detailed-hispanic-origin-2012 (accessed May 14, 2015).
2. Ibid.
3. "2010 Census Shows Nation's Hispanic Population Grew Four Times Faster than Total U.S. Population," *Newsroom Archive United States Census Bureau*, United States Census Bureau, May 26, 2011. https://www.census.gov/newsroom/releases/archives/ 2010_census/cb11-cn146.html (accessed May 7, 2015).
4. Krogstad, Jens Manuel, "A View of the Future through Kindergarten Demographics," Fact Tank: News in the Numbers. Pew Research Center, July 8, 2014. http://www.pewresearch.org/fact-tank/2014/07/08/a-view-of-the-future-through-kindergarten-demographics/ (accessed May 4, 2015).
5. "2010 Census Shows Nation's Hispanic Population Grew Four Times Faster than Total U.S. Population."
6. "inspiration, n." *OED Online*. Oxford University Press, December 2014. Web. http://www.oed.com/view/Entry/96980?redirectedFrom=inspiration (accessed February 27, 2015). "A special immediate action or influence of the Spirit of God (or of some divinity or supernatural being) upon the human mind or soul; said *esp.* of that divine influence under which the books of Scripture are held to have been written. Various views have been held as to the inspiration of Scripture, such as those of *verbal inspiration*, according to which every word written was dictated by the Spirit of God; *plenary inspiration*, according to which the inspiration of the writers extends to all subjects treated of, so that all their statements are to be received as infallibly true; *moral inspiration*, according to which the inspiration is confined to the moral and religious teaching imparted; *dynamical inspiration*, mechanical inspiration (see DYNAMICAL adj. 3)."
7. Ibid. Emphasis added.
8. Like most families, my family worked hard to keep our secrets. We were not allowed to speak of them, and they certainly were not to serve as the embers that ignited my creative activity.

   On the other hand, I truly didn't understand the mechanics of directing, and it was also a gendered creative activity—from observation as a young person, I learned that men directed, women acted or made costumes or stage-managed.

9. "inspirit, v." *OED Online*. Oxford University Press. http://www.oed.com/view/Entry/96997?rskey=eqMABD&result=1&isAdvanced=false#eid (accessed March 17, 2015).
10. Truth be told, to this day I have to fight the impulse to self-silence. And more often than not, I can easily spot this notion in my students of color as well. Despite the forward movement of time, there it is in the young women—Latina, Black, Asian, and Native American—in my classrooms.
11. Oddly, that year the Venezuelan Moises Kaufman was one of the O'Neill directors, but for another playwright/project. When we met up at the conference, he and I both wondered why we hadn't been paired up together for my project, which would have made perfect sense to us both. We regretted the missed opportunity. Quién sabe.
12. My play required six Latina/o actors and one white, male actor who should read twenty-five to thirty-five years old. "That," the agency's rep told me over the phone when she called from New York, she could fill—"easy!"
13. Peripheral note of interest. Although the O'Neill could not afford a full cast of LA actors, they did front for one LA-based Latina actor. A very, very young America Ferrera, fresh from doing the film that made her famous (*Real Women Have Curves*) and pre-*Ugly Betty*, was contracted by the O'Neill to take up the role of my play's young protagonist.
14. Brian Eugenio Herrera, *The Latina/o Theatre Commons 2013 National Convening: A Narrative Report* (Boston: HowlRound: A commons by and for people who make performance, 2015), 17.
15. Avila, Kat. "TENAZ (Teatros Nacionales de Aztlan) XVI International Theatre Festival." TENAZ (Teatros Nacionales de Aztlan) XVI International Theatre Festival, a review by Kat Avila. http://www.katavila.com/articles/ teatro-chicano/tenaz-xvi-text.html (accessed February 13, 2015).
16. Herrera, *The Latina/o Theatre Commons 2013 National Convening*, 19.
17. Herrera, *The Latina/o Theatre Commons 2013 National Convening*, 1.
18. "About." HowlRound: A commons by and for people who make performance. http://howlround.com/about (March 3, 2015).
19. A commons, in the briefest of explanations, is a "social system for the long-term stewardship of resources that preserves shared values and community identity." Eschewing the nonprofit model that has become ubiquitous to theatre companies, HowlRound believes that "commoning is the most effective way to revive the creativity and relevance of theater for ordinary people." "Commoning" is an activity of "open collaboration without hierarchy, [without the impetus for] commercial success, and top-down control." In their decision to form a commons, HowlRound consciously decided to, in the words of its director Polly Carl, "let go of things that you think are really valuable [like conventional structures for nonprofit theater] and experiment."
20. Herrera, *The Latina/o Theatre Commons 2013 National Convening*, 19.
21. Steven Leigh Morris, "The Fantastic Encuentro 2014 Festival Showed the Power of Latina/o Theater." http://www.laweekly.com/arts/the-fantastic-encuentro-2014-festival-showed-the-power-of-latino-theater-5207079 (accessed March 6, 2015).

Part IV

BOOK REVIEWS

Preaching to Convert: Evangelical Outreach and Performance Activism in a Secular Age. By John Fletcher. Ann Arbor: University of Michigan Press, 2013. 412 pp. $44.00 cloth.

Part ethnography, part polemic, John Fletcher's new book provides a landmark survey of contemporary American evangelicalism's vibrant culture of performance. It is also a provocation addressed to "secular Left" scholars who might (falsely) believe they have cornered the market in theatre for social change. These two themes—the range and sophistication of evangelical performance versus the smug hypocrisy and dismissiveness of antitheistic critics—form the double helix of Fletcher's well-researched and closely observed study. It deserves to be widely read and debated.

As the lengthy introduction explains, Fletcher sets out to identify and categorize the array of performance strategies that "evangelicals in the United States use to change their world, to win converts to their faith and worldview" (5). Fletcher places particular emphasis on "the challenges they face, and the solutions, innovations, or compromises they create" in the context of a society whose norms are regarded as increasingly antireligious and tolerant of difference, that is, the "secular age" of his title, which he takes from the Canadian philosopher of identity Charles Taylor (5). Structured as eight lengthy chapters, Fletcher covers everything from traditional door-to-door "soul winning" (or "kerygmatic" performatives) to alternative Halloween immersive theatres known as "Hell Houses," from Ken Ham's Kentucky-based Creation Museum to "seeker-sensitive [Church] services" pioneered by Rick Warren's Saddleback Church. Fletcher also discusses evangelical debates about "sexual orientation change efforts," also known as "conversion therapy," in the penultimate chapter of the book. In most of these case studies, Fletcher's rhetorical criticism is grounded in firsthand "thick descriptions" based on his wide-ranging fieldwork.

But Fletcher is no disinterested observer on these travels. Eschewing "paranoid criticism," which he defines as the reflexive ascription of "hegemonic ideologies" to anything but the most politically radical practices, he instead adopts the perspective of "critical generosity," or the "good faith" approach (29). Drawing on scholars of activist performance such as Jan Cohen-Cruz and David Roman, Fletcher seeks to employs "deep empathy" with American evangelicals in order to render their aims and methods with greater nuance and complexity. (For a work that engages so many theorists so well, it may seem ungenerous to wish Fletcher had employed others. However, one cannot help but wonder how he might have engaged with Michael Walzer's notion of "connected criticism.") Further, this challenge to the values of left-progressive theatre historiography is intended to lift "significant limitations on the critical and political imaginations of theatre and performance activist-scholars" (29). Fletcher demonstrates that evangelicals are social-change innovators whose practices are worthy of admiration and possibly even theft.

The chapter "Hell and Judgment: House of Distinction" may be the strongest application of this method for the way in which it complicates the premise that all evangelical performance is "preaching to convert." Originally devised by Colorado pastor Keenan Roberts during the 1990s and now circulated nationally through so-called Outreach Kits (sold for $299), the typical "Hell House" stages a procession of harrowing tableaux depicting the wages of sin, especially teenage forms of moral misadventure: fatal drunk-driving accidents, drug overdoses, rape, abortion, and demonic possessions brought on by dabbling in the occult, all of which consign the victims to the just torments of hell. As Fletcher records, Roberts's original has inspired numerous variants, including Judgment House, Revelation Walk, and Rapture House. According to Fletcher, all of these productions create what he memorably terms "interactive eschatological theatre" (160). However, in one of the more important takeaways from this study, Fletcher problematizes the notion that Hell Houses are designed to interpellate the unconverted. Drawing on Baz Kershaw's theory of "authentication" in community-based theatre, Fletcher writes, "In order to 'work,' Hell House relies on an audience of people willing to buy into (authenticate) the picture of reality that Hell House presents. For those who do not already believe in demons or God or the evangelical definition of sin, Hell House offers at best a kind of curious fantasy world, an inauthentic reality vulnerable to ridicule" (169).

Hell Houses, thus, are *not* "preaching to convert."

Neither is Ken Ham's Creation Museum, according to chapter 5's patient decoding of this $27-million-dollar temple to antievolution propaganda. Memorably calling it "a creationist wolf in scientific costume," Fletcher asserts that, in spite of its "surface professionalism," the museum "speaks not primarily to unbelievers but to evangelicals" (193). Like Hell House, it "preaches to the converted" (200). I have to confess, these chapters struck me as describing a different critical trajectory than the one promised by Fletcher's introductory apologia for evangelical's proselytizing mission. But if there is a bit of bait and switch going on here, I liked the switch. Hell Houses and other modes of intramural evangelical performance merit further attention from scholars researching—and practicing—community-based theatre. This is Fletcher's claim, of course, and it is a convincing one.

Less persuasive is Fletcher's analysis of recent debates about "conversion therapy," and this chapter's inclusion is problematic for two reasons. First, there is little actual performance to analyze in these pages. Second, Fletcher's apologetics on behalf of the baby steps toward recognizing the humanity of LGBTQ folks taken by some "Gay Explanatory Framework" (283) theorists and other, more moderate evangelical groups falls short of fulfilling the hope narrative promised by the chapter title: "Change Is Possible" (262). In this case, his principle of critical generosity is strained.

Fletcher concludes his study by insisting that "the time when religious conviction could be dismissed as an endangered species in the face of regnant secularism has long passed" (314). We secular-progressive-leftist theatre scholars and activists are called upon to reject our Enlightenment project illusions and accept that people of faith, and the increasing power of their cultural performances, are defining the real terms of meaningful political debate in the United States. It is a kind of domestic corollary to Samuel P. Huntington's "Clash of Civilizations" thesis, which was also meant as a realpolitik wake-up call for dreamy liberals. All of this may be.

However, I think the immediate value of Fletcher's work will be to open up new possibilities for scholarship on the varieties of religious performance in the United States. Presenting evangelicalism as a predominantly white, Southern, and Protestant phenomenon allowed Fletcher to give his study valuable focus. Other readers of this book, though, will want to know more about African American and Latino evangelicals, for example, or the many modes of Mormon outreach. *Preaching to Convert* will supply them with many of the critical and methodological instruments they will need to map the broader landscape of faith-based performance.

—JAY BALL
Central Washington University

Imagining Human Rights in Twenty-First-Century Theater: Global Perspectives. Edited by Florian N. Becker, Paola S. Hernández, and Brenda Werth. New York, NY: Palgrave Macmillan, 2013. xii + 248 pp. $85.00 cloth.

Editors Becker, Hernández, and Werth respond to and comment on the ongoing conversation regarding the intersection of human rights and theatre in their collection of essays, *Imagining Human Rights in the Twenty-First-Century Theater: Global Perspectives*. Although we are only a decade and a half into the twenty-first century, this book addresses how far we have come in that time, and how much father we have still to go with the use of theatre and performance to effect change in improving human rights. The foreword, "Postnational Theater Studies," written by Jill Lane, provides an example of a male flamenco singer whose song lamented a poor man who was forced into the streets by a bank in Seville, Spain, in 2012. Lane notes that this event offers a strong point of entry into "the role that theater and performance can play in relation to human rights practice today," because of its targeted use of the body in performance to react against injustice (ix).

The editors introduce key concepts such as theatre as public imaginary and Habermas's notion of the critical public sphere, as well as describing how the two come together: "The establishment and operation of human rights has depended and continues to depend at every turn on efforts of imagination" (8). The editors argue that human rights are a "core concern" for the twenty-first century. Through its focus on the intersection of performance and activism, this collection of essays sheds new light on performance aesthetics and sites of inequality. The contributors recognize how theatre and performance act as a "distinctive representational practice" in the fight for human rights (2). This volume has two central aims: first, "to chart the extraordinary diversity, depth, and complexity of the encounter between theater, performance, and human rights over the past two decades," and second, "to open the way toward understanding the character and significance of this encounter" (1). The book is thus an exploration of how theatre and performance are used in support of human rights.

The book is divided into three thematic sections: Transnational Justice and Civil Society, The "War on Terror" and the Global Economic Order, and Transnational Publics. The three sections and twelve chapters examine plays and performances across six continents. The theatrical and performance events are closely analyzed in an attempt to investigate phenomenological and physical experiences of theatre and their impact on human rights. The editors asked their contributors to consider the aesthetics, ethics, and effects of theatre and performance as a tool for social change.

Section I investigates how theatre and performance assist spectators in reimagining the politics of human rights in the face of large-scale social and national traumas. Ann Lambright focuses on how dead bodies and the mimetic embodiment of the dead can serve in the commemoration of national tragedy as she examines the relationship between the Peruvian Truth and Reconciliation

Commission and an activist theatre troupe, Grupo Cultural Yuyachkani (chapter 1). Essays from Luís Madureir (chapter 2) and Paola S. Hernández (chapter 3) investigate contrasting spaces (urban vs. rural, military vs. public) in Mozambique and Buenos Aires, respectively. Brenda Werth examines two plays from Latin America's Southern Cone that reference the Bosnian War and the Beslan schoolhouse massacre in Russia in order to question dramatic violence as a means for addressing state violence (chapter 4).

Section II examines how theatrical practices have met challenges and obstacles (cultural and financial) in the wake of September 11, 2001, and President George W. Bush's declared War on Terror. In this context, Lindsey Mantoan and Christina Wilson address the use of documentary theatre. Mantoan looks at Victoria Brittain and Gillian Slovo's play *Guantánamo: Honor Bound to Defend Freedom* (2004) (chapter 5) and the play's pushback to the media's spectacle of war. Wilson discusses Christine Evans's *Slow Falling Bird* (2003) (chapter 6) as a means of staging human rights activism. Sarah M. Misemer seeks to "understand how economic neoliberal practices lead to porous borders" (chapter 7) through which money and goods flow unrestrained while people and politics are restricted through her analysis of two plays: Víctor Hugo Rascón Banda's *Hotel Juarez* and Gabriel Peveroni's *Berlin* (137). Within the US context, Ana Elena Puga highlights the journey of Elvira Arellano, an undocumented migrant artist, to sanctuary and her embodiment of the "heroic suffering-as-virtue and political-as-personal" (chapter 8) (155).

The final section addresses innovations in twenty-first-century transnational performances of human rights, with a focus on the public sphere. Camilla Stevens analyzes citizenship as she looks at dramatists—Frank Disla, Claudio Mir, and María Isabel Bosch—who travel between the United States and the Dominican Republic (chapter 9). Joi Barrios takes a personal approach by sharing her own work in street performance at the University of the Philippines in 1984 (chapter 10). Elizabeth Anker analyzes Tony Kushner's *Homebody/Kabul* (2001) to critique the Western perspective on non-Western suffering (chapter 11). In the final chapter (chapter 12), Kerry Bystrom contrasts Western plays and performances, such as Eve Ensler's "V-DAY" campaigns and Lynn Nottage's *Ruined* (2009), as sites of a "convergence of aesthetics and activism" and the importance of the balance between aesthetics and activism (228).

Imagining Human Rights argues that theatre and performance are "representational, and the representations they produce arise through shared acts of imagination about actually present human bodies" (4). A strength of this collection of essays is its breadth of coverage of performance art and theatre texts alike. Overall, *Imagining Human Rights* goes beyond the more expected topic of theatre for social change to include a transnational perspective on the spaces where theatre, performance, and human rights meet. This book would serve well for courses in performance, trauma studies, transnationalism, human rights activism, and more.

—AMANDA BOYLE
University of Kansas

Making Make-Believe Real: Politics as Theater in Shakespeare's Time. By Garry Wills. New Haven, CT: Yale University Press, 2014. ix + 414 pp. $30.00 cloth.

Garry Wills's monograph *Making Make-Believe Real: Politics as Theater in Shakespeare's Time* is a thought-provoking contribution to the realm of Shakespeare Performance Studies and political history, although the title itself is somewhat misleading. The subtitle suggests the book will focus extensively on Shakespearean drama. However, Shakespeare is not the only Elizabethan writer included in Wills's analysis, and the book itself actually focuses principally on Queen Elizabeth I. Further, Shakespeare and Elizabeth share the limelight with the poet Edmund Spenser, and it is Spenser's *Faerie Queene* (and not a Shakespearean king or heroine) that Wills employs continuously to comment on Elizabeth's performativity. Although the book's title is slightly problematic, its overall content offers a cultural and political study of the Elizabethan era that is relevant and insightful to anyone interested in Shakespeare Performance Studies as outlined in W. B. Worthen's *Shakespeare Performance Studies* (2014). The monograph examines how Elizabeth's reign relied entirely on her ability to "make-believe" elements of her monarchy, since her position as an English queen (and not king) was "unimaginable"; thus, "she would just have to be *imagined* into office, and imaginatively retained there" (7).

Wills divides his book into six sections that focus on aspects of Elizabeth's reign in which the queen created an illusion of power: (courtly) love, (divine) monarchy, (cosmic) religion, (faerie) nation, (chivalric) war, and (courtier) warriors. The first section, "Make-Believe (Courtly) Love," analyzes Elizabeth's exploitation of courtly love as one way to strengthen her reign. Since Parliament fretted constantly over the question of an heir, Elizabeth created the illusion that the prospect of her bearing a child (by means of a potential marriage) was always possible. Thus, "all the conventions of her court were tempered by the conventions of courtly love" (31). To illustrate this argument, Wills claims that Renaissance courting was "a clever way of going back into English tradition without revivifying its Catholic elements," (17) and it successfully kept Elizabeth's Parliament, patrons, and suitors temporarily placid.

Wills's second section, "Make-Believe (Divine) Monarchy," figures Shakespeare's plays more prominently as a parallel to Elizabeth's reign alongside Spenser's *The Faerie Queene*. As a presumed bastard child of Henry VIII, owing to her father's paranoia regarding her mother's faithfulness, Elizabeth manipulated make-believe to solidify the idea that she was the *blood* heir to the throne and spent a majority of her reign "downplaying coronation, since it remembered a vestigial machinery for choosing a king apart from heredity" (64). This section argues that Shakespeare's characters Richard II, Cleopatra, and Henry V served as dramatic representations of Elizabeth's theatricality regarding succession, but the section diverges from the main argument concerning Elizabeth's theatricality considerably in order to rebuke theories commonly associated with these plays in modern scholarship such as the New Historicists' "Hal Haters" (91).

"Make-Believe (Cosmic) Religion" argues that Elizabeth's personal religious beliefs were and remain something of a mystery, which is why the façade of a make-believe religion needed to remain strong. Elizabeth's father, Henry VIII, notoriously broke away from the Roman Catholic Church but still firmly supported many of its beliefs and practices. As Wills argues, Elizabeth also struggled to solidify England's new religious affiliation: "She had some longstanding ties to her father's Catholicism without the pope—she preferred, for instance, a robed and celibate clergy, and she kept a gold crucifix in her chapel. But she also had a pent-up resentment of the half-sister [Mary, Queen of Scots] who so stormily preceded her" (171). This new religion had very blurred boundaries, but Elizabeth was determined to create the perception of a strong religious underpinning for her nation, something she did successfully by cultivating comparisons of herself to key religious figures. In this section, Wills highlights Elizabeth's comparisons to: Deborah (a powerful prophet and warrior of the Israelites from the biblical Book of Judges) during her coronation procession of 1559 (143–45); St. George in illustrations of the queen such as Thomas Cecil's equestrian portrait of Elizabeth (149–52); and the Jesuits' superior Henry Garnet and Shakespeare's characters in *Macbeth* (161–68). By the end of her reign, Elizabeth had successfully strengthened the new Anglican Church through these comparisons and the façade of its strength, building itself up "as a spiritual force" (180).

The fourth section, "Make-Believe (Faerie) Nation," examines Elizabeth's ability to create a nation that supported a queen similar to Spenser's Faerie Queene—a nation that encouraged noble and chivalrous acts reminiscent of a fictional Arthurian court. Her processions throughout the country were arguably a "ceremonial 'palimpsest' of routes" and held "elements of the old order, but they were continually stamped with new Renaissance emblems" (199). Focused on Arthurian pageantry, Elizabeth's gentry were required to constitute her Camelot, and her entire make-believe nation functioned under this "mythical cover" (217).

"Make-Believe (Chivalric) War" argues that Elizabeth's wartime strategies were particularly fitting for a woman on the throne, claiming: "She had far more to gain from make-believe war than from real war" (232). Although Elizabeth constantly warned against Spanish and French interference, war never became a reality during her reign, except during her defensive triumph against the Spanish Armada. Rather than on actual military violence, her kingdom was instead based on honor, since honor was easier to make-believe: "To achieve noble status and courtly standing was the reward of make-believe war in the tilt, as much as (sometimes more than) reward in actual battle" (253). She required her militants to always be ready for battle by "training" in tournaments and jousting. Wills argues that in doing so, these tournaments became "make-believe war" and allowed Elizabeth to convince the nation that in hosting such tournaments, she was capable as head of state and commander of the nation's military forces without ever having to go into battle.

Wills' final section, "Make-Believe (Courtier) Warriors," focuses once more on Elizabeth's suitors and their military endeavors, both make-believe and real. The section's inclusion of James I's son, Prince Henry, and his continuance of theatricality within the monarchy concludes the argument that Elizabeth's reign was principally based on her theatricality and ability to re-create illusion as necessary. This conclusion illustrates the effectiveness of Elizabeth's theatricality, since it continued and magnified under her successor. However, the theatrical political game was not to last: "With Henry's death, [the court] learned [the illusion] was not to be. Having to learn it all at once, so unexpectedly, was a stunning blow. The many make-believes of Elizabethan rule were no longer believable" (344).

Garry Wills's *Making Make-Believe Real: Politics as Theater in Shakespeare's Time* is an insightful read for any Shakespeare Performance Studies or Elizabethan England enthusiast. Although the book does not critically examine Shakespeare's work in great detail, Wills offers an anthropological investigation into the Elizabethan society that surrounded Shakespeare and morphed the "real" with the "make-believe." In doing so, *Making Make-Believe Real* presents a fascinating study of cultural performance and political theatricality and—though lacking in Shakespearean exploration—should be praised for its thorough analysis of politics and society in the Shakespearean era.

—ALEX CAHILL
University of Missouri

Violence Against Women in Early Modern Performance: Invisible Acts. By Kim Solga. New York: Palgrave Macmillan, 2013. vii + 212 pp. $30.00 paper.

Kim Solga's valuable study directs critical attention to a particularly problematic issue: to perform violence against women during England's early modern period, whether in the playhouse or the public square, was also to perform its transformation and erasure. In other words, when violence against women was reenacted as public spectacle, particularized experiences of pain and trauma were generalized to make them comprehensible to social and theatrical audiences. Solga sets out to make these mechanisms of disappearance discernable for modern practitioners and audiences alike by conducting a comparative analysis of the legal commentary, conduct literature (which provided instructions on household matters such as wife beating), and dramatic texts that survive early modern performances of gendered violence. Although it attends to early modern plays' originating social contexts, this is not a book about reconstructing the original practices of Shakespeare and his contemporaries. Rather, it is concerned with formulating an ethical, feminist strategy for producing and witnessing these plays today. Solga coins the term "in/visible" to refer to a bimodal means of witnessing both violence and the mechanisms of its disappearance in the act of performance. This redirects the reader's attention to the importance of staging an encounter with what has gone missing and how.

In order for abuse of women to be rendered legible within early modern England's masculine social sphere, victims had to graft their experiences of pain and abuse onto highly prescriptive behavioral models. For instance, Solga delves into how rape protocol required its victims to publicly frame their personal experience of violence as a crime against the household. In this process, women's internal, physical, and emotional experiences of rape, battery, and in some cases death are streamlined and sanitized in terms of their effects within a patriarchal system. Solga's introduction effectively roots this thesis in feminist scholarship and performance analysis in order to foreground the production-oriented case studies that follow. These case studies successfully elucidate the ways in which marriage manuals and instructional morality texts surrounding rape and wife beating not only deal with shifting definitions and legalities surrounding gendered violence but also make allowances for that violence's inevitability. The comparative analysis of these sources illustrates how the texts that survive representations of women's bodily distress in the Elizabethan and Jacobean periods inform one another and work in conjunction to displace particularized experiences of assault and abuse. Solga selects *Titus Andronicus, A Woman Killed with Kindness, The Duchess of Malfi*, and *The Changeling* not only because they reference, enact, and perhaps place pressure upon culturally determined reactions to sexual molestation, corporal punishment, and psychological torment but also because each play has enjoyed a recent production that strategically challenges passive spectatorship to denaturalize violence as well as its occlusion. For instance, Deborah Warner's production of *Titus Andronicus* for the Royal Shakespeare Company made Lavinia's rape central to the production rather than a peripheral catalyst for her father's revenge trajectory. Warner's staging emphasized how quickly the male characters made Lavinia's experience of sexual violence entirely about themselves. The actress playing Lavinia utilized an increasingly catatonic physicality. She remained off to one side, in low light, while her father took center stage to express his offense and self-pity while forgetting his violated daughter entirely. The character's constantly collapsing body was either ignored or repositioned as a kind of living marionette until her father snaps her neck in the final moments of the play.

Each chapter centers around one of these plays and conducts a similar performance analysis of a recent production that engages with the selective utilization of acting techniques, audience demographics, and directorial innovations intended to trouble scripts that render the female body-in-pain dumb or transform dying women into stoically suffering icons of grace. These case studies present models for ethical, feminist production strategies for approaching otherwise problematic works. They also shed light on discourses of gendered embodiment circulating around the turn of the seventeenth century and place pressure on their cultural persistence today. Solga's deft performance analyses of Deborah Warner's *Titus Andronicus*, Peter Hinton's *Duchess of Malfi*, Katie Mitchell's *A Women Killed by Kindness*, and Cheek by Jowl's *The Changeling* delineate the ways in which these productions attempt, with varying degrees of success, to make conventional, male-authored acts of violence strange.

These productions place pressure upon stock depictions of women as self-erasing symbols of religious salvation or objectified accessories to masculinity and probe the counterdiscursive possibilities and limitations of moving toward what Frederick Burwick refers to as a "meontic" mode of representation (60). This mode, which is held in tension with the mimetic, endeavors to stage what is not there, that which resists or has been denied signification in relation to presupposed realities. This kind of dual perception holds what is visibly demonstrable in tension with what is invisibly operative in performance. It also promotes a critical reception of performances that make harm to women's bodies and selves meaningful only in relation to how their injuries affect their male relatives.

Solga's book ends by encouraging practitioners and feminist spectators to engage with hidden violence as they approach early modern performance texts. She asks us to embody ghosts, acknowledge pain, and articulate what has been unnamed, as a means of combatting this vanishing act. The urgency of this project cannot be underestimated. *Violence Against Women in Early Modern Performance* reinvigorates political and ethical questions surrounding gendered violence, the shaping modes that bring that violence to consciousness, and the potentialities for theatre as an embodied medium that appropriates, historicizes, and hopefully defamiliarizes an experience that should never be reduced to shorthand. This important contribution to the field of performance studies is useful reading for all scholars and students of theatre history and early modern drama, especially those who have an interest in gender and the political implications of observing violence against women as readers, practitioners, and audience members.

—RACHEL PRICE COOPER
University of Illinois

Theatre/Performance Historiography: Time, Space, Matter. Edited by Rosemarie K. Bank and Michal Kobialka. New York: Palgrave Macmillan, 2015. 270 pp. $90.00, cloth. $85.50, electronic.

In the introduction to their new volume on the theory and use of theatre historiography, *Theatre/Performance Historiography: Time, Space, Matter*, editors Rosemarie K. Bank and Michal Kobialka waste no time and pull no punches in establishing their collection of essays as a direct challenge to what they identify as shortcomings of the seminal 1989 anthology *Interpreting the Theatrical Past.*

Editors Thomas Postlewait and Bruce McConachie introduced that work, Bank and Kobialka note, "without defining 'historiography,'" and, subsequently, any use of the term, or its derivatives, "could be perceived as apart from theatre history, cross-disciplinary (if not interdisciplinary), and synonymous with 'methodology,' 'interpretation' (criticism), and 'theory' (and so, with 'terminology' per se)" (1). *Interpreting the Theatrical Past*, Bank and Kobialka argue, was published at the crest of an academic and social sea change—the former in the field of theatre studies, precipitated by the introduction and rapid popularizing of the performance studies model, and the latter exemplified by the fall of the Berlin Wall and the political and social assumptions that crumbled with it. Such shifts "would underscore the problems created in theatre and performance scholarship by the absence of a 'historiography' that is not conflated with 'methodology,' 'interpretation,' and/or 'theory'" (2). In other words, through failing to specifically define "historiography" at a time of almost unprecedented social and academic change, *Interpreting the Theatrical Past* was out of date before it was released.

It is no accident that this critique informs the three thematic pillars that organize *Theatre/Performance Historiography*'s essays: Bank and Kobialka "want to recoup a definition of historiography as the arrangement of the historical record," they write. "To that end, we called for essays that addressed theatre and performance history in terms of the historiography of time, space and matter" (2). What results is a diverse group of eleven theoretically rigorous essays from a varied collection of academic heavy hitters and exciting young scholars, all of whom model creative and scholarly (re)arrangements of theatrical and performative historical records around concepts of time, space, and matter.

The anthology follows an organizational strategy implied by the theoretical insights. Following Bank and Kobialka's introduction, "Part I: The Space of Formations" offers four essays, each of which is focused on how historical narratives are arranged by space, time, and matter. "Part II: Temporal Matter" comprises three essays on "the polychronic and multitemporal construction of archival matter" and how such constructions are used to generate "aesthetic memory" (9). "Part III: Material Spaces," which includes four essays that draw from theories of dialectical materialism, challenges concepts of historical fixity through the piecemeal construction of theatrical history. While these three themes organize the essays, there is considerable productive crossover with each section's organizing principle. The result is a collection of essays that manages to address a wide swath of topics without sacrificing cohesion, delivering on Bank and Kobialka's promise to "target a historiography that *is* the time, the space, and the matter it takes . . . a historiography whose function is to *be* a mode of thinking, to explore how time, space and matter mediate historical subjects" (7). The epistemological argument for Bank and Kobialka's approach to theatre historiography echoes Diana Taylor's argument that performance is a way of knowing; Bank and Kobialka define historiography as being intrinsically defined by, and composed of, time, space, and matter. Twelve images—frozen time and space given material form—included in the book are confined to two essays: Angenette Spalin and Scott Magelssen's "Performing Speciation" and Patricia Badir's "The Design of Theatrical Wonder in Roy Mitchell's *The Chester Mysteries*," and I wish that some of the other contributors would have included images, as well. Gwyneth Shanks' "The Ground of (Im)Potential," for example, takes the reader through an intimate exploration of a Shanks family binder of personal stories about the San Francisco earthquake. Much of the text of that essay is devoted to describing the visual affect of "a sort of unsettledness, a twisting narrative of retraces, back steps, and add-ons" implied by Shanks' experience with the text (220). Including images may have saved Shanks some narrative space to further the construction of "historiography as Earthquake."

While all eleven essays are worthwhile and contribute in various measures to using time, space, and matter as organizational keystones in thinking about and practicing theatre historiography, a handful stand out for both the quality and accessibility of their scholarship. The aforementioned "Performing Speciation: The Nature/Culture Divide at the Creation Museum" is a remarkably strong essay to kick off the volume. By positioning the Petersburg, Kentucky, Creation Museum's fossil reconstructions as an example of a "historical narrative shaped by the concepts of space, time, and matter" that participates in antiscientific arguments against evolution, Spalin and Magelssen effectively demonstrate the value of historiography as a way of thinking (7). The Creation Museum's displays shape a historical narrative that must be understood as being implicated in, and shaped by, political, religious, and corporate interests. Will Daddario's essay, "Adorno, Baroque, Gardens, Ruzzante: Rearranging Theatre Historiography," seeks to reposition central questions of theatre historiography from asking "what really happened?" toward a philosophical understanding of the encounter between a historical event and the historian. Repositioned as an encounter, rather than a description, Daddario illustrates the potential of moving away from positivist historical work and toward the act of historiography as a way of knowing the past.

Theatre/Performance Historiography is, to borrow a phrase from Daddario, a collection of eleven works that are "reinvigorated and theoretically nimble." A bold and brash addition to the field of theatre historiography, the anthology has left me genuinely excited to see what kind of new work is inspired by the arguments and insights developed by the contributors and skillfully curated by Bank and Kobialka. I anticipate that many young scholars working their way through the essays will find themselves challenged, impressed, and inspired. Just as *Interpreting the Theatrical Past* entered the graduate studies canon, *Theatre/Performance Historiography*'s carefully cultivated essays should prove to be required reading on theatre historiography syllabi going forward.

—DANNY DEVLIN
Bismarck State College

A History of Collective Creation and *Collective Creation in Contemporary Performance*. Edited by Kathryn Mederos Syssoyeva and Scott Proudfit. New York: Palgrave MacMillan, 2013. 276 pp.; 252 pp. Each volume $85.00 hardcover.

Epic serves as an apt description of Kathryn Mederos Syssoyeva and Scott Proudfit's double collection of scholarship on collective creation. Genealogies about epic dramaturgy via Piscator and Brecht indeed get discussed in many chapters, but really it is the wide sweep of topics and transnational approaches in exploring the long story of collective creation in the twentieth century that make these volumes epic. Syssoyeva and Proudfit's big project provides an effective overview of the state of scholarship on collective creation. The strengths of the books include documentation of many different types of collaborative processes and serious provocations to categories for conceptualizing work patterns in theatre rehearsal rooms.

The first volume in the pair, *A History of Collective Creation*, concentrates on early twentieth-century precedents in Russia at the Moscow Art Theatre, in Poland with Reduta, and in France through Copeau's methods before opening into studies of "collective creation's second wave" between 1945 and 1985. The examples in the postwar period range from the expected Living Theatre, Theatre du Soleil, and San Francisco Mime Troupe to the less frequently covered Theatre du Nouveau Monde and Grand Cirque Ordinaire in Quebec, the partnership of John Cage and Merce Cunningham, early Chicano theatre, Lilith: A Women's Theatre, and the Family Circus Theatre of Portland, Oregon.

Driven by Syssoyeva's revisionary focus on Meyerhold and Stanislavsky, plus her sophisticated inclusion of dance, improvisation, and public pageants in the framing historiography, this first set of scholarship goes deep and detailed. Atillio Favorini's analysis in his chapter, "Collective Creation in Documentary

Theatre," effectively bridges the time periods and geographies traversed in the first volume. Proudfit's study, "Shared Space and Shared Pages: Collective Creation for Edward Albee and the Playwrights of the Open Theatre," showcases a smart method: marrying a history of ideas with analysis based on a materialist consideration of performance venues. Overall, this volume forms a powerful foundation that on its own feels like a necessary contribution to and key resource for the field of theatre history.

Collective Creation in Contemporary Performance serves as a companion to the first volume while also pursuing its own project of figuring out "what happened to collective creation after the 1970s" (*Contemporary* 13). Whereas the first volume's studies feel densely networked in their concern to rehistoricize collective creation, the selections in the second volume are more like snapshots of working methods and pedagogy, reflecting the contemporary proliferation of compositional approaches. The scholarly methods employ more introductory overviews of a region or approach, artist self-analysis, and participant-observer studies. The effect is saved from feeling scattered by the sequence of informally paired chapters that produces interludes of focus on contemporary British theatre, Eugenio Barba and Jerzy Grotowski, the pedagogy of LeCoq training and the Dell'Arte International School of Physical Theatre, and contemporary US collective creation via the SITI Company and the Nature Theatre of Oklahoma.

Naming a "third wave" of collective creation—launched by the founding of several companies between 1976 and 1983, punctuated by the death of Julian Beck in 1985, and ultimately achieving critical mass in the 1990s—doesn't so much delimit the second volume's exclusive focus as it allows for the rethinking of continuities in practice and contestations of definitions, especially in relation to ideology, leadership, and the use of text. Such shifts mark the interaction between this project and the existing scholarship on collective creation and devising, like that by Mark Weinberg, Dierdre Heddon and Jane Milling, and Bruce Barton. The most valuable part of volume 2 is its preface, "From Margin to Center: Collective Creation and Devising at the Turn of the Millennium (A View from the United States)." The argument of the second volume about the still visible role of politics in collective aesthetics develops here with examples from the Occupy movement, queer and feminist theatre, performance art, the global "third theatre," immersive theatre, and rock bands like Gogol Bordello and Pussy Riot. The field of theatre studies should continue to respond to the force and provocation of this volume's frame.

Between the two books, a set of key ideas track clearly, and the way they are flagged indicates strong editorial attention. The most consistent thread through all the studies is concern for the continuums between authority and egalitarianism and individuality and collectivity as played out in collaboration and creation. Second, the writing highlights issues of politics, ethics, power, and aesthetics to probe both the linking of collective creation to countercultural movements and artistic interest in popular forms. Finally, the scholarly methods provide strong emphasis on "lines of transmission": genealogies of influence, especially in the interactions of teachers and students, masters and apprentices. Many aspects of this history sit firmly in the realm of Diana Taylor's concept of "repertoire," and the spatio-temporal models evoked to understand historical relationships between events include grids and broken traditions as well as waves.

The decision to refuse strong dichotomies between individuality and collectivity grounds both the scope and the depth of these volumes. Starting with Syssoyeva on Meyerhold and Jane Baldwin on Copeau, different configurations of groups and leaders receive a wide range of treatment and prompt very detailed discussions of working methods among directors, writers, and "actor-creators" to chart exactly how collectivity and sense of ensemble function. Particular attention is paid to where agency shifts, gets acknowledged, or is withheld. The introduction to volume 1 valuably notes that "just as we may find authoritarianism lurking beneath the surface of an egalitarian rhetoric, we may find ample examples of collaborative devising lurking beneath the surface of directorial dominance" (*History* 7). Such tensions underline Victoria Lewis's "From Mao to the Feeling Circle: The Limits and Endurance of Collective Creation," about the individual/group dynamics in the San Francisco Mime Troupe and Lilith as well as other radical West Coast US theatres of the 1970s that she experienced as a member of those groups and now theorizes elegantly.

Likewise, Roger Bechtel's discussion of the role of the writer in British devising processes of the 1970s and 1980s takes on three different cases about authority and authorship in relationship to collectivity. Although the information about Caryl Churchill and Joint Stock is well-worn ground, this direct discussion of playwriting attribution dimensionalizes the many times where other chapters record who is acknowledged or credited as a writer in different practices. Across the volumes, the contributing scholars search for and propose language to describe the paradoxical copresence of independent self and interconnected group experienced in collective creation. This quest drives Laura Cull's application of Deleuzian philosophy to the Living Theatre in "Collective Creation as a Theatre of Immanence." Proudfit, following Lorraine York, calls this type of unity and plurality "fused independence." Uniquely, his analysis of the effect of SITI company workshops in Los Angeles in the late 1990s on the collaborative process of two experimental companies identifies a triad of factors that impact the ability of groups to create together in a healthy way (*Contemporary* 138–39).

In discussing the collaboration of John Cage and Merce Cunningham through the lens of queer theory, Michael Hunter suggests a distinction between what might be called "good government" and "no government" models of collaboration. He posits that Cage and Cunningham's almost invisible, anarchic mode of collectivity through collage renounced "communication and expression (including discussion) bound up with power" (*History* 152). By contrast, most of the studies in these volumes demonstrate that many of the famous collective creation companies struggle(d) to find "good government" modes of collaboration. What good government does is manage power, not remove it, and this notion underlies the insistent discussion of ethics and politics across the two books.

If it is a given that aesthetic work expresses political content and that politics are a form of aesthetic expression, then writing about collective creation demands a fresh addressing of these interrelated trajectories. Syssoyeva and Proudfit resist the urge to take as given the links between countercultural movements and collective processes; instead, they trace the arc from 1930s-era radicalism to 1960s-era agitation, from 1990s-era backlash to contemporary political expression with nuance. They also frame interpersonal, ethical dimensions of theatrical processes as political, so interpersonal as well as ideological hierarchies receive specific discussion.

The crux of the political issues around collective creation is the question of whether the techniques of artistic process correspond directly to aesthetic result. How does the way the artists work interact with the ideas they express and the forms in which the ideas find expression? Since scholarship on postwar and 1960s-era collective creation usually emphasizes the utopian or revolutionary dimension of the work, David Calder's excellent neo-Marxist "Against Efficiency: Théâtre du Soleil's Experimental Relations of Production" proves to be the best self-contained rehistoricization in the collection as it enlivens the political stakes and strategies at play in May 1968. In this vein, Alex Mermikides contextualizes and critiques the employment patterns resulting from reconfigurations of "collectivity" in British devising theatres under the current neoliberal model of the "creative industries" while brilliantly forwarding the collection's discussion of individual authorship, improvisational rehearsal practices, and the 'brands' of specific directors.

"Brand" comes across as a distasteful term, but one of the major accomplishments of these volumes is to follow the movements of signature styles, methods of training, and approaches to rehearsal that travel among collaborators within companies and between teachers and students in schools. In recognizing those lines of transmission, the material finds interesting patterns about the use of a "rural retreat" or a type of monastic dedication to solidify collective creation processes and about the dynamics of gender in different organizations, as well as the incredibly pervasive influence of Viola Spolin's writing in the genealogies of collective creation.

Spolin's influence is only one of the genealogies carefully followed in the collections. Kris Salata also makes two contributions, one in each book, that track the connections from Poland's radically collective Reduta laboratory theatre between the world wars, through Grotowski's work in Poland and at the Workcenter in Pontedera, Italy. Unfortunately, because of the combination of Salata's pieces and Ian Watson's deep exposition of Eugenio Barba's working methods, the collection temporarily feels dominated by Grotowski's ethos in a repetitive way.

The legacies of Copeau and LeCoq receive equally deep treatment, however, through Claire Canavan and Maiya Murphy's contributions, respectively. Murphy's chapter demonstrates an innovative scholarly form by presenting a participant-observer analysis of studying at the London International School for the Performing Arts in a program that employed the LeCoq-based strategy of the *auto-cours* (self-course). Her narrative intertwines with responses from Jon Foley Sherman, who trained under a similar program at L'École Internationale de Théâtre Jacques LeCoq. Their dialogue contradicts and deepens the picture of how pedagogy plays out across institutions and over generations.

Such modes of self-reflection employed in the volume deepen the specific information about working methods contained in the scholarship. Thomas Riccio's piece about his own work blends descriptions of exercises with carefully positioned contextualization about his guidance of collective creation processes with indigenous communities. Riccio's self-reflection acknowledges the uncomfortable neocolonial dimensions of his artistic leadership in this area. Yet, it is one of the strengths of Syssoyeva and Proudfit's curation that this chapter pushes the discussion of community, transnational lines of transmission, and the adaptability of working methods farther than their largely Western-focused scope is able to go in every selection.

The epic effect of these two volumes is impressive: This is a dense, comprehensive, and authoritative set of readings, many of which will be useful to other scholars as specific case studies in any number of considerations of particular geographies, periods, and genres, all of which advance the study of theatrical practice and the documentation of how and why theatre artists work they way they work.

—SARA FREEMAN
University of Puget Sound

Women's Voices on American Stages in the Early Twenty-First Century: Sarah Ruhl and Her Contemporaries. By Leslie Atkins Durham. New York: Palgrave Macmillan, 2013. 1 + 215 pp. $90.35 hardcover, $85.83 Kindle.

Until Leslie Atkins Durham's new book, James Al-Shamma had the Ruhl market well and truly cornered with his thorough 2011 volume on the (then) complete works of Sarah Ruhl: *Sarah Ruhl: A Critical Study of the Plays.* But with her latest text, Durham makes an admirable contribution to the discussion surrounding one of the most well-known and frequently produced women playwrights of the current century. What makes this book particularly useful, though, is that Durham does not stop with Ruhl; rather Ruhl's popularity is the wedge in the academic door that allows entry to a much broader and deeper conversation. Durham claims that "Ruhl's work should not be read in isolation, because her work is part of a larger conversation by female playwrights about the values present in and missing from contemporary American culture" (5). With this in mind, *Women's Voices* is a rigorous exercise in context and consciousness raising and an excellent exploration of the works of a handful of noteworthy contemporary women playwrights of the American stage—some of whom are already widely recognized in their own right (e.g., Lynn Nottage and Young Jean Lee), and some of whom who have yet to receive as much mainstream attention (e.g., Kia Corthron and Bathsheba Doran).

In the introduction, Durham describes the twenty-first-century stage as one that is not particularly welcoming to women's voices, citing the dearth of women playwrights in production on Broadway and their under-representation on the lists of winners of major playwriting awards. However, Ruhl has undeniably achieved great success despite the inhospitable environment, so Durham lays out Ruhl's career, achievements, and prominence, painting a careful picture of her importance. Rather than her well-known association with Paula Vogel, this account focuses on Ruhl's early years with the Piven Theatre Workshop in Illinois, including the adaptations of pieces by Virginia Woolf and Anton Chekhov commissioned by Piven. Durham shows Ruhl's pool of dramatic inspiration to be deep and varied, making her work fertile ground for the intricate readings Durham will undertake in the following pages. And her overall project to use a commercially prominent writer as a springboard for the elevation of other "famous and not-yet-but-should-be famous" writers (8) is definitely a worthy and engaging one.

Once the study gets going, each chapter is anchored by analysis of one of Ruhl's plays, which then expands into that play's conversation on a specific topic as it is borne out by two additional plays by two additional writers. In the chapter titled "Emotional Journeys," Durham reads Ruhl's ode to her deceased father, *Eurydice*, against Joan Didion's *The Year of Magical Thinking* and Jenny Schwartz's *God's Ear* through their shared concern with mourning and grief. "They disarm conventional gendered expectations of the look and sound of grief while they show how important it is not just in the lives of dramatic characters but in the lives of those in the audience who hurt with them" (52). The next chapter, "Caring Labor," centers on one of Ruhl's most well-known works, *The Clean House*, connecting its depiction of domestic service and homemaking to Lisa Loomer's *Living Out* and Diana Son's *Satellites*. Durham invokes feminist economist Nancy Folbre's questions about the economic value of the traditionally female work of caring for the family as a critical foundation for her observations about the dynamics at work in all three plays. "Theatrical Devotion" is, unsurprisingly, a treatment of the role of religious devotion in Ruhl's ambitious *Passion Play*, alongside *100 Saints You Should Know* by Kate Fodor and *Church* by Young Jean Lee, with particular attention paid to the reappropriation of Christian symbology for feminist ends. In the chapter "Mobile Lines," Durham addresses the intersection of technology and intimacy as she engages Ruhl's play *Dead Man's Cell Phone*, Bathsheba Doran's *Kin*, and Quiara Alegría Hudes's *Water by the Spoonful*. In an increasingly digital world, Durham finds in these plays the questions of "how and where [the characters can] ground the relationships that define them and how they might distinguish the moral from the immoral as they create the maps for shaping and maintaining these relationships" (99). Finally, in her chapter titled "Natural Forces," Durham brings an ecofeminist lens to the issues of sexual freedom at work in *In the Next Room or the vibrator play*, Lynn Nottage's *Ruined*, and Kia Corthron's *A Cool Dip in the Barren Saharan Crick*. She uses these plays to explore the "important connections between women's liberation and a just relationship with and respect for the natural world and its forces" (131).

Durham's approach to all the plays she discusses is focused and fluid. She has chosen culturally noteworthy topics as the nuclei of her chapters, and her discussion of those elements within the plays is thorough, thought-provoking, and clear. Through careful close reading and insightful critical engagement, she leads the reader along detailed trails that connect the central idea or conceit of each play. But, for my money, the most exciting thing about Durham's study is her treatment of fifteen plays by eleven women as deserving works of art in their own right, without having to treat them as "women's plays" on "women's subjects." She argues that the women in her study "have boldly claimed a post at the center of American theater . . . the characters they craft, the stories they tell, the questions they pose, and the ideas they materialize have the potential to shape the cultural imagination of a large group of theatregoers as a complex new era unfolds" (5). Recognizing the power of women in the public sphere, she walks the delicate line of celebrating the work of a handful of women without essentializing it.

As Durham notes in her final chapter, the work of these mid-career playwrights is anything but over, and the same could certainly be said for her own project. Durham's book is a beginning. It is a call to value the unheard voices of the stage, an invitation to look deeper into the threads that connect them, and a challenge to continue to seek out more.

—JENNIFER GOFF
Frostburg State University

Bigger, Brighter, Louder: 150 Years of Chicago Theater As Seen by "Chicago Tribune" Critics. By Chris Jones. Chicago: University of Chicago Press, 2013. 357 pp. + 16 illustrations. $27.50 cloth.

Chris Jones's anthology may not be scholarly, but it is valuable to theatre scholars. The lead theatre reviewer for the *Chicago Tribune*, Jones was able to plumb that newspaper's archives in search of landmark reviews from the paper's mid-nineteenth-century beginnings to the present, from which he selected one hundred and one, most not seen since their original publication. Jones's collection includes reviews of both homegrown and touring productions, representative reviews from several generations of *Tribune* critics, and long-forgotten accounts of performances by prominent theatre artists and even some celebrities better known for their film and television work. (Imagine seeing *Waiting for Godot* with Harvey Korman as Didi and Mike Nichols as Lucky!) Jones includes vivid accounts of key events, most notably the 1904 Iroquois Theatre fire. Unlike many historical accounts of theatre in given cities, here the reader sits right beside the critic, experiencing memorable moments up close.

Jones's book serves as a nice companion to Richard Christiansen's *A Theater of Our Own: A History and a Memoir of 1,001 Nights in Chicago*, much as a baseball color commentator complements the ongoing spiel of a play-by-play announcer: Jones's book is like the former, providing contextualizing anecdotes that enliven and heighten the stakes of Christiansen's narrative. Combined, the two books trumpet the theatrical highs and lows of the proverbial "Second City."

Chicago has long been a generator of noteworthy theatre, sending its artists and productions off to the East Coast hub for national consumption and cultural validation. For example, Chicago Little Theatre artists Susan Glaspell and husband Jig Cook subsequently migrated east to help found the Provincetown Players. Similarly, Chicago newspaperman Ben Hecht relocated to New York City to extend his playwriting, and later screenwriting, career. Chicago nurtured Tennessee Williams, invented Second City improvisation, generated the satire *Chicago* and the musical *Grease*, and still later birthed the imaginings of director Robert Falls and the acting ensemble Steppenwolf. In the last three decades, no fewer than five of Chicago's roughly three hundred theatres have won a Tony Award as best regional theatre.

Despite its prominence, relatively little has been written about Chicago's profound theatrical contributions. Beyond Richard Christiansen's aforementioned history, Harvey Young and Queen Meccasia Zabriskie coauthored *Black Theater is Black Life: An Oral History of Chicago Theater and Dance*, a collection of interviews with some of the city's most notable modern black theatre and dance artists. The story of Second City's improvisational comedy has been well documented by Jeffrey Sweet and Janet Coleman. But *Bigger, Brighter, Louder* still fills an important historical niche.

Jones organizes his reviews chronologically, bringing to light a progression of memorable events in Chicago theatre history. It opens with an 1853 notice of a show at Mr. Rice's theatre and follows that with an 1868 review of Joseph Jefferson III as Rip Van Winkle—though still fledgling, nineteenth-century Chicago was a destination for touring stars. Subsequent reviews then chart major Chicago theatrical activity up to the 2012 Robert Falls production of Eugene O'Neill's *The Iceman Cometh*, restaged in the spring of 2015 at the Brooklyn Academy of Music. Intriguing nuggets are found along the way: the 1890 Chicago debut of *A Doll's House*; the original (Chicago-generated) production of *The Wizard of Oz*, from 1902; pans of both *Tobacco Road* and *Waiting for Lefty*; first looks at *The Glass Menagerie*, *All My Sons*, *Waiting for Godot* and *Long Day's Journey into Night*; debuts of *American Buffalo* and *Working*, *The Grapes of Wrath* and *Gem of the Ocean*, *Clybourne Park* and many more. Here is indeed a firsthand account of American theatre as seen through Midwest journalistic eyes.

Jones's book also accounts for several generations of noteworthy reviewers. Percy Hammond started off at the *Tribune* before heading to New York (where he famously died shortly after reviewing Orson Welles's *Voodoo Macbeth*). Later came the conservative Charles Collins (who panned Odets on political grounds), the gentler Cecil Smith, and then the formidable and legendary Claudia Cassidy. For over twenty-five years, Cassidy's caustic wit and highest possible standards proved a thorn to Broadway producers bent on sending second-rate tours to Chicago. Cassidy's power was such that she helped launch Tennessee Williams's career, among others. Later *Tribune* critics included William Leonard, Linda Winer, and Sid Smith. Perhaps most influential was Richard Christiansen, who had much to do with nurturing the Off-Loop theatre in the 1960s, which blossomed in the 1970s and continues today. Jones appropriately includes his own criticism here as well. If Jones's book serves as a primer on differing approaches to stage reviewing, it also offers a Whitman's Sampler of entertaining and articulate essays, even as it demonstrates the critics' power to make or break productions.

Following each review are comments by Jones, designed to contextualize and/or explain the proclivities of that particular critic, artist, or production. His comments tend to be more descriptive than analytical. They are also uneven, as some explain more than others, and some do not explain enough. It leaves the reader a bit frustrated to have a thread introduced but not carried out; one wants more consistency from entry to entry, beyond obligatory segues linking to the following review. Still, Jones's better comments add depth, texture, and significance, pointing out important characteristics and historical value, often enhanced with an entertaining insider's anecdote.

Like much Chicagoana, this collection is often guilty of civic boosterism, coming off as self-congratulatory and parochial. Overshadowing Chicago theatre is a cloud of second-city-ism, a reflexive defensiveness in the face of New York City's cultural dominance. When Jones deems a production "famous" or "significant," is that only within Chicago's own story, only looking inward? Local legend-making sometimes substitutes for aesthetic quality, a dilemma that reviewers no doubt needed to untangle when assessing worth. Yet productions like *Warp!*, though essentially meaningless outside Chicago, are intrinsic to the evolution and perpetuation of that city's legacy and aesthetic and are happily included here.

In interest of full disclosure, I must note that I had the good fortune to work on two productions reviewed in this collection, both directed by Robert Falls: *In the Belly of the Beast* and *Hamlet*. Too often good theatre work conceived outside of New York gets lost due to the form's inherently ephemeral nature, forgotten in the larger swirl of many regional theatres operating in the proverbial hinterlands. How refreshing it is to have Chris Jones salvage the traces of so many past productions and, in the process, reconstruct a city's theatrical heritage.

—**STUART J. HECHT**
Boston College

Embodied Consciousness: Performance Technologies. Edited by Jade Rosina McCutcheon and Barbara Sellers-Young. New York: Palgrave Macmillan, 2013. xii + 229 pp. $85.00 cloth.

Jade Rosina McCutcheon and Barbara Sellers-Young's collection of essays, *Embodied Consciousness: Performance Technologies,* contributes to "the discursive shift in the humanities and the arts from the textual to the performative," specifically focusing on the body as a locus of knowledge and technique within performance and theatre (1). McCutcheon and Sellers-Young select essays that combine recent neuroscience with theories of performance in order to contemplate, question, and ultimately understand embodied consciousness through theatre and performance technologies. They define embodied consciousness as "an integration of the brain and the body as they interact with the environment." In other words: "We think and act from an integrated neurological system, which structures our processes of thinking and is referred to as embodied cognition: an idea that cognition is situated in the body as well as the brain" (2–3). Taking this definition as a starting point, McCutcheon and Sellers-Young bring in contributors with a diverse array of backgrounds in "neuroscience, history, philosophy, performance pedagogy and the artistic endeavors of acting, directing, and community-based practice" to more fully explore the potential interaction between neuroscience and performance (4).

The collection comprises fourteen essays grouped into four different parts. The first essay, by neuroscientist D. W. Zaidel, "Consciousness and the Brain: A Window to the Mind," serves as an introduction to consciousness studies in the field of neuroscience. Zaidel's essay quickly outlines the history of consciousness and its connection to the brain and provides us with a map of where consciousness studies has gone in the last decade by highlighting some of the field's major concerns: biological and evolutionary issues, embodiment, notions of the self, and awareness versus nonawareness. The essay serves as a fine primer for the rest of the collection's four parts.

The book's first two parts, "Pedagogy of Performance Training" and "Eastern Influences on Western Performance Technologies," provide detailed accounts of how neuroscience has been and might further be used to understand and improve our methods of actor training. Elizabeth Carlin-Metz's piece, "The Neuroscience of Performance Pedagogy," provides the most all-inclusive examination of neuroscience's place in performance pedagogy by engaging neuroscience as a way to explore the complicated nature of the age-old Cartesian debate of mind versus body. Relying on the concept of embodied consciousness, Carlin-Metz succeeds in arguing for a pedagogy of experiential practices by focusing on neuroscientific structures such as mirror neurons, the physical sensory feedback system, and the construction of memory. Importantly, Carlin-Metz never loses site of the analytical, rational, and logical requirements of acting. Conversely, Bella Merlin, in the same section, delivers a personal account of stage fright to investigate the dual nature of an actor's consciousness (actor/character) through a neuroscientific approach to subjectivity and the self. Merlin ultimately suggests a specialized warm-up regimen that she argues will help reduce the risk of fragmentation of the actor's consciousness, something she believes is one of the causes of stage fright. Other essays focus on the ability of certain actor training techniques to create altered states of consciousness (ASC), such as Devika Wasson's "Pause in Breath: Potential for Altered States of Consciousness in Traditional Indian Performance" and R. Andrew White's "Altered States: Radiating Consciousness in Michael Chekhov's Technique." These essays work to explicate and justify established training techniques through the use of neuroscience. Thus, within these two parts there are two different kinds of essays: those that attempt to develop and alter actor training based on neuroscience, like Carlin-Metz's work, and those that seek to explain and justify acting practices through neuroscience, like White and Wasson's work. Both implementations of neuroscience will be of interest to those who want to learn how such interactions can be applied to a diverse array of performance practices and pedagogies.

The final two parts focus on the primary relationship of the theatrical experience: that between the audience and the performer. While "Reception and Reflection in Contemporary Performance" focuses almost exclusively on reception, "Theorizing the Consciousness of Postmodern Performance" delves into the interplay between the audience and the performer through a focus on philosophical antecedents to neuroscience's work on consciousness. McCutcheon's "The Performance Mirror: Self, Consciousness and Verbatim Theatre" serves as the quintessential example of the reception section. In her essay, McCutcheon scrutinizes a unique event in which audience members, who also served as interviewees, experienced their replicas onstage in verbatim theatre. This literal mirroring of an audience member onstage reflects the way mirror neurons operate. Through the case study we gain an understanding of the physical and mental changes that occur in audience members at a theatrical event. Other essays in the section examine the disruptive power of performance on the biopolitical ideology of systemic child abuse in Ireland (Gabriella Calchi-Novati) and on understanding the formation of an ASC in online viewership of commercial flash mobs through the use of game theory, cognitive studies, and ritual theory (Mary Elizabeth Anderson). The final part of the book takes the reader on a tour of philosophies of consciousness. It begins with Doug Rosson's reclamation of Martin Heidegger's definition of Being, in his 1927 book *Being and Time*, in order to form a concept of performance, the performative, and the 'Real' that speaks to to an 'authentic' mode of being that relies on contemplative performance within theatre, as well as how this cognitive awareness operates as both a feature of theatre and that which consciousness desires from theatre. The essays in these two sections will serve anyone interested in the larger philosophical and theoretical issues of the theatrical and performance arts.

Embodied Consciousness provides an impressive look at the possibilities of integrating consciousness studies into theatre and performance. The essays share a common vocabulary while also staking claims in a diverse array of theatrical and performance concerns. The collection spurs questions and leaves room for additional exploration in the study of presence, technologically mediated performance, and historiography, among others. This volume will be of great value to theatre and performance scholars seeking to engage cognitive neuroscience to answer fundamental questions about the nature of performance.

—**SCOTT C. KNOWLES**
Southern Utah University

Audience Participation in Theatre: Aesthetics of the Invitation. By Gareth White. New York: Palgrave Macmillan, 2013. 240 pp. $29.00 trade paperback.

Gareth White opens his *Audience Participation in Theatre: Aesthetics of the Invitation* with the simple observation that "there are few things in the theatre that are more despised than audience participation" (1). While this sentiment might be somewhat overstated, I suspect few artists or audience members would claim total freedom from apprehension when participation is called for at a performance. As White points out, however, participatory theatre continues to be an integral part of practice at all levels of theatre. The dissonance between the trepidation of the audience and the proliferation of these techniques in approaches such as applied theatre, immersive theatre, and theatre for social change suggests that they offer at least some degree of efficacy. In seeking to resolve the gap between audience resistance and performance affect, White focuses his study on the aesthetic framing that enables and authorizes this type of theatre: the invitation to participate.

For White, this "moment of invitation" is critical to the success of the participatory performance, to the strength of the audience's engagement, and even to the ethical implications of the public transformation of an audience member from spectator to spectated. He suggests, however, that this critical moment has been sometimes dismissed as merely a necessary structural component of any participatory performance. By way of response, White uses this study to argue that the process of extending an invitation to join in a performance should be understood as a method of art-making. In this sense, the moment of invitation is not only an aesthetic device but also, through its conventions, repeated structures, and capacity for meaning-making, an aesthetic in its own right. In that these moments are actively negotiated and revised during performance and embodied by presumably untrained participants, however, the aesthetic suggested by these practices raises important questions of access, agency, and danger. White's framing of invitation-as-aesthetic is supported by the fact that these questions can contribute to potentially profound shifts in audience experience and point of view (9).

White's study is organized into four chapters. The first three, "Process and Procedure," "Risk and Rational Action," and "Irrational Interactions," are devoted primarily to the implications, ethics, and potential dangers of the preinvitation period, as well as the actual extension of the invitation to participate. In these chapters, he covers theoretical lenses ranging from performance studies to cognitive neuroscience in an effort to approach the act of invitation from a variety of perspectives. Chapter 4, "Accepting the Invitation," moves into the actual experience of responding to the invitation and the repercussions of that response. In each of these chapters, White opens with a review of relevant scholarship and an application of these theories to the moment of invitation before turning to a practical example. As he cautions in the introduction, however, "nothing here is articulated with the rigour of a case study" (3).

This caution aside, out of these examples comes the most exciting material in the book. In these readings, spanning work by Armadillo Theatre, Jonathan Kay, De La Guarda, and Tim Crouch, White hits his stride and demonstrates his own considerable experience with applied theatre and theatre in education. It is in those sections, rather than in the theoretical reviews that precede them, that the importance and artistry of invitation is made clear. Also important here is White's work in extending the notion of "horizon of expectations" developed by Gadamer, Jauss, and Bennett. His adapted "horizon of participation" begins by drawing on the earlier theory's framework of signals and characteristics that condition any audiencing experience and locate interpretation, at least in part, as a process that presupposes exposure to the text or performance. White's major point of departure is that while both the horizon of expectation and the horizon of participation rely on the audience member (or reader) to interpretatively bridge gaps and make meaning in the dissonance between expectation and actuality, the horizon of participation is distinct because the "choices are about action rather than interpretation" (59). In his chapter on risk, White adapts this concept still further into a "horizon of risk" (81). This extended framework covers the danger, ranging from embarrassment to actual physical or psychological risk, that partially conditions how an audience (or individual audience member) reacts to an invitation to participate.

As compelling as White's play with "horizons" and his work with risk are, the scope of his study raises some questions. Insofar as exploring the moment of invitation also means engaging with larger and still contested debates in performance, art, aesthetics, and reception, White here opts for a strategy built around continually retuning to the moment of invitation with new theories and lenses, thereby "taking a thin slice across audience participation as a whole" (28). While this approach admirably demonstrates the complexity of the issue, his study suffers in the lack of more thorough engagement with each of these theories and their application to the moment of invitation. This structure also forces White to engage in a considerable amount of literature review, which occasionally makes reading a slog. As such, the payoff that comes with the application sections at the end of each chapter can be somewhat fleeting. Also fleeting is White's engagement with the ethics and politics of audience participation. In the introduction, he promises to only "defer the political analysis of them very briefly" (14). Unfortunately, the book is littered with these sidesteps until finally, toward the end of the conclusion, he acknowledges that it is time to "make good that promise" (203). While this is the structure White outlines from the beginning, I could not help but feel that addressing these questions as they arose could have only strengthened the study.

Ultimately, White sets out to explore the complexities and aesthetic value of the performative act of invitation in participatory theatre. In this, he is successful. On the other hand, his theoretical framework seems to get away from him, leading to some dense and unnecessary explanations of otherwise canonical theories. To a certain extent, this will restrict the audience for the work. That noted, a scholar/artist with interest in applied theatre or theatre for social change will likely find this a valuable resource.

—**PATRICK M. KONESKO**
University of Wyoming

Eugene O'Neill: A Life in Four Acts. By Robert M. Dowling. New Haven: Yale University Press, 2014. xi + 569 pp. $35.00 cloth.

Eugene O'Neill: The Contemporary Reviews. Edited by Jackson R. Bryer and Robert M. Dowling. New York: Cambridge University Press, 2014. xxxvi + 991 pp. $160.00 cloth.

The mitigated highs and abysmal lows of Eugene O'Neill's complex personal life are well established in important biographies by Louis Sheaffer and by Arthur and Barbara Gelb as well as in psychological studies like that of Stephen A. Black, political and religious contexts by John Patrick Diggins and Edward L. Shaughnessy, respectively, maritime influences analyzed by Robert A. Richter, broadly humanistic examinations like that of Thierry Dubost, and many more. What Robert M. Dowling's new biography adds to our understanding of the only Nobel Prize–winning American dramatist is a structured context for the way O'Neill's inner demons impacted his relationships and his work. Dowling's creative unearthing and use of neglected documents and interview subjects, along with some never-before-published photographs, enhance the contribution he makes with *Eugene O'Neill: A Life in Four Acts.*

Robert Dowling's virtually simultaneous coeditorship (with Jackson R. Bryer) of a monumental collection of reviews from the original productions of O'Neill's plays informs his biographical writing on a playwright whose attention to published criticism of his own plays "bordered on the pathological" (343). It makes excellent supplementary reading alongside Dowling's fluidly written narrative. For example, Dowling notes that after Heywood Broun's review of *Gold* (1921), "O'Neill's low opinion of Broun curdled into a rancid hatred" (226), and the reader is alerted to notice the trajectory of Broun's increasingly negative balance of scathing versus constructive commentary over the course of his many pieces reprinted in *Eugene O'Neill: The Contemporary Reviews.* The timely publication of both the biography and the anthology gives rise to endless rewards of cross-referencing.

Taking a cue from O'Neill's frequent use of the four-act structure for his plays, Robert Dowling's biography divides his subject's life into four parts. The exposition (act 1) covers O'Neill's early childhood on the road with his father, actor James O'Neill, who was consciously selling out his artistry for commercial success in *The Count of Monte Cristo*, while his mother suffered her own recriminations over the death of her second son, Edmund, and her morphine addiction resulting from the painful birth of the unwanted "replacement" son, Eugene (35). Years of boarding school, the beginning of O'Neill's lifelong struggles with alcohol, loss of religious faith, expulsion from Princeton in his freshman year, his first two marriages (interspersed by affairs with Louise Bryant, Dorothy Day, and others), odd jobs at sea, a long stay in Buenos Aires, returning to New York and hitting bottom in a suicide attempt, a job at the *New London Telegraph*, six months in a sanatorium for tuberculosis, a year in George Pierce Baker's playwriting seminar at Harvard, and another descent to the dregs in New York together comprise the action of that first act, interwoven with background material on the squalor of places he lived and the people he met who would eventually be reincarnated as characters in his plays. Act 1 also establishes the leitmotif that haunts most of O'Neill's life story: the curse of alcohol. O'Neill consumed prodigious quantities of liquor before, during, and after Prohibition, and he went on drunken binges that lasted for days, unleashing horrifying acts of violence, destruction, and cruelty from a personality generally seen by theatre artists with whom he worked as "very gentle" and "charming" (452).

The rising action of act 2 takes us from 1916, O'Neill's first summer in Provincetown, to his 1922 success with *The Hairy Ape*. This period encompasses his early one-act plays produced at Provincetown Playhouse in Greenwich Village and a steady output of full-length plays, two of which won Pulitzer Prizes: *Beyond the Horizon* (1920) and *Anna Christie* (1921). Traditionally in the four-act structure, Act 3 is the locus for a play's determining crisis immediately preceded or followed by an emotional climax, and this structuring conceit probably works in terms of O'Neill's personal life if his 1929 divorce from Agnes Boulton and marriage to Carlotta Monterey are identified as crisis and climax. The chapter traces a generally upward career trajectory shadowed by the deaths of his parents and brother and by his deteriorating second marriage. Act 4, the so-called denouement of O'Neill's life, covers his remaining quarter century, 1928–1953. While his playwriting—interrupted by a twelve-year hiatus—did achieve its maturity with the plays we recognize as his masterworks, those years proved to be as emotionally action-packed as earlier periods, given the often-tempestuous nature of his marriage. Interestingly, this aberrant dramaturgical structure for his life story echoes a frequent criticism of his plays: he did not know when to stop. His nemesis Heywood Broun said it best in a review of *Desire Under the*

Elms: "When his tale has come to an end he must add more. It is not enough that we have been cleansed by pity and terror. We must be scrubbed" (407).

Eugene O'Neill: A Life in Four Acts includes numerous photographs, ample notes, an index, an appendix listing of completion years for most of the plays, a brief prologue, an introduction, and a postscript with information about the autopsy and burial of Eugene O'Neill as well as about Carlotta Monterey's early release of *Long Day's Journey into Night*. Dowling's reader-friendly storytelling approach makes it a contribution that will undoubtedly lead many to take a deeper look at the plays. His habitual use of "he'd" for "he had" or "he would" may have economized several pages in the book's length. The chronology gets muddy in 1928–29, but the only actual error I found is the misspelling of Elisabeth Marbury's name (318, 562).

Eugene O'Neill: The Contemporary Reviews offers many revelations, including the fact that it is surprisingly easy to read thirty or so reviews of the same production at a sitting! Indeed, there is much to learn from the various ways of describing and evaluating a work in good, lively prose—or in faux Spoon River verse in the case of Alexander Woollcott's review of *Desire Under the Elms* (434). It must be noted that of the 967 pages of reviews, fully 628 pages are devoted to plays of the 1920s. Dowling's biography makes it abundantly clear that the 1920s were O'Neill's most prolific years, but separating the decades with sticky notes drives the point home when the 1920s encompass two-thirds of the thick book. Beginning in 1916 with the New York City production of *Bound East for Cardiff* (two reviews), each play is prefaced by a page listing of the complete cast and the date of any move to another venue. Each review is set off on the page by a big header with all the publication data, including source page numbers. Beginning with *Beyond the Horizon* (1920), many plays get over thirty reviews, which are followed by a bibliographical listing of additional reviews. The index makes it easy to track all entries by any one critic or—an interesting aid—reviews that contain comparisons to other O'Neill plays. I noticed how very often the early reviews identify the playwright as son of the great actor James O'Neill, a tag that disappears after 1920 except for an occasional reference to the author's latent melodramatic tendencies. There is much to savor in this volume and, juxtaposed with Robert M. Dowling's biography, it will surely contribute importantly to O'Neill scholarship and production.

—FELICIA HARDISON LONDRÉ
University of Missouri-Kansas City

Celebration, Entertainment, and Theatre in the Ottoman World. Edited by Suraiya Faroqhi and Arzu Ozturkmen. Kolkata, West Bengal: Seagull Books, 2014. xiv + 514 pp. $25 paper.

The disicipline of Ottoman studies frightens away theatre historians like a scarecrow: most seem to avoid the topic, perhaps because they want to avoid falling into the trap of orientalism. Meanwhile, those who do attempt to approach Ottoman performativity tend to do so solely from a Western social and political ideology. Over the course of its six-hundred-year history, Ottoman society developed a variety of customs, traditions, and ceremonies owing to the incorporation of myriad regions, ethnicities, and religions. Naturally, the formulas of theatre historiography generated by scholars to analyze Western performativity are partially inoperable when they are practiced on a realm like the Ottoman Empire. The Ottoman impact on Western art, social life, and innovations, however, is impossible to sidestep or ignore. Arzu Ozturkmen touches on this issue in her introduction to *Celebration, Entertainment, and Theatre in the Ottoman World* by noting that "some works have approached historical events with an eye on dramatic structures. But the analysis of the political, social and cultural history of the Ottoman world has not yet benefitted much from the paradigm change known as the performative turn" (4). This suggests that an examination of Ottoman courtly attitudes "as performance" instead of "is performance," following Richard Schechner's schema, is necessary. In this regard, Suraiya Faroqhi and Arzu Ozturkmen provide in their well-structured collection a wide-open gate and a research guide especially for theatre scholars to enter the Ottomans' sophisticated and multifaceted world.

Including Faraqhi and Ozturkmen's individual introductions, the book contains twenty-four essays by twenty-four Ottoman studies researchers, organized into three main parts: Celebration and Entertainment, Ottoman Theatre and Theatricality, and European Encounters. The first part examines Ottoman festivals, birthday and circumcision celebrations, and fetes starting in the sixteenth century and progressing through the late Ottoman reign. In chapter 1, for instance, "Evaluating Three Imperial Festivals: 1524, 1530 and 1539," Zeynep Yelce interrogates the grand vizier Ibrahim Pasha's wedding celebration and the circumcision ceremonies for Sultan Suleiman the Magnificent's two sons. In order to focus on the "formation and demonstration of power" (71), Yelce examines the participants' roles in these celebration rituals and the political messages inherent to their nature. Her essay gives the reader an opportunity to glimpse the motives, symbols, conventions, and arrangements of these three Ottoman ceremonies in order to discuss the performative messages conveyed in the social and political contexts of each.

Efdal Sevincli's "Festivals and Their Documentation" also investigates ceremonies in the Ottoman court. Sevincli, however, focuses on the multilayered documentation of pictorial festival books called "surnames." While his research focuses specifically on the surnames of Abdi and Etienne Robolly, which cover wedding and circumcision festivals in 1675, and an anonymous surname from the National Library of Vienna, which depicts events in 1724, he also considers the conflicting statements of historians studying this era. Although he remarks that these festivals served as "cathartic" events, Sevincli doesn't investigate this aspect thoroughly, so his approach to the term remains obscure. Despite this, a reader may grasp the festivity styles of the Ottoman elite from Sevincli's essay and also become acquainted with the antique form of documentation art, the surname, from illustrated examples.

While Yelce and Sevincli examine the most visible and documented side of Ottoman festivals and ceremonies, Suraiya Faroqhi's "When the Sultan Planned a Great Feast, Was Everyone in a Festive Mood?" tries to draw readers' attention to the underdocumented side of these events: the financial aspects, the role of women, the role of servants, and non-Muslim spectators. She does this by relying on drawings of the ceremonies plus foreign authors' transcriptions. The data, however, remain too limited to understand these background characters thoroughly. Faroqhi's essay seems a short version of a larger study, and although she mentions women and servants, for instance, her discussion of them is fleeting. Nevertheless, the essay still provides an important glimpse into a mostly uninvestigated side of these festivals.

Meropi Anastassiadou, who contributes the essay "Making Urban Identity, Dividing up Urban Time," also seems to want to say too much in the space allotted. Although the density of information may cause the attention of Anastassiadou's readers to drift over some crucial points, her article contains rich enough material to visualize both the historical and current Greek communities of Istanbul and their religious festivals, ceremonies, as well as the Greek population's social life and interactions with Muslim and other religion's societies. For instance, Anastassiadou examines the Epiphany Day (January 6), considering its historical importance, traditional performativity, and how Muslims, especially now in modern Turkey, perceive this ceremony. In this way, she not only examines Greek society's current place in modern Turkey but also highlights the political dilemma of ongoing nationalist ideology in that region.

The second part of the book focuses on theatrical performances in the Ottoman world. Cigdem Kilic writes about crossgender acting, necessitated by gender segregation. Nur Gurani Arslan looks at Turkish language musicals and the development of Western-style theatre in the nineteenth-century Ottoman Empire, and Fahriye Dincer considers female identity in Ottoman theatrical space. Daryo Mizrahi, who examines the popular shadow theatre form Karagoz in "Language and Sexuality in Ottoman Shadow-Puppet Performances," writes "puppet plays are comic performances foregrounding language, communication and sexuality, in which spectators see not a carefully administered law-abiding urban community but a reversal of social norms" (275). This argument provides a perspective much different from previous assumptions about this form. Indeed, despite common perceptions of Muslim performance as socially conservative, European visitors frequently mentioned the erotic aspects of this genre.

The third section of the book contains perhaps the most appealing theme for Western scholars and general audiences alike: Ottoman representation in Western society. The authors discuss how Ottoman identity developed in European courts and even in North America from the sixteenth century to the end of the nineteenth century. In her article "Summa Turcica: The Image of the Turk in Eighteenth-Century Viennese Opera," Lale Babaoglu Balkis provides a close reading of Ottoman characters primarily from eighteenth-century Habsburg operas. While she points out that "the two Vienna stages subject to courtly control created an image of Ottomans which allowed the powers that be to manipulate local society" (425), she highlights the political power of these operas and explains how this relationship allowed the Viennese cultural elite to influence Western opinion regarding the Ottomans.

To completely examine the performativity of the Ottoman court at large, of course, is impossible even in a 514-page book. Certainly, then, any deficiency in this work can be attributed primarily to the sheer breadth of the subject. While the space of a review prevents detailed consideration of all but a few of the twenty-four articles in this volume, each article by itself opens another window into a previously understudied and underanalyzed aspect of the Ottoman court and its members' civic lives. *Celebration, Entertainment, and Theatre in the Ottoman World* therefore allows scholars to raise important questions, starting new conversations about the Ottoman world.

—DUYGU ERDOGAN MONSON
University of Washington

Paratexts in English Printed Drama to 1642. 2 volumes. Edited by Thomas L. Berger and Sonia Massai. Cambridge: Cambridge University Press, 2014. xx + 1040 pp. $250.00 hardcover.

Navigating the world of Renaissance publication can be a tricky business. As the often febrile disputations over whether Hamlet's flesh was too solid or too sullied testify, the mutable world of the early modern printing press can throw up issues seemingly small in size but substantive in nature. Therefore, any attempt to catalog the erratic corpus of sixteenth- and seventeenth-century publications can be fraught with difficulty. Archival work is tremendously time consuming, and while online databases such as *Early English Books Online* (EEBO), *Database of Early English Playbooks* (DEEP), and the Folger Shakespeare Library's extensive collection of digitized images have empowered scholars to access important material speedily, those who produce concordances and other similar cataloguing texts are to be commended, most especially for their bravery in engaging with such an idiosyncratic body of literature.

The two-volume *Paratexts in English Drama to 1642*, as the title suggests, follows a similar vein. It endeavors to produce a readily accessible reference work of all material appended to early modern dramatic texts up to the start of the English Civil War. According to its editors Thomas L. Berger and Sonia Masai, "paratextual materials . . . represent a substantial, yet largely untapped, repository of information about all aspects of the production, reception and transmission of dramatic literature in the period" (1:xi). As such, addenda like prefaces, frontispieces, and marginalia retain a special interest for scholars of the Renaissance English drama, containing a whole host of nuggets of information that can further illumine our understanding of this extraordinary period in theatrical history. "Especially prominent," observe the editors, "are references to the changing status of dramatic authorship, to the impact of censorship, to theatrical trends and styles associated with different theatrical venues, and to the popularity of individual plays on the stage and to early modern readers" (1:xi). Considering the potential of such avenues of scholarly investigation, the overall aim of this project—to collate and catalog the paratextual material of the period's dramaturgy—is an admirable one.

There are, however, a number of problems with the catalog that hinder its usefulness as a reference book. Not the least of these is the layout. The two volumes are, the editors admit, indebted to Walter W. Greg's foundational study *A Bibliography of the English Printed Drama to the Restoration*, published from

1939 to 1959. Berger and Masai utilize Greg's ordering system for their own catalog, listing entries following the earlier *Bibliography*'s chronology. Thus, for example, John Skelton's satirical morality play *Magnificence*, which was written circa 1525, is listed as "Greg 11, *Magnificence*, John Skelton," (1:11), meaning that the primary frame of location is the play's position in Greg's catalog. A more useful ordering system for a reference work of this kind would undoubtedly be a relatively strict temporal chronology, as adopted for instance in Martin Wiggins and Catherine Richardson's excellent ongoing series *British Drama, 1533–1566: A Catalogue*. Instead, the editors, in subscribing to a large extent to Greg's own ordering system, render an important aspect of the plays catalogued, namely the publication date, to (literally) a footnote at the bottom of each page.

A secondary though related problem is the font used for each entry. The above example, for instance, has the title as well as the paratextual material in bold typeface. This means that it is difficult to distinguish new entries when scanning the page. Such homogeneity can make discerning the many texts catalogued overly difficult. Renaissance texts, by their very nature, come with a degree of abstruse bibliographical and typographical quirks. However, clarity for a twenty-first-century audience (alongside fidelity to sixteenth- and seventeenth-century authorship) must always be paramount.

Nonetheless, there are a number of very valuable editorial additions to the works collated. Among these are the appendices to the second volume, titled "Finding List." Here, each entry is laid out in diagrammatic form indicating which of a number of categories its paratextual material fulfills. These include dedicatory epistles, addresses to the reader, commendatory poem/poems, content list, actor list, errata, graphic ornamentations, and colophon. Such an ordering enables cross-referencing between texts published in the period considered. For instance, we are able to compare and contrast the paratexts of Ben Jonson's folio of his plays (1616) with that of his great contemporary William Shakespeare (1623). One of the most notable aspects flagged up by Berger and Masai's organization is the relative paucity of addenda to Jonson's 1616 edition—unlike Shakespeare, for example, we do not have an actor list, colophon, or dedicatory epistle. Such physical differences serve to emphasize the contrast between the two works and their respective authors. The included list of contemporary actors in Shakespeare's first folio, for example, reminds us of the fundamentally stage-oriented and even collaborative nature of his dramatic works. Perhaps by contrast, Jonson himself dominates the paratext, suggesting that he should be considered the only presence in the production of his plays.

This example is just one instance of many insights that may be gleaned from comparing and contrasting the physicality of published early modern dramatic texts. While this catalog does have its faults on a stylistic level, its overall project is to be commended for opening new areas of investigation with regard to how we understand and relate to the world of the Renaissance stage and page.

—PATRICK J. MURRAY
University of Glasgow

Tennessee Williams: A Literary Life. By John S. Bak. New York: Palgrave Macmillan, 2013. 341 pp. $100.00 hardcover.

As Jon S. Bak makes clear in his preface, "any new biography of [Tennessee Williams] is likely to tread on well-beaten ground" (viii), and the mission undertaken in writing the book, as he states, echoing a turn of phrase from Strindberg's preface to *Miss Julie*, is "new wine, as it were, in old bottles" (viii). What Bak has written is a thoroughly researched, engaging, but at times exasperating portrait of Tennessee Williams the writer. To be clear, it is Tennessee Williams that is exasperating and not Bak's book, for the book is a meticulous and rewarding exploration of a "literary life." It is a biography that is provocative and illuminating and is especially valuable in challenging the reader to reconsider the post–*Night of the Iguana* years as a time that was productive, creative, and artistically (if not commercially) rewarding for Williams and not simply two decades of personal and literary decline.

Williams's restless—some might argue neurotic—energy permeates the book, so much so that although it is organized chronologically, the chapter titles reference travel patterns and destinations but not time—the first chapter, "Columbus to Columbia (via St Louis): Separating Fact from Fiction," begins the narrative in 1918, when Tennessee is already seven years old; the fifth chapter, "Hollywood to Rome (via Chicago): The 'Catastrophe' of His Success," chronicles the months leading up to the Broadway premiere of *The Glass Menagerie*; and the last chapter, "Chicago to St Louis (via Vancouver): '*Right (Write) On!*,'" covers the last few months of his life. It proves to be a useful framing device that captures the nomadic wanderings/haunted wanderlust of Williams. Bak suggests that while Williams's constant motion stemmed in large part from his inability to escape ever-present low spirits and depression, what Williams called the "blue devils," this restlessness was essential to how he worked as a writer. Bak suggests that despite the overwhelming movement in his life and travels, much of it, at least in terms of enjoying the exotic or escaping his depression, was unsuccessful. As a tourist, Williams found travel unrewarding, but he was constantly writing, and his inability to "stay put" was mirrored in a work ethic that often saw him working on four or five projects at any one time. Williams could not let his work sit any more than he himself could sit. Working on several pieces at once was a method of combating writer's block, but it was also Williams's way of keeping at bay the mental illness he so feared.

Bak's narrative conceives Williams's literary career through tropes of endurance and tenacity. This is perhaps not surprising from someone whose motto was *en avant*, but Bak makes it clear that when Williams was committed to a notion, good or bad, he refused to surrender. Williams spent more than eight years working on *The Glass Menagerie*, and Bak traces the development of earlier and shorter works like "Portrait of a Girl in Glass," "Blue Roses and the Polar Star," and "If You Breathe, It Breaks," arguing that they "were essentially steps in the achievement of his first masterpiece" (109). One of the delights of this book lies in gaining an understanding of how Williams would develop ideas, characters, and situations into a variety of narrative forms and then slowly collage those elements into a long-form play. As one might expect, this is a painstakingly slow way of working, and there was no prescribed gestation period: *Cat on a Hot Tin Roof* took months to write, *Sweet Bird of Youth* took years, and *Orpheus Descending* took decades. This said, Bak does observe that "the more [time] Williams spent writing a play, the less likely were its chances of success" (149). Nothing, however, demonstrates Williams's tenacity better than how he endured the ongoing personal attacks levelled against him and his work by a misunderstanding and often homophobic press. He and his work had been vilified since *The Glass Menagerie* opened, and Bak demonstrates the emotional toll these attacks took on the already fragile playwright, but he also celebrates Williams's resolve not to be destroyed by the attacks as well as his desire to demonstrate through his essays and other published nonfiction works how wrong the critics were in their attacks against him. Even though he knew the war was unwinnable, Williams was unable to retreat despite the physical, emotional, and artistic toll that waging the war cost him.

Throughout the book, Bak champions a rereading and reassessment of Williams' large and, thanks to a number of unpublished writings that have been contested by the estate and the publisher, possibly still growing oeuvre. He argues that in 1940, during Williams's brief residency in New York City, when he witnessed Clifford Odets's experimental *Night Music* fail miserably, Williams became concerned that his theory of the "plastic theatre" was at odds with the economic realities of Broadway (78). His theory of the plastic theatre, also referred to as "sculptural theatre," was a rejection of "the exhausted theatre of realistic conventions" (110). Inspired by the stream of consciousness writings of Joyce, "Williams made use of numerous devices outside of speech to help disrupt the linear representation of human thought patterns" (111) and was key to Williams's commitment to finding and presenting "the truth" onstage.

The traditional narrative suggests that after the success of *Night of the Iguana* (1961), Williams fell into two decades of moral decline and a literary abyss culminating in his death in 1983. Bak argues that while it is true that Williams never had the Cinderella comeback he always dreamed of, his artistic and creative output then more than equaled his pre-1961 output, and the dramatic texts of this period are complex, multilayered experimentations in postmodern writing and should be understood as extensions of the plastic theatre. Bak suggests that in the academy, if not in the world of professional theatre, there is a growing assessment that Williams was tragically ahead of his time. Seeming failures such as *Two Character Play, Vieux Carré, Clothes for a Summer Hotel*, and even *Small Craft Warnings* (which in 1972 enjoyed modest Off-Broadway success) are recontextualized, reanalyzed, and presented as radical yet natural developments of a playwright doing what he had always done—pushing the theatrical form in order to uncover human truths. The inability of audiences and critics to understand that his new works were simply a logical extension of his early (also radical) work proved especially difficult for Williams. Bak argues that "in particular the mountains of draft fragments that he left of his work . . . show how conscious Williams was of his struggle not to write a better play but to convince his public that indeed he already had" (211).

It should be noted that this is not an introductory biography insofar as it assumes that the reader has, at times, more than a passing familiarity with the Williams narrative, and Bak often skims well-known biographical details in order to more fully explore the literary implications of lesser-known events. The nonjudgmental candor with which Bak treats Williams's voracious sexual appetite is also refreshing, and those looking for scandalous exposés will be disappointed. If the book has a weakness, however, it is that the portrait that emerges of Tennessee Williams is rather unlikable. In the preface Bak writes, "There was enough pleasurable love, sex, and success in his life . . . that also allowed him to laugh. . .. It is *that* Williams that I wish to capture more extensively in these pages" (ix). Yet Bak seems unable to capture *that* Tennessee Williams at all and instead presents Williams as a man who could be variously petty, loyal, neurotic, paranoid, and full of regret. Even so, throughout the book, Bak presents his subject as a man who was always committed to his art. It is a pity that Bak could not have captured at least a glimpse of *that* other, laughing, Tennessee Williams.

This, however, is a small concern that in no way detracts from the valuable contributions that this book makes to furthering the scholarship around Tennessee Williams. Importantly, the reanalysis and reassessment of the post-*Iguana* years will do much in terms of reclaiming aspects of Tennessee Williams's literary reputation. Bak's book will be invaluable to Tennessee Williams scholars but will also be of interest to a variety of academics working in a range of fields including modern American theatre aesthetics, literary theory, and cultural studies as well as, of course, anyone with more than a passing interest in understanding the artistry of this iconic playwright.

—WES D. PEARCE
University of Regina

Ira Aldridge: The Early Years, 1807–1833. By Bernth Lindfors. Rochester, NY: University of Rochester Press, 2011. 387 pp. $49.50 cloth.

Ira Aldridge: The Vagabond Years, 1833–1852. By Bernth Lindfors. Rochester, NY: University of Rochester Press, 2011. 244 pp. $55.00 cloth.

Ira Aldridge: Performing Shakespeare in Europe, 1852–1855. By Bernth Lindfors. Rochester, NY: University of Rochester Press, 2013. 350 pp. $55.00 cloth.

Being dead for almost 150 years hasn't stopped Ira Aldridge from making yet another comeback. This nineteenth-century black actor is the subject of a three-volume biography by Bernth Lindfors with a possible fourth volume on the way. Aldridge is also the subject of the 2012 play *Red Velvet*, by Lolita Chakabariti; a production of *Red Velvet* starring Adrian Lester transferred from London to New York for a brief run in 2014 and reopened in London in 2016. Perhaps the fortuitous timing of these works will finally lift this fascinating actor out of semi-obscurity, giving him the respect and fame he has so long deserved.

Bernth Lindfors, professor emeritus of English and African literatures at the University of Texas, Austin, has been a leading Aldridge scholar for many years and is perhaps best known for editing and contributing to the 2007 book *Ira Aldridge: The African Roscius* as well as other articles offering new insights into Aldridge's career and personal biography. In this new multivolume biography,

Lindfors expertly merges his new research with the body of Aldridge scholarship over the decades, including the first biography of Aldridge, *Ira Aldridge: The Negro Tragedian*, published by Marshall and Stock in 1958. There is plenty of fresh information and new perspectives on Aldridge to be found in Lindfors's new volumes, even for those familiar with Lindfors's previous publications. The first two volumes, published in 2011, *The Early Years* and *The Vagabond Years*, cover the first fifty years of Aldridge's life and career, most of which were spent in England and Ireland. Volume 3, published in 2013, covers 1852–1855, focusing on Aldridge's international success as a Shakespearean actor in Europe, mostly outside of the United Kingdom. The final ten years of Aldridge's life are tantalizingly left to future volume(s); however, the three volumes currently available are already a colossal achievement, following Aldridge through scores of theatres in over a dozen nations.

Lindfors has crafted a gloriously deep history, the result of decades of digging into the theatrical and cultural backgrounds of the places and people Aldridge touched. Lindfors goes beyond a chronological tracing of Aldridge's major life and career events to excavate the cultural context of the texts he performed, the spaces he performed in, the popular contemporary actors and acting styles, the prevailing politics of slavery/abolition, and racial stereotypes of the various places he performed. All three books inspire a profound respect for Aldridge's range of talent, the political and moral effect of his performances, his business ingenuity, his perpetual experimentation with repertoire, and his courage to continue acting and innovating in the face of disappointments, setbacks, and racism. The itinerancy of Aldridge's career is often given as the reason why his story has slipped through the cracks, yet Lindfors demonstrates the profound rewards of analyzing peripatetic subjects for the larger perspective they offer on the theatre culture, theatre economy, and political landscape.

The Early Years covers the first twenty-six years of Aldridge's life, starting in New York City, where he was born, educated at the African Free School, and had his first theatre experiences. Aldridge may have been involved with the African Theatre in New York, and Lindfors details Aldridge's connections with the African Theatre's leading actor, James Hewlett, as well as the burlesquing of Hewlett and the African Theatre by English comedian Charles Matthews. Whether or not Aldridge ever acted at the African Theatre in New York (there is no conclusive extant record), Aldridge capitalized on Matthews's popular burlesque of an African Shakespearian actor throughout his career in the United Kingdom, inviting audiences to compare his skill with Matthews's mockery. The bulk of this volume, however, follows the beginning of Aldridge's career in England, particularly his London engagements in 1825, 1829, and 1833. It has generally been accepted that Aldridge's London debut was at the Coburg Theatre (now the Old Vic) in October 1825, but Lindfors has uncovered evidence that his debut was actually at London's Royalty Theatre in May 1825. Lindfors charts Aldridge's subsequent provincial tours through England, Ireland, and Scotland, his return to London at the Sadler's Wells' Theatre in 1829, and finally his crucial, brief engagement at London's prestigious Theatre Royal Covent Garden in 1833, the critical failure of which led Aldridge to abandon hopes of London engagements for the next fifteen years. Lindfors comprehensively explores Aldridge's ever-expanding repertoire, including his experiments with white tragic and melodramatic roles, as well as a short-lived stint as actor-manager of a small-town theatre in Coventry. Of course Aldridge's racial identity and the politics of slavery were major factors in Aldridge's career and reception from the start, and the question of whether novelty or true talent was driving his box office appeal always followed him. Lindfors argues that Aldridge's "Africanness was an engaging riddle" for reviewers and audiences, who time after time debated whether his acting style was "African or Western . . . natural or learned . . . original or derivative" (1:127). Yet Lindfors convincingly argues that Aldridge was not simply a racial novelty but a formidable theatrical talent and that "through his art he was deliberately challenging conventional ideas about black people generally, not just Africans . . . forcing [audiences] to reconsider their ingrained racial assumptions" (1:1). Rounding out this volume are early comparisons of Aldridge's acting style with Kean and Macready, the two most famous English actors of the period.

The Vagabond Years, 1833–1852 takes us through the aftermath of Aldridge's unsuccessful 1833 London engagement at the Theatre Royal Covent Garden, through nineteen years as an itinerant actor/manager, success in Ireland, his return to London in 1848, another return to provincial touring, his adaptation of Shakespeare's *Titus Andronicus* and its London reception in 1852, and finally his decision to seek out new engagements in continental Europe. After his failed brief run at Covent Garden, Aldridge did not return to London for over a decade. Lindfors explains the forces keeping Aldridge out of London, including the backlash to the abolition of slavery in British colonies in 1833 and the popularity of T. D. Rice's blackface performances starting in 1836. So Aldridge stayed out of London, and he toured, spending the first six consecutive years after Covent Garden performing in Ireland. It was there that Aldridge developed a one-man show that showcased his diverse talents and that was also economical for touring. Lindfors is the first to recount this period in Aldridge's life, a time between Aldridge's big city accomplishments but nevertheless fascinating. Aldridge's one-man show was titled a "Grand, Fashionable, and Dramatic Entertainment" (2:45), which included an argument for the moral value of theatre, a narrative of his fictional royal African origin story, and scenes and songs to highlight the full range of Aldridge's talents—from tragedy to musical comedy. Aldridge was very successful with this one-man show. He also did well touring with a mini-company of four or five other actors to perform abbreviated versions of full-length plays. Lindfors notes how anomalous this success was during a period of across-the-board theatrical decline. Even though Aldridge wasn't performing in London during these years, Lindfors argues that Aldridge's impact on the surrounding theatre culture is evident in the multiple comedies burlesquing Aldridge that were written and produced during this period, including: *Stage Struck*, by William Dimond (later titled *Stage Mad, or the African Roscius*), *Othello: The Moor of Venice, Travesty*, by Maurice G. Dowling (later titled *Othello, by Act of Parliament*), and the skits and songs popularized by the American T. D. Rice, who debuted in London in 1836 and immediately became a popular success. Lindfors considers the influence of Rice's London career on Aldridge, particularly Aldridge's incorporation of Rice's blackface skits and songs into his own act, which Lindfors argues had a significantly different effect on audiences. Aldridge's performances of Rice's skits and songs were always presented in contrast to a serious role, highlighting Aldridge's broad range of skills and focusing audience admiration on the performer instead of the role. Lindfors argues this presented a stark contrast with Rice's performances, which were interpreted as an accurate portrait of African Americans. This volume also details Aldridge's steps toward a comeback starting in 1845, when he disbanded his mini-company and returned to the legitimate stage to perform with resident companies. Lindfors takes us through Aldridge's return to London in 1848 at the Surrey Theatre, followed by his new adaptation of *Titus Andronicus* in 1849. Lindfors argues this new *Titus* may have been born out of Aldridge's need for new material to secure another London engagement, which Aldridge secured in 1852 at the Britannia Saloon. When this engagement didn't attract the attention Aldridge had long hoped for, he set his sights across the English Channel.

The third volume in this series, *Performing Shakespeare in Europe, 1852–1855*, follows the most critically successful period in Aldridge's career, when he left touring the British Isles after twenty-seven years and found greater success in continental Europe as a Shakespearian actor. In these new contexts, where generally neither his audience nor his fellow actors spoke English, both criticism and praise of Aldridge was gauged on three axes: Aldridge's racial identity, Aldridge's perceived English style of acting, and local Shakespearian performance traditions. Although Aldridge demonstrated a larger repertoire in the United Kingdom, Aldridge's performances during this four-year period on the continent were limited to a handful of Shakespearian tragic roles: Othello, Shylock, Macbeth, and Richard III, plus the comic role of Mungo from the old English comedy, *The Padlock*, as the comic afterpiece. Lindfors provides a detailed breakdown of the versions of Shakespeare's plays Aldridge performed and the history of Shakespearean performance in each nation or state (now the areas encompassed by Belgium, Germany, Austria, Hungary, Poland, Lithuania, Denmark, Belgium, Czech Republic, and Switzerland). Lindfors also analyzes Aldridge's performances of each role, teasing out what was innovative in Aldridge's interpretations. To help illustrate Aldridge's acting style, Lindfors analyzes published comparisons made between Aldridge and famous contemporary actors including the French actress Mademoiselle Rachel (Elisa Rachel Félix) and the French actor François-Joseph Talma, the English actor William Charles Macready, the German actors Ludwig Devrient, Karl Seydelmann, Ludwig Dessior, and Emil Devrient, and the Polish German actor Bogumil Dawison. Lindfors also recounts how Hungarian officials monitored Aldridge as a potential spy during these travels.

Taken together, these three biographies by Lindfors are a perfect introduction to the existing scholarship on Aldridge as well as a welcoming platform for the next wave of scholars. There is no question these are the new definitive biographies of Aldridge, and they should be required reading in the fields of nineteenth-century theatre history, performance of race, Shakespeare, melodrama, and political activist theatre. Although the third volume offers a rough sketch of the final twelve years of Aldridge's career, when Aldridge bounced back and forth between the United Kingdom and Europe, the brevity of this sketch leaves this reader longing for more. These final adventures were among Aldridge's most glamorous—performing for queens and dukes and receiving the Verdienst Medal, which elevated Aldridge to the ranks of nobility in the Royal House of Saxony (3:250). Meanwhile, Lindfors just released a fourth volume to flesh out Aldridge's final twelve years, and the first three volumes indicate that the whole collection will be a treasure trove for nineteenth-century theatre historians.

—**KATE ROARK**
Blackburn College

International Women Stage Directors. Edited by Anne Fliotsos and Wendy Vierow. Urbana, Chicago, and Springfield: University of Illinois Press, 2013. x + 327 pp. $60.00 cloth.

Although directors such as Anne Bogart, Elizabeth LeCompte, Ariane Mnouchkine, Julie Taymor, and others have gained significant recognition, scholarship dedicated to exploring the artistic work and experiences of women stage directors is still minimal. Thus, Anne Fliotsos and Wendy Vierow's *International Women Stage Directors* fills a distinct gap in theatre scholarship surrounding the work of women directors and serves as a natural and necessary expansion of the work begun by the duo in *American Women Stage Directors of the Twentieth Century* (2008).

In this edited volume, Fliotsos and Vierow bring together twenty-four essays, each chronicling the work of women directors around the globe from countries including Argentina, Canada, Greece, India, Pakistan, South Africa, and more. In addition to highlighting the work of prominent women directors from each country, each chapter also provides a look at the surrounding social, cultural, political, and economic contexts in which these women are working—a wise strategy, as many readers may be unfamiliar with the specific sociopolitical workings of each country and, perhaps more importantly, many of the women directors highlighted in the text are confronting or subverting these sociopolitical contexts as part of their theatrical work. Thus, the text's goal is twofold: to expose readers to women directors from around the world "who could not be ignored for their [artistic] contributions" and to illuminate the geopolitical contexts that inevitably shape the directors' work and experiences as women and as artists (2).

The book's introductory materials firmly establish the project's import and concisely articulate its parameters. Roberta Levitow, cofounder of Theatre Without Borders, is a logical author for the foreword; her passion for global theatre practices and international theatre artists, particularly women, provides an exciting opening and a credible endorsement; as Levitow powerfully notes, "The stories of these women theatre artists . . . are larger than the confines of their theatre buildings or performance spaces" (ix).

In the introduction, Fliotsos carefully spells out the inspiration for the book. Particularly striking is her refreshingly candid articulation of the limits of the project. She notes that the text does not "claim to include a scientific sample representative of the entire globe" and admits that one of the limitations in coverage was finding qualified contributors—theatre scholars and practitioners who speak from "a point of authenticity" because they are from or have lived and worked in that country (1). However, this limitation becomes one of the text's great strengths, as the authors' firsthand knowledge gives each chapter credibility and rich details about the directors' work. Fliotsos also astutely situates this work amid other scholarly works on women and directing such as Aston and Case's *Staging International Feminisms*, Donkin and Clement's *Upstaging Big Daddy*, and others, thus contextualizing the project and offering readers additional sources to explore.

Despite any limits, the selection of countries featured in the book is sensible and thorough, with nearly every continent represented as well as several unexpected but fascinating countries such as Egypt, Kenya, and Bulgaria included. Admittedly, I was surprised not to see countries such as Italy and Spain included, considering their significant legacies in theatre's historical development, and the text would benefit from the inclusion of more Asian countries such as Japan or Korea. However, this is a minor quibble, as my appreciation for the diversity of the countries included trumps any concerns about exclusions.

Organized alphabetically for easy navigation, the essays are written in clear, accessible prose. Drawing from interviews with directors as well as articles and reviews, the authors pack an impressive amount of information into their chapters. For consistency, all the essays follow the same basic structure, first addressing the broader sociopolitical context for women's rights in that country, then considering the country's directorial fore-mothers, then describing contemporary artistic working conditions, and finally featuring biographical and artistic profiles of three to five directors. These profiles of individual directors are the most compelling and interesting aspects of the chapters. They provide tangible examples of the aesthetic and artistic strategies women directors are employing to create provocative, powerful, and often political art. In more than one instance, I found myself jotting down the name of a director to explore further.

Bibliographies provided at the end of each chapter offer additional resources for those who wish to delve more deeply into a particular area or director, and several chapters include photos of the various directors' works, although it would have been beneficial to include even more, as they provide useful visual reinforcement for the directorial work described.

Some essays also include brief sidebars—shorter, highlighted sections that provide additional information on a related topic or director. While somewhat inconsistent in the regularity of their appearance, the sidebars help broaden the scope of the text by including references to other geographical areas or aspects of women's international directorial work that could not be covered in a single chapter but still merit attention. For instance, the sidebar "Women Directors in the Arab World: Lebanon and Syria" by Fliotsos and Watfa Hamad offers a truly fascinating extension of the already insightful and illuminating discussion of women directors' work in Egypt.

In an increasingly globalized society, Fliotsos and Vierow's text provides a necessary intervention in the scholarly study and documentation of women's theatrical work and directing practices. Because of its accessibility—both in its encyclopedic organization and clear writing—this book will be an incredible resource for theatre students, scholars, and practitioners as well as readers interested in women's and gender studies or transnational discourses. Through their text, Fliotsos and Vierow open the doors to an understanding and awareness of the work of women directors on a global scale and, perhaps more importantly, offer a strong starting point for other scholars and students to undertake further in-depth investigation of these women's directorial work. I, for one, would eagerly welcome a second volume of *International Women Stage Directors.*

—EMILY A. ROLLIE
Monmouth College

Theatre & Violence. By Lucy Nevitt. New York: Palgrave Macmillan, 2013. xii + 83 pp. $10.00 paperback.

Continuing the mission of the *Theatre &* series, Lucy Nevitt's *Theatre & Violence* compellingly engages with a broad interdisciplinary subject through examples from theatre and performance, providing thought-provoking lines of inquiry for further discussion. Using examples ranging from the plays of Sarah Kane to the spectacle of World Wrestling Entertainment (WWE), Nevitt argues that "it is necessary and desirable to use theatre and performance to help us to contemplate violence" (8). Importantly, her text both explores the role of violence in performance and studies the performative qualities of violent action outside the theatre space.

The book, which includes a preface by series editors Jen Harvie and Dan Rebellato and a forward by Catherine Cusack, is expansive in its scope despite the standard brevity of the *Theatre &* series format. Nevitt begins her book by exploring case studies of theatrical violence and observes the tendency of violent action in works such as Sarah Kane's *Blasted* to "overshadow spectorial responses" and even to "obscure the [work] as a whole," reducing it to just "a violent play" (10). As she develops this argument, she expands the scope of the work, examining the performative aspects of real-world events such as hunger strikes and acts of terrorism. Ultimately, Nevitt advocates that those who stage acts of violence in performance do so not because they enjoy spectacles of violence but because "they profoundly dislike it and seek to contribute to the making of a more peaceful and less violent world" (75).

The core theoretical concerns of Nevitt's study relate to simulation, actuality, and spectatorship. She argues that spectatorship of both theatrical and actual violence has its effects and asserts the possibility that simulated violence in performance can sometimes offer a more visceral reality than actual violence, while actual violence can, in certain circumstances, feel performed or unreal. In the theatre, audiences have emotional, physical, and psychological responses to the carefully choreographed violent actions they witness onstage. Audiences may also witness performances in which an artist chooses to inflict bodily harm to him- or herself or have harm inflicted upon them, thereby blurring the line between witness and participant. Although Nevitt is vigilant not to draw too strong a boundary or to collapse the distinctions between actual and performed violence, the limitations of the short text prohibit more extensive theoretical approaches to the complexities within these divisions.

In considering the causes and effects of simulated violence, Nevitt participates in the dialogue on how representations of violence foster or cause actual material violence. She argues that these debates frequently foreground what the "performance in question *shows*, rather than . . . what the portrayal *does*, in a broader social sense" (28). By foregrounding an analysis of performativity and ideology, Nevitt deepens her commitment to the ethical considerations of violence and its effects. Her example of simulated rape in performance demonstrates the challenging terrain of showing violence to critique it without being able to control its effects on the audience and explores the more disturbing possibility of this kind of violence depicted without critique. She also reminds her readers that assumptions of violent content are deeply dependent on a variety of factors including historical context, a work's canonical status, or the rules of the performative world in which the violence is enacted. While this argument is compelling, it could be strengthened by a lengthier discussion of other influences that contribute to this understanding, such as cultural, political, and religious norms that factor into individual and social determinations of violent actions and behaviors.

Theatre & Violence offers a significant analysis of the complexities of violence in performance as well as the performative aspects of real violence. Its high quality and reasonable cost make it an ideal text for a variety of literature, theory, and history courses in theatre and performance studies. Her discussions of violence are imperative and need to be made central to scholarship in theatre and performance. The text might easily be utilized to enhance an undergraduate dramatic analysis course examining the violence in canonical works such as Sophocles's *Oedipus Rex* and Shakespeare's *Macbeth* or in a performance studies course exploring how artists have explored self-harm or violence in their work. Nevitt's work also suggests multiple uses in the ongoing conversations about ethics, representation, and intention in many fields, particularly those of media and cinema studies, sociology, and psychology. Any course that engages in discussions of violence or its affects would certainly benefit from this exceptional challenge to rethink how such acts are sensationalized, disregarded, or normalized instead of thoroughly examined and understood. Through foregrounding this vital intervention, Lucy Nevitt's *Theatre & Violence* makes an essential contribution to theatre and performance studies.

—**MICHELLE SALERNO**
University of Illinois at Urbana-Champaign

Shakespeare's Medieval Craft: Remnants of the Mysteries on the London Stage. By Kurt A. Schreyer. Ithaca, NY: Cornell University Press, 2014. xi + 177 pp. $46.20 hardcover.

What if the original ass's head fixed on Bottom in the first production of *A Midsummer Night's Dream* was a renovated stage property originally employed in a Chester mystery play? What if the ghost of Hamlet's father first entered through a trapdoor that, for early modern spectators, symbolically merged the portal to purgatory and hell? And what if Jacobean audiences heard the Porter's knocking in *Macbeth* as echoes from the raps on hell's gate in the *Harrowing of Hell* pageants? In *Shakespeare's Medieval Craft: Remnants of the Mysteries on the London Stage*, Kurt Schreyer poses these and other historiographical questions and pursues answers through a deft analysis of the lingering traces of medieval culture situated within Shakespeare's dramaturgy. Calling attention to the signifying plurality of staged objects, Schreyer unsettles the typical privileging of Renaissance performance by considering: "What would it mean if in fact the material remnants of the mysteries were vital and direct agents, not rude precursors, in the production of some of the most famous plays in the Shakespeare canon?" (4).

Much of Schreyer's compelling study hinges on two premises. First, his argument assumes that Shakespeare's audience was generally familiar with, or even had firsthand experience of, the largely provincial practice of mystery performance. Relying on the fact that widespread in-migration from the provinces to London occurred during the late sixteenth century, Schreyer contends that many early modern audiences were theatrically primed to view plays on the London stage by their earlier experiences with the pageants. Second, *Shakespeare's Medieval Craft* claims that material and immaterial remnants "have the ability to produce memory even as they are being resituated in new cultural contexts" (9). Consequently, the remnants that Shakespeare dramaturgically evokes afforded a kind of "synchronic diachrony" for Elizabethan and Jacobean spectators—lifting up the (Protestant) present while simultaneously reifying the (Catholic) customs of the past (7).

Building upon these introductory premises, Schreyer's first and second chapters outline a historiographical approach. Chapter 1, "Toward a Renaissance Culture of Medieval Artifacts," examines traditional literary and historical criticism (Thomas Warton, E. K. Chambers, Jacob Burckhardt), which generally views medieval artifacts as lost to early modern performance. Refuting these claims and, in contrast, arguing that pre-Reformation artifacts were indispensable to Renaissance culture, Schreyer examines three early modern discursive modes that "preserve contact with past matter: exemplarity, palimpsests, and anachronism" (19). The three discourses offer reinforcing historiographies, which each participate in Schreyer's chief piece of evidence, and the topic of his second chapter, "The Chester Banns: A Sixteenth-Century Perspective on the Mysteries." As the official proclamations that announced the upcoming cycle of pageants, the Banns present a summary of the local mystery tradition. Yet, as Schreyer astutely demonstrates, the two surviving versions of the Chester Banns—an "Early" or "Catholic" account and a "Late" or "Protestant" record—provide distinct renderings (48). The second chapter, then, demonstrates via comparison between the two how the Late Banns reframed Chester's dramatic tradition as a harmless civic practice that honors the town's history and does *not* celebrate popish idols. The rewriting of the Late Banns performed a kind of historiography that "knowingly antiquate[s] dramatic remnants in order to justify their present resurrection and return to the stage" (55). Schreyer finds the "synchronic diachrony" of the Late Banns to be a valuable example of the period's temporal blend and, therefore, an important model by which to examine the historiographical complexities of Shakespeare's plays (68).

The subsequent chapters investigate particular medieval remnants situated in Shakespeare's plays. Chapter 3, "Balaam to Bottom: A Sixteenth-Century Translation," is the strongest of Schreyer's case studies and is both persuasive and engaging. The focal remnant in this chapter is the headpiece that "translates" Bottom's character into an ass. Tracing the genealogy of the ass's head from its use in the Chester mystery play, *Moses and the Law: Balaack and Balaam*, to the "Popish Asse," which was a widespread image in Reformation discourse, and then to Shakespeare's use of the "ass's nole" for Bottom, Schreyer skillfully details the secular and sacred meanings of the ass's head in the sixteenth century. Moreover, the chapter outlines how, while on tour to the provinces, the Queen's Men could have acquired the showy and popular headpiece from the hard up cappers guild of Chester.

Chapter 4, "'Then Is Doomsday Near': *Hamlet*, the *Last Judgment*, and the Place of Purgatory," addresses the doctrine of purgatory in post-Reformation England by way of the Globe Theater's trapdoor. Integrated into the materiality of the London stage, Schreyer claims the trapdoor allowed a dramatization similar to that of the Doomsday pageants, which typically featured a cosmography of heaven, Earth, purgatory, and hell. While most Renaissance drama discarded purgatory as a staged site, *Hamlet* materially incorporates both purgatory and hell into the trapdoor from whence the ghost ascends. The trapdoor, in effect, "joins the material remnants and thematic language of the *Last Judgment* in order to, on the one hand, create an atmosphere of impending tragedy and, on the other hand, defer Hamlet's revenge" (127).

The fifth chapter, "Here's a Knocking Indeed! *Macbeth* and the *Harrowing of Hell*," examines an immaterial "aural prop": knocking (137). Employed in both *Harrowing* and *Macbeth*, Schreyer contends the sound effect directs the speech and action of *Macbeth*'s Porter, causing him to behave like a comedic devil in the mysteries. Thus, Shakespeare (synchronically) re-creates the knocking from the *Harrowing* only to distance himself (diachronically) from the medieval world the Porter recalls. Such simultaneity allows Shakespeare, like the Porter, to equivocate and "toys with the audience's interpretation of the knocking" (160).

The book's epilogue, "Riding the Banns beyond Shakespeare," demonstrates the value of applying the book's historiographical approach to other works of English Renaissance drama. Investigating the throne set piece in Shakespeare's *King John* and the use of the devil character in Ben Jonson's city comedy *Devil of Edmonton*, Schreyer reveals the continued influence of the mysteries long after the last pageant wagon performance.

As a work of scholarship, *Shakespeare's Medieval Craft* is meticulously researched and provides powerful textual readings. Schreyer's underlying, plausible argument concerning the audience's mnemonic reception anticipates further work on human memory in early modern performance history. What the book does exceedingly well is to argue that Shakespeare was a "play-wright" who crafted plays out of the medieval remnants that were within his dramatic reach (19).

—CLAIRE SYLER
University of Missouri-Columbia

BOOKS RECEIVED

Alford, Terry. *Fortune's Fool: The Life of John Wilkes Booth*. Oxford: Oxford University Press, 2015.

Barnett, David. *A History of the Berliner Ensemble*. New York: Cambridge University Press, 2015.

Bial, Henry. *Playing God: The Bible on the Broadway Stage*. Ann Arbor: University of Michigan Press, 2015.

Bianchini, Natka. *Samuel Beckett's Theatre in America: The Legacy of Alan Schneider as Beckett's American Director*. New York: Palgrave, 2015.

Bryer, Jackson R. and Mary C. Hartig, eds. *William Inge: Essays and Reminiscences on the Plays and the Man*. Jefferson, NC: McFarland & Co., 2014.

Camp, Pannill. *The First Frame: Theatre Space in Enlightenment France*. Cambridge: Cambridge University Press, 2014.

Duckett, Victoria. *Seeing Sarah Bernhardt: Performance and Silent Film*. Urbana: University of Illinois Press, 2015.

Erdman, Harley, and Susan Paun de García, eds. *Remaking the Comedia: Spanish Classical Theater in Adaptation*. Cornwall, UK: Tamesis, 2015.

Farabee, Darlene, Mark Netzloff, and Bradley D. Ryner, eds. *Early Modern Drama in Performance: Essays in Honor of Lois Potter*. Newark: University of Delaware Press, 2015.

Kim, Ju Yon. *The Racial Mundane: Asian American Performance and the Embodied Everyday*. New York: New York University Press, 2015.

Mazer, Cary M. *Double Shakespeares: Emotional-Realist Acting and Contemporary Performance*. Madison: Fairleigh Dickinson University Press, 2015.

Monrós-Gaspar, Laura. *Victorian Classical Burlesques: A Critical Anthology*. New York: Bloomsbury, 2015.

Nicholson, Steve. *The Censorship of British Drama, 1900–1968*. Volume Four: *The Sixties*. Exeter, UK: University of Exeter Press, 2015.

Osborne, Elizabeth A., and Christine Woodworth, eds. *Working in the Wings: New Perspectives on Theatre History and Labor*. Carbondale: Southern Illinois University Press, 2015.

Pérez, Hiram. *A Taste for Brown Bodies: Gay Modernity and Cosmopolitan Desire*. New York: New York University Press, 2015.

Peschel, Lisa, ed. *Performing Captivity, Performing Escape: Cabarets and Plays from the Terezin/Theresienstadt Ghetto*. London: Seagull Books, 2014.

Sauter, Willmar, and David Wiles, eds. *The Theatre of Drottingholm—Then and Now: Performance between the 18th and 21st Centuries*. Stockholm: Stockholm University, 2014.

Schmitt, Natalie Crohn. *Befriending the Commedia dell' Arte of Flaminio Scala: The Comic Scenarios*. Toronto: University of Toronto Press, 2014.

Simon, Linda. *The Greatest Shows on Earth: A History of the Circus*. London: Reaktion, 2014.

Vey, Shauna. *Childhood and the Nineteenth-Century American Theatre: The Work of the Marsh Troupe of Juvenile Actors*. Carbondale: Southern Illinois University Press, 2015.

Watermeier, Daniel J. *American Tragedian: The Life of Edwin Booth*. Columbia: University of Missouri Press, 2015.

Weintraub, Stanley. *Bernard Shaw before His First Play: The Embryo Playwright*. Saline, MI: ELT Press, 2015.

White, Ann Folino. *Plowed Under: Food Policy Protests and Performance in New Deal America*. Bloomington: Indiana University Press, 2015.

White, Timothy R. *Blue Collar Broadway: The Craft and Industry of American Theatre*. Philadelphia: University of Pennsylvania Press, 2015.

Williams, Simon, ed. *The Cambridge Encyclopedia of Stage Actors and Acting*. Cambridge: Cambridge University Press, 2015.

CONTRIBUTORS

KAREN BAMFORD is a professor of English at Mount Allison University, New Brunswick, Canada, where she teaches modern drama and Renaissance literature. Author of *Sexual Violence on the Jacobean Stage*, she is also coeditor of several volumes, including *Maternity and Romance Narratives in Early Modern England.*

BRIAN E. G. COOK is an assistant professor of theatre at the University of Alaska Anchorage. He received his PhD in theatre arts from the University of Oregon and his MA from the Royal Academy of Dramatic Art and King's College, London. His research focuses on contemporary British theatre, particularly on the work of the Cherub Company in the United Kingdom and abroad between 1978 and 2003. Brian has presented at conferences including "Subsidy, Patronage and Sponsorship" at the Victoria and Albert Museum in London, the Mid-America Theatre Conference, and the American Society for Theatre Research and has published articles and reviews in *Performing Arts Resources* and *Theatre Survey.*

JENNIFER DOUGLAS is the program director of Graduate Studies at the American Public University System, where she leads initiatives to support graduate students in their journey toward a graduate degree. She received her PhD in English at the University of Rochester. She was an assistant professor of English at Trinity Christian College, Chicago, before transitioning to the role of graduate professional development director at West Virginia University.

ANN HAUGO is an associate professor in the School of Theatre and Dance and core faculty with the Women's and Gender Studies Program and the minor in Native American Studies at Illinois State University. She coedited with Scott Magelssen *Querying Difference in Theatre History*. Her publications on American Indian and First Nations theatre have appeared in books such as *The Color of Theatre: A Critical Sourcebook in Race and Performance*, *American Indian Theater in Performance: A Reader*, *The Cambridge Companion to Native American Literature*, and Blackwell's *A Companion to Twentieth-Century American Drama*, as well as various academic journals and periodicals. She is a past president of the Mid-America Theatre Conference and she formerly served on the advisory board for Project HOOP (Honoring Our Origins and People through Native Theatre, Education, and Community Development).

CHANDRA OWENBY HOPKINS holds an MFA from Virginia Commonwealth University and a PhD from the University of Kansas. Her articles, reviews, and chapters have appeared in *Theatre Survey*, *Theatre Annual*, and the collection *Performing Objects and Theatrical Things*. As a dramaturg, she has worked with Georgia Shakespeare and the Tennessee Shakespeare Company. In 2013, Chandra joined the faculty of Converse College as an assistant professor of theatre, teaching and directing within the School of the Arts.

RHONA JUSTICE-MALLOY is a professor of theatre at the University of Mississippi. She is a coeditor of and contributor to the book *Enacting History*. She has served as the editor of *Theatre History Studies*. She is a member of the National Theatre Conference and a fellow of the Mid-America Theatre Conference.

JOZEFINA KOMPORALY is a London-based linguist and academic working on cultural exchanges between Anglophone and European literary traditions. Her publications include *Staging Motherhood: British Women Playwrights, 1956 to the Present* and numerous articles in edited collections and academic journals. Jozefina is the editor and cotranslator of the first English-language anthology of Matéi Visniec's plays, *Matéi Visniec: How to Explain the History of Communism to Mental Patients and Other Plays*, and she is currently working on a monograph on radical revivals as adaptation for Palgrave. As a translator, she champions the literatures of small European nations, in particular Hungarian and Romanian, and is preparing a critical edition of plays by Transylvanian playwright and dramaturg András Visky.

KARIN MARESH is an associate professor of communication arts at Washington & Jefferson College in Washington, Pennylvania, where she teaches theatre, film, and gender and women's studies courses. She is also a director and performer. Her scholarship has appeared in the journals *Theatre Journal* and *Theatre Survey* and in the book *International Women Stage Directors*.

A native of San Antonio, Texas, IRMA MAYORGA is a Chicana scholar/theatremaker. Working with collaborator Virginia Grise, she conceived and wrote the solo work *The Panza Monologues*, which focuses on the intersections of race, class, gender, obesity, and institutionalized racism in Mexican American communities; *The Panza Monologues* was published in 2014. Her play *Cascarones* earned ATHE's Jane Chambers Playwriting Award (student division) and went on to become the first play written by a Chicana to be developed at the prestigious Eugene O'Neill Theater Center's Playwrights Conference. Her research explores contemporary theatre and performance by US people of color and Latina/o expressive culture. Her current manuscript project focuses on theatricality in Chicana cultural production. She holds a PhD in drama and the humanities from Stanford University and currently teaches as an assistant professor of theatre at Dartmouth College.

SHEILA RABILLARD is an associate professor of English at the University of Victoria. She has published on modern and contemporary British, American, and Canadian drama and is the editor of *Essays on Caryl Churchill: Contemporary Representations*. She currently serves as the "Drama, Theatre, and Performance" subject editor for the *Routledge Encyclopedia of Modernism* and is at work on a monograph study of mothering in contemporary theatre.

REBECCA ROVIT is an associate professor in the Department of Theatre at the University of Kansas. She is also the editor of the *Journal of Dramatic Theory and Criticism*. Her microhistory *The Jewish Kulturbund Theatre Company in Nazi Berlin* earned a *Choice* Outstanding Title for 2013. In addition to *Theatrical Performance during the Holocaust: Texts, Documents, Memoirs*, which she coedited with Alvin Goldfarb, she has published widely on theatre history, performance, and the Holocaust in such journals as *PAJ*, *TDR*, *Theatre Survey*, *The Journal of Holocaust and Genocide Studies*, and the *Journal of Dramatic Theory and Criticism*. Her article on remembrance, identity, and the Holocaust accompanies the 2014 DVD rerelease of Siegfried Kühn's feature film *The Actress* (*Die Schauspielerin*, GDR, 1988).

MARGARET SAVILONIS is an assistant professor of English at the University of New Haven, where she serves as the resident dramaturg for the university theater. Her publications include "Value, Voice, and Identity in *Three Birds Alighting on a Field*," in *International Dramaturgy: Translation and Transformation in the Theatre of Timberlake Wertenbaker*, "Got to Get Over the Hump: The Politics of Glam in the Work of Labelle and Parliament," in *Taking it to the Bridge: Music as Performance*, and "Choreographing Diversity and the American Experience: Myra Kinch & Group, Federal Theatre Project, 1937–1939," in *Experiments in Democracy: Inter-racial and Cross-cultural Exchange in American Theatre and Performance, 1900–1950*.

ARDEN ELIZABETH THOMAS received her PhD in theater and performance studies from Stanford University and is the cofounder and executive director of MACH 33: The Festival of New Science-Driven Plays at Caltech. She has published essays in performance and ecology in *Reading Contemporary Performance: Theatricality Across Genres* (ed. Meiling Chang and Gabrielle Cody) and *Readings in Performance and Ecology* (ed. Theresa May and Wendy Arons). Arden is also the Los Angeles managing regional editor of the online journal *New International Theatre Experience: World Theatre News* at www.nitenews.org.

STEVE TILLIS is the author of *Toward an Aesthetics of the Puppet* and *Rethinking Folk Drama*, as well as articles on world theatre history published in *TDR*, *Asian Theatre Journal*, *Theatre Survey*, *New Theatre Quarterly*, and *Theatre Topics*. He teaches at Saint Mary's College of California.

SCOTT VENTERS is currently a student in the University of Washington's PhD program in theatre history, theory, and criticism and a member of UW's Critical Animal Studies research cluster. Scott received his BFA in drama from the University of Oklahoma, his BA in English and philosophy from CUNY-Hunter College, and his MA in theatre from Oklahoma State University. His research focuses on animals in cultural and scientific "performance" during the rise of liberalism, political contractarianism, and colonialism between the seventeenth and nineteenth centuries in Europe and the Americas. He is the recipient of the Ruth Limmer Bequest for graduate study in the humanities and the Outstanding Paper Award from ATHE's Religion and Theatre focus group and has presented multiple papers at ASTR, ATHE, and MATC.

JENNIFER WORTH is a graduate of the Theatre Department at CUNY's Graduate Center. Her reviews and articles have been published in *Western European Stages*, *Theatre Journal*, and *Theatre Research International* and she serves on

ATHE's Pedagogy Subcommittee. Having previously taught at Washington University, York College-CUNY, and Wagner College, she now works as the administrative manager of the Reacting Consortium at Barnard College, where she collaborates with faculty around the world to spread the active-learning pedagogy Reacting to the Past, and teaches using RTTP in the First Year Program.

www.ingramcontent.com/pod-product-compliance
Lightning Source LLC
LaVergne TN
LVHW050557110926
847619LV00018B/80